WHATEVER HAPPENED TO THE MUSIC TEACHER?

WHATEVER HAPPENED

to the MUSIC TEACHER?

How Government Decides and Why

DONALD J. SAVOIE

McGill-Queen's University Press
Montreal & Kingston · London · Ithaca

© McGill-Queen's University Press 2013
ISBN 978-0-7735-4110-8

Legal deposit second quarter 2013
Bibliothèque nationale du Québec

Printed in Canada on acid-free paper that is 100% ancient forest
free (100% post-consumer recycled), processed chlorine free

This book has been published with the help of a grant from the
Canadian Institute for Research on Regional Development at the
Université de Moncton.

McGill-Queen's University Press acknowledges the support of the
Canada Council for the Arts for our publishing program. We also
acknowledge the financial support of the Government of Canada
through the Canada Book Fund for our publishing activities.

Library and Archives Canada Cataloguing in Publication

Savoie, Donald J., 1947–
Whatever happened to the music teacher? : how government decides
and why / Donald J. Savoie.

Includes bibliographical references and index.
ISBN 978-0-7735-4110-8

1. Public administration – Canada – Decision making – Textbooks.
2. Political planning – Canada – Decision making – Textbooks.
3. Canada – Politics and government – Decision making
– Textbooks.   I. Title.

JL86.D42S29 2013   352.3'30971   C2012-906173-5

Set in 10/13 Sabon with Trade Gothic
Book design & typesetting by Garet Markvoort, zijn digital

TO MICHAEL AND LÉA

CONTENTS

PREFACE

The idea for this book was born out of a conversation between one of Canada's leading businessmen, the newly elected premier of Nova Scotia, a senior provincial public servant, and myself. At the informal gathering, the businessman spoke of his village life some fifty years earlier. The small village school had had a music teacher who taught him how to appreciate music, something he has retained over the years. He told us that there was a barber shop in the village and next to it was an office that the provincial Department of Natural Resources rented for fifty dollars a month. The department had a staff of two looking after "all the trees, the rivers, the deer and moose and everything else that needed to be looked after in Cumberland County." He added, "Today we are told that we can no longer afford a music teacher in our community. However, the Department of Natural Resources is now housed in two fine buildings, employing a staff of 150. Yet, Cumberland County has the same acreage, about the same number of trees, rivers, and deer and moose as it had fifty years ago."

"How," he asked the premier, "can you explain this?" The newly elected premier was naturally at a loss to offer any reasons on the spot. I subsequently asked several senior Nova Scotia public servants whether the situation was as described. One chuckled and said it probably was, particularly if one included Truro, an adjoining community.

Bureaucracy has become the butt of jokes and the object of derision. As the saying goes in Ottawa, young university graduates join the public service for its generous maternity and paternity leave and then stay for the pension plan. Popular belief and humour may point to a perception problem, but they can hardly answer the question: "What happened to the music teacher?" I hasten to inform the reader that this is not an Agatha Christie story. The book's central purpose is to show how policy and budgetary decisions are made in today's public sector. The focus is on the federal government and how Ottawa decides, not on Nova Scotia or small Canadian communities.

I have published extensively on accountability and machinery of government issues and have served as adviser to policy makers on a number of occasions to governments in Canada and abroad. As a result, I know my way around government – what information one needs in order to answer the question about the music teacher and where to find it. The vast amount of information that government departments make available on the Internet may not be easily accessible or comprehensible to many Canadians, but it is to me. The reader familiar with some of my earlier work will see that I borrow from it, notably when dealing with the role of the prime minister in shaping government policies and decisions.

My hope is that readers of this book will gain fresh insights on how government decides. Those who view this work as an exercise in bureaucracy bashing will entirely miss the point. Yet more than one senior government official in Ottawa urged me not to write the book. They were worried that it would be misunderstood and very likely create problems for the public service. One said grimly, "We have enough problems as it is without you pouring gasoline on the fire."

My intention is the opposite. The book is a cry for reform – to fix an institution that continues to lose credibility. I strongly believe that the Canadian public service is vital to our country's continued prosperity. It is precisely for this reason that I decided to speak truth, at least as I see it, about this important institution so that Canadians will understand it better and both political and public service leaders may be encouraged to take steps to improve its operations. In brief, I have come to the view that the Canadian public service is in urgent need of repair if it is to regain the trust and respect of those it is asked to serve. My hope is that this book will make a contribution to this end.

The book's cover – a piano in a dark setting with no one playing – is an original painting by my cousin, the well-known artist Roméo Savoie. The photo was taken by my son Julien Z. Savoie.

I once again want to thank three outstanding women who have always been there for me: my wife Linda, for her patience, support, and gentle ability to run interference on my behalf so that I can concentrate on my writing; Ginette Benoit, for her continued good cheer, her competence, and her incredible ability to read my handwriting; and Joan Harcourt, for her professionalism and her ability to make my sentences read better. I want to thank Carlotta Lemieux for her sharp eye and her fine work in editing the manuscript.

I dedicate this book to our grandchildren, Michael and Léa, for bringing pure joy to our lives.

I also want to express a special thank-you to the two persons who reviewed the manuscript. They provided valuable insights and suggestions for improving it. I would like to stress, however, that I myself am answerable, responsible, and accountable for this book and for any of its errors and deficiencies.

Donald J. Savoie
Canada Research Chair in Public Administration and Governance
Université de Moncton

WHATEVER HAPPENED TO THE MUSIC TEACHER?

A retired deputy minister explained to me over breakfast, in no uncertain terms, what was wrong with the Canadian public service. He said, "It is seriously, seriously overstaffed. There are far too many people running around pretending to be busy, creating mindless work for themselves and others. One should just decide one day to cut the size of the public service by half and you would see a dramatic improvement. That is the solution we need to look at, nothing else will work. We have tried everything else and nothing has ever worked."[1] Strange thing about recently retired senior public servants – they are quick to see that the service is too big soon after they leave government. It is quite a different matter while they are in office. I recall, as a young public servant in Ottawa, telling my deputy minister that I felt that there were too many people in the department for the required work. His reaction was swift. He proceeded to tell me that I was showing a disturbing level of disloyalty to the department. He pointed out that if I truly felt this way, I should seriously think about leaving.

I did leave, both the department and the government. When I saw him several years later in Ottawa, he too was no longer in government. He had just left a meeting at the Privy Council Office where, he reported, he had met with some fifteen to twenty public servants to go over what he described as a relatively minor issue. He commented on the waste of talent and resources in government and said that things were not like that in his current work in the private sector. Obviously, he had completely forgotten our conversation of several years earlier. When I reminded him, he replied, "There is an old saying in government – in matters of public policy, you stand where you sit."[2] What it told me was that there is no point asking a public sector manager if his or her department, agency, or unit has too many employees. You will never get a straight answer. Indeed, you are most likely to hear that more staff and more resources are needed and that things are stretched to the limit.

This is not a Canadian phenomenon. It will be recalled that Margaret Thatcher declared a freeze on hiring the day she came to office and scrapped plans to add new positions. She ignored the claim in the civil service briefing books that the 733,000-strong civil service was already stretched to the limit and that "even modest" cuts in staff would inhibit departments from functioning effectively. Early in her first mandate, she directed that the civil service be reduced in size by nearly 15 percent. By the time she left office, it had been cut by over 22 percent, down to 569,000.[3] Essentially, Thatcher imposed cuts simply by outlining targets and underlining the importance of management reform. It can hardly be described as a sophisticated approach, but it worked, at least from her perspective. Convinced that more could be done without a reduction in services, she simply declared that cuts could be absorbed through superior management practices, by importing private sector approaches, and just by old-fashioned cuts throughout government departments. She stuck to her position and met her objectives.[4]

I asked Sir Robert Armstrong, one of the authors of the briefing books, if Thatcher had it right when she ignored their claim and imposed cuts by picking a number out of the air. Yes was the answer. "Why, then," I asked, "did you attempt to persuade her to hire more public servants?" The answer: "Permanent secretaries made their claim, and we packaged the various requests and made the case for more resources."[5] The suggestion is that it is up to politicians to determine the size of the public service, particularly when it needs to be cut down, and also to decide whether departments truly need more people. However, this implies that politicians can, on their own, somehow secure the knowledge and generate the necessary interest to establish the proper size of the public service. In one of my earlier books, I wrote that it is no longer sufficient to ask senior public servants to speak truth to power, to their political masters; they also need to speak truth to one another and to their own organization.[6]

Like the Nova Scotia businessman, many people intuitively suspect that there is something not quite right with government bureaucracies. According to public opinion surveys, Canadians are convinced that the bureaucracies engender massive waste. For example, one survey reported as far back as 1997 that Canadians believe that of every dollar Ottawa spends, it wastes forty-seven cents.[7] Things have hardly improved since the late 1990s.[8]

To be sure, there is now a reluctance to defend the role of government on any grounds – from efficiency to promoting the collective interest.[9] The few who still argue against tampering with the existing machinery of government and its "armies" of entrenched officials are on the defensive and are discounted by both the political left and political right. Even people who had supported the ideas and social welfare programs of leaders such as Franklin Roosevelt, Clement Attlee, T.C. Douglas, Lester Pearson, and Adlai Stevenson are now calling for changes to the apparatus of government. A serious candidate for the presidency of the United States in the run-up to the 2012 election pledged to make Washington "irrelevant" in the lives of Americans.[10]

Why is this so? Though the pursuit of a "just society" led governments to introduce new policies and programs in the 1960s and 1970s, one can hardly argue "mission accomplished." Certainly, a variety of programs were introduced, but there is no sign that a just society has arrived. Indeed, there is ample evidence that inequality in society is more pronounced today in most Western democracies than it was in the 1950s, 1960s, and 1970s. Tony Judt writes that the greatest extremes of private privilege and public indifference can be seen in the United States and Britain – "the epicentres of enthusiasm for deregulated market capitalism." He notes that Britain "is now more unequal – in incomes, wealth, health, education and life chances – than was the case in the 1960s and 70s."[11] In Canada, inequality in income has been on the rise. Before the mid-1990s the ratio between the wealthiest and poorest Canadians was eight to one; it is now ten to one.[12]

Is bureaucracy the problem? John Kenneth Galbraith, himself a leading proponent in the twentieth century for a greater role for government in society, maintained that bureaucracy had given government a bad reputation. Defending the system had become "more than the liberal task," he insisted. "It is far more important now to improve the operation than enlarge and increase its scope. This must be the direction of our major effort."[13] A good number of left-of-centre and centrist politicians do not hesitate to point their fingers at bureaucracy to explain why the public sector has fallen out of favour. Tony Benn, for one, asserts that "the power, role, influence and authority of the senior levels in Britain have grown to such an extent as to create the embryo of a corporate state."[14]

Centrist politicians who have worked with public servants in the past have become openly critical of them once out of office. Shirley Williams, for example, writes: "My impression of the British Civil Service is that it is a beautifully designed and effective braking mechanism. It produces a hundred well argued answers against initiatives and change."[15] In Canada, left-of-centre politicians such as Allan J. MacEachen and Lloyd Axworthy have openly questioned the work of public servants.[16] Reg Alcock, a senior minister in the Paul Martin Liberal government, called bureaucrats "the enemy," and as Treasury Board president he declared that he hoped to bring the public service "back to its glory days."[17] Nor can public servants look to right-of-centre politicians for support. Margaret Thatcher said that she disliked bureaucrats as a breed, Ronald Reagan said he went to Washington to drain the swamp, and Brian Mulroney pledged in 1984 to give bureaucrats pink slips and running shoes if he was elected to power.[18]

What are voters to make of this? It takes only a moment's reflection to appreciate that citizens will find it extremely daunting to try to understand how government, let alone bureaucracy, operates and decides. We are now told that Parliament itself is at its "weakest in the control and scrutiny of public money."[19] If members of Parliament – who presumably are there to hold the government to account and who have staff and resources to turn to for help – are unable to scrutinize government spending, one can imagine what it is like for the average citizen. The inherent opacity of government documents, the horizontal nature of government decision making, and the many informational obstacles that exist make it virtually impossible for citizens, preoccupied as they are with the daily demands of their own lives, to understand how government decides and why.

Public servants are not free to engage politicians in a public debate about the merits of their work or the reasons why the public sector no longer enjoys the credibility it once had. However, they do not hesitate to voice their views in private. Bev Deware, former deputy minister of defence and associate clerk of the privy council, likely spoke for a number of senior public servants when he said, "Politicians should learn to heal themselves and their institutions before they try to heal the public service."[20] At the same time, many politicians are equally convinced that the problem lies not with themselves but with public servants and the public service.

From time to time, citizens will get a glimpse of waste in government when a financial audit reports that someone broke the rules or when the results of an access-to-information request uncovers financial or administrative abuses. It will be recalled, for example, that the auditor general revealed in 2001 that the federal government had sent home-heating cheques to 1,600 prison inmates and a year later declared that senior bureaucrats had broken "just about every rule in the book" in mismanaging the

Chrétien government's sponsorship program.[21] Such incidents are widely reported in the media, and they give bureaucracy a bad name. But they are often isolated cases and represent a minuscule amount of the government expenditure budget. In any event, they can never tell the whole story of how government decides and why. Often they speak to the problem, not to the cause.

In this book we set out to answer a number of questions. How well are government operations managed? What has been the impact of private-sector-inspired management practices on government operations? How does the government shape and manage its expenditure budget? Students of public spending maintain that taxpayers have "implicitly come to understand that there are underlying forces that invariably lead both bureaucrats and politicians to be inefficient and wasteful in public expenditures."[22] What are these forces? What forces also shape relations between elected politicians and public servants in managing government expenditures? How does the relationship influence government spending?

Politicians on the outside looking in have a greater capacity to see a need to cut spending than those in power do. Politicians on the campaign trail often point to waste in government spending, but more often than not they sing a different song once in power. The mayor of my own community stressed the need to be "cautious with spending" in his first mayoralty campaign and pointed to the previous council's growing operating budgets as a serious problem. After four years in office, the city's operating budget grew by about 30 percent.[23] What happens to politicians after they assume office?

This *volte face* is hardly limited to my community. Stephen Harper in opposition and as head of the National Citizens Coalition called on the government to initiate "tough government spending cuts." Stephen Harper in government has apparently held a different view. Between his accession as prime minister in 2006 and his March 2012 budget, government spending grew to the tune of 5.5 percent per annum, outpacing the rate of inflation.[24]

Control in either the public or private sector allows managers to assess whether or not their plans are implemented effectively.[25] The budget arguably is the most important instrument of control in both sectors. In allocating funds, private sector firms expect a healthy return on their investments. The feedback is direct, quick, and blunt. What about the public sector? Governments in the Western world have, over the past thirty years or so, sought to make the public sector look like the private sector, at least when it comes to management. One can now ask, how has the budget process in government changed to accommodate this new reality? This study seeks to answer that question.

The politics of public spending is a well-travelled territory.[26] Little wonder, since virtually all government activities take place in the shadow of money. In government, the expenditure budget steals the stage and declares winners and losers, much as the market does in the private sector. One deputy minister in Ottawa summed it up well when he said, "Success in Ottawa is measured by – Can you get money?"[27] It is easy to measure if a minister and his or her deputy are able to secure more money for their department. Sir Humphrey Appleby, a senior public servant in the popular BBC-TV series *Yes Minister*, had this to say about measuring success in government: "The civil service does not make profits or losses. Ergo we measure success by the size of our staff and budget. By definition, a big department is more successful than a small one. This simple proposition is the basis of our whole system."[28] However, almost everything else in government is not so easily measured.

We have witnessed in more recent years an explosion in the literature on government spending.[29] For the most part, the studies have looked at the point where politicians and public servants meet or where politics and public administration meet. This study seeks to go further; it explores both how government operates and decides and how it manages operations. Thus, we look not only at where politicians and public servants meet but also where government operations simply roll on in the vast complex world of public administration. In brief, it explores not just how decisions are made but also why and how government bureaucracies operate the way they do.

There have been a number of attempts to overhaul the management of the public sector over the past thirty years or so. We have seen efforts to relax procedural rules and processes, to introduce explicit performance standards; we have seen competition between public and private sector units, centralization of the policy-making process, and the disaggregation of activities, most notably a split between policy and delivery.[30] These efforts were designed to make the management of the public sector resemble that of the private sector. Governments in all Anglo-American democracies, for example, decided to borrow a page from the private sector in introducing pay-for-performance schemes. But these, like most other reform measures, have met with limited success.

Western countries are now confronting a crisis in public spending, and an overhaul – ranging from pensions, social services, and education to health care – is being called for. The managing director of the International Monetary Fund (IMF) has, at least on the face of it, a simple cure for a country's debt crisis: cut public spending and increase taxes.[31] Prime Minister Stephen Harper had a message for the G20 leaders shortly before he hosted them in Canada in 2010, noting that the Western world is confronting a very serious fiscal challenge and "to meet this challenge, we must deliver firm, credible plans that will put our countries on a path of fiscal sustainability."[32] However, he waited until he secured a majority mandate before unveiling sweeping spending cuts.

Where does one look for the answer? I have laboured through many government documents, consulted elected politicians and public servants, read the literature, and published extensively in this area. My own experience as an adviser to various governments at both the provincial and federal levels, as well as abroad, suggests a pattern: politicians want to squeeze savings from government operations and bureaucracy; but public servants insist that if significant savings are to be realized, the politicians must generate the political will to cut programs.

New theories have emerged in recent years to explain growth in public spending. Public choice, rational choice, and principal-agent theories have been in fashion for the past forty years or so. These theories borrow more than a page from the economics discipline and have come to dominate many departments of political science as well as the public policy literature. However, the theories seek to explain growth in the public sector rather than cuts in spending.[33] The relatively small public administration community of which I am a member has, for the most part, stayed on the sidelines in this theoretical debate – many rejecting the theories but unable to come up with anything more convincing. To some observers, the public administration community has been essentially left to defend the indefensible – government bureaucracy – against powerful theories and bureaucratic inefficiencies.

To be sure, there is a strong link between the public administration community and bureaucracy. The relationship may not be as close as it is between schools of business and the private sector, but it is close. Many government officials are drawn from graduate programs in schools of public administration, public policy, or political science. A good number of adjunct faculty members are former senior public servants, and some faculty members are asked to serve in government as consultants or special advisers.

The public administration community will more than likely make the case that public choice or related theories may have some merit, but they can never tell the whole story. In trying to define a world that is inherently complex, the theories are too simplistic. Still, the community remains haunted by the words of Dwight Waldo, a pioneer in the field, when he observed that public administration is "a subject matter in search of a discipline."[34]

I share the views of my colleagues that economics-inspired theories do not and never can tell the whole story. I do, however, recognize that, *faute de mieux*, the theories continue to make an important contribution to a greater understanding of how government decides and operates. Accordingly, the purpose of this study is not to assess the relevance and viability of these theories; rather, it is to offer what I hope will be new insights into the politics that shape what bureaucracy does and why, and into the relationship between politicians and public servants and between them and citizens. In brief, it offers material to add to what Chris Pollitt and Geert Bouckaert, in their classic *Management Reform*, call our "shopping basket … of assorted insights."[35]

Although I looked mainly to Canadian governments for material and inspiration, I also drew on the experience of other countries. I have, in the past, written about public administration in Britain and the United States,[36] and I have had the good fortune to spend time in these and other countries, meeting with colleagues and government officials. This has enabled me to test my ideas and gather material on government bureaucracies and government spending.

I also drew on my own varied experience. Over the years, I have had a ringside seat as new public spending took hold and as several efforts were made to cut spending. I served on several transition-to-power teams at both the federal and provincial levels. At the request of Prime Minister Brian Mulroney, I wrote the report on the establishment of the Atlantic Canada Opportunities Agency (1986–87). I also wrote the report on the establishment of the Canadian Centre for Management Development and became its first deputy principal (1988–90). The centre was later renamed the Canada School of Public Service, an agency of the Government of Canada. I served as director of provincial analysis in the Privy Council Office and later as assistant secretary (1987–88), Corporate Policy and Public Affairs; later still, as the Simon Reisman Visiting Fellow at the Treasury Board (2004). In this role, I was asked to work on measures designed to strengthen accountability requirements in the immediate aftermath of the sponsorship scandal. Subsequently, I was director of research for the second phase (the recommendations phase) of the Commission of Inquiry into the Sponsorship Program and Advertising Activities in the Government of Canada (2004–05). In Nova Scotia, I chaired the Economic Advisory Panel for the newly elected Dexter government (2009) and served as the external adviser to the Strategic Review of the Atlantic Canada Opportunities Agency (2010). Strategic review exercises were designed to identify spending reductions in line departments, and all departments were requested to have an external adviser in order to provide an independent assessment of the recommendations. Lastly, I worked as policy adviser in two ministers' offices and in one deputy minister's office in Ottawa. Since the early 1980s, I have also published extensively on public administration, public spending, and regional economic development.

In planning this book, I consulted the work of the pioneers in the political science and public administration fields. I hold that both fields have lost sight of the more important issue: "Who Gets What, When, How." Harold Lasswell's classic, published in 1935, sought to establish a lasting model by exploring the politics of multilateral bargaining between interest groups.[37] His work resonates today as much as it did some eighty years ago, and it applies more to the Canadian setting than at any time in the past. Canadian politics and its public sector remain fundamentally about "Who gets what, when, how." This brings us back to the question, Why can a village no longer afford a music teacher while a government department in the area has grown from a staff of 2 to 150 in some sixty years?

The political science field has, to some extent, lost interest in the question of who gets what and why. Much of its focus today is on behaviour, stressing the scientific study of individual and group behaviour. Economic imperialism has made its presence felt in both the political science and public administration fields. Edward Lazear makes the case that "the power of economics lies in its rigor. Economics is scientific; it follows the scientific method of stating a formal refutable theory, testing the theory, and revising the theory based on the evidence. Economics succeeds where other social sciences fail because economists are willing to abstract." The starting point for economists is that an individual or a business sets out to maximize something – a benefit, utility, or profit.[38] Many political scientists have emulated economists in their search for a rigorous science, embracing rational choice modelling of human behaviour.[39] Their studies incorporate public opinion surveys, political behaviour, political attitudes, opinion change, and voter choice.

The public administration literature, meanwhile, also has moved away from the study of institutions. Many still regard it as a subfield of political science. As a result, it too has come under the influence of economics, taking an interest in human behaviour. However, as Donald Kettl writes, "Political science has long been impatient with public administration, a field grounded in the search for clear, convincing, prescriptive solutions to problems that rarely have good answers – and few answers remain good for long."[40] Many have bought into the idea that market competition and the private sector are invariably superior to public administration. Harold Lasswell argues that the study of politics is or should be the study of influence and that "the influential are those who get the most of what there is to get."[41] Influence and the influential are never static; they evolve. New approaches to public administration can hold far-reaching implications for influence and the influential. This study explores how.

This study is also a call for the public administration discipline and the public sector to return to their roots. Efforts to make the public sector look like the private sector have been misguided, are costly to taxpayers, and have entailed a profoundly negative effect on the public service as an institution. These and other developments have knocked the public service off its moorings, played havoc with its internal logic, and left individual public servants uncertain about their role and about who their allies are.

I recognize that traditional public administration is not without problems. Nevertheless, I believe that New Public Management is not an appropriate model for the public sector. The key to understanding the public sector is to focus on tasks. This in turn explains why there are two fairly distinct spaces inside government. One is based in Ottawa, where public servants look up to their ministers, to deputy ministers, and to the prime minister and his courtiers. The other is staffed by front-line managers and workers who look to clients.[42] This is one of the reasons why the public and private sectors are intrinsically different. There are very few opportunities for applying private sector approaches and management techniques to government.[43] Attempts to do so explain why the public service culture, along with the values of public servants themselves, have become more individualistic, rather than having a more collective orientation as in years past.[44]

Outline of Study

In the 1980s, traditional public administration came under attack by the leading politicians of the day. Senior public servants, meanwhile, saw little wrong with their institution and hardly any need to pursue ambitious reform measures. Politicians such as Margaret Thatcher (famously, "not for turning") looked to the private sector for solutions, and some leading UK business executives agreed to serve in government for a set period to look at government programs. In North America as in Britain, private sector management practices were considered to be far superior to public sector ones, and sustained efforts were made to introduce them to government.

Public servants who identified their work with traditional public administration discovered that they could no longer look to their long-standing allies in the academic community for support. The field of economics itself lost interest in moral philosophy and political economy. Economists, in their desire to speak the language of science, turned to mathematics and to rational expectations theory. A body of literature and economic theories emerged based on assumptions of rationality, efficiency, and equilibrium in the marketplace.[45] Political science and students of public administration borrowed a page or two from the economists and also sought to speak the language of science. In the process, new theories emerged, based on a morality of individualism and rational self-interest. In chapter 1, we consider how the study of public administration has evolved in recent years and how it squares with attempts to reform the machinery of government and government operations.

Parliament's role is intimately tied to the spending of money. It is Parliament that authorizes spending and new taxes or tax increases. It is Parliament that holds policy makers to account. In brief, the government's revenue and expenditure management system is directly tied to parliamentary authority and control. However, many observers, including many members of Parliament, increasingly believe that Parliament has lost its way. Nowhere is this more evident than in the approval of expenditures. Mountains of documents sent to Parliament every day are either skimmed or not read at all; MPs readily admit that they spend little time reviewing spending estimates. Chapter 2 looks at the role of Parliament and MPs in reviewing the government's expenditure budget.

Chapter 3 discusses the changing role of cabinet ministers in the government's policy and decision making. Ministers no longer hold the power and influence they once had in shaping policies, programs, and new spending. Like other MPs, they continue to press for new initiatives for their constituencies and regions; regional grievances remain strong, and politicians are expected to give voice to them and to seek redress in Ottawa. Accordingly, the forces that shape the government's expenditure budget are the same as they were in years past. But the decision-making process that determines the expenditure budget has taken a new form. The prime minister and his courtiers, together with the finance minister, are today's architects of the expenditure budget. Decisions of any consequence – including new spending commitments or spending cuts – are struck by the prime minister, the minister of finance, and their key advisers.

The above has created a power vacuum in the machinery of government in Ottawa, and chapter 4 explores the implications for the expenditure budget process. It strengthens the hand of those in government who favour the status quo, because only the prime minister and his closest advisers can jolt the machinery into action. The result is that new spending commitments and cuts in the expenditure budgets are unveiled like bolts of lightning from above. This has been the case in both the ambitious program review (1994–97) and Harper's strategic and operational review exercises (2011–12).

Chapter 5 explores recent changes to the machinery of government. It looks at the horizontal nature of the policy- and decision-making processes and the way the machinery has been adjusted to respond. Some of the changes are having an effect on the spending of public money. Many affect individuals personally. The arrival of permanent election campaigns, the call for greater transparency and the need to handle real or potential political crises have created a fault line between senior government officials, who look up to politicians, and front-line workers and their managers (the music teacher types), who look to citizens. The former not only hold the upper hand, but they have grown in number in recent years. Their never-ending demands for more information from front-line managers have shifted resources to managing processes and away from managing programs and services.

The call to let the manager manage goes back fifty years in Ottawa. The call was given a new lease on life with the arrival of New Public Management in the 1980s. A theme that runs through chapter 6 and elsewhere is the decision by the Government of Canada and other Anglo-American governments to import private sector management measures to strengthen government operations. If public sector management was somehow made to look like private sector management, a bottom line comparable to that in the private sector would have to be invented. As a result, we now have a plethora of reporting requirements designed to assess the performance of departments and their managers. Chapter 6 reviews these developments, the role of central agencies, and the role of officers of Parliament in public sector management and government spending.

Chapter 7 looks at one of Ottawa's growth industries of the past forty years: program evaluation. It traces the budget process from line item to program budgeting and makes the case that the Treasury Board Secretariat lost a great deal of influence when it moved away from its traditional guardian role as it sought to implement the management board concept. Treasury Board's role in the expenditure budget is now more akin to overseeing a production line of evaluation and performance assessment reports than of producing a thorough review of departmental spending plans. The chapter also makes the point that the changing Treasury Board role and the attempts to make public sector management look like the private sector has come at a significant cost to taxpayers.

Chapter 8 compares public and private sector compensation. It reports that the great majority of federal public servants enjoy higher salaries and considerably more generous employee benefits than their private sector counterparts. This chapter also looks at how the workforce of the federal public service has been restructured in recent years. Occupational groups that provide front-line services and deliver programs have lost employment, while management, financial, administrative, and policy groups have seen a substantial increase in new positions.

Chapter 9 looks at management practices in the federal government. It revisits the progress (if any) made in recent years in implementing new private-sector-inspired management measures and their impact. The chapter also looks at what truly matters to senior public servants, what motivates them, and what it takes to make it to the top. It reviews mobility in the senior ranks and its implications for program and service delivery in line departments. The chapter also considers the challenges of public sector management under collective bargaining.

Chapter 10 explores the transition from public administration to public management in government operations. Public administration was about centrally prescribed rules and processes, while public management is about outputs, the evaluation of programs, and individual performance. One concentrated on inputs, the other looks at outputs. The chapter makes the case that the transition has failed. Public sector management reforms have not lived up to even modest expectations, while many of the benefits that traditional public administration holds have been lost. The chapter also reviews the role of public servants in policy and decision making and recent changes to the relationships between public servants and politicians.

Chapter 11 considers the impact public management reform measures have had for front-line managers and their staff (the music teacher types). The reforms have, if anything, given life to the theories that borrow from the economic discipline. In brief, rather than solving the problem they set out to fix, they have made matters worse. The chapter affirms the need for public administration and the public service to return to their roots in order to regain credibility both with politicians and with taxpayers. It concludes that the chain of accountability in public spending can be repaired only by recognizing that the public and private sectors are fundamentally different in virtually all aspects and by embracing a Weberian perspective on how the state apparatus should operate.

1

Public Administration without Romance

At about the same time as government bureaucracies came under sustained attack from the political right, political left, the media, the private sector, think-tanks, and the academic community, the study of political science also underwent far-reaching changes. Many in the field began to cast government bureaucracy in a negative light, and public servants were suddenly left with few allies. Even their traditional allies, politicians and students of government and public policy, were now aiming their guns at government bureaucracies rather than jumping to their defence.

It will be recalled that by the late 1970s, politicians had decided to run for office by running against Ottawa, Washington, entrenched government bureaucracies, or whatever else stood in the way of change. The argument went that not only was bureaucracy incapable of generating new ideas, but it invariably stood in the way of those wanting to promote change. Politicians projected an image of government bureaucracies as self-serving, wedded to the status quo, and simply incapable of making their institutions more efficient. Bureaucracy, they argued, had a well-honed capacity of giving the appearance of embracing change while in fact standing still. To this day, politicians who run under the banner "Time for Change" continue to meet with success. Public servants had become the whipping boy, with no one left to defend them.

It was not always thus. There was a time when public servants were trusted by citizens and when politicians – on the government side, at least – had a strong working relationship with them. Politicians would come to their defence if attacked. This was the time when there was what Heclo and Wildavsky described as a "village life," with its own culture, where politicians and public servants shared common beliefs.[1] There was also a traditional bargain that guided relations between politicians and public servants in a Westminster-styled parliamentary system.[2] The bargain brought benefits to both sides: politicians were able to turn to a professional non-partisan public service, dedicated and loyal, while public servants enjoyed tenure and served under the cover of anonymity. That bargain is now broken, in part because it can no longer operate hidden from public view.[3]

Pioneers in the study of political science and public administration, meanwhile, were largely preoccupied with institutions and the proper workings of government departments and their links to centrally prescribed rules and processes. Scholars were largely, if not wholly, preoccupied with the traditional bargain – how institutions should work and the relations between political and bureaucratic actors. It is no exaggeration to say that the roots of public administration and, indeed, of political science itself, can be found in the study of institutions and that they can be traced as far back as Aristotle and Plato.[4] Institutions were what mattered, and individuals were expected to serve the greater good through them. Aristotle and Plato believed that public servants should set aside their personal interests because of their duty to their communities. Plato's guardians were ideal public servants for whom a special type of education was prescribed. They were expected to have no personal possessions.[5]

In its early years at least, political science and public administration sought to define institutions and processes that provided for good government. In Canada, for example, we have R. MacGregor Dawson's *The Civil Service of Canada*, *The Government of Canada*, and *Democratic Government in Canada*. His focus in all three books was on the constitution, the proper workings of Parliament, and the machinery of government.[6] J.E. Hodgetts, the dean of public administration in Canada, also wrote about institutions, including a seminal contribution from an historical perspective: *The Canadian Public Service: A Physiology of Government, 1867–1970*.[7] Another leading Canadian political scientist, James Mallory, attached a great deal of importance to the mechanics of governing and relations between Parliament and government, as demonstrated in his *The Structure of Canadian Government*.[8] Many students of public administration who followed the pioneers in the field continued to focus on the mechanics and processes of governing, again from an institutional perspective. Peter Aucoin, Herman Bakvis, and Paul Thomas, among others, have written extensively about the importance of the merit principle, account-ability, the political neutrality of public servants, and the working of the machinery of government in recent years.[9]

Public servants felt that the pioneers understood their challenges well and knew how political institutions and the machinery of government worked – or, better yet, should work. In their early years, faculty members in political science departments and public administration programs sought to identify ways to structure institutions and organizations in order to shape the behaviour of individuals in pursuit of efficient administration. It will be recalled, for example, that Woodrow Wilson, some 125 years ago, wrote in the second volume of *Political Science Quarterly* that politicians should establish policies and then let administrators run government programs. He went on to argue that the "administration lies outside the proper sphere of politics. Administrative questions are not political questions. Although politics sets the tasks for administration, it should not be suffered to manipulate its offices."[10] The dichotomy was important, he believed, not simply for establishing efficient administration but also for strengthening democracy itself. To separate the two realms would constitute a powerful counterweight to "centrifugal" democracy, since it would create an apolitical public service. In turn, an apolitical public service would provide the institutional underpinning for public servants to go about their work, to provide policy advice to politicians without fear or favour, and to deliver public services free of any partisan considerations.

Public servants saw merit in the work of institutionalists, if only because they generally sided with bureaucracy in its continuing struggle to secure more autonomy from politicians in recruiting and promoting individual public servants and in managing government operations. The work of Dawson, Hodgetts, and Mallory made sense to them because it dealt with how their institutions and organizations operated, or should operate, and how they should relate to politicians. In brief, public servants felt understood and knew that their work was appreciated by the leading political scientists of the day. Moreover, public servants and academics shared common values.

There have been many examples of close cooperation between public servants and students of public administration. The Institute of Public Administration of Canada, for example, was built by public servants from the three orders of government in close cooperation with a small but active circle of faculty members from the public administration community. Robert A. Wardhaugh writes about the close ties between the faculty members at Queen's University and senior public servants in Ottawa in the 1920s,

1930s, and 1940s and discusses how professors such as O.D. Skelton and Clifford Clark shaped both the public service and public policies.[11]

It is perhaps more than a coincidence that institutionalists came under attack about the same time that politicians started to badmouth bureaucrats. Departments of political science began to give way, some forty years ago, to new theories centred around the behaviour of individuals rather than around institutions or organizations. A new generation of political scientists – particularly in the United States but also in Canada and other Western countries – took a markedly different approach to the study of government operations by looking at politics and public administration from the perspective of rent-seeking individuals. In short, both institutionalists and public servants were faced with new fashions and fads in public policy that painted their work in a negative light. One keen observer of government operations writes about a "behavioural revolution" that "fundamentally challenged the discipline of political science and to a lesser extent other social sciences" by looking to the individual rather than to institutions.[12] Institutionalists, the traditional allies of bureaucracy, became *passé* and stood accused of looking at the world from a deeply flawed perspective.

The purpose of this chapter is to review the evolution in the public administration literature as institutionalists gave way to rational, public choice, and principal-agent theories. I have borrowed the title for the chapter from James Buchanan, a leading proponent of public choice theory, who argued that public choice theory should be considered as "politics without romance."[13]

Institutionalists

As already noted, public servants looked to the pioneers in the political science field for both support and guidance. These pioneers sought to put public administration on a more solid non-partisan footing by promoting the establishment of a professional bureaucracy to manage the affairs of state. Institutionalists argue that institutions and organizations are essentially a collection of rules and routines laying out appropriate action for individuals. Institutions, they insist, should provide the basis for members to behave even in ways that may run against their own self-interest.[14]

The important point is that institutionalists believe that institutions have the power to mould the behaviour of individuals and provide meaning for their participation in shaping public policy and delivering public services. Amitia Etzioni, for example, writes that institutions and organizations have three types of incentives with which to shape the behaviour of individuals: coercive, remunerative, and normative.[15] Centrally prescribed financial and administrative rules and processes serve as a check against inappropriate behaviour of public servants and force them to take decisions that have little to do with their own economic self-interest.

J.G. March and J.P. Olsen maintained that public institutions and organizations rely more on normative incentives – the integration of institutions – rather than on coercion to shape the behaviour of their members. They attach a great deal of importance to the "logic of appropriateness" as the critical force in shaping behaviour.[16] Put differently, there are things that public servants would not do after they have been part of the public service for any length of time, simply because they are public servants and because their institution would frown on such behaviour. It is important to stress that in this version of institutionalism, the preferences of individuals are endogenous and are formed once people are in the institution.

Thus, Ottawa operates the way it does because the federal government is home to a number of organizational cultures that shape how individuals react to circumstances and even to managing the demands of the day. Public servants react in certain ways, the argument goes, because their organizations have norms to which they must adjust. Institutions and organizations have their own distinct culture that lay down the appropriate behaviour to which their members should adhere. If they do not, they will find it difficult to operate in the system.

The Ottawa mantra goes: "On policy, you stand where you sit." Accordingly, one can predict how a Department of Finance official will react to a spending proposal. That same official would react quite differently if moved to a spending department such as Transport Canada. It is expected that Finance officials will look for all the weaknesses in spending proposals, whereas Transport officials will marshall the best possible arguments to expand departmental programs and secure new funding. The logic of appropriateness for Finance officials is to oppose all, or most, spending proposals from line departments, and for line departments it is to present the best case possible to protect or expand their departments' sphere of influence, program activities, and budget, and to let someone else worry about the government's fiscal framework.

Gérard Veilleux, a former senior public servant, tells the story of how, early in his career at the Department of Finance, he was called on the carpet by the deputy minister, Simon Reisman. Veilleux had been asked to prepare a briefing note to accompany a proposal to increase widows' pensions, and he had argued that the proposal was sensible, given recent inflationary pressure. Reisman told Veilleux, in the strongest possible terms, that his responsibility was to "shoot holes in departmental proposals, no matter their merit." It was not up to him, but to line departments to sell new spending plans. Veilleux had learned a quick lesson in the behaviour the department expected of its employees – an important lesson if one wanted to climb the organizational ladder.

Historical institutionalists, meanwhile, maintain that initial choices on policy and organizations contribute a great deal to understanding the behaviour of organizations and individuals because they invariably shape subsequent choices and decisions. Put differently, policies, decisions, and behaviour are shaped by initial decisions. There is a body of literature on "path dependency" which maintains that, once launched, institutions, policies, and processes will persist unless a major force jolts them into a new direction.[17] Historical institutionalists believe that the problem with the management of public finance is not that governments spend more on new things but that they are spending too much on old things.[18]

While institutionalists believe that institutions shape the behaviour of individuals, they are less certain that individuals influence the behaviour of institutions. Individuals may well arrive in an institution with their own values and strongly held beliefs, but unless they rise to the top very quickly, unless they lead small organizations, and unless the organization is ready for change, they will soon conform to its "logic of appropriateness."[19] This can take several forms. Government departments, for example, have well-established routines, processes to deal with citizens, and role models that point the way for public servants to adapt to the organization's expectations. Nils Brunsson and Johan P. Olsen, as normative institutionalists, underline the importance of leadership in changing the values of an institution. This squares with much of the private sector management literature.[20]

The above is to make the point that institutions have an inherent logic that members are expected to embrace. There is a "socializing" process that turns individuals into institutional members to the point that some observers maintain that individuals can become "depersonalized" as they adapt to a logic of appropriateness and, perhaps more importantly, to the logic of consequences of their institutions or organizations.[21] The important point here is that institutions and, more specifically, institutional factors, require us to focus on organizational structure in order to gain a better understanding of how and why government officials operate the way they do.

Public servants working under the Westminster parliamentary model learn very early that they are expected to be loyal both to the government of the day and to the culture and rules of their institutions, which should embody honesty, integrity, self-discipline, and respect between politicians and public servants. One only has to read Peter Hennessy's *Whitehall* to gain an appreciation of how British public servants learn the ways of the institution soon after they became members.[22] These values are not always rooted in statutes. Rather, they are rooted in the institutional culture and how members look to long-serving role models for guidance or to gain a rite of passage to the upper echelons.

Canada is no different. Indeed, senior Canadian public servants looked to their British counterparts in creating Canada's machinery of government. Arnold Heeney, the first modern secretary to the cabinet, readily admitted that the modern Privy Council Office was modelled after the Cabinet Office in Britain.[23] The importance of institutional values shines through any reading about the work of public servants in both Canada and Britain, at least, from the 1930s to the 1960s.[24] Canadian public servants have – or at least had – a long-shared common understanding that the public interest differs substantially from private interests. It was their vocation to pursue the public interest, however defined, and they did so while promoting a parsimonious culture and a team spirit.[25]

Growth in government, starting in the 1960s, gave rise to concerns about the people being recruited. Village life was becoming too big, populated by individuals from different backgrounds, many arriving in Ottawa from newly established universities. It was no longer clear what was the right path to the upper ranks, and there was growing uncertainty about the appropriate behaviour of all members. Peer pressure took different shapes because individual public servants identified with different groups. Graduates of Oxford and Queen's University no longer formed the majority of top public servants as francophones, then women, and then visible minorities began to make their presence felt.

Growth in government also involved an important shift in the logic of appropriateness. Public servants were rebranded "rational and budget-maximising bureaucrats." Village life was replaced by a relatively hostile environment. New theories surfaced that captured both the academic community and politicians such as Margaret Thatcher, theories that would have been dismissed by practitioners twenty years earlier as hopelessly unconnected to their real world. Still, Thatcher and like-minded politicians and observers pointed to these theories to explain growth in public spending.

Until the 1960s, the Canadian public service was characterized by a relatively small number of poorly paid civil servants who shared the belief that public service was a civic virtue, a vocation. On size, J.L. Granatstein writes: "Through the Second World War and well beyond, most of the key officials had offices in the East Block. Indeed, it is now difficult to believe that in this building so much political and bureaucratic power was concentrated. The Prime Minister, the Clerk of the Privy Council Office, and the Under-Secretary of State for External Affairs all had their offices there ... The officers of the Department of External Affairs, the staff of the Prime Minister's Office, and the Privy Council Office, were also located there. Finance was close by."[26]

It is also difficult to appreciate how the machinery of government could possibly function with so few people. In 1873 Prime Minister Alexander Mackenzie had no secretary and answered all correspondence himself.[27] In 1909 the newly created Department of External Affairs was entirely housed above a barber shop in Ottawa.[28] Gordon Robertson reports that the 1950 federal-provincial conference involved only about 75 officials; the same conference today would involve at least 375.[29] Moreover, the prime minister now receives about 1.4 million pieces of correspondence annually – letters, emails, faxes, postcards, petitions, greeting requests – and also telephone calls.[30]

On remuneration, Granatstein writes that salaries were low: "Robertson was negotiating trade agreements ... wearing suits that were shiny with use ... Of course, they wanted a comfortable salary, but almost all would have remained at their posts without it."[31] He reports that "they felt a duty to serve their country and its people. If that sounds trite and pious today, it is only because our age is more cynical."[32] Senior public servants believed that they were serving a collective purpose that transcended their personal interests. Anyone claiming that they were rational budget maximizers would have been dismissed out of hand as completely disconnected from reality.

The work of institutionalists and that of senior public servants, however, would soon be challenged, and the impact would be felt throughout academe and government bureaucracies. Critics of institutionalism insist that it can never provide the complete answer because the focus on institutions overlooks the most important factor of all – the personal. Underpinning the new theories was a focus on the role played by individually motivated agents in shaping bureaucratic outcomes and managing government operations.

David Stockman, Ronald Reagan's head of the Office of Management and Budget, publicly applauded the new theories that looked to individuals rather than institutions to explain growth in government spending. Stockman summed up the work of public choice theorists well when he observed, "Do you want to understand why government officials behave the way they do? All you need to know is that they are trying to maximize the budgets of their agencies. Do you want to understand what drives politicians? All you need to know is that they want to be re-elected."[33] Similarly, Margaret Thatcher not only approved of the public choice theorists, she urged her senior bureaucrats to consult them.[34] There is a clear link between public choice, rational choice, and the rise of neoliberalism thinking in Anglo-American democracies.[35]

Public Choice: Look to the Individual, Not to the Institution for Answers

Public choice theorists have introduced a new vocabulary to government: free riding, coalition forming, and agenda setting. They see government not as an institution but as a collection of "budget-maximising" bureaucrats and self-interested politicians pursuing what works best for them and for their personal and economic interests. Apparently, they have a simple remedy for fixing government: have less of it.

Public choice starts with the premise that the "basic behavioural postulate is that man is an egoistic, rational utility maximizer."[36] Economists were the first to develop public choice theory, seeing no reason why individuals should behave differently because they were employed in the public sector. As Alasdair Roberts observes, the theory produced a "bleak view" of politicians, bureaucrats, and indeed of "liberal democracies."[37] Bleak or not, that view is accepted by many observers and politicians in today's more secular and less deferential society. Public choice theorists essentially view government from the perspective of the political and bureaucratic actors who constitute it, assuming that such officials pursue goals and take decisions always with an eye to maximizing their own economic benefits. But what about the actions and decisions of political and bureaucratic actors who are not motivated by economic reasons? As anyone who has worked in government for any length of time can attest, there are numerous public servants who work without having an eye to their own interests. Public choice has precious little to say about them.

The same can be said about rational choice, which has become the dominant theory in many political science departments in Anglo-American democracies. B. Guy Peters maintains that its growing dominance was what motivated March and Olsen to promote their "normative version of new institutionalism."[38] The fundamental logic supporting public choice and rational choice theories is the same: the focus is on the individual, and the theory is that individuals are essentially self-interested agents. Many of the things they do make economic sense to them personally but likely do not benefit the overall population. Indeed, public and rational choice theories see little merit in such terms as "the community" or "the people."[39]

To politicians and many senior public servants, both theories exude an aura of otherworldliness. While they may see some merit in them, they believe that neither theory can paint a full picture of how and why governments decide. They acknowledge that actors at both the political and the bureaucratic level do matter, but they are aware that all are not motivated in the same fashion or for the same reasons; and they claim that institutions, organizations, and processes also matter. Practitioners point out that they do not operate in a vacuum and that we are still far from having an underlying theory to explain why and how government operates.

Principal-Agent Theory

The principal-agent theory has been in fashion in recent years to explain relationships between voters and politicians, politicians and public servants, and how government expenditure budgets are shaped and managed.[40] Like the two above theories, it is rooted in the economics discipline, but it also borrows a page from law. The argument is straightforward: principals cannot have all the information needed to determine whether the agent has performed the tasks expected of him or her. Principal-agent theorists offer a simple and oft-quoted example to make their point: "If you – the principal – hire a gardener – your agent – to mow your lawn while you are away, all you can observe is how the lawn looks when you come back. He could have mowed it every ten days, as you agreed, or he could have waited until two days before you were due home and mowed it only once. By prevailing on a neighbour to monitor your employee's behaviour, you could find out what he actually did, although at some cost."[41]

Principal-agent theory thus refers to the contractual relationship between buyers and sellers. The theory centres on delegation, on the principal turning to an agent or agents to accomplish tasks that the principal cannot perform. Two issues – adverse selection and moral hazard – are central to the theory. The first focuses on whether the right agent is hired; the second on whether the agent does the job appropriately. Moral hazards become a problem because the principal and agent can have conflicting objectives and because the principal cannot always assume that the agent will pursue the principal's best interest. One can monitor the agent's performance, but this can be costly, difficult, and is often uncertain.[42]

One also needs to establish the level of discretion that one is prepared to delegate to the agent. One can attempt to design fairly specific contracts or bargains to establish the relationship between principal and agent, but there are at least two issues that will inhibit this: (1) both principal and agent will try as best they can to maximize their own benefits under the arrangement; (2) it is extremely difficult in modern government to articulate with any degree of precision what will be expected under contractual arrangements. Individuals in government can look to any number of measures to protect their interests, to hide their errors or inactivity, and to explain their inability to perform. They can always point to the work of central agencies, the lack of adequate funding (always a popular one and very difficult to counter), and the role of their political masters (even more difficult to counter). They can make the case that no policy issue belongs to a single government department. Public policy increasingly cuts across orders of government and government departments, so individuals can blame the requirements of horizontal government to explain why things did not work out as planned. A principal can always decide not to delegate responsibilities, but this too is difficult. When you overlay all of this with an emphasis on the individual and a shift away from formal processes, you pose even more challenges for accountability requirements.

Principal-agent models have been widely employed to gain a better understanding of the interactions among groups of institutions or between individuals. They have also been employed to explore issues in public budgeting. Fighting for one's corner and managing the flow of information have been central features of a number of studies on public budgeting.[43] The Prisoner's Dilemma, part of public choice and game theories, is designed to study short-term decision making where actors rely on a process of mutual cooperation to pursue an objective. It is popular in Canada, given the country's political structure. Why would a department, a region, or a constituency agree to see cuts in its sphere of activities only to see another department or region gain new spending or sidestep spending cuts?

In my 1990 book *The Politics of Public Spending in Canada*, I borrowed a page from the Prisoner's Dilemma literature to guide the research. I compared the politics of public spending in Canada to ten people meeting for the first time over lunch. They must decide whether they will share one cheque or ask for ten separate ones. In theory, I argued, if they decided on one shared cheque, they would all choose the most expensive items. But if each were paying individually, they probably would make a different choice: nobody would want to miss the best food while paying for someone else to have it.[44] Given the state of the Canadian federation and Ottawa's machinery of government, I argued that this goes a long way to explaining the dynamics shaping the expenditure budget.

It Depends

There is no optimal form of organization in the public sector, nor is there a widely accepted theory to explain how government decides and why. It depends. It seems that everything depends on key individuals in any organization, on institutional history, political culture, the nature of the programs to be delivered, and many other independent variables.[45] The key to a better understanding of public administration is to focus on both the political actors and the public servants, on the organization, organizational values, available resources, types of clients, the machinery of government, and even the demands of the day. As Paul Thomas has pointed out, politics causes policy, but policy also shapes the patterns of partisan politics and administrative actions.[46]

Long-serving practitioners are convinced that the answer to the question, how and why does government decide? depends on so many forces and variables that it is simply not possible to go with one supposedly all-encompassing theory and declare, "That's it!" Because one theory can never be it. Gérard Veilleux, former secretary to the Treasury Board and head of the Canadian Broadcasting Corporation, echoed a good number of senior government officials when he explained: "Public choice theory contains more than an element of truth and probably the same can be said about principal-agent theory and so on. We know from experience that a department's history and culture will shape thinking and how one views issues. But none can provide the full picture because the full picture is never complete – it is always changing. Circumstances change, actors change, conditions change, the way we do things change. It is not possible to wrap a theory around all of this and make it stick."[47]

Many agree with Veilleux. The exchange between Kenneth Kernaghan, Ian Gow, and Vince Wilson in some ways speaks to the unsuccessful search for theoretical underpinnings. Gow and Wilson offer a revealing title labelled "oppositions impossible to fully resolve in public administration," the oppositions being accountability/horizontal management, accent on results/accent on process, ideology/evidence, employees/taxpayers' rights, and accountability/partnerships.[48]

No less an authority than James Q. Wilson maintains that "reality often does not conform to scholarly theories." He adds, "Some interesting theories of bureaucratic behaviours have been produced by making reasonable assumptions, but the theories so far have not explained very much."[49] Barbara W. Carroll, former editor of *Canadian Public Administration*, argues that there is still considerable distance between theory and practice in public administration and that not much can be done to bridge the gap.[50] I take all these warnings to heel, and I too see little merit in pursuing theoretical purity. I can do no better on this point than quote Don Kettl: "What will it profit the field to gain theoretical purity at the cost of answers that matter to no one?"[51]

Guardians and Spenders

The search for a greater understanding of how and why government decides has led some students of government to examine relations between actors inside government, a popular approach for those interested in public sector budgeting. The public administration literature on government budgeting that divides government actors into guardians and spenders originated with Aaron Wildavsky[52] and still makes good sense. I have employed the guardians-spenders framework in my own work, as have many others studying government budgeting in Western democracies.[53] Wildavsky explains the framework: "Administrative agencies act as advocates of increased expenditure, and central control organs function as guardians of the treasury. Each expects the other to do its job; agencies can advocate, knowing that the centre will impose limits, and the centre can exert control, knowing that agencies will push expenditures as hard as they can. Thus, roles serve in calculating mechanisms. The interaction between spending and cutting roles makes up the component elements of budgeting systems."[54]

David Good, in *The Politics of Public Money*, confirms that practitioners relate well to this framework. However, he makes a convincing case that the framework alone can no longer explain how Ottawa's budget process takes shape. He argues that spenders now incorporate guardian functions in their roles and vice versa; further, there are new actors making their presence felt. He points to the role played by what he labels "priority setters" in shaping and implementing the expenditure budget. These priority setters are central agencies other than Finance (i.e., the Privy Council Office and the Prime Minister's Office) and financial watchdogs, including officers of Parliament, notably the Office of the Auditor General.[55]

More to the point, Good's findings demonstrate that we cannot look to a single framework or to a comprehensive theory to explain how government budgets are formulated, how government decides and why, and how politicians and public servants interact. There are many rivulets of thought, many institutions, many actors, and many forces – at times contradictory ones – that invariably come into play. The world of government has its own distinct characteristics and it is vastly different from the private sector in both important and unimportant ways.[56]

Accountability: Rules or the Individual?

While a good number of public servants I worked with dismiss out of hand the relevance of public choice and rational choice, they do not so easily dismiss the Herman Finer/Carl Friedrich debate on accountability. The classic debate remains as pertinent, if not more so, than when it was first given voice over seventy years ago.[57] Finer insisted that accountability can best be assured by putting in place detailed processes, rules, controls, regulations and sanctions. The objective is to limit discretionary judgment as much as possible, and when it is not possible to rely on hierarchy, on a clear chain of command that stops with the elected leaders. Finer was clearly inspired by the work of Max Weber and the military model.

Weber sought to specify exactly how a bureaucratic organization should function.[58] He believed that officials should be organized in a clearly defined hierarchy of offices; that each office should have a clearly, legally defined sphere of competence; that work in the office can constitute a career; and that officials are subject to strict and systematic descriptions and controls in the conduct of their respective offices. Weber saw distinct roles and responsibilities not only for government departments but also for each position, so that the incumbents would understand clearly what was expected of them and then be held to account for their activities. In Weber's bureaucracy, with its clear lines of authority and subordination, hierarchy and technical skills are important for a host of reasons. The defining of the necessary technical skills not only ensures an efficient organization but also insulates it from "dilution by influences from outside and corruption from within the organization."[59] Hierarchy provides clear lines of authority through which commands can be transmitted, and it allows "calculability of results" for those in positions of authority.[60] Moreover, a hierarchical division of responsibility and authority ensures that the higher office does not take over the work of the lower and also gives the "governed" a clear line for appealing "the decision of a lower office to the corresponding superior authority."[61]

Carl Friedrich, on the other hand, attached more importance to the ability of public servants for self-direction, self-regulation, and sound judgment than to rules and regulations. Finer believed that individuals are generally flawed, so rules and sanctions are necessary; Friedrich thought that individuals have wisdom, good judgment, and can make good decisions, and he argued that, in any case, one could never design controls and sanctions to deal with all circumstances and all contexts. No matter the level of controls, at some point citizens and politicians need to rely on the judgment of public servants.

At least on the face of it, the traditional public administration model squares with Herman Finer's view while, to some extent, New Public Management (NPM) measures correspond to the work of Carl Friedrich. The public administration literature attaches a great deal of importance to elaborate and standard accountability requirements, while NPM ostensibly seeks to "let the manager manage," a call that has been heard time and again in Ottawa for the past fifty years.

From Public Administration to Public Management

It seems that by the 1980s a number of practitioners and students of public administration had given up on the public administration discipline. It had become associated with government inefficiency, outdated rules, regulations, and processes, and the apparent inability of political leaders to steer the ship of state. The search was at first led by Margaret Thatcher and her consultants as they sought to introduce a private sector organizational culture to the United Kingdom's machinery of government.[62] Many senior public servants preferred to stay on the sidelines – wedded to the Weberian model with its emphasis on hierarchy and "calculable rules without regard for persons" – having decided that it was time to batten down the hatches and wait for the latest storm to pass.[63] The storm did not pass. Thatcher and her followers had limited interest in Weberian practices. They had a bias for action and wanted results and better management, and if public servants could not come up with new approaches, then they should look to their private sector counterparts for solutions.

Public servants – with enthusiasm or not – went about implementing measures largely conceived in the private sector or at least inspired by it. Program reviews in the 1980s were led or co-chaired by leading private sector executives in Britain (Derek Rayner), the United States (Peter Grace), and Canada (the Nielsen Task Force).[64] Senior public servants were told that they were not very competent managers and should look to their private sector counterparts for inspiration and best practices. Many public servants came to believe this. As a result, a new approach – New Public Management – was born in Britain under Thatcher and soon spread to all Anglo-American democracies.

Essentially, NPM was designed to give political leaders the ability to re-orient policies so that public services were delivered in an efficient, businesslike fashion.[65] A new vocabulary, if not a new way of thinking, found its way into government operations. If public servants were no longer trusted in steering the ship of state, things were different when it came to management. Front-line managers and their workers were to be empowered, to have the freedom to manage their operations with a minimum of constraints, much like their private sector counterparts. A number of centrally prescribed rules governing human and financial resources were done away with, and new agencies were established and given a mandate to focus on management. The goal was straightforward: make the public sector look like the private sector because private sector executives are much better managers than those in the public sector.

Without doubt, the accepted wisdom of the political leadership of the past thirty years or so in Anglo-American democracies, both right and left, is that private sector management practices are far superior to those found in government. The public service bureaucracy and the "old" public administration, with its emphasis on centrally prescribed rules, were the villain, and a lack of solid management practices was the problem that needed fixing – hence the introduction of NPM.

Margaret Thatcher, Tony Blair, Bill Clinton, Jean Chrétien, and many other political leaders turned to the private sector to reform their bureaucracies, *faute de mieux*.[66] In their attempt to introduce a stronger management culture to government operations, they had nowhere else to turn but to the private sector. After all, senior public servants were not about to admit that their management practices were inadequate. In any event, they had not historically attached much importance to management; centrally prescribed rules and regulations were there to take care of it. Management matters properly belonged to those "who are seen by the mandarins as not being able to make it to the top."[67] Put differently, for the more senior public servants, management was of less concern and importance than policy work. They believed that politicians could talk a fine line on management, but when push came to shove, their political masters would turn to them to fix things and to define policy on the run.

The introduction of a private sector management culture to government did, however, need the support of senior public servants – hardly a given. Although the political leadership considered that the policy role of the civil service was "deeply illegitimate," public servants could not be expected to acquiesce in this view.[68] Regardless, many politicians insisted that nonelected officials had become too powerful in shaping policy and that they should be sent back to a more legitimate role – that of implementing policy decisions and managing government resources more efficiently. Adjusting to the new role would not be easy. The road to the top for career public servants had usually been through policy rather than administration. "Have policy experience, will travel" had long been the byword for the ambitious in government. In any event, senior career public servants are trained as professionals and over the years have developed considerable policy expertise in their areas of work.

Gordon Robertson, described as the "gold standard" by at least some of his colleagues when he was clerk of the privy council and head of the Canadian civil service from the mid-1960s to the mid-1970s, did not discuss management issues in his memoirs.[69] He did, however, mention that administrative matters frequently left him insufficient time to deal with major policy issues.[70] Al Johnson, a deputy minister in the 1960s in Ottawa, published an article titled, "The Role of the Deputy Minister" in which he never once employed the word "management." He wrote: "The role of the deputy minister is to make it possible for the minister and the cabinet to provide the best government of which they are capable – even better if either of them happens to be weak."[71]

So long as centrally prescribed rules governed financial and administrative decisions, senior public servants were free to focus on policy and help cabinet ministers provide the best government of which they were capable. This approach promoted a parsimonious culture in government operations: input costs were carefully controlled, and pre-spending comptrollers were in place to ensure that departments had the financial resources before spending commitments could be made. Establishing a new position or re-classifying an existing one required a great deal of paperwork and a hierarchy in departments and central agencies that were not easily convinced. Government was smaller then, and anything of consequence was brought to the attention of senior officials. Lester Pearson, at the time a senior official at External Affairs, became exasperated with the kind of details requiring a ministerial signature. He wrote a memorandum in October 1941 to his deputy minister asking how he was "going to show the Prime Minister how to win the war and make the peace," if he had to "spend two hours each day talking about the cost of Désy's table linen or the salary of the newest stenographer."[72]

It is important to note that NPM has little in the way of theoretical underpinnings. For traditionalist public servants, it was an unwelcome baby left on the doorstep by politicians who were convinced that public servants had too much influence, if not power, in shaping policy; and that government bureaucracy cost too much and delivered too little. NPM is not wedded to a comprehensive theory other than the view that the private sector and its superior management practices hold the key to better and more efficient government.

Yet, to this day, no one has been able to duplicate market forces inside government operations. It is not for want of trying. We have seen a plethora of performance measurement schemes, management targets, and oversight bodies, and we have witnessed an explosive growth in the program evaluation industry. Performance pay schemes also have been in vogue since the days of Thatcher, Reagan, and Mulroney. Neither program evaluation efforts nor pay-for-performance schemes, however, have ever been able to live up to expectations.[73] Indeed, there is evidence that both have given rise to gaming and attempts on the part of departments and public servants to distort government priorities.[74]

Notwithstanding various NPM measures, performance in government is in the eye of the beholder – hardly an objective criterion on which to base a performance pay scheme. It may explain why whatever amount of money is allocated to performance pay schemes is invariably used up; and why, several years ago, well over 90 percent of public service managers in the Government of Canada received a performance reward. This prompted the private sector chair of the advisory committee on retention and compensation of senior managers to observe that the committee "will refrain from recommending further increases ... until the government shows a commitment to ensuring the program does not reward poor performers."[75] However, the chair did not explain how one could determine poor performance among the senior ranks of the public service.

There have been other developments that suggest that the parsimonious culture that once was an important component of the values that defined the public service has faded. NPM's removal of a number of centrally prescribed rules has, to some extent, empowered government managers. This, in turn, has allowed the public service and, more specifically, individual departments to act as self-governing organizations on a number of management matters. For example, we increasingly hear about "classification creep," which increases the payroll.[76]

NPM has important implications for representative democracy. Some NPM measures were based on an individual-economic model. The thinking was that all management challenges are similar and therefore should be approached in similar ways.[77] It assumes that there is little difference between political and management accountability and between the public and private sectors, at least when it comes to management. Yet NPM differs from traditional public administration and the latter's accountability requirements, with the emphasis on input costs, processes, hierarchical control, and culture traditions. It quickly became apparent that NPM accountability requirements were lacking, and this gave rise to other shortcomings, including lack of adequate policy and program coordination.

It Is Now All about Governance

Although NPM has been found wanting, precious few voices are being heard for a return to the old public administration paradigm. Even left-of-centre politicians have continued to sing the praises of business management practices.[78] Many public servants, too, are in no mood to move away from NPM's management flexibility and return to centrally prescribed rules and regulations. In many ways, NPM has become the new status quo.

Meanwhile, the search is on to adjust NPM more to the realities of the public sector. By the 1990s, governance, however defined, had become the new fashion in Anglo-American democracies. It will be recalled that the National Academy of Public Administration dropped the term "public administration" in favour of the new buzz word, "governance."[79] Governance has come to mean virtually anything and everything: "steering at a distance," "managerialism," "network management," "oversight and transparency," "governing through network," "a shift from a bureaucratic state to a hollow state," "governance without government" ... and the list goes on.[80] H. George Frederickson summed it up well when he wrote: "Governance is fashionable – not only the flavour of the month but also of the year and the decade ... The concept is imprecise and, when applied, it is so broad that virtually any meaning can be attached to it."[81]

Peter Aucoin has written about New Public Governance (NPG) which, he maintains, has integrated permanent election campaigns in the art of governing. He has noted three main features of NPG: the rise of partisan political staff as a third force in governing; the politicization of appointments at the senior levels of the public service; and public service loyalty to the government of the day to the extent that it now borders on being promiscuously partisan.[82] NPG also speaks to the concentration of political power at the centre of government, either to move policy initiatives or to manage permanent election campaigns.

The reader may well conclude that both government bureaucracy and the public administration discipline now suffer from an identity crisis. They do. Economics has had a profound effect on the discipline with attempts to identify incentives that decision makers in the public sector follow. Public administration, meanwhile, remains concerned with prescriptions, with normative rules and processes for public servants to follow in order to make decisions that benefit all of society. Students of public administration have been on the defensive in recent years, and the impact has been felt in government. Jon Pierre maintains that some thirty years ago, public sector reformers looked to their own institution and its history for reform. Now, he notes, reformers look to outside forces, to the private sector as a source for reform.[83]

Few in the academic community or in government still speak of public administration, yet New Public Management and New Public Governance have not been able to fill the void. The public sector is still regarded as inefficient, overly large and cumbersome, and unable to deal with stubborn deficits, both financial and democratic. Bureaucracy's traditional allies have been increasingly critical of governmental performance, and many observers continue to cling to the individual economic model to explain the public sector's inherent problems.

Few believe that the search for a comprehensive theory in public administration or public management has been successful or that there is much merit in pursuing the search. Some students of government argue that we should simplify the objective and search for a "proper and universally acceptable definition of public administration, given there is little agreement on what constitutes principles of public administration."[84] Some of the leading scholars of public administration, from Dwight Waldo to James Q. Wilson, have sought to advance the discipline by focusing on what works best in different circumstances and different organizations. They have avoided the search for a comprehensive theoretical design, insisting that there is no one best way to organize and that the search will not meet with much success, if any.[85] Christopher Pollitt put his finger on the problem when he argued that developing and testing theoretical propositions requires a consistency of objectives, terminology, and capacity measures over time.[86] As students of public administration know full well, and as the chapters below illustrate, we have witnessed a plethora of constantly changing reforms and new approaches to public administration that inhibit theoretical advancement.

John L. Manion, former Treasury Board secretary, associate clerk of the Privy Council Office, and founder of the Canadian Centre for Management Development – later renamed the Canada School of Public Service – lamented the work of the academic community. He once told me, "Academics are quite good at telling us what's wrong about government and why things are the way they are. They have a point. However, I cannot think of a single academic in recent years telling us: Here is how things should work, here is how you can improve government operations or here is a solution. I can tell you that I would truly welcome such a contribution, and I am sure many of my colleagues feel the same way."[87] This book's last chapter attempts to answer his call.

2

Parliament: Try a Blank Piece of Paper

In a parliamentary system, voters confer authority on Parliament, Parliament confers authority on the prime minister and cabinet, and, leaving aside some notable exceptions, the prime minister and ministers confer authority on government departments and agencies. The accountability of the prime minister, the ministers, and their departments to Parliament is fundamental to our system of responsible government. Every year, departments, crown corporations, and agencies submit to Parliament reams and reams of documents in the name of accountability.

It is now widely acknowledged that accountability in government is in a state of disrepair and that the massive piles of government documents sent to Parliament are of little help. Shawn Murphy, the former chair of Parliament's Public Accounts Committee, said as much when he met with senior financial officials, including those from the Treasury Board Secretariat, at a retreat in 2008. He challenged them to insert some blank pages in their documents to see if MPs would notice. He felt confident that the MPs would not. He reminded the committee that one year the Department of Justice simply "forgot" to include financial statements for the firearms registry, a controversial initiative widely reported in the media.[1] No one noticed. Murphy concluded by observing that what they were sending to Parliament was too complex, too voluminous, and too convoluted to be of any use either to parliamentarians or to anyone else.[2] What in fact he was saying is that the principal-agent theory holds considerable promise in explaining how and why governments decide.

The role of Parliament is intimately tied to the spending of public money. In many ways Parliament, under the Westminster model, was born out of a desire to control public spending better and to hold the spenders accountable for their decisions. The history of the Westminster parliamentary system is essentially a story of the struggle between the monarch and Parliament over money. In brief, parliamentary control of the public purse is directly tied to the ability of the House of Commons to establish a spending cap every year on the amount of funds that the government can spend and to hold the government to account.

The Magna Carta, the Bill of Rights, and the Act of Settlement were all designed to limit the power of the crown and then to hold it to account. It was during the reign of Edward III (1327–77) when Parliament started to take form. Although monarchs would learn ways to get around it, the precedent was set that no tax could be imposed without Parliament's consent. In time, this right became established, and in 1868 C.D. Yonge was able to state that the first principle of the British constitution was "the omnipotence of Parliament."[3] Parliament's omnipotent role in the spending of public money is also made clear in Canada's constitution (Constitution Act, 1867, s. 53). No public money can be spent without parliamentary approval. In addition, only the crown or the government can initiate a request for public spending.[4]

There was a time when Parliament was omnipotent, when it really did rule. Vernon Bogdanor labels this era as Parliament's "golden age" – the postwar period until the 1960s, before judges became assertive.[5] He could have gone farther back in history to the years that followed government by the crown but preceded government by parties. Between the two Reform Acts of 1832 and 1872 in Britain, no less than ten governments lost power because they lost the confidence of the House of Commons. Adam Tomkins explains that with the arrival of the modern, centralized organization of the political party came the "greatest single challenge that the system of political accountability had yet to face."[6]

Practitioners, no less than students of government, may well suffer from a case of "golden ageism." But whatever the reasons, our national political and administrative institutions no longer command the respect that they once did. In the case of Parliament, its members are the first to admit this. The purpose of this chapter is to consider Parliament's role in the budget process and in holding the spenders to account.

Parliament: Bella Figura

Parliament's role is to provide a forum where representatives from across Canada come together to meet and *parler*. But it is more than this, or at least it should be. Parliament represents the country's leading and legitimate deliberative body. It establishes a legitimate government, makes government work by allocating resources and adopting legislation, makes government behave and holds it accountable, and provides for an alternative government. It also functions to express the "mind of the people, teach society and inform both government and citizens of grievances and problems."[7]

Is Parliament fulfilling its historical role of allocating resources and making government work? Hardly. All is not well on this front and has not been so for some time. No less an authority on the subject than Robert Marleau, former clerk of the Canadian House of Commons, maintains that the Commons has "almost abandoned its constitutional responsibility of supply."[8] Lowell Murray, a highly respected minister in the Mulroney government's cabinet, recently had this to say: "Parliament – specifically the House of Commons – over a period of more than forty years, has allowed its most vital power, the power of the purse, to become a dead letter, their Supply and Estimates process an empty ritual."[9] The problem is not new. More than fifty years ago, Norman Ward, in his widely quoted book *The Public Purse*, stated that "the record of the Canadian House of Commons in the scrutiny of executive expenditures is not good."[10]

Things have only deteriorated since Ward published his book. Parliament – like other institutions – has dropped several notches on the "trust" scale in recent years. Indeed, study after study reports this phenomenon in much of the Western world.[11] Politicians and public servants now deal with a vastly different and more complex society than existed thirty years ago. Richard Wilson, cabinet secretary in Britain, 1998–2002, observed in 2006 that "the public are no longer patient or deferential."[12] Neil Nevitte's work on the "Decline of Deference," in which he compared Canadian values from a comparative perspective, is, if anything, even more pertinent today than when it was first published in 1996.[13]

The *Hill Times*, an independent Ottawa-based publication about Parliament, MPs, their staff, and government bureaucracy, ran an editorial on 25 April 2011 declaring that "Parliament is broken" and MPs "should fix it."[14] In a lead editorial, the Toronto *Globe and Mail* argued on the eve of the 2011 election that "the next House of Commons must find new ways to protect Parliament, the heart of our democracy."[15] The editorial was not clear about whom the House of Commons had to protect Parliament from or what had caused Parliament to need protection, but it received the endorsement of many academics and practitioners. The decline of the role of Parliament in the nation's business has given rise to a variety of studies and task forces in recent years, all intent on making Parliament more relevant.[16] A well-known student of politics wrote an article asking, "Is the decline of Parliament irreversible?" He concluded with a plea for Canadians to "rediscover the relevance of political institutions."[17]

At the heart of the problem is the fact that senior government officials, and at times the government, all too often regard Parliament as a nuisance, an obstacle to be ignored or overcome, an institution whose members are essentially concerned only with scoring partisan political points. It will be recalled that the Speaker of the House of Commons ruled on 9 March 2011 that "on its face," the government was in contempt of Parliament for failing to disclose information requested by the House's finance committee.[18]

Members of Parliament have also been vocal about the state of their institution. A bipartisan committee of MPs concluded in 2003 that Parliament "has, in a sense, lost its way."[19] More recently, Samara, an independent research organization, has teamed up with the Canadian Association of Former Parliamentarians to produce insightful reports based on "exit interviews" with MPs. The reports speak of "frustrations," "confusion," and even "embarrassment" with their institution.[20] The group has thus far published three reports, including one with a revealing title: *Welcome to Parliament: A Job with No Description*. This report reveals that there is little "consistency" among MPs about their proper role. It discusses their arrival in Ottawa "largely unprepared for what lay ahead," and it notes that they have "little initial sense of where to focus" and that "their assignments seemed to be allocated at random."[21]

A member of Parliament is essentially expected to perform three roles: review, refine if necessary, and pass legislation; authorize the spending of public money and hold the government accountable; and decide to support or withdrew confidence in the government. On the face of it, one could conclude that these functions belong to a different era. Unlike in nineteenth-century Britain, MPs are hardly free to decide to support or withdraw confidence in the government. It is a news item of considerable interest when an MP decides to disregard party discipline, if only because it is so rarely done and because it challenges the party leader openly. Party discipline is alive and well in the Canadian Parliament, and no majority government is at risk of losing the confidence of the House of Commons.

Samara's report *It's My Party: Parliamentary Dysfunction Reconsidered* discusses the politics of party discipline. One MP said that in Question Period, MPs are like "potted plants," moved around for decoration. The report reveals that in their exit interviews, "MPs spoke of seemingly juvenile punishments" meted out by their party's leadership for actions or even opinions that met with disapproval.[22]

Of course, it was considerably easier for members of Parliament to authorize the spending of public money and to hold the government to account in the days when government was smaller and issues were straightforward. Earl Grey had to debate in Parliament the merits of the sale of a surplus horse, and there was a time when ministers had to defend before Parliament the hiring of an engineer, a clerk, or a secretary by their departments.[23] Things are vastly different today, in view of the size and complexity of government departments. The same can be said about reviewing and refining legislation in the era of the Charter of Rights and Freedoms, since policies and programs – in both orders of government – are increasingly interwoven.

Losing Its Way

If, as the bipartisan committee of MPs argued, Parliament has lost its way, nowhere is this more evident than in the approval of the spending of public money and the accountability of policy and decision making. There are several reasons for this: first, the process has become inaccessible to parliamentarians; second, there are too many hands and voices involved, thus confusing the non-specialists; and third, we have a new approach to government decision making that does not square with the workings and realities of the public sector. This is not to suggest that Parliament no longer has a process by which to approve government spending plans. In fact, the process never ends. Pick any month of the year, and there is intense activity in government or in Parliament in approving and monitoring the government's spending plans. Ottawa's budget process has been well described elsewhere, so here we need only highlight the more salient points.[24]

More often than not, the minister of finance tables the budget speech in February. The speech is the proverbial tip of the iceberg. The budget refers to the country's economic circumstances, outlines planned spending by departments, and provides for unallocated reserves to support new initiatives established during the coming year, changes in expenditure forecasts, and emergencies. Several months before the budget speech – in October of the previous year – departments and agencies will have submitted to the Treasury Board Secretariat their Annual Reference Level Update (ARLU). The purpose here is to establish funding for the existing authorities, the existing level of services, and all previously approved measures. Treasury

Board officials then undertake a review of these estimates, looking for errors or attempts to pad existing budgets. They were, however, much better at doing this twenty or thirty years ago, and more is said about this below.

At about the same time, the minister of finance makes a presentation to cabinet to provide an economic and fiscal update. This takes stock of the economic circumstances and the government's fiscal situation – spending, revenues, and surplus or size of the deficit. The cabinet is in fact briefed on budget issues throughout the year, including, whenever possible, a June retreat to ponder broad political, policy, and budgetary issues. There are also ongoing discussions with private sector economic forecasters. These discussions, including presentations to cabinet, deal with broad economic or fiscal issues and rarely if ever address specific issues.

Preceding the budget, the minister of finance also initiates wide-ranging consultations with the House of Commons Standing Committee on Finance. These involve an "Economic and Fiscal Update," in which the minister outlines the economic circumstances and the government's budget objectives. The minister and senior departmental officials then conduct a series of consultations with expert witnesses and interest groups, while the Standing Committee holds public hearings. The discussions deal with very broad economic and budgetary issues. Parliament has no decision-making authority in these prebudget consultations.[25]

Effective decision-making authority in government rests with the prime minister and the minister of finance. The two, along with their most trusted political and bureaucratic advisers, determine the broad contours of the budget, decide which new spending commitments they are prepared to support, and agree on how to deal with the spending departments and the departments' ministers. Both the prime minister and the minister of finance are sure to be subjected to intense pressure from ministers and their departments to support new initiatives. Thus, they manage the budget process carefully, often paying attention to the various consultations only to the extent they find them useful or support their perspective. The point is that the true architects of the budget are the prime minister, the minister of finance, and their more senior advisers.[26]

The day the budget is to be tabled in Parliament, the minister of finance informs cabinet of the highlights of the budget speech. A budget lockup is held on budget day to which journalists and interest-group representatives are invited to put questions to government officials. The budget establishes the government's fiscal framework, the level of revenues and expenditures, and proposed new spending initiatives or tax measures. The budget is one of the government's major planned events every year.

Not long after the minister of finance has read the budget speech, the president of the Treasury Board tables the government's spending estimates. The House of Commons begins its deliberations (the Business of Supply) and refers the estimates to its standing committees. Each department and agency is tied to a specific standing committee, and its ministers and officials are invited to appear before the committee to answer questions on its spending plans. The standing committees are able to draw from a variety of documents in reviewing departmental spending estimates: the budget, the government's expenditure plan, the estimates and the Reports on Plans and Priorities (RPPs), and Departmental Performance Reports (DPRs).

Several points need to be underlined here. First, if by 31 May the standing committees have not reported back to the Commons, they are "deemed" to have reported. Second, the work of standing committees has been questioned by a number of people. The authors of a parliamentary study of the supply process, for example, concluded that "the vast sums of money spent by government are subjected to only perfunctory parliamentary scrutiny."[27] A longtime observer of the Canadian Parliament wrote that "most committee meetings on estimates involve wide-ranging and relatively partisan exchanges over political priorities and the policy directions of departments, minimal attention to the substance of the estimates, and predictable votes in support of the estimates as proposed by government majorities on committees."[28] A twenty-year veteran at the Library of Parliament, assigned to work with parliamentary committees, reports that it has become increasingly difficult for staff to encourage committee members to take a strong interest in the spending estimates. She says that staff always press committees to allocate more days to review the estimates, and committee members always push back for fewer days. She explains: "Committee members by and large do not see the importance of reviewing the estimates to gain a better understanding of what departments do and why. It is sad, really."[29] All in all, the Commons allocates twenty days to review the spending estimates. However, the opposition often decides to employ these days for other purposes. Regardless, the appropriate legislation has to be approved by June.

Three students of Parliament went to the heart of the matter by looking at incentives or de-incentives for MPs in reviewing the estimates. They argue that there "is little or nothing to motivate MPs and lots to de-motivate them from seriously delving into the estimates." For one thing, voters do not reward MPs for spending the time required to scrutinize estimates. In addition, difficult or awkward questions "may not be rewarded in the

Ottawa" environment. Moreover, most MPs do not have the skills – or the time to develop the skills – to assess the government's spending plans, nor do they have access to people with the knowledge to do so. Lastly, the tabling of the estimates coincides with what is often the busiest period for standing committees.[30]

There are two kinds of expenditures: voted and statutory appropriations. Voted appropriations require parliamentary approval every year, while statutory expenditures are authorized on a continuing basis through legislation. In 1963, voted appropriations represented 58 percent of all expenditures, but by 2004 the number had dropped to 35 percent. Today, the number is 36.5 percent.[31] The point is that the annual discretion of Parliament, ministers, and public servants over government spending has been substantially reduced during the past fifty years or so.[32] Statutory items may not be amended; they are included in the estimates only "for information." In addition, proposals to transfer funds from one vote to another under voted appropriations are ruled out of order because they would have the effect of increasing a vote. Given that only the crown or the government can initiate new spending, all that committees can do is reduce the amount of a vote. They have no authority either to increase a vote or to decrease one in order to increase another.

To sum up, the business of supply hinges on three fundamental points: The executive must have some assurance that its requests for funds will be dealt with by certain fixed dates if it is to continue providing services to Canadians; Parliament must have a reasonable opportunity to examine proposed expenditures; and failure to grant supply by not approving the estimates is an established means for demonstrating non-confidence in the government.

A series of measures, including special review committees, were launched in 1963 to overhaul the business of supply. The efforts came to a close in 1968, when the House adopted the report of a special procedural committee and agreed to substantial changes to supply. The committee had concluded that "among the most time consuming, repetitive and archaic procedures inherited by the Canadian Parliament are those relating to the business of supply."[33] The new standing orders adopted in December 1968 introduced several changes. First, debate of the estimates moved from the House (Committee of Supply) to standing committees. The Committee of Supply, however, was still meeting, but under another name and under relaxed rules. The House, it was thought when the reforms were introduced, could now focus on other matters, including the government's legislative agenda. Second, the changes gave the government a firm financial calendar, which strengthens its hand in its dealings with Parliament. All estimates were now to be referred to standing committees on or before 1 March and, as noted above, the committees must report back to the House by 31 May, otherwise they are simply "deemed" to have approved the estimates. Third, under the old system, opposition parties used filibusters to extract concessions from the government. The changes provided twenty-five days as "allotted days," during which two motions could be tabled as motions of non-confidence in the government, and the allotted days became "supply" or "opposition days."

There have been further adjustments since 1968, but the broad outline remains intact. The more recent changes have, for example, reduced the number of allotted days from twenty-five to twenty; in the early 1970s, changes to the estimates allowed spending plans to correspond to broad program objectives; and in 1981–82 the estimates were overhauled (divided into three parts) to provide more background information.

Before 1968, MPs could focus on administrative details or inputs (numbers of public servants, their salaries, travel expenses, and so on) and urge spending cuts in these areas. They could easily grasp salary and travel budgets and compare the operation of one department to another and even one administrative unit to another. This process came under heavy criticism in some quarters – mostly in government and among senior public servants – because it tended to focus political debate on administrative issues rather than on policy or program objectives. While we have fewer debates on the administrative or input cost of programs, we have not had much of an increase in debates in the Commons on policy or program objectives. The changes assumed that MPs would have the same level of interest and knowledge to plow through information on program evaluation as they had on administrative issues.

There is now broad agreement that the 1968 changes made things worse. It is extremely difficult to find anyone, other than perhaps ministers and public servants, satisfied with the current arrangement. Scholars have argued that "from all sides the view is the same: the review of the estimates is often meaningless" and MPs have "been relegated to a role in the financial process of government that is very marginal."[34] In 1993 the chairs of all standing committees tabled a report that stated: "As a result of the 1968 decision to transfer estimates from Committee of the Whole to Standing Committees, Canadian MPs in a majority Parliament have effectively lost the power to reduce government expenditures. Members are therefore making the very rational calculation that there is no point devoting time and effort to an exercise over which they can have no influence."[35]

Herb Gray, a veteran MP who served before 1968, observed, as government House leader under Jean Chrétien, that "the Estimates are complex and difficult to analyse and are, for constitutional reasons, difficult to change. In addition, their consideration is subject to a rigorous timetable. As a result, the examination of the Main Estimates has become rather cursory and there has been no focus for parliamentary debate on government spending before its spending priorities are actually set."[36] Robert Giroux, former deputy minister of public works and government services and secretary to the Treasury Board, reports that in all his appearances before a House standing committee, he could remember only "once when actually a question was asked on the document we called Part III of the estimates." He added that when briefing ministers he always said, "Don't worry about all that information, you will not get a question on that. We know what to expect and that is what will enable the opposition to score political points."[37] Committee meetings on estimates involve for the most part relatively partisan exchanges, paying minimal attention to the estimates.[38]

Some career officials are no more positive about the estimates process. John L. Manion believed that the 1968 changes altered Parliament's relationships with the government and with career officials, and that only the government and senior public servants obtained long-term benefits. Because of the fixed calendar for approval, Parliament could no longer delay supply indefinitely and apply pressure to lower spending plans. Manion revealed that opposition parties accepted the changes in return for some funding to support activities in their consistency offices and in Ottawa.

But he argued that this advantage came at a tremendous cost, since it "caused Parliament to lose its main function, i.e., holding the Government to account." In a report to the Office of the Auditor General, he explained: "The new procedures produced significant advantages for the government, principally a fixed supply calendar, greater freedom to advance its legislative program and some reduction of the potential for opposition harassment offered by the Old Supply process. By 1991 [opposition MPs] were complaining that ministers had reduced attendance at committees to a minimum, often restricting their input to a pro forma opening statement at the commencement of the review of the estimates, then have their officials handle all but policy questions. This practice has continued and reflects an erosion of the principle of ministerial responsibility, while exposing officials to the sometimes hostile treatment of frustrated MPs." He added, "Within the new committees, there was seldom much interest in expenditures – except to demand more for their constituencies and ferret out information for political purposes. Committee proceedings are generally of little interest to the media, are not televised, and many members have lost interest."[39]

Career officials report that they have sought to do their part in improving the estimates process by providing Parliament with more and better information. The estimates now involve thousands and thousands of pages of detailed information.[40] They are tabled in three parts over a four-week period. Part I provides an overview of federal spending and summarizes key elements of the main estimates. Part II presents a detailed listing of the resources required by individual departments and agencies for the next fiscal year. (In the 2002–03 estimates, these two parts covered 338 pages; by 2011–12, the number had risen to 405 pages.) Part III outlines individual expenditure plans for each department and agency, but not for crown corporations.

For 2001–02 there were 87 reports. That for Agriculture and Agri-Food Canada, for example, contained 67 pages. Part III also provides for a report on departmental performance (DPR). It is designed to report on "the government's commitments – to improve accountability for results." All federal government organizations receiving appropriations must now report their performance to the Treasury Board Secretariat and to Parliament.[41] For the fiscal year 2009–10, Agriculture and Agri-Food Canada's DPR had three distinct sections dealing with departmental programs, the department's contributions to the government's strategic outcomes, and on risks and spending plans, all in 50 pages for a single department. But that is not all. The Treasury Board president regularly tables documents such as *Results for Canadians: A Management Framework for the Government of Canada* to explain financial-management practices further. The president also tables expenditure plans for crown corporations on behalf of the ministers who preside over them.[42] Finally, the government annually tables thousands of pages of information under the rubric of public accounts. Today, there are 92 reports tabled as part of the estimates.[43] These reports are essentially communication tools rather than accountability documents, and MPs see little merit in reviewing them.

MPs now complain that they are inundated with data and documents. When the estimates under the present format were introduced in the early 1980s, they had to be hauled into the House on heavily laden carts, much to the amusement of MPs.[44] There is considerable evidence to suggest that MPs do not read the material. Those whom I met tell me that they do not, and career officials have expressed frustration that they have answered questions in standing committees simply by *reading* sections of Part III.[45]

Quite apart from the estimates documents, there is a constant stream of program evaluations made available to MPs, but most are inconclusive and are rarely understood by the non-specialist. MPs, like anyone else, can understand the elements of a straight itemized budget, such as the number of public servants required to run a program or the level of resources allocated to travel expenses. The information is concrete and easily grasped. But Bob Bryce, a former clerk of the privy council and deputy minister of finance, was sceptical about the new, "elaborate systems of goal-setting and the evaluation of efficiency and effectiveness in many fields where these defy measurement."[46] If these evaluations, as it is claimed, were designed to assist Parliament to hold the government to account, they have failed where it matters most – namely, in helping those whom they were intended to help: the MPs. Geoff Regan, a long-serving MP who has sat on both the government and the opposition branches, said, "It's amazing, considering how thick the documents can get, how little valuable information you can actually find in them."[47]

Most of the mountain of information that the government sends to Parliament every year is simply ignored. A former secretary to the Treasury Board suggests that even ministers no longer understand the process. He writes: "The annual Estimates cycle is the engine of a frantic annual process which has been so impossibly burdensome that Ministers and Parliament alike have effectively given up."[48] The answer that a government MP gave to my question – Do you believe that civil servants speak truth to power when they appear before your committee? – is telling: "They speak volumes, not necessarily truth."[49] An MP cannot properly interpret results without having detailed information on the staffing, budgets, and geographical location of spending patterns – information which they no longer receive.[50] The territory today is a great deal murkier than it was before the 1968 changes. Forty years ago, the estimates process held valuable advantages for MPs. The information was accessible and easy to grasp, given its focus on input costs. This is no longer the case.

Parliament: On Top of Very Little

It is hard to deny that Parliament is on the outside looking in when it comes to reviewing the government's expenditure process. The review is superficial, and when it actually takes place, it amounts to little more than political theatre. In 1976, the auditor general observed that "Parliament – and indeed the government – had lost or was close to losing effective control of the public purse."[51] A flurry of activities followed, including the establishment of the Office of the Comptroller General, which was later merged with the Treasury Board Secretariat, and later still recreated as an autonomous body. New approaches to budgeting have since been introduced, then scrapped for even newer approaches.[52] Yet the auditor general's observation is more relevant today than it was in 1976.

Parliament sits at the very end of an assembly line after all spending decisions have been struck and the competition between demands has been sorted out. As we have seen, the final product handed over to Parliament at the end of the assembly line consists of thousands and thousands of pages of not easily accessible material.[53] Notwithstanding the reams of documents, David Crane, a leading journalist and an astute longtime observer of public policies, wrote in the summer of 2011 that the Government of Canada is "dedicated to providing as little information as possible to Canadians on how their tax dollars are spent or on how spending priorities are chosen."[54] Yet the problem is not a lack of information provided to Parliament.

It is extremely difficult to find anyone who believes that Parliament has much of an impact in reviewing the government's expenditure budget. Sheila Fraser argued, shortly before she stepped down as auditor general, that members of Parliament are "failing Canadians" on one of their most fundamental roles – the scrutiny of yearly spending estimates. It is interesting to note that only a week later – on 3 June 2011 – MPs essentially rubber-stamped more than $250 billion in government spending.[55] It will be recalled that the spending estimates for 2012–13 tabled in late February 2012 did not reflect the spending cuts that were unveiled in the March 2012 budget. Accordingly, the estimates were outdated while under parliamentary review. As Susan Riley asked, "Why would MPs waste time studying them?"[56]

Parliament does not control spending in the sense of determining the levels of expenditures for particular departments, functions, and levels. Although it reviews government spending plans, it rarely influences them. Government MPs, not wishing to embarrass one of their own ministers, avoid raising substantive issues on departmental spending in the House. Opposition MPs, meanwhile, limit their participation to calling for increased spending on a particular program or problem and take little interest in pursuing more substantive issues related to the budget, either in the House or in standing committees. In any event, members are not privy to the decisions made in preparing the expenditure budget. They see the final product, the estimates books, only when these are tabled in Parliament and thus publicly released for the first time. To see the real forces shaping the expenditure budget, we have to look inside government to see how spending policies and programs are defined.

The role of MPs on the government side of the House is to support the government's spending plans. One may be a neoconservative who sees little merit in government intervention in the economy or one may hold strong views that a certain program should be scrapped or sealed back, but once the budget and estimates are tabled in the Commons, the government MP's role is to support them, no questions asked. Certainly, government MPs are free to raise concerns or voice their opinions in the privacy of a caucus meeting, but caucus meetings are not conducive to a productive discussion on the government's spending plans. For one thing, they are often free-wheeling sessions covering a wide range of issues. For another, caucus, no less than Parliament, is at the end of the assembly line when all decisions have already been struck. By the time government MPs see the documents, they see the final product. In any event, much more often than not, an MP will be looking to the estimates to see if a project that he or she has been promoting for the constituents back home has been approved.

Opposition MPs, on the other hand, are free to be critical of the budget and the government's spending estimates, and they invariably are. Indeed, one would be hard-pressed to recall many instances when an opposition MP rose in the Commons to applaud the government's spending priorities. One would also be hard-pressed to find an instance where an opposition MP was able to influence the government's expenditure budget in any tangible way.

What, Then, Do MPs Do?

Samara conducted exit interviews with 65 MPs and asked them to describe their "job." The answer: "50 different answers from 65 people."[57] The report concluded that "among the 65 MPs to whom we spoke, there is little shared idea of what forms the central elements of the actual job itself. This was a surprise coming from a group who had served in the job for, on average, over ten years."[58] An MP's job description and expectations are so uncertain that one MP, albeit an Independent, decided to take up a sideline job as a tour bus driver. He drove the bus once a week mostly in his home province, but occasionally went as far as Florida.[59]

MPs are, of course, expected to make laws, to hold the government to account, to support their political party, and to represent constituents. That in essence is an MP's job description. In pursuing their work, they split their time between Ottawa and the constituencies that elected them. They operate under the tight control and direction of their party leaders. However, so long as they toe the party line and do not challenge their leaders, at least publicly, they are free to focus on whatever issues they select, pursue whatever interests they choose, and carry out their work in the manner they see fit.

The Samara study and other reports press home the point that MPs are "unprepared for their roles as Parliamentarians" and receive "little or no formal training or orientation."[60] Virtually all jobs in modern society require formal training and periodical skills-development sessions to perform at expected levels. Not so for members of Parliament. Before being elected to Parliament, MPs do a variety of jobs; they are lawyers, business executives, teachers, union activists, small-business people, partisan political advisers, students, career politicians, and former journalists. There is no school or university where one can learn how to become and perform as an MP. There is no question that many of them are amateurs when it comes to understanding the ways of Parliament or government. Indeed, a good number regard their amateur status and their lack of national political experience as a plus.[61]

How, then, do candidates prepare to serve in Parliament? Some do very little, especially those who do not expect to be elected. But others commit long hours to becoming an MP. David Docherty reports that community service is "the strongest motivating factor in many MPs' initial decision to seek office." He adds that unlike policy work, working on behalf of one's constituency is "encouraged by the Commons preference rule."[62] MPs who run for Parliament to promote the interests of their constituencies are more likely to be successful than those who run to contribute to policy or to hold the government to account or who find flaws in the spending estimates.[63]

Once elected, MPs' training and orientation sessions are thin on the ground. One MP explained, "You get there, they take you in the House, they give you a book on constituency rights and responsibilities, the former Speaker talks about being in the House, and that's it. There is no orientation. There is no training. There is nothing on how to be effective." Another MP summed it up: "You learn by the seat of your pants."[64] Little wonder that the Samara study revealed that although two-thirds of the MPs consulted spent at least a portion of their time in Ottawa on the opposition benches, "only a few mentioned holding a government accountable as part of their job."[65]

Training or not, all MPs are expected to serve on at least one parliamentary committee. Here again, you learn by the seat of your pants. Party leaders and their advisers assign committee responsibilities for a variety of reasons. Committee memberships from all parties have, to the extent possible, to square with regional, language, and gender balance. As one MP put it, "You are on a committee because that's where you're put."[66] An MP may have some interest, background, or expertise in, say, health, only to be asked to serve on the Justice committee because it will fill a hole for the party.[67]

The lack of proper orientation and training, the mismatch between expertise and committee membership, and the turnover of MPs after general elections make parliamentary committees considerably less effective in Canada than in Britain.[68] But this hardly tells the whole story. Parliamentary committees, like the House of Commons itself, operate in a highly partisan environment. Scoring political points matters more than having reasoned debates about public policy. As one example, consider the following: The government Operations Committee spent weeks in 2010 on the lobbying efforts of Rahim Jaffer, a former MP, and only hours on the government's estimates.[69] The estimates held little potential for scoring partisan political points, but the Jaffer affair did.

Newly elected MPs arrive in Ottawa having proved that they were able to secure their party's nomination (difficult in some cases, not in others) and to win a constituency in a general election or by-election. They know the ways of partisan politics and the communities they represent. But they are short on other knowledge, and the obstacles to securing it are formidable. Simply understanding the ways of Parliament – their workplace – is a daunting challenge. On arrival, they need to hire staff in two offices (no small challenge for someone who has never hired or managed staff), find housing or lodging in Ottawa, and make weekly travel arrangements when the House sits. This is just the beginning. Parliament has its own distinct culture and its own rules that are different from those in other organizations. Few MPs make the effort to understand parliamentary rules and procedures. "Next to nobody knows the rules of the House," observed a former MP.[70] The novices learn on the job or by consulting those who have travelled the territory before them; or they ask mentors who may be willing to extend a helping hand. There is little interest in Ottawa for putting together training or development programs for them. It is as if parliamentary democracy requires that MPs must learn to fend for themselves.

Public servants consider it highly inappropriate for them to tell MPs how they should go about their work – how to become more effective, how to understand the government's expenditure budget, or how to hold the government to account. Public servants are loyal to the government of the day, and the great majority of them intuitively avoid partisan politics. The prime minister and his or her courtiers, meanwhile, have no interest in helping opposition MPs, and they look at their own MPs as a group to be managed, if not controlled. This is no small task, given the constant demands of the twenty-four hour news cycles. In any event, the prime minister and courtiers are kept busy with the demands of the day and rely on the party whip and the caucus liaison official in the Prime Minister's Office to keep the government caucus in line.

Even universities hesitate to create development programs for MPs. Carleton University recently put together a program for current and aspiring ministerial staff, but no university has come forward with a similar program for current or aspiring MPs.

If We Have to Keep Our Promises, It Means That We Won

The House of Commons is a collection of people from diverse backgrounds, ranging from longtime career politicians to one-term MPs. There is, however, a common thread linking all of them: each represents a constituency. Constituencies, whether urban or rural, "have" or "have-less," are their lifeblood. Many factors explain their electoral success, starting with the performance of their leaders during the campaign. Yet MPs and aspiring MPs have little say in the national campaign, their leader's political strategy, or the party platform. They focus on their own election campaigns and their own constituencies.

Local candidates make local campaign commitments, and the successful ones arrive in Ottawa with a "to do" list. In my own community of Moncton in the 2011 campaign, the Conservative candidate, Robert Goguen, pledged, if elected, to secure federal funding for a new convention centre and a rebate on RCMP policing costs for the Moncton–Dieppe–Riverview communities.[71] This type of commitment is not an isolated case, nor is it limited to constituencies in "have-less" regions. The Liberal candidate in the 2011 election in Gatineau, for example, pledged to secure funding for a new bridge linking Ottawa and Gatineau – hardly a "have-not" region.[72] A few months after being successfully elected, Goguen was able to return to his constituency on a late Friday afternoon to declare that he had "delivered" on a federal rebate for RCMP policing costs. The local newspaper, the *Times and Transcript*, ran an editorial applauding Ottawa's decision to provide a 10 percent subsidy to cover the costs of the RCMP policing. The editorial added, "We commend the hard work in particular of Moncton–Riverview–Dieppe member of Parliament Robert Goguen. Mr. Goguen shepherded this project through within just a few months of taking power after his predecessors, sitting on the wrong side of government all this time, toiled fruitlessly for almost 13 years."[73]

During an election campaign, the pressure to respond to the needs of constituencies, of which there is never a shortage, is great. The thirty-six days (the minimum under Canada's election act) are politically charged and highly competitive, at least between the two leading candidates. Meanwhile, not a word is heard from Finance and Treasury Board officials assessing the potential benefits of any proposed initiative. Nor is the Office of the Auditor General heard commenting on the financial implications of the campaign commitments. The state of the country's fiscal health is rarely, if ever, the ballot question at the constituency level.

Dominic LeBlanc, MP for Beauséjour, reports that during discussions leading up to the 2011 election, a sitting MP made this revealing observation: "If we have to keep our promises, it means that we won."[74] The overriding goal for local candidates and party workers is to win, leaving to a later day and often to others the task of picking up the pieces. The result is that there are a lot of pieces to be picked up or discarded after a general election. MPs on the government side are not easily convinced to give up their campaign commitments. They know that they will be held to account by the local media and by their constituents when the next election rolls around, if not sooner.

When it comes to the expenditure budget, virtually all MPs walk around Ottawa seeking support for initiatives for their constituencies. Few come with specific ideas on how to cut spending, though many will call on the government to get its deficit under better control. Many will also see waste in government operations, in the ways of the bureaucracy, in regional programs that do not apply to their own constituencies, or in measures that favour one region over their own – of which, given Canada's history and geography, there is never a shortage.

Many newly elected MPs do not fully appreciate that the actual role of government is to govern and that of the Commons is to subject political power to certain controls, to provide legitimacy to government action and activities, and to hold the executive to account.[75] They see that government and public servants run policies and programs, and they want to participate; they want to be part of the action and party to the decision-making process. Poring through thousands of pages of material in an attempt to hold the government to account holds little appeal for them, especially in an institution where party leaders hold sway and where knowing the rules and procedures requires a high level of expertise.

The bulk of MPs want to focus their efforts on their own constituencies. It is a world in which they are comfortable – more comfortable than with bureaucratic Ottawa or even Parliament, with its archaic rules. Moreover, it holds more potential as a re-election strategy. Dominic LeBlanc summed it up well. "I get elected in the towns and villages of Beauséjour, not in the city of Ottawa," he said, adding, "All politics is indeed local." When I visited LeBlanc's constituency office in July 2011, the visitor he received before me was calling on him to sort out an employment insurance issue, and the visitor after me was there to inquire about old age pensions for his parents.[76]

A good number of MPs are content simply to play an ombudsman role for their constituencies. They are there to promote projects for the ridings and to look after the concerns of their constituents. Rural MPs will be asked to intervene on behalf of social programs or to secure a project or a government office for the riding. An MP stands a better chance of success if he or she is on the government side. For example, in 2011, when Service Canada sought to implement a national downsizing plan, Gerald Keddy, MP for South Shore–St Margaret's, was able to keep the local Employment Insurance (EI) office open in his constituency while several EI offices in Liberal constituencies were closed.[77]

MPs in urban areas attend to different issues. They may be asked to help someone obtain a passport or to assist new Canadians or aspiring immigrants navigate the government's "complex and sometimes frustrating system." A Toronto-area MP reports that about "80 percent of his constituency office's work is devoted to citizenship, immigration and passport issues." A Winnipeg MP claims that "MPs offices have become de facto immigration offices."[78] Another member of Parliament points out, on the Parliament of Canada website, that he is "first and foremost a representative of the people and accountable to those who elected me."[79]

MPs as ombudsmen have implications for the public purse. Accountability is geared to their work on behalf of their constituents and their ability to deliver initiatives to their own regions. Ombudsmen are more successful as spenders than as guardians. Being able to deliver on campaign commitments and being perceived in the constituency as someone who can bring home the bacon matters a great deal more than holding the government to account in managing its expenditure budget or influencing public policy.

The government party in the Commons has a different relationship with its MPs than opposition parties have with theirs. A government party with a majority mandate has its hands on all the levers of power to decide, appoint, finance, and produce legislation, while opposition parties are on the outside looking in. Some of the government's MPs have access to power, and some of them have access only to levers of influence, but neither power nor much influence, if any, are available to opposition MPs. Something like one in five government MPs will be ministers, about twenty will be parliamentary secretaries, twenty will chair a committee, one will be Speaker, and another will be government whip. All in all, some seventy or more government MPs hold a position of power or influence. The rest enjoy a privileged position in Parliament because they are members of the government caucus, where they hear about legislative proposals before they are introduced into Parliament. More importantly, they have weekly opportunities to challenge the prime minister and other ministers in private and to voice opinions about government policies or operations. Government MPs reveal that some of these caucus sessions can be quite stormy, with strongly worded criticism directed at individual ministers. C.E.S. Franks observed, "An MP on the government side has a good chance of holding a position of power; those left out have a good prospect of achieving a position of power someday, and backbenchers have more direct contact with cabinet. Nor should the prospects of future rewards be neglected."[80]

The prospect of future rewards in turn strengthens the hand of the prime minister. Although some MPs are quite happy not to be in cabinet, they are very much in the minority. One minister suggested that "at least 90 percent of the government caucus, if not more, would welcome an opportunity to sit in cabinet. For the great majority of us, that is why we run for Parliament."[81] A member of Parliament has to make a run at the party nomination and then for several weeks is involved in political campaigning, knocking on doors, speaking to local service clubs, and attending all-party meetings. Chances are that anyone who successfully navigates this obstacle course is highly motivated and ambitious. He or she will probably want a seat at the cabinet table. But that is not all. MPs know full well that the prime minister appoints viceroys, senators, judges, ambassadors, and members of boards, task forces, and commissions. This power of appointment constitutes an indispensable tool to ensure party discipline, and the latter is essential if the government is to maintain the confidence of the House.

Prime ministers emphasize party discipline and do not easily tolerate dissent, no matter what they may have said when in opposition. As David Docherty points out, Brian Mulroney rejected the recommendations of the McGrath Committee "that dealt with confidence," and Jean Chrétien "did not follow through on the Red Book" commitment to treat gun control as a matter of conscience. MPs are expected to be "guided by longstanding notions of party solidarity and, with few exceptions, defy the logic and function of discipline in the day-to-day workings of the Commons at their own expense."[82]

Similarly, opposition MPs are expected to endorse their party's policies, voting with the party on legislation and falling in line behind the leader. Opposition leaders can always hold out the promise of appointment if they ever achieve power. In addition, they can remove some MPs from relatively high-profile "shadow-cabinet" positions. Members of the opposition know that internal dissension can hinder their party's chances in the next election. Yet they have a much freer hand in speaking out on policy issues and government operations than government MPs do.[83] The goal is often to humiliate the government and to gain a profile in the media. So long as one does not harm one's party's image or embarrass one's leader, everything seems to be fair game. John Nunziata, a member of the so-called rat pack of four Liberal members who taunted the Mulroney government in Question Period, explains, "We were carefree and at times careless. We were a hot commodity." He reported that fellow rat-pack member Brian Tobin repeatedly rehearsed ripping up a report in private before performing it publicly during Question Period. The line was going to be, "It's not worth the paper it's printed on," said Nunziata, and Tobin practised "tearing it in half and in half again and throwing these bits of paper up into the air; that was the TV clip."[84]

Docherty's research reveals that opposition MPs spend more time on policy development and legislative work than government MPs do. First, there are more government than opposition MPs, and the latter have to assume more policy work. Second, government MPs have access to far more resources. Still, for most MPs, Docherty concludes, policy work is "not a strategic activity. Members invest a good portion of their working time on such work, but not necessarily for self-interested reasons."[85] Since policy work does not give MPs much of a media profile, they do not see it as helping in the next election.

The prime minister, his advisers, and the more senior ministers would much sooner see government MPs leave serious policy work and the expenditure budget to them. It is their turf. They regard policy not only as complex but as filled with potential regional, interdepartmental, and political pitfalls. Unless one can connect all the dots and ensure that the finer points of policy requirements are met, a crisis may well be in the making. Government MPs have access to resources, but with limits, particularly vis-à-vis expertise in departments. Public servants are uneasy about sharing their policy work with MPs, even when their ministers ask them to do so. MPs may run off with information prematurely to score political points, and information may be misinterpreted outside. There are also no rewards for career officials engaging MPs in policy work.

The risks are even greater in regard to opposition MPs. Career officials know that their ministers would not like them to share policy work and spending plans before they become public. The adversarial nature of politics affects the public service, even though officials assiduously distance themselves from politics. C.E.S. Franks does not mince words: "In the question of the formation of policy and legislation ... the member of parliament (i.e., both government and opposition) is virtually excluded from the process ... There are two separate worlds in Ottawa: the public world of parliament and the media; and the private world of the public service, cabinet, central agencies, and their contacts with interest groups." He adds that "senior public servants in Canada tend to relegate MPs to the periphery of the policy-making world more so than those in Italy, Germany, the United States, or the United Kingdom."[86]

Canada has a high turnover of MPs in general elections, which adds to the challenge. Docherty and Franks both stress the impact of this high turnover on the work of the House and its ability to hold the government to account. Docherty observes that "the lack of long-serving members is problematic and viewed as detrimental for a number of reasons ... Simply put, it is difficult for both government backbenchers and opposition members to keep Cabinet accountable when they lack the experience and parliamentary savvy of members of the executive."[87] Franks compares British and Canadian experience: "The average Canadian member of Parliament is a newcomer who is likely to leave before he has served ten years and is most unlikely to serve for fifteen years. The average British member has been in the house for at least ten years, and is very likely to serve for at least fifteen years ... This comparison of parliamentary experience of MPs and of time in office of prime ministers shows there is a very different relationship of power between the two bodies in Britain and Canada. In Canada, a strong, solidly entrenched prime minister faces an insecure and transient House of Commons; in Britain, an insecure and transient prime minister faces a strong and solidly entrenched House."[88]

It appears that many members of Parliament are able to see the light on policy and the expenditure budget only when they are in government, particularly in cabinet. Tobin, as a member of Chrétien's program review committee in the mid-1990s, went "after the deficit with missionary zeal."[89]

One senior official reports that "Tobin in opposition when the Mulroney government was trying to introduce spending cuts was a far cry from Tobin as a member of the cabinet committee on program review. It was like night and day."[90] Tobin told his colleagues, "I've become the right-wing fiscal conservative of this government." He reported that his conversion took place on a trip to Japan, which impressed on him Canada's vulnerability to the "whims of foreign lenders."[91] Some officials scoffed at this observation, saying that if Tobin could add, he would have known much earlier about Ottawa's serious fiscal difficulties. They argued that it was simply convenient for him to oppose spending cuts when Mulroney was in government but to change his tune when Chrétien was in power.[92]

Doug Young, while an opposition MP, launched a high-profile campaign to fight the Mulroney government's plan to reduce VIA Rail services in Atlantic Canada and to introduce cuts to the Unemployment Insurance (UI) program (as it was then called). He urged New Brunswickers to help him stop the government dead in its tracks, on the grounds that both measures would hurt the provincial economy.[93] He even offered to organize public hearings to enable all New Brunswickers to demonstrate their opposition to the plans. It was good politics, particularly for his constituents in the economically depressed region of northeast New Brunswick. Now, fast forward to Chrétien's first mandate, where that same Mr Young turned all his energy to fiscal concerns. He took to the program review exercise with gusto and promoted a policy to sell the country's air navigation system, privatize CN Rail, reduce still further subsidies to VIA Rail, and do away completely with freight rate subsidies for Atlantic manufacturers.[94] Moreover, he came out in favour of substantial cuts to the Unemployment Insurance program. What explains his remarkable about-face? One can only assume that it was not political ideology or sound policy work that changed his mind. Rather, it was the pursuit of political power and a recognition of the reality of public policy once he was in power. He went down to defeat in a traditionally strong Liberal constituency in the 1997 general election.

At the risk of sounding repetitive, career officials instinctively shy away from bringing MPs into their department's decision making. They see a clear dividing line between ministers' roles and that of other MPs. They also draw a line between Parliament and themselves. The world of Parliament and party politics is vastly different from the one in which public servants operate, and they will go to great lengths to keep it that way. A former MP showed me his correspondence with the prime minister and other ministers complaining about certain bureaucrats' insensitivity to his concerns. Former ministers have also provided me with written exchanges with their deputy ministers designed to encourage their departments to brief MPs on their activities. The material is both revealing and instructive.

One former government backbencher complained to the prime minister on behalf, he claimed, of several of his colleagues (all of them government MPs) about the insensitivity of an assistant deputy minister to MPs' views. The letter was sweeping and general, identified no specific charges or problems, and asked for the removal of the bureaucrat. The author insisted that his letter should not be interpreted "strictly in terms of partisan political consideration" and claimed that the official regarded all MPs as "unnecessary evils." What MPs wanted, he wrote, was "someone who can communicate effectively with us."[95] The relevant minister decided not to intervene on behalf of the official. The prime minister never responded, although four months later changes occurred with senior personnel in the department, including that of the deputy minister and later the assistant deputy. It was not at all clear that the letter provoked the changes.

A former minister handed me copies of correspondence with his deputy minister in which he and his staff were encouraging the "involvement of MPs in the decision-making process." The deputy minister and senior officials responded by acknowledging that the minister had "on many occasions expressed the wish that MPs be kept fully informed of departmental activities." One side spoke of "involvement," the other of "information." The minister and his staff wanted an all-encompassing process, while the officials strongly recommended a "pilot briefing basis." The minister and his staff saw no difficulty in quick action. The deputy minister and senior officials did. They brought up a number of issues: the fear of raising MPs' expectations of influencing programs; the problem of "truly confidential or privileged information," whose "operational premise is that information placed before MPs becomes public information; and the question of whether to treat opposition MPs the same way."[96] The matter was never resolved, and the issue came to an end when the minister was moved. Public servants often have the luxury of putting things off forever – to the Greek month of calends. Ministers do not.

MPs and public servants are connected through the work of their institutions, but the connection is uneasy because the two institutions operate differently and each regards the other with a jaundiced eye. One is home to partisan politics and views the world from the bottom up. Its boundaries are defined by geography and regional interests. It is a world shaped by the ability to score political points and by fifteen-second linear bursts of bombast. In politics and in Parliament, perception is reality. A long-term perspective is four years. Competition is intense and ongoing in an era of permanent campaigns. By contrast, the public service consists of skilled policy analysts and administrators, and its boundaries are established by hierarchy. It is a very patient realm and places a premium on achieving a consensus. It looks at partisan politics with detachment and has every reason to avoid being drawn into that world. Sectors ranging from agriculture to industry to health care – and, of course, their own departments – are what matter to public servants. They leave it to politicians to worry about constituencies and communities.[97] Both institutions and their actors have interests to promote or to protect.

The expenditure budget belongs to the government, and Parliament is now left on the outside looking in. It is worth repeating Lowell Murray's observation: "Parliament – specifically the House of Commons ... has allowed its most vital power, the power of the purse, to become a dead letter, their Supply and Estimates process an empty ritual."[98] There is no shortage of information for MPs, as this chapter has shown. As Paul Thomas argues, "It is the long standing problem that parliamentarians are stuffed with information and starved for understanding."[99] The arrival of "permanent election campaigns" in Canadian politics has made it more difficult to "fix" Parliament's supply process and make it more meaningful to MPs, the media, and Canadians.

It is left to the prime minister and a handful of advisers, including a few ministers, notably the minister of finance, to shape the expenditure budget. The next two chapters explore how they deal with constant pressure for more spending.

3

Ministers: Where Have All the Characters Gone?

In my 1990 book, *The Politics of Public Spending in Canada*, I sought to describe what characteristics typify ministers. In doing so, I grouped ministers under four broad headings: *status, mission, policy,* and *process* participants.[1] One can still use the four labels in describing ministers' characteristics, though they mean much less today than they did twenty-three years ago. The rise of court government has changed all that, leaving most ministers scrambling to have any real influence, let alone contributing to policy making or having a hand in major new government initiatives.

Consider the following. Several important decisions on Canada's military deployment in Afghanistan – one by a Liberal government and another by a Conservative – were taken by the prime minister, with a handful of partisan advisers, public servants, and military officials. The two relevant ministers – of Defence and Foreign Affairs – were not even in the room when the discussions took place.[2] We are now informed that the defence minister was "blindsided" when the prime minister and his senior advisers decided to establish a "blue ribbon panel" to review Canada's mission in Afghanistan. The minister explained, "It wasn't discussed with the broader cabinet," adding, "I didn't know all of the specifics."[3] It is now apparent that all major policy and budgetary decisions are taken by the prime minister, the minister of finance, and a handful of carefully selected advisers, or courtiers.[4] Former prime minister Paul Martin recognized that governing from the centre had become a reality in Ottawa when he wrote, "It is also true that policy making in most areas has gradually been centralized in the Privy Council Office – a process that began in earnest under Pierre

Trudeau. Probably only Finance ... has fully retained its independent capacity through the recent decades."[5]

The above sums up how court government differs from cabinet government. Authority is now highly concentrated in the hands of prime ministers and their courtiers. The courtiers are drawn from the cabinet, from partisan political staffers, from the bureaucracy, and from outside government, including selected lobbyists and think-tanks. Policy making and decision making follow two separate paths. When prime ministers and their courtiers want something, funding is easily secured and decisions are quickly struck. However, when they have limited interest in a proposal, the formal decision-making process takes over. It is elaborate (it can involve other governments, a number of government departments and agencies, and outsiders) and is slow, porous, and consultative.

This is not to suggest that all ministers have lost power or influence. Some are members of the prime minister's court, and they have considerable power and influence. All ministers are involved with various policy- and decision-making processes. Many sit on top of large bureaucracies that deliver a multitude of programs and services. All have "some" access to the prime minister and his court, especially when cabinet meets. Some have the full confidence of the prime minister and, as members of his court, can shape initiatives. Others, in the words of a senior deputy minister, are "kept on a very short leash."[6]

All ministers continue to lead very busy lives, even though most have lost the kind of power and influence they once had. Consider this: ministers need to meet regularly with their political staff, attend to House duties, and meet with their deputy ministers and other senior departmental officials; they must also meet with constituents and with client groups or individuals tied to their departmental mandates; as well, they must attend cabinet and cabinet committee meetings, see to the affairs of their political parties, deal with correspondence, answer or return numerous telephone calls, attend caucus meetings, deal with provincial governments, and participate in Question Period. However, in government, simply being busy does not equate to having power or influence. Unless a minister has access to the prime minister and his court, he or she will have limited influence, despite a very full agenda.

Motivation

In a wide-ranging discussion with Bernard Valcourt, a minister in the Mulroney and Harper governments, I asked his views on public choice theory, after outlining its more salient points. His response: "Do we really need a bunch of academics to tell us that politicians, like everybody else, are motivated by self-interest?" He added, "Show me a politician who does not look for ways to help win an election and I will show you a politician who will not be successful at anything. The world of politics is highly competitive, and one enters it to win and continue to win. You will be looking after your people and your communities. Why on earth should this be an important discovery for academics?"[7] Valcourt's point was that while politicians most certainly are motivated by self-interest, one needs to go beyond this and look at the underlying forces that shape both their self-interest and the government's expenditure budget. In the Canadian setting perhaps more than elsewhere, the self-interest of politicians only partly explains why and how public policies and government decisions are made. The nature of Canadian regionalism and federalism also explains the pressure that federal politicians apply on the government's expenditure budget.

Leaving aside the one or two senators invited to sit in cabinet, ministers are drawn from the House of Commons, which means they had to win an election. Three keen observers of Canadian politics made the point in the immediate aftermath of the 2011 general election that "Canada doesn't have a national election. It has a series of regional elections with different competitors, different issues, and different dynamics."[8] In Canada, although party leaders and their advisers manage national campaigns with a firm hand, the regional factor is crucial to a party's electoral platform, and party leaders need to tailor their messages to take in regional identities and economic circumstances as much as possible.

All regions – and indeed all communities – have problems, and their resolution all too often entail public funds. Imagine a candidate in any constituency in any federal election campaign saying, "We have no problems here, everything is fine, and if elected, I pledge not to support local projects in the interest of the government's fiscal challenges or financial integrity." Local politicians speak to local interests, not to the national interest. They know their communities well, and it has become *de rigueur* to make commitments to deal with challenges and opportunities during election campaigns. The financing of a convention centre or a bridge, or aid to an ailing economic sector, among many other possible scenarios, have somehow become the responsibility of the national government through election campaigns.

The national interest, meanwhile, is left to others to define – no easy task. To residents of Atlantic and western Canada, "national interest" is a code for Ontario and Quebec.[9] Quebec remains uncertain what the national interest may hold but is forthcoming about its own provincial interest. Ontario, because of globalization and other economic forces, has increasingly focused on provincial concerns, if only because the national economy no longer holds the kind of economic benefits it once did.[10]

The point is that every national election campaign is sure to bring Ottawa new spending commitments. Hardly ever does one involve specific measures to cut spending. Spenders, not guardians, shape national electoral platforms: election promises don't require a rigorous evaluation process. The overriding goal in general election campaigns is to win, and if it requires a new spending commitment, so be it, as long as it does not paint the party as fiscally irresponsible.

The voice of spenders is heard loud and clear at both the regional and constituency level during election campaigns. There is always pressure from local candidates for the party to commit to specific high-profile projects. Just this one project, the aspiring MP will argue, and I can win the constituency for the party. Again, the long list of potential projects can include anything from a ring road for a mid-size city to new investment to promote IT activities. The observation that "if we have to keep our promises, it means that we won the election" resonates in every region and every party. And invariably it results in an over-supply of spending commitments. Governments in Canada have worked around a rigid constitution by signing flexible federal-provincial agreements to side-step which jurisdiction is responsible for any given sector. This has enabled the federal government to fund a wide variety of initiatives in a wide variety of sectors, and it has served the interest of the spenders at the expense of the guardians.

During an election campaign, when MPs or aspiring MPs debate potential spending restraint measures, they do so in abstract terms, invariably pointing to "fat" in government bureaucracies or to wasteful spending in other regions (not in their own). When asked about possible spending cuts, they will refer to what they regard as flagrant cases of wasteful spending, such as that of Christine Ouimet, the former "disgraced" integrity commissioner. It will be recalled that Ms Ouimet received from "whistleblowers" more than two hundred allegations of wrongdoing but investigated only seven and issued "zero" findings of wrongdoing. The auditor general, in a special report, revealed that Ms Ouimet had failed to fulfill her mandate and faulted her as well for "berating and bullying staff." Still, the government gave her a $500,000 payout as she left her office.[11] So an MP on the campaign trail will ask, "Why impose restraint on my constituents when the government allows such cases of wasteful spending?"

I have been a lifelong student of public administration and regional economic development policy and have yet to see a single region in Canada that does not think that another region benefits more than it does from the federal government.[12] Those who do not live in Ontario have long believed that Ottawa favours that province. Ontario is home to Parliament, to the head offices of most federal departments and agencies, and it has benefited more than the other regions from "national" policies. They have a point. A substantial part of Canada's manufacturing sector was born out of Canada's war effort during the Second World War. The bulk of the war effort went to central Canada, and not a single crown corporation of the thirty-two created at the time was established in any of the Maritime provinces or in western Canada. The national government signed an auto pact with the United States that created thousands of jobs in southern Ontario but made the cost of purchasing a new car everywhere in Canada more expensive. In addition, whenever there is a sign that Canada's industrial heartland may hit a rough patch, Ottawa rushes in headlong with a helping hand, as it did for the automotive sector in 2008–10 and the manufacturing sector in 1981–83.[13]

Ontario, however, is now convinced that other regions are benefiting at its expense. The Mowat Centre, financed at least in part by the Government of Ontario, has produced a number of reports since it was established claiming that Ontario has been short-changed in various federal transfers to the provinces (transfers in health care and social services) and to individuals (employment insurance). Quebec has long-standing grievances against the federal government, and much has been said and written about western alienation.[14]

Canada has many regional myths that are seriously believed, but it has few national ones.[15] The case has been made that in some ways, Canada's federal system acts like a unitary state. The country's political institutions ensure equality between individuals through the House of Commons but not the equality of the regions through an effective, elected, and equal Senate.[16] Members of Parliament and cabinet are left to fight for what they can to bring more government spending to their constituencies and regions.

Many newly elected MPs may well believe that Ottawa needs to impose fiscal discipline, but they will likely point their fingers at other constituencies or other regions or to sectors that have little or no relevance to their own constituencies. The New Brunswick media and local observers applauded the appointment of two ministers in the Harper government in 2011, convinced that the province would now be in a better position to secure more federal funding. It is interesting to note that much less is being heard about western alienation since Stephen Harper became prime minister and several senior ministers from the western provinces sit at the cabinet table. The view in the West is that they are now in a position to bring home the bacon.

The regional factor in Canadian politics is unlike that of other Western democracies. The United States, Australia, and Germany have an effective Senate, or Upper House, that represents the regional factor in national policies and programs. Canada does not. The heavily populated provinces of Ontario and Quebec, both rich in seats in the House of Commons, opposed reforming the Canadian Senate to give a regional voice to national policies. The McGuinty government in Ontario had stressed the importance of "representation by population" for the House of Commons but at the same time would have liked to see the Senate abolished. The Charest government in Quebec had threatened to take the Harper government to court if it pursued legislation to change how senators are appointed.[17]

Regional grievances and the perception, if not the reality, of regional bias in federal government spending, along with the importance of being able to "bring home the bacon," continue to have an impact in the shaping of Ottawa's expenditure budget, particularly with regard to new spending. Given our Westminster-style parliamentary system, the battle for new spending is fought behind closed doors in the Prime Minister's Office, the Department of Finance, and among key advisers to the prime minister. Ministers push and pull whatever levers may be accessible to them to secure new funding for their regions or their departments.

Ministers

MPs on the winning side assemble in Ottawa shortly after their victory. As Jean Chrétien is reported to have said after his 1993 election victory, it is the best day they will have for "a long, long time."[18] Some of the MPs are confident that they will be invited to sit in cabinet. These are senior party members who have sat on the front bench, or else they are star candidates, the lone winning candidate in a province, or a close supporter of the party leader. Others know that they are unlikely to receive a call from the prime minister. These are newly elected MPs or those who come from a province that already has a number of star candidates or long-serving and competent MPs, who are more likely to be chosen.

In putting together the cabinet, the prime minister and his close political advisers review the list of potential ministers and also consult officials in the Privy Council Office. There is extensive literature on the practice of cabinet making in Canada, so there is no need to go over all the points here.[19] Suffice it to note that ability is not necessarily a prerequisite. Some government MPs may be ideally suited for a particular portfolio but are overlooked because of the need for a regional, gender, or linguistic balance in cabinet. As the *Toronto Star* once reported, "Politicians don't fall from heaven. They are the folks next door."[20] There is no special training required. All that is required is a security check, which is now carried out on all possible cabinet appointees.

Canadian MPs and cabinet ministers have a variety of backgrounds. The typical MP from the 2011 class spent the bulk of his or her working life outside politics. It is interesting to note that 90 percent of NDP MPs spent 90 percent of their adult lives outside elected politics, compared with 78 percent of the Conservatives and 67 percent of the Liberals. "Elected politics" refers to the federal Parliament, a provincial legislature, and municipal councils. There are, however, a number of "career politicians" in all three parties: one in 7 of the Liberal MPs, one in 25 of the NDP, and one in 12 of the Conservative MPs.[21] But it should be noted that the percentage of freshman MPs representing the NDP was an exceptional event, reflecting the surge of party support in Quebec.

The prime minister, along with his chief of staff, invites the MPs selected for cabinet to his office, to 24 Sussex Drive, or to his summer residence at Harrington Lake a day or two before the new cabinet is made public. He informs the new ministers of their portfolios and tells them that the appointment must remain confidential until they meet again at Rideau Hall for the swearing-in ceremony. The ministers are given "mandate letters" from the prime minister that outline the government's policy objectives for their respective departments.[22] These letters have been drafted by officials in the Privy Council Office and reviewed by close associates of the prime minister. Accordingly, the minister has had very little, if any, say in the direction his or her department is to follow.

Shortly after leaving the swearing-in ceremony, ministers meet their deputy ministers and are given a number of briefing books. They are also expected to attend a series of briefing sessions with senior departmental staff. They have immediate access to a chauffeured automobile and are told that they have funds to hire a politically partisan staff, including a chief of staff. The latter holds a senior position, even when compared with permanent positions in the career public service; it is ranked at the assistant deputy minister level, or one level below the deputy minister.

The Prime Minister's Office, in tandem with the tendency to govern from the centre, now has a strong say in who makes it as chief of staff to a minister. It all depends on who the minister is. A senior minister, such as the minister of finance or those who are members of the prime minister's court, have a freer hand in selecting their chiefs of staff, but in all cases the Prime Minister's Office retains the right to recommend or even reject the choice. The prime minister's courtiers know that partisan political advisers play an increasingly important role in bringing a political perspective to bear on the work of departments. Liane Benoit writes that ministerial political staff "can, and often do, exert a substantial degree of influence on the development and in some cases on the administration of public policy in Canada."[23]

As already observed, newly appointed ministers soon discover that they lead busy lives and that the demands of their departments must compete with those of Parliament, cabinet, cabinet committees, government caucus, their own regional caucus, their home provincial governments, interest groups, their constituencies, lobbyists, relevant sectoral associations, and their own political staff. Cabinet ministers who arrive in their departments planning to reorient their departments substantially and rethink their policies and programs, without a specific mandate from the prime minister and the clerk of the privy council, are certain to fail. A highly respected former clerk has this advice for ministers: "Having many roles, you will be under constant and unremitting pressure to allocate some of your time to this or that worthy endeavour. They [ministers] must establish priorities and the time frame within which they want to accomplish them and allocate their time accordingly. If they don't do this, and do it well, they will be lost."[24] He added that ministers work between seventy and eighty hours a week but that "surveys indicate that they often have only three hours a week to spend with their Deputy Ministers."[25]

It was not always so. Prime Minister Pearson ran a cabinet government. J. Stephen Dupré described it as a "departmental cabinet system," in which ministers were responsible for departmental policies and administration, while cabinet and central agencies had limited capacity to develop and promote policy coordination instruments. Ministers brought their policy and spending proposals from their departments and had it out with their colleagues at the cabinet table.[26] Prime Ministers Trudeau and Mulroney also sought to involve ministers in putting together the expenditure budgets. The Trudeau government introduced a new approach to budget making in 1980 – the Policy and Expenditure Management System (PEMS). The objective was to impose a discipline on spending ministers by setting limits to the expenditure budget in advance of spending proposals and decisions.[27]

The thinking was that the central problem with Ottawa's expenditure budget was that spending ministers and their departments made demands on the budget and were constrained only by those responsible for the total expenditure budget – the traditional guardians, namely the prime minister, the minister of finance, the president of the Treasury Board, and their officials. PEMS was meant to change this culture by making spending ministers themselves responsible for making expenditure decisions in light of the government's overall priorities and plans, but within specific limits.[28] The view was that PEMS would create a spending discipline among ministers, which would make it easier for the guardians to go about their work.

The structure adopted to this end was based on a system of cabinet committees, each with its own budgetary "envelope," within which the spending ministers on each committee were to integrate their policy and expenditure decisions collectively. In brief, PEMS was meant to force spending ministers to face the expenditure and thus the fiscal consequences of their policy and program decisions. The thinking was that once ministers had spent their allocated envelopes, they would have to look at ongoing programs to reallocate resources – hence placing responsibility for budgetary decisions squarely on their own shoulders.[29]

PEMS never lived up to expectations, and it was scrapped in the mid-1980s. Spending ministers were quick to allocate their envelopes among themselves but had no interest in reallocating resources from existing programs. In addition, they made end runs to the prime minister and the minister of finance in search of funds that they could not obtain from their own or another cabinet committee's envelope. The size of Canada's federal cabinet, with anywhere between thirty to forty ministers, also made the practical operation of PEMS unwieldy. Still, it enabled ministers to carve out a role for themselves and to compete for financial resources. Although it had a short life, the role of ministers in search of new spending is evident to this day. As a result, one can still identify the four character types among ministers.[30]

Characters Matter Less

It is still possible to identify ministers as *status, mission, policy,* and *process* participants, though the characteristics are much less pronounced than they were. Status participants still seek public visibility at every turn and look to any and all departmental activities to secure a positive public profile. The emphasis of status ministers is not on what they do in government or what they achieve, but how they appear to the electorate and to their colleagues. To the extent that they influence public spending, they sit in the spenders' camp. They much prefer being the bearer of good news. Cuts in spending are rarely popular or easy to sell, and they would rather leave that task to others.

Mission participants, meanwhile, continue to bring to government strongly held views. Examples abound: Stéphane Dion and the place of

Quebec in Canada; Jason Kenney and his goal to make new Canadians take a more sympathetic view of the Conservative Party; Paul Martin in the Chrétien government and his "come hell or high water" approach to fighting the deficit in the 1990s; Eugene Whelan in the Trudeau cabinet and the economic interests of farmers ... and the list goes on. Mission participants can be found in both the spender and the guardian camps, though politicians on a mission tend to tax the public treasury. Great causes cost money more often than not.

Policy participants bring strong knowledge of a policy field or an economic sector to Ottawa. They are not career politicians. They are medical doctors (e.g., Carolyn Bennett), tax experts (e.g., Donald Johnston), lawyers (many), business executives (e.g., Joe Oliver), and community activists (e.g., Peter Julian). However, policy participants have had limited success in government. Having expertise in a policy field is one thing, but knowing how the government policy process works is quite another. The process, given its highly consultative nature, is now a field of specialization in its own right. Policy participants who have been cabinet ministers and have later written about their experiences often report their deep frustration over their inability to change policy.[31] Those who do claim to have had some success report that they had to go to extraordinary lengths to bypass the formal policy process, and a minister can only do this by having access to the prime minister's court.[32] Policy participants are more often found on the spenders side. Rare is the policy field that does not have problems which do not require public money to fix.

Process participants, meanwhile, seek to strike deals to help their constituencies, their constituents, their regions, and specific client groups. They have limited interest in the policy process, the substance of policies, government organization, or management issues. They believe they are in Ottawa and on the government side for a limited period, and they want to leave their mark or a legacy in national programs or, more often, at home in their region or constituency. They are on the lookout for projects – the more, the better. They have no interest in challenging their departments or the system, and they have problems only with their permanent officials if the officials are uncooperative in putting deals together. Process participants are generally easygoing extroverts and are popular with government backbenchers. They are clearly in the spenders' camp.

All four character types are still in evidence in Ottawa, but all are considerably less effective than they once were. Court government has made life extremely difficult for all four. All of them, particularly the mission and policy participants, need a formal setting such as cabinet meetings and formal processes in order to be effective, to voice their views, to debate the merits of their ideas, and to win the argument.

The prime minister and his court now keep a tight control over the government's policy agenda, the decision-making processes, the expenditure budget, and relations with the media. The prime minister wants to be front and centre when major initiatives are announced, and his courtiers manage any bad news as best they can. In brief, ministers are no longer as free as they were in managing their department's relations with the media. Public servants have been instructed to label announcements or initiatives as being from "the Harper government," rather than from the Government of Canada, so that the prime minister is always at the centre of good news.[33] One former Privy Council Office official explained how the centre controls media relations: "We discussed every single issue and micromanaged every news release – everything."[34] As a result, status participants can no longer expect their own political or departmental staff to manage their public profile. They need the blessing of the prime minister's court if they are to gain favourable media coverage.

Ministers now have a limited say in planning media events, even in their own departments. The process is managed by the Prime Minister's Office (PMO) and Privy Council Office (PCO) under their "message events proposal." Everything goes up to these offices for decisions in planning events, and the PMO-PCO control every detail, even "the dress code."[35]

The government spends a substantial amount of money every year on "manipulating the message." Central agencies and line departments and agencies employ hundreds of "highly paid people" to manage communications and relations with the media. But all communication roads lead to the PMO-PCO. It will be recalled that the government spent $54 million in 2009–10 to promote its Economic Action Plan at a time when the plan was coming to an end. The strategy was tied to paid advertisements, announcements by ministers and MPs on the government side, and a website – all managed by the PMO-PCO. A PCO document explained that content development was a "joint PMO-PCO responsibility, final content approval rests with PMO."[36] Total government-wide spending on advertising alone in 2009–10 was $136 million.[37] The report detailing the activities was to be published in May 2011, the month Canadians went to the polls, but it was released only after the general election. As the above makes clear, the prime minister and his courtiers have a strong hand in managing the government's communications strategy and can secure funding for it at the stroke of a pen. They have no one to ask for funding but themselves. Status participants, meanwhile, have been relegated to playing a supporting role.

The practice of labelling initiatives as coming from "the Harper government," following a directive from the PCO, is also not without implications and controversy. The approach not only makes life difficult for status participants, but it brings public servants too close to partisan activities. Ralph Heintzman, a widely respected former senior public servant and at one point head of the Office of Values and Ethics in Treasury Board, made this observation: "I would say that any public servant who's involved in communications activities of that type is in breach of both Communications Policy and the Values and Ethics Code. And any deputy minister who directs or permits public servants to be involved in those activities is in breach of the Values and Ethics Code."[38]

The prime minister's courtiers argue that relations with the media are different today because the modern media are different – more subjective, less deferential, more intrusive than in the past, and forever watching for flaws and missteps by the government and waiting to see what the prime minister will do in response. This also explains the change from "the Government of Canada" to "the Harper government." The desire is to have the prime minister front and centre on positive announcements and thus to control the government's media relations.

Access to information legislation has made it far easier for the media to ferret out scandals. The sponsorship scandal likely would not have come to light had it not been for a *Globe and Mail* journalist who pursued the story through access to information legislation. Gotcha journalism is "easy to write." David Taras argues that "the quality of journalism has deteriorated" to the point that "citizens are increasingly deprived of the vital information they need to make decisions about their communities and their lives." This in turn has had a profound effect in the relationship between the media and the government.[39]

One veteran Canadian journalist admits that working in a highly fragmented media and competitive environment is forcing print journalists to produce articles too quickly. He explains: "Before our newspaper went online, a journalist was expected to produce a solid article a day. Now, journalists are expected to report all new developments online. There is no time for reflection or in-depth reporting."[40] Michel Cormier, a veteran CBC/Radio-Canada journalist, agrees. He talks about the prevalence of mobile telephones, which enables everyone to become a photojournalist. "This and blogs," he says, "have put enormous pressure on the mainstream media to run after stories as they develop. This comes with a price – more substantive and reflective work is less and less evident."[41] This in turn has made life difficult for status participants: they are cut out of good news stories because the prime minister and the prime minister's court now micro-manage media relations so as to cast the government in a positive light.

Status participants can no longer freelance. The Internet, Google searches, and political bloggers have introduced a new dimension to governing. The Internet is highly accessible, easily searchable, and a virtual permanent repository of everything the media publish, and this strengthens the impact of journalism. As a *Toronto Star* journalist put it, "A news organization's journalism can now reach more people, in more places around the world, at greater speed than ever before. No longer does today's printed news become tomorrow's recycling bin throwaway."[42] This often makes the individual politician the centre of attention, rather than the political party or a policy proposal. One only has to Google a name to uncover a cabinet minister's past deeds, good or bad.

There is no question that the wings of status participants have been clipped. Given the new media, the need to protect the government against gotcha journalism and the role of the prime minister's courtiers in managing media relations, the best news for ministers is often no news.[43] This contrasts sharply with Maurice Lamontagne's observation that "if a minister enjoys a good press, he will be envied and respected by his colleagues. If he has no press, he has no future."[44] Things are different today. Indeed, having no press can now put one in good stead with the prime minister's court. Although good press, to the extent that it can be promoted, is now managed by and usually reserved for the prime minister, even so, status participants continue to push for projects and new initiatives in the hope that they will at least play a supporting role in any announcement.

Mission participants may still be present in Ottawa, but here again, their presence is not as strongly felt as it once was. The prime minister and his courtiers keep a tight leash on mission participants in order to control the government's brand, its policy agenda and message. The challenge for mission participants is to find a forum in which to voice their views now that cabinet has been transformed into a kind of focus group for the prime minister. Mission participants are also handicapped by their mandate letters. They had no say in drafting these letters, which they received when they were appointed. It was not always thus. For example, Roméo LeBlanc told Trudeau, before his appointment to cabinet, that he wanted to be the minister for fishermen, much as Eugene Whelan was the minister for farmers. LeBlanc gave two speeches within nine months of his appointment to cabinet to outline "his vision for the future of Canada's fisheries and the steps he intended to take to bring it about."[45] A minister would have no such authority today. Even strong mission participants now have to shape their speeches around their mandate letters or, failing that, in close consultation with the prime minister's court.

A new vision for the fisheries sector would, to be sure, involve the minister responsible, but it would also involve many other federal departments and agencies, and a countless number of meetings, unless the prime minister made it his own priority. It would also involve provincial governments and international organizations. The process would unfold under the watchful eye and guidance of the PMO-PCO. Opposition to mission participants is now found more often within the machinery of government than on the opposition benches in Parliament.

The same can be said about policy participants. They continue to have limited success, for several reasons. Sectoral expertise matters less today because it is no longer possible to isolate policy issues in a single department or even to a single perspective. Unless the prime minister pursues a policy change – and there is a limit to how many he can pursue – there are many hands from many departments and agencies involved in all policy debates and reviews in Ottawa. The prime minister and his court can successfully pursue a limited number of policy changes, but with the rest, the elaborate and slow-moving policy process, involving many hands, takes over. Leaving aside initiatives pursued by the prime minister and his courtiers, making life difficult for policy participants favours the status quo in all other areas of government activities. It explains in part why the government's expenditure is more about repeated choices than new choices.[46]

Notwithstanding the rise of court government in Ottawa, there will never be a shortage of process participants. The desire, if not the ability, to bring home the bacon is as strong today as it was even forty years ago. Only the approach has changed. Horse trading between ministers has given way to a new approach because ministers, for the most part, have few horses to trade. Under such budgeting processes as the PEMS, ministers were able to manage policy reserves and allocate new spending.[47] Today, the prime minister, the minister of finance, and selected courtiers – not cabinet – shape new spending. Process participants have had to redirect their efforts to them, not to one another, to be successful.

From Focus Group to a Search for Relevance

How does cabinet now operate? It is no longer clear that it has much standing, even as a focus group. It depends on the issue and on who sits in the prime minister's chair.

Chrétien essentially used cabinet as a focus group, as his memoirs reveal. Major new spending commitments and key policy decisions were taken outside cabinet.[48] Harper essentially looks to his cabinet to plan Question Period when the House sits and, from time to time, to hold broad political and policy discussions. Harper does not meet his cabinet as regularly as past prime ministers did. It remains useful for ratifying decisions made elsewhere and to plan broad political strategies, but it is no longer the forum where one goes to strike policy and spending decisions.

Cabinet committees matter under Harper, as they did with all previous prime ministers since Trudeau. The cabinet committee that truly matters and is emerging as the new focus group is the Priorities and Planning (P and P) Committee. It matters because the prime minister chairs it, and as a result, it has effective decision-making power. It also matters because its members are for the most part members of the prime minister's court. The key P and P members all chair other cabinet committees.

If the prime minister and his courtiers – who invariably include the minister of finance – govern from the centre, one might assume that it would be easier to control the expenditure budget. Things are not that simple. Whether or not ministers are involved, the forces to increase spending and to protect the status quo do not disappear. The focus has simply shifted away from cabinet and cabinet ministers to the prime minister's court. Ministers and government MPs can always appeal to the prime minister and his court to secure new funding or to protect existing programs, and most do. The prime minister and the minister of finance are subject to the same political forces as cabinet and cabinet committees were subject to under earlier budget processes. The actors may change, but the forces do not.

To cut a program may make a great deal of sense from an Ottawa perspective, but not to Atlantic Canada or Quebec. Similarly, to cut a program or a government unit may make a great deal of sense to Atlantic Canada, but not to Ottawa. Tensions between new spending for new initiatives and reducing spending on existing initiatives remain strong, no matter the actors. The only change is the locus of the decision.

Ministers and Their Departments: A Different Kind of Bacon

Prime ministers and their courtiers may well launch all major policy initiatives and hold effective decision-making power over many issues. The prime minister – as Jean Chrétien was fond of saying – is "le boss." Within departments, ministers are the "boss," but only up to a point. Although ministers are "responsible" for their departments, it is not at all clear that they are "the boss." The fourth Samara report, based on sixty-five exit interviews with MPs, one-third of whom had served in cabinet, reveals that they saw themselves as "powerless and outside the system." Yet they reported little interest in "changing the system so that it's workable" and instead opted to pursue issues of interest to them "in other ways, which meant fighting for their constituency, their region or department."[49]

Ministers are part of the system in that they are expected to promote and defend the interests of their departments. David Good correctly makes the point that success in government is measured by the ability to secure new spending. He writes: "Ask any retired minister to reflect on what he or she accomplished and almost to a person the immediate response has to do with putting in place some major economic, social or international spending initiative." He adds that the prime minister will move weak ministers who cannot make the case for government priorities "to less important and less visible priorities."[50]

Departments want to have strong ministers who are members of the prime minister's court or have access to it in order to protect their interests and sell their plans. Departments are never short of ideas for new spending. They monitor the party's campaign commitments, the media, and what departmental clients, the premiers, and business and community leaders are saying. They arm their ministers with the most persuasive arguments to sell whatever the department has in its planning stages.

In many ways, ministers are lobbyists for their departments. They are expected to be there for the department at every turn – before Parliament, before the media, and before the prime minister's court. They can challenge what the department is proposing (mission participants will often want to do this, others less often) and pick and choose what they think will sell better politically. However, if they are not willing to sell and protect the department, the minister's relations with the department will not be happy, and in some instances the officials may decide to down tools.

Like MPs and ministers who try to see where money flows – to which regions and constituencies – senior departmental officials keep a tab on which department is receiving new funding. Given their knowledge of the machinery of government and the time they have to focus on such matters, public servants are often more successful than politicians in assessing who gets what. Like political constituencies, departments want ministers who can bring home the bacon. Given the demands on their time, the way court government operates, and Canada's political and bureaucratic cultures, it is not too much of an exaggeration to say that the role of ministers can now be summed up as follows: they are lobbyists for their constituencies, regions, and departments.

Tony Clement spoke both to court government and to his role as a minister when he declared that he was "working on establishing a Budget with the Prime Minister's Office" to develop a "G8 Legacy Fund." The fund was to be spent on "border infrastructure."[51] The auditor general, however, subsequently reported that Clement had used the fund more to support special projects and to improve "the look of downtowns" in communities in his constituency than to support border infrastructure.[52] Projects were approved on Clement's advice with little in the way of supporting documents. Public servants were not involved in selecting projects, some of which were a hundred kilometres from the summit site. Parliament, meanwhile, was "left in the dark on the total cost of hosting the G8 summit."[53]

The above raises a number of questions. Why did Clement go to the Prime Minister's Office to establish a G8 legacy budget? There was a time when a minister would have knocked on the door of the Department of Finance and the Treasury Board with this request. It also begs the question: What do Finance and Treasury Board officials now do? What are the minister of finance and his department responsible for, if not the budget? Where were Treasury Board officials in reviewing these projects?

The above also speaks to the minister's ability in bringing home the bacon. Clement is the MP for a relatively well-endowed constituency not far from the Greater Toronto Area, one of the strong "have" regions in Canada's industrial heartland, which has long benefited from national policies. If Clement could secure $50 million from the prime minister's court, at least in part to shower his constituency with projects, what are the other MPs and ministers – especially those representing "have-less" regions – to think or, better yet, to do?

As noted above, ministers focus their efforts on securing their share of government largesse for their regions; this is more rewarding, more tangible, and more easily understood than thousands of pages of government documents tabled in Parliament every year. When new government initiatives are unveiled, ministers and their staff and officials in provincial governments pore over them to see whether they can be applied to their constituencies or regions. This explains why government constituencies received more than their share under the Harper government's Economic Action Plan. As much as 57 percent of the projects with more than $1 million in federal funding went to Conservative ridings, even though the party held only 46 percent of the seats in the Commons before the 2011 general election. Ontario, the heart of Canada's manufacturing and financial services sector, but also the province in which any party has to win a large number of seats to form a majority government, secured 54 percent of all projects, although it accounts for only 39 percent of the population.[54]

Process participant ministers thrive in this environment, and government MPs quickly identify who they are. Court government has served to push more and more ministers into the process participant camp. Providing that they can influence the prime minister's court, they now stand a greater chance of success than mission, policy, or status participants do. Consequently, process participants and the charges of pork-barrelling associated with them attract the attention of the media more than the other three participant types do: pork-barrel politics is easier to understand and document than a complex public policy issue or the finer points of a federal-provincial agreement.

In addition, the presence of ministerial exempt staff is much more tolerated in government operations today than it once was. Access to information legislation, the new media, and permanent election campaigns have made government operations more sensitive to politics and political direction within departments. Exempt staff want to get to the bottom of any potential news story in order to brief the minister and possibly the PMO on its development and political implications. Going up through the traditional bureaucratic channels to the deputy minister and then to the minister and the PMO will no longer do. That takes time, and the media, with their 24-hour news channels, won't wait. Many public servants have no objection to exempt staff members being present in government operations because they recognize that matters that have become issues of partisan controversy are not appropriate for formal briefings, and they welcome any opportunity to isolate themselves from the partisan political process. In any event, it is often better for them to have exempt staffers brief PMO officials than to do it themselves.

Access to information legislation holds challenges for government operations, and it comes at a cost for taxpayers. Simply responding to access to information requests and managing actual or possible controversies can consume a great deal of time and resources. Andy Scott, the minister of Indian affairs and northern development in Paul Martin's government (2004–06), reports that the department's communications branch employed 118 officials and that 111 of them spent most of their time on work related to access to information requests.[55]

Ministers: Hands Off Management

A minister described his position at the top of his department as follows: "It's like I was suddenly landed on the top deck of an ocean liner and told that the ship was my responsibility. When I turned to the captain [i.e., deputy minster] I was told that he was appointed there by someone else and any decision to remove him would be made elsewhere. When I turned to others on the ship, I soon found out that they all report through the deputy minister, owe their allegiance to him and more importantly their future promotions. When I asked for a change in the ship's course, the ship just kept on going on the same course."[56] The minister made this observation in 1983 when court government was in its early stages, when horizontal government was not as evident as it is today, and before access to information legislation was born. If anything, the ocean liner, or line departments, are today considerably more difficult to steer.

Ministers are told in subtle and less than subtle ways to keep their hands off management issues. The deputy minister will explain that he or she is the department's general manager, who serves to free the minister to focus on politics and policy matters. There are also statutes that inhibit ministers from playing a management role. The Financial Administration Act (FAA), the Public Service Employment Act (PSEA), and the Official Languages Act (OLA) declare certain areas to be off limits to ministers. More recently, the accounting officer concept has sought, albeit with uncertain success, to establish a distinct administrative space for senior career public servants.

Canadian public servants hold a number of statutory responsibilities. These responsibilities originate from different sources – from the Interpretation Act and other departmental acts and from powers assigned directly to them in their own right under the FAA, PSEA, and OLA. Ministers cannot by law – not just because of a constitutional convention – issue specific directions to deputy ministers on matters covered by these statutes. The Government of Canada itself has made clear that "deputy ministers are responsible for financial regularity and probity; economy, efficiency and effectiveness; financial management systems for departmental programs and public property."[57] The above makes the point that public servants in Canada have a direct responsibility as servants of the crown and not simply to the government of the day or to their ministers.

The recently introduced accounting officer concept seeks to define further the boundary that separates the political from the permanent public service. The concept is designed to give the accounting officer (or the deputy minister in the case of a line department) a personal responsibility for ensuring that the estimates presented to Parliament are consistent with the statutory powers and that the use of resources in the department is consistent with the estimates. The accounting officer must also answer to Parliament for the stewardship of these responsibilities. The concept was introduced in the aftermath of the Chrétien government's sponsorship scandal.[58] The message to ministers is clear: the deputy minister has specific statutory responsibilities for the management of the department, and if ministers move into that territory, they may well create political problems for the department, themselves, and ultimately the government. More is said below about the accounting officer concept and its application in the Canadian government.

When it comes to management, ministers need considerable knowledge and technical expertise in a subject if they choose to "take on officials." As one minister explained, "You need a great deal of knowledge that you are unlikely to get from the deputy minister or officials down the line reporting to him."[59] It is important to underline the point that ministers have no or very little say in the appointment either of their deputy ministers or in any public service appointments. Deputy ministers, as is well known, are appointed by the prime minister on the advice of the clerk of the privy council. In addition, as we saw earlier, the Prime Minister's Office now has a direct hand in the appointment even of a minister's chief of staff.

Thus, management issues usually hold little interest for ministers, and even when they are interested, their management role in financial and human resources is very limited. However, ministers do expect their deputy ministers to keep the department out of political hot water, and here they have the support of the prime minister and the PMO. Robert Adie and Paul Thomas went so far as to suggest that the first duty of a deputy minister is to keep the minister "out of trouble."[60]

In the eyes of the prime minister's court, a competent deputy minister is one who can keep his or her minister – and by extension, the government – out of trouble; from the department's point of view, a competent minister is one who can promote and defend departmental interests and secure new funding. At the risk of sounding repetitive, there is never a shortage of ideas from departments to expand existing programs and establish new activities. David Good summed it up when he wrote, "Talk to any minister or deputy minister in Ottawa about how the town works and one is immediately struck by how much they view the world from the perspective of the allocation of public money and how much of their time and effort is devoted to trying to get new money for new policy initiatives."[61]

Just as gaining a greater share of the market and a strong bottom line are the measure of success in the private sector, securing new money, protecting one's turf, and avoiding negative press are what truly matters in government. The two worlds are vastly different, despite recent efforts to make the public sector look like the private sector. Ministers are told in many ways that management responsibility belongs to career officials over whom they have no power of appointment or dismissal. This way of operating is completely foreign to the private sector. When it comes to policy issues, leaving aside a few exceptions, ministers have come to terms with the reality that the "centre," or the prime minister's court, controls the policy agenda. It is little wonder, then, that some ministers and MPs consider themselves "powerless and outside the system."

Yet ministers are involved when departments are asked to reduce spending through across-the-board cuts or strategic reviews. The minister leads the discussion for the department before Treasury Board, explaining why the cuts will be difficult to implement and politically difficult to sell to Canadians. The minister then has to convince Canadians of the need for the cuts. The department's public servants know that this is the minister's role, not theirs. The prime minister and his courtiers also expect it, as part of the minister's duty to protect the prime minister from negative media in an era of permanent election campaigns. A minister is always expendable politically, but never the prime minister, of course. Ministers know that even cuts to "low priority" programs are not easy to sell. Nor do they want their departments or the region they represent to be on the losing end of spending cuts, unless others are in the same boat. Low-priority programs are in the eye of the beholder and ministers are all too aware that someone, somewhere, will voice strong opposition to the cuts.

When the minister of public works and government services, for example, announced that 150 "term employees" would be terminated at the public service pension centre in Shediac, New Brunswick, because the project they were working on had come to an end, the local member of Parliament spoke to the media to say that he "was shocked" that Ottawa would cut staff in his constituency. He called the decision "cruel" and "frustrating," comments that were widely reported in the local media. Not to be outdone, the mayor of Shediac and the vice-president of the Public Service Alliance [i.e., the public sector union] labelled the cuts "a huge loss for the community."[62] Nothing was said by any of them about whether there was sufficient work to keep the term employees busy. This, it seems, was simply beside the point. Try that for size in the private sector.

This point was brought home to me in the mid-1970s when Eaton's, then a large Canadian retailer, decided to close its catalogue operations in Moncton, throwing a thousand people out of work. Monctonians looked on the matter as essentially a business decision, and there was little protest by the local media and community leaders. Governments were asked to intervene with special job-creation measures, but there were no demonstrations against Eaton's itself, and the company was not asked to keep open its catalogue operations. It left Moncton quietly, with a minimum of fuss.

In contrast, when Canadian National Railways (CN) decided in the early 1980s that it no longer required its repair and maintenance shops in Moncton, Roméo LeBlanc, a powerful minister in the Trudeau cabinet representing the riding adjoining Moncton, made it clear to CN that closing "the Moncton shops would not be acceptable – period."[63] CN knew full well that it would not be any easier to close the Winnipeg shops, a city then represented by Lloyd Axworthy, another powerful minister in cabinet, or those in Montreal, which was represented by Marc Lalonde and Trudeau himself.

With the election of the Mulroney government, CN again sought to close the Moncton shops, and this time there was no longer any senior cabinet minister to fight for Moncton. With only one junior minister representing New Brunswick at the time, CN was finally able to close the Moncton shops. The reaction in Moncton was swift, highly vocal, and determined. The local member of Parliament was asked to resign, a "Save Our Shop" committee, consisting of leading community spokespersons, was established, several widely reported demonstrations took place, and the matter dominated the local media for three years.[64] Municipal, provincial, and some federal politicians insisted that the "federal government" was treating Moncton unfairly. CN subsequently announced a delay in implementing the shop closure and created a special fund to attract new jobs to Moncton. In short, Monctonians had one set of expectations for government, even for crown corporations operating in a competitive environment, and another for the private sector. When a leading member of the Moncton community was asked to comment on this discrepancy, he responded that "business must make business decisions. There is a bottom line to look after. Otherwise the business will not survive long. Eaton's is a business and it must compete. In government, especially in the federal government, there is a great deal of waste and inefficiency. Moncton is not getting its share of the waste. In losing the CN shops, we are now getting even less of our share."[65]

This chapter has discussed how the role of ministers has been redefined, albeit by stealth, in recent years. They no longer debate policy issues in cabinet, where mission participants, for example, used to be able to make the case for a new policy initiative. Instead, the prime minister and his courtiers now engage in bilateral discussions with ministers to decide policy issues and to identify new spending measures. A handful of strong ministers who are members of the prime minister's court can still influence policy and new spending commitments. Others, however, are left to represent their departments to the media, departmental stakeholders, and their constituents. The dominant actors in government today are the prime minister and his courtiers in all key policy issues and also in budget making. The next chapter explores their role and how they manage the budget process.

4

The Prime Minister: Give Me Time to Learn

Tony Blair warns that the one phrase a prime minister must never utter from the very moment of being sworn into office is "Give me time to learn."[1] The minute one sits in the prime minister's chair, power and responsibility flow into the hands of the incumbent, who is expected to have all the knowledge necessary to lead the government and take important decisions. B. Guy Peters dismissed the suggestion that we are witnessing the "Presidentization of the Prime Minister in Canada," insisting that the United States president does not have anywhere near the power that our prime minister has.[2] The shift from cabinet government to governing from the centre in Canada is now complete. Events, circumstances, and developments in society and within the machinery of government have all conspired to strengthen the hand of the prime minister. The prime minister and some carefully selected courtiers have the power. Others may have influence, but even that is frequently tied to their ability to gain access to the prime minister's court.[3]

It is interesting to note that "governing from the centre" is not a Canadian phenomenon. A ten-country survey recently revealed that the trend is now evident throughout the Western world.[4] Canadians believe that the Prime Minister's Office has too much power and that the House of Commons does not have enough.[5] A senior deputy minister observed that "no one debates whether or not we govern from the centre anymore. It is now a fact. The more important question is what does it mean for decision making and the work of the public service and what does it mean for the work of policy analysts?"[6]

There is no need to go over again the instruments that enable the prime minister to govern from the centre.[7] Rather, this chapter looks at the dominant role the prime minister and the PM's court play in government, in shaping the government's expenditure budget, and in managing government operations.

The Prime Minister Rules

Prime ministers lead incredibly busy lives. They have all the responsibilities that MPs and cabinet ministers have, and then some. They cannot possibly meet all the demands on their time as they operate in several overlapping worlds, including the world stage. They also have family matters to attend to. Prime ministers, like other senior executives, have a finite amount of energy and time to devote to the job. More to the point, they have a "hectic, fragmented, episodic, pressured and stressful" agenda, despite the efforts of their staff to plan and organize their activities.[8] Certainly, no prime minister can attend every important meeting in government and read every important document.[9]

The prime minister's power is thus limited by the scarcity of time. In addition, the global economy and the "interconnected" world of public policy issues has caused some power to move out of national governments, drifting up to international or regional trade agreements or organizations, and down to local government.[10] Power has also flowed to the courts as the Charter of Rights and Freedoms continues to make its presence felt in many policy sectors. Canada's chief justice recently made clear her views on the role of the judiciary when she wrote, "I believe that judges have the duty to insist that the legislative and executive branches of government conform to certain established and fundamental norms, even in times of trouble." She added that "the debate is not about whether judges should ever use unwritten constitutional norms to invalidate laws, but rather about whether norms may justify such actions."[11] One can hardly imagine a judge making a similar observation even as recently as the 1970s.

Still, within the government, perhaps because there is less power to go around, prime ministers and their courtiers can rule with a heavy hand. Yet there is no job description or any statutes outlining the prime minister's role and responsibilities. Issues of any consequence invariably flow to the PM for resolution, and well over a hundred officials have some form of reporting relationship with the prime minister. Management and organizational theories suggest that a suitable span of control for a senior executive in the private sector would have anywhere between three and twelve sub-ordinates. The literature also suggests that the farther you spread the span of control, the less effective the senior executive will be.[12] Private sector executives would not tolerate, let alone try to cope with, having more than a hundred individuals reporting to them.

Prime ministers, at least the ones perceived to be effective, also have their own policy preferences to pursue. They climb to the top for a reason, presumably not simply because they want to be "le boss." It will be recalled that Trudeau set out to bring Canada's constitution home, Mulroney embraced a free trade agreement with the United States, and Chrétien wanted to be a competent manager and to promote national unity, while Harper, it seems, wants to redefine the role of the federal government. Prime ministers focus their efforts on policy initiatives and projects that matter to them, knowing that they can have their way and that their time in power may be brief. They also focus on appointments they want to secure for their supporters and those who promote their policy agenda.

As for the rest, the government machinery is essentially allowed to run on its tracks – unless, of course, a scandal or a crisis that generate strong media interest comes along to upset things. The prime minister, his chief of staff, and the clerk of the privy council are in frequent – if not daily – contact to deal with the pressing issues of the day, of which there is never a shortage.[13] Prime ministers are not allowed to say "give me time to learn" or to press the pause button to put an emerging crisis on hold while reflecting on how to resolve the issue.

Prime ministers learn on the job, for the most part, and by turning to a handful of senior government officials for guidance. Some, such as Chrétien, had wide experience in government before becoming prime minister; others, including Harper, had very little. Prime ministers certainly do not want to consult their predecessors for advice. One only needs to read Paul Martin and Jean Chrétien's accounts of their political careers to see that Martin would not have consulted Chrétien for a variety of reasons.[14] Harper, in turn, very likely concluded that he had no lessons to learn from Martin.

Prime ministers soon learn that although they have the power to rule within government, they spend the bulk of their time reacting to events. When asked to name the biggest challenge he had faced when in office, former British prime minister Harold Macmillan famously replied, "Events, my dear boy, events."[15] Indeed, no prime minister can avoid dealing with crises, unforeseen events, or significant political or economic developments. A senior PCO official once told me that an important part of his job was "to fall on hand grenades." He added that in government, officials deal with known crises (those that are reported in the media) and unknown crises (those that the Ottawa system has been able to manage without the media reporting on them).[16] Crises, scandals, potential scandals, administrative miscues, charges of favouritism, conflicts between ministers or with provincial governments, leaks of sensitive material, media reports that a parliamentary secretary had exchanged flirtatious emails with a reporter from China, conflicts between some ministers and their senior departmental officials, reports from officers of Parliament ... all such matters are part and parcel of what needs to be managed in the age of 24-hour news channels and access to information legislation. These issues dominate the agenda of politicians and senior public servants in a way that is foreign to private sector executives and their employees.

While the prime minister may want issues and government operations to run quietly on their tracks, things can easily go wrong, as is all too evident. Low-profile departments or programs can quickly run off their tracks, and then the prime minister and the courtiers have to play a central role in managing the fallout. This in turn can consume a great deal of prime ministerial time. There is never a shortage of crises in an organization that has some 40 cabinet ministers and nearly 300,000 public servants operating in a highly charged political environment. It is no exaggeration to suggest that the ability to keep oneself or one's department out of public controversy may well be the most important criterion of success in government, at least when viewed from the prime minister's perspective.

Governing is also made more difficult, more complex, and more unpredictable in an era of permanent election campaigns, given that governing now requires continuing public approval.[17] As Paul Thomas writes, "The techniques for winning power have been transferred increasingly to the processes of government."[18] The prime minister is the central player in managing permanent campaigns, no less than in general election campaigns. The PM and the courtiers are "the" important source of news; they set the government agenda, manage media relations, organize "spin" and "the spin doctors," and to the extent they can, they manage the news.[19]

The prime minister and the courtiers value ministers and public servants who avoid negative publicity, can manage a real-time or emerging crisis, and are willing to fall on hand grenades. The bold and daring initiatives, meanwhile, are best left to the prime minister's court to unveil and manage. This encourages lack of action in enterprises and government operations that are of little interest to the prime minister and his courtiers.

The Prime Minister's Court

Who are the members of the prime minister's court, and what issues do they address? These two questions are important if one wishes to understand how the government decides and why. The prime minister's political court is partisan and consists of both outsiders and insiders. The outsiders include media relations specialists, selected lobbyists, and close political confidants of the prime minister. The insiders include the prime minister's chief of staff, the minister of finance, and a handful of favoured ministers.

The prime minister's court also has a non-partisan component. The clerk of the privy council is invariably a member of the court, as are a few senior officials in the PCO and the deputy minister of finance. If the prime minister loses confidence in the clerk, he or she will be quietly moved on or, if lucky, rewarded with a highly sought-after ambassadorial appointment. Similarly, senior PCO officials who make it to the prime minister's court are usually rewarded with deputy ministerial appointments.[20]

The prime minister's court carefully controls the government agenda. One of Chrétien's former policy advisers essentially confirmed, perhaps unwittingly, that court government has replaced cabinet government. He explained that final decisions on priorities are "made solely by the prime minister and the minister of finance rather than by the whole Cabinet."[21] "In my experience in Ottawa," he wrote, "cabinets don't seem to work in a way to achieve a consensus on what overall government spending priorities should be." He went on to say that cabinet ministers are not able "to take into account the whole mix of considerations," including unanticipated events.[22] He never answered the question "What, then, do cabinets do?" Nor did he explain how the prime minister and advisers are able to understand "unanticipated events" better than the cabinet does. It seems that only minor policy issues and other small matters are now submitted to the formal policy- and decision-making processes, decisions that have been carefully monitored by the prime minister's court or matter little to it.

In brief, the prime minister's court, not cabinet or cabinet committees, now decides "overall" government spending priorities. If one is to accept the argument from the Chrétien adviser – and there is ample evidence to suggest that he was correct – one can only conclude that the key actors who shape Ottawa's expenditure budget, particularly when dealing with new spending or spending cuts, are the prime minister, his courtiers, and the minister of finance.

When Guardians Become Spenders

The traditional battle lines between guardians and spenders were once clear. In recent years, court government and the apparent inability of cabinet ministers "to achieve a consensus on what overall government spending priorities should be" have turned guardians into part-time spenders and pushed some spenders to the sidelines.

It is worth repeating that the power over new spending decisions is now concentrated in a few hands in Ottawa. The prime minister and his courtiers are not in the habit of bringing their spending proposals to cabinet for consideration. Indeed, by the time ministers are briefed on the initiative, the die has been cast. Meanwhile, the minister of finance is brought on side to ensure the budget makes provisions for the initiative. One of Chrétien's policy advisers explained why the prime minister decided to ignore the policy process when he introduced the $2.5 billion Millennium Scholarship Fund, described as the federal government's most significant millennium project: "If we had respected the process, the idea would never have come out at the other end the way we wanted it. Intergovernmental affairs would have argued that the matter was provincial, not federal. Human Resources Department would have argued that the idea was in its jurisdiction, while Heritage Canada would have made a similar claim. The prime minister asked one of us to call Paul Martin [minister of finance] and his deputy minister to let them know what we were doing. In that way he got what he wanted."[23]

The above explains why policies and major initiatives are now made by announcement or, as Arthur Kroeger said, "like bolts of lightning." Very little of consequence now happens without a strong push from the centre. A strong central push does not require formal cabinet processes or many written documents; only the most essential interdepartmental consultations have to be undertaken. A deck, a PowerPoint presentation, a review by selected central agency officials, and a nod from the prime minister are frequently all that is needed to launch a costly initiative. News management, always important in a permanent campaign era, is also easier to manage when only a handful of individuals is involved.

The advantages of court government, especially from the prime minister's perspective, are many.[24] Policy changes are quickly established and decisions are taken in short order in a fast-changing global economy. The prime minister has a sense of being in control of the policy process and the machinery of government at a time when the media expect a quick response to emerging issues. However, it is not without drawbacks, particularly when it comes to managing the government's expenditure budget. Decisions of any consequence, including spending cuts or new spending commitments, can be made only by the prime minister and the PM's court. This has created an overload problem, a bottleneck of issues to be decided by the prime minister and the court, with the result that many matters are left unattended in the pending basket.

If the prime minister does not call for or give his blessings to spending cuts, nothing happens. Since the prime minister and the courtiers can never possess the necessary information or have time to gather the information to initiate specific spending cuts, they rely on across-the-board cuts. Having things run on their tracks holds distinct political advantages for the prime minister and his courtiers, but the downside is that no one has any incentive to challenge the status quo in order to see whether government operations and programs could be run more efficiently.

Give Me Time to Manage

Court government has created a power vacuum in various parts of the machinery of government. In areas that hold limited interest for the prime minister and his court, decisions are either not made or are simply put off, as we noted above. The court is happy to allow the elaborate and formal decision-making process take over issues in which they have little interest. The goal is to avoid negative publicity in the era of permanent election campaigns. When things are at risk, it is best to have them massaged by a number of oversight bodies, risk assessors, and accountability requirements, thereby minimizing potential problems for the prime minister's court.

A crisis, however, can jolt the prime minister's court into action and derail its political and policy agenda, at least temporarily. Harry Swain, a former deputy minister of Indian affairs and northern development, showed how a crisis or a story that gains a high profile in the media can move the government to act, suggesting that at times it is the only way to get the government to move on an issue.[25]

The government machinery, broadly defined, is quite content to lie at rest. This serves the government's political and bureaucratic interests, and is true at all levels of government. The various levels are relatively isolated from one another. One level – the prime minister's court – has an oversupply of power, while the other levels have too little, spending an inordinate amount of time avoiding errors, guessing what the court may think about issues, managing media relations, and avoiding errors that could cause political problems for the government. The same is true to some extent in line departments. Unless the prime minister's court makes its views clear, deputy ministers can attempt to move issues and proposals forward as best they can, put things on hold, promote aspiring public servants, and block initiatives that hold little or no advantage to their departments. Meanwhile, public servants down the line do not have this authority and are left to manage programs to deliver services without bringing attention to themselves or to the department.[26] This favours the status quo in many policy sectors and government operations, and has obvious implications for the government's expenditure budget.[27]

Elites Meet with Elites

The prime minister's court meets on a regular basis with political, economic, and public service elites. Its members read the papers or have someone monitor the media, keep in contact with provincial premiers, look to world events and stay in touch with world leaders, and are in regular contact with the most senior bureaucrats, notably the clerk of the privy council, the deputy minister of finance, and the deputy minister of foreign affairs. The most senior lobbyists with strong links to the governing party and their more influential clients also have access to the prime minister's inner circle.

Hierarchy still matters. Like the Lowells of Boston who talked "only to Cabots," and the Cabots who talked "only to God," the prime minister's courtiers speak only with a select few. They continually have to respond to requests for meetings, turning down many more than they accept, and very rarely have to seek out individuals they wish to meet. They also have to respond to proposal after proposal for new spending commitments from ministers, government MPs, provincial governments, lobbyists, and a variety of associations or groups and business executives – but dealing only with individuals at the most senior levels.

One cannot overemphasize the fact that the prime minister and his court operate in a world of elites. A recent two-year review of who has access to the prime minister reveals that top executives from industry lead the list; 75 percent of the lobbying directed toward the prime minister came from senior representatives of Canadian industry, with the Canadian Council of Chief Executives topping the list. Harper's deputy press secretary explained why: "The government's priority for the last two and a half years has been the economy ... It is no surprise that the prime minister has met quite a few times, and predominantly with business and industry representatives."[28]

Political and economic elites have come to share a view of the world that is increasingly focused on the competitive nature of the global economy. This view has somehow to accommodate several uncomfortable facts: the never-ending cry for greater transparency; a more aggressive media and a less deferential society; the need to respond quickly to questions and emerging problems for fear of being perceived as weak or not in control; and the reality that no public policy issue can belong to a single government department or agency.

Given the above, one can appreciate that from the prime minister's perspective, governing from the centre makes sense. It enables him and his court to exert a greater degree of control over what they invariably regard as a potentially hostile and chaotic world. Chrétien summed up the life of a present-day politician as "learning to walk with your back to the wall, your elbows high, and a smile on your face. It is a survival game played under the glare of light. If you don't learn that, you're quickly finished. The press wants to get you. The opposition wants to get you. Even some of the bureaucrats want to get you. They all have an interest in making you look bad."[29] Governing from the centre enables the prime minister to protect his own and his government's political interest.

It takes a strong wrench of the wheel for those outside the court to see one of their proposed initiatives put on the government's to-do list. The challenge for them is to present their ideas and proposals in a way that will matter to the courtiers. Political survival in the era of permanent campaigns is tied as much to the court's ability to keep a lid on things as on shaping new policy initiatives. Chrétien's sponsorship scandal, for example, did far more damage to the Liberal Party than its ambitious 1994–97 program review exercise.[30] Chrétien's court designed and managed the sponsorship program to a greater extent than it was ever prepared to admit.[31] There were no effective checks and balances from cabinet or from the public service, and, to some extent, there were no statutes to prevent the prime minister's court from grabbing power and abusing it.[32] The same cannot be said of the rest of the machinery of government.

Scandals and bureaucratic missteps very often entail in their immediate aftermath new oversight bodies, new rules, and new administrative processes to prevent such disasters recurring and to ensure that the machinery of government continues to run on its tracks. The prime minister's court and central agencies sit at the centre of a schizophrenic world, insisting on their right to change course and to introduce schemes like the sponsorship program in order to promote national unity, and they also have the flexibility to deal with such issues as emerged from the G8 meetings, for instance, and from fast-changing economic circumstances. There is little inside government to hold them back.

The goal for the prime minister's court is to control the message and to put in place a focused, coherent, and disciplined communications strategy while pursuing its political and policy agenda. Paul Thomas explains: "The emergence of a multi-channel, aggressive, adversarial and negative 24/7 media system has reflected and reinforced a political culture of scandal and caused the public to further mistrust government as a messenger" – all of this in a more "legalized, regulated" environment. Permanent election campaigns, he adds, have had a profound effect on governing.[33]

The prime minister's court monitors very carefully those issues that may cast the government in a positive or negative light. It will be recalled, for example, that a federal fisheries scientist published a paper in the journal *Science* after she had discovered a virus that could be killing large numbers of Fraser River salmon before they could reach their spawning grounds. The Privy Council Office, not the Department of Fisheries and Oceans, decided to prohibit the scientist from speaking to the media about her findings. The thinking was that the risk of things going off the rails was too high to allow a public servant to speak publicly about her scientific findings.[34]

The Department of Fisheries and its minister had no choice but to sit back and let the PCO take the lead on an issue that in years past would surely have been resolved by the department. The point is that issues, both large and small, are increasingly being managed at the centre of government. Discussions are between the political and bureaucratic elites, with the deputy minister of the relevant department consulted or simply informed. The views of front-line employees – the scientist or the music teacher type of staff – are rarely heard within the prime minister's court. There are too many layers of central agencies, oversight bodies, and bureaucratic units between them and the decision makers for the front-line workers to be heard.

In brief, the prime minister and his courtiers have an agenda to promote. They take decisions on matters that are of interest to them and on those that in some way come into the court's orbit. This orbit encompasses political, economic, and media elites representing interest groups and political constituencies. The point of reference for the court remains fairly constant in terms of elites, and the flow of information is relatively circular.

Prime ministers do not have the luxury of saying "give me time to learn," but they do have easy access to experts in all policy fields. In Ottawa, the experts – more than a thousand strong – have no programs or services to deliver to Canadians. They are there to plan, coordinate, monitor, and assess for prime ministers and their courtiers, and if necessary to fall on hand grenades. The Prime Minister's Office and the Privy Council Office are now more than three times larger than they were in the late 1970s.[35] Many of their members put in very long hours. We are informed that prime ministers' chiefs of staff, for example, are on the "job before 7 a.m. and remain certainly reachable on their BlackBerries until 10 or 11 o'clock at night, when they supposedly turn them off. But sometimes they don't turn them off and they ring in the middle of the night."[36]

The prime minister's court also has access to Canada's leading pollsters and policy consultants. Given the prime minister's power of appointment and the capacity to marshall resources, the court can have its way on any issue and can handle difficult situations even when they belong in line departments. Line department officials support their ministers, but if the minister is in conflict with the prime minister's court or does not enjoy its support, they will quickly sense this – in which case, they may well, as one director-level official explained, adopt a "3D strategy: drop, delay, or delegate."[37] A former PMO staffer pointed out that when MPs or cabinet ministers make mistakes, "it sometimes falls to PMO to pick up the pieces."[38] Ministers, parliamentary secretaries, and even government MPs are no longer left to their own resources to resolve their own controversies.

If, as many political scientists now argue, one governs by network, where vertical lines of authority have to be reconciled with horizontal lines of action, the prime minister's court sits at the centre of the network.[39] One deputy minister in Ottawa, commenting on where power lies within government, noted, "Actually you can find power in most mornings when the Clerk and the Prime Minister meet. The Prime Minister has a list of things he wants the Clerk to look after and the Clerk has a series of recommendations for the Prime Minister to consider. In some ways, they trade power. If what they decide should happen in a department, it happens. If they decide that it should not happen, it will not happen … Line departments have power in delivering their programs, but nothing compared to the PM-Clerk. I am not saying that this is not the way it should be. It may be the best way to get things done. What I am saying is that this is the way it is."[40]

The prime minister has his agenda for the clerk: initiatives that he wants to pursue, ministers he wants kept on a short leash, problems in the bureaucracy that he has heard about, an appointment that he wishes to make, a media story that he wants to be briefed on, or a looming problem that needs to be addressed. The clerk also has an agenda. He or she wants to protect the interests of the public service. The ability to do this often distinguishes strong clerks from weak ones – at least, in the eyes of public servants. Indeed, one should never underestimate the clerk's desire to be seen as the defender of the public service. Since 1993, one of the clerk's three key responsibilities has been to act as "the head of the public service." It will be recalled that the authors of Public Service 2000, a high-profile effort to overhaul how the Canadian public service functions, argued that the clerk should take the lead on "issues of management" and become "the leader of the Public Service."[41]

Keith Beardsley, former senior adviser and deputy chief of staff to Stephen Harper, reports that the prime minister "typically participates in a morning meeting with nine or 10 senior advisors. They brief him on issues bubbling up in the media, mostly."[42] This session and the prime minister's morning meeting with his chief of staff and the clerk of the privy council, define the government's political and policy agenda of the day. If one wants to see evidence that urgent matters can crowd out important ones, one needs look no further than these meetings. However, if one wants to see quick decisions taken on the back of an envelope or after looking at a ten-minute Deck presentation, this also happens at those morning meetings.

The front pages of the Globe and Mail and La Presse, and the lead stories on the evening news at CBC, CTV, and Radio-Canada – as Beardsley points out – often determine the content of these morning discussions. This explains why inactivity is so seductive. It provides a sense of safety to the prime minister's court and also to senior public servants in their desire to protect the public service as an institution. The ability to keep your minister and your department below the parapet is an important measure of success. This is no easy task in an era of 24-hour news, social media, and access to information legislation. To avoid difficult decisions and to let programs run on their tracks are sure ways of staying below the parapet and avoiding controversy.

The Prime Minister's Court and the Expenditure Budget

David Good describes the important role that PMO-PCO plays in approving new spending and turns to a series of interviews with senior govern-

ment officials to build his case. He writes that "for one skilled departmental spender, there is no doubt where he goes for new funding. You go to
PMO."[43] Another senior official explains how you do so: "With the prime
minister, you play the angle – you say – either you want it or you don't.
This is not a cabinet issue. It is your issue. Your ministers will rag the puck
until you take it."[44]

Having access to the court is both crucial and limited. Ministers take
great pride in being part of the court or of having access to it to get things
approved. It separates influential ministers, who are able to get new spending commitments, from weak ones. Stéphane Dion, for example, claimed
with pride before Justice Gomery that he had been a member of Chrétien's
court. He told Gomery that he had an extremely strong working relationship with the prime minister, insisting that "few ministers had that kind
of direct relationship with him."[45] Dion was able to secure substantial new
funding from the Chrétien government for new initiatives in support of
official languages minorities.[46]

There is never a shortage of ideas for new spending that are presented
to the prime minister's court. Ministers and deputy ministers always have
an agenda to pursue which, more often than not, costs money. Yet hardly
ever do any of them go to the court with ideas on how to cut spending in
their departments. Even in periods of expenditure restraints or program
reviews, they are rarely in the mood to offer spending cuts. Ministers and
deputy ministers are in the business of leaving a legacy, a program, a project, or an initiative which they can point to as their accomplishment. But
legacies cost money, and few line department ministers or deputy ministers
want to look back and say, "I was responsible for cutting a program, gut-
ting a department, eliminating a service, or getting rid of 5 or 10 percent
of the staff."

The fact that the prime minister's court decides on major initiatives
means that in pursuing their legacy projects, ministers now turn to the
prime minister's court rather than to one another, to cabinet committees,
or to full cabinet, as in the past. A successful minister is one who has been
able to gain the confidence of the prime minister and his courtiers and has
come away with a costly legacy project. For example, Elmer MacKay, who
temporarily gave up his constituency to Brian Mulroney, can legitimately
claim credit for construction of the fixed link between New Brunswick and
Prince Edward Island; Marc Lalonde could say that he was responsible for
delivering part of the contract for building navy frigates to the Davie shipyard in Quebec in the early 1980s; David Dingwall can claim that he delivered capital expenditure projects to the University of Cape Breton during

the 1990s; Roméo LeBlanc could point to his success in locating a Department of Supply and Services office in Shediac, a small community in his constituency; Lloyd Axworthy secured several infrastructure projects in Winnipeg; Jean Chrétien won a Revenue Canada office for his riding; and Tony Clement spent $50 million of G8 money throughout his constituency. The list goes on and on.

Protecting the "A" Base

Ottawa regularly holds expenditure or program reviews, budget exercises, and strategic and operation reviews, all designed to reduce spending from a department's A base or its ongoing programs and operations. In some cases, as in 1978, the prime minister acts without such reviews. Trudeau returned from a trip to Germany – where the idea was gaining traction that growth in government spending was fuelling inflation – and announced a series of expenditure reductions. After consulting only a handful of his closest advisers, he announced $2 billion in spending cuts.[47] He insisted that "we must have a major re-ordering of Government priorities. We must reduce the size of government." Failing that, he pointed out, "Canadians within several years would almost certainly be faced with a fiscal crisis."[48] As is now well known, Trudeau did not even consult his minister of finance, Jean Chrétien, before announcing the cuts, nor did he provide any details on where the cuts would be made.[49] He simply declared that the government needed a $2 billion spending cut and that somehow the system would identify where and how. It was his way of challenging the status quo, an approach that remains in fashion to this day.

Since then, we have seen a variety of strategic policy, program, or operations reviews.[50] Some (circa 1994–97) were more ambitious than others (including some fourteen expenditure cutting exercises between 1984 and 1993). Throughout it all, targets and processes were established by central agencies with the centre pushing line departments to come forward with possible spending cuts.

Departments always resist cuts. They attempt to avoid them, but if there is no escaping them, they may offer up their most politically appealing or high-profile programs – the musical ride approach, so named after the popular RCMP musical ride, whose demise would cause a political uproar. Officials know that politically embarrassing spending cuts will ultimately be rejected by the prime minister's court.[51] This is another reason why the prime minister insists on signing off on all spending cuts of any significance.

Ministers fight for their departments and many go to the prime minister's court in an attempt to reverse proposed spending cuts. Traditional guardians, ministers who have long called for less government spending, often have a change of mind when it comes to their own departments. John Manley, a senior minister in the Chrétien government who liked to portray himself as a friend of the business community and to favour less government intervention in the economy (particularly when it involved regions outside his own Ottawa area), went directly to the prime minister in the 1994–97 program review to make the case that his department should be spared.[52] He wrote to Chrétien arguing that the guardians were about to "make a major political mistake" in cutting one of his programs at Industry Canada.[53] Chrétien never replied to Manley, in effect supporting the decision to strip the program of government funding.[54]

Manley was not the only minister to make impassioned appeals to protect his department. Ralph Goodale, the minister of agriculture, asked the guardians, "What gives you the right to act as judges on what generations of other people have created? From what divine right do you derive the power to decide that fifty of my scientists will be without work tomorrow?"[55] Still other ministers, like André Ouellet, who had served under Trudeau and was also a member of the ministerial program review group in the Chrétien government, expressed deep concern that the review would have grave political consequences for the government. Still, the prime minister and the minister of finance stood firm and substantial spending cuts were made.

As noted earlier, ministers learn soon after their appointment that an important part of their responsibilities is to defend the interest of their departments. They invariably point to other departments, other programs, or other services where cuts should be made. They want to look strong to their senior departmental officials, to clients of the department, to the media, and to their constituents. The perception in Ottawa is that strong ministers have easy access to the prime minister's court and are capable of defending their departmental interests and budget. Weak ministers have limited access to the court and, consequently, little ability to promote or protect their departmental budget. Ministers who become strong advocates for their departments very seldom get themselves in political difficulty, since most publicized political problems stem from ministers ignoring advice from their officials.[56] Meanwhile, they enjoy the support of their departmental officials for projects or initiatives they may wish to pursue.

David Good, echoing the principal-agent theory, writes that in Ottawa "spenders don't naturally give information to guardians ... no spender wants a guardian to use the information later to turn down a request or, worse yet, to cut a program."[57] Spenders have no interest in feeding central agencies information about their activities, unless it bolsters the argument for more spending or for preserving the status quo. This is not helped by high staff turnover in central agencies – indeed a stint in a central agency is very often necessary for ambitious public servants who wish to make it to the top.[58]

Thus, the prime minister's court is left to call for across-the-board cuts whenever it has to introduce expenditure restraint measures. Even the much-vaunted 1994–97 program review in the end was tied to across-the-board cuts that departments had to meet. The cuts were divided into three categories: very significant (up to 50 percent), substantial (up to 25 percent), and smaller (up to 15 percent). Harper's strategic and operations reviews have also been tied to across-the-board cuts (anywhere from 5 to 10 percent, or higher in some cases). Across-the-board cuts hold some advantages: they do not require an intimate knowledge of line departments and their programs; it is somewhat easier to sell them in the system because everyone has to share the pain; and they generate suggestions and recommendations from the departments, with the result that the prime minister's court has the last word.

Harper's 2012 budget, his first under a majority mandate, looked to across-the-board cuts to generate spending reductions of $5.2 billion over three years. All departments and agencies were asked to submit scenarios for 5 and 10 percent reductions which included employment cuts in the public service.[59] Members of the prime minister's court, including central agencies, maintain that across-the-board is the only way to achieve spending cuts. Why is this so? As we have seen, ministers arrive in Ottawa as MPs determined to represent the best interests of their constituencies and regions. But they soon discover that their role in shaping policy is limited by the horizontal nature of the policy-making process and by the concentration of power in the hands of the prime minister and his courtiers. Their ability to manage their departments is also limited by time constraints, statutes, a lack of knowledge about the machinery of government, and by Ottawa's culture.

Successful ministers quickly realize that the way to get things done, to avoid political pitfalls, and to secure some level of influence in the system is to align themselves with their departments. They recognize that they have few allies in the system, and in time they come to rely on their own senior departmental officials. For their part, these officials press their ministers to protect and promote their departmental interest. The prime minister and his courtiers have all the levers to push back ministers and their departments if they so choose, and to select which proposed initiatives they will support. This enables the prime minister to be a guardian or a spender, depending on the circumstances. Prime ministers, especially since Trudeau, have been both active guardians and spenders.

This flies in the face of traditional public administration, which argues that guardians can only be guardians, never spenders. Traditionally, central agencies did not have programs to deliver. If they did, they would be in a constant conflict of interest, since they would be tempted to promote their own programs at the expense of the line departments. As in so many other things, this aspect of traditional public administration has been tossed aside. The prime minister and the minister of finance have become important spenders and, together with their immediate advisers, have become the "new priority setters."[60] No longer is this role played by the cabinet. Priority setters decide who wins in the continuing competition for new funding and also who loses in expenditure review exercises. As Good writes, "Priority setters directly shape current budget decisions."[61]

The priority setters constitute the new village, in contrast to the one described in Heclo and Wildavsky's *The Private Government of Public Money*.[62] The village is today considerably smaller, more coherent, and more decisive. Its strength, however, is also its weakness. While it can make decisions quickly and most of the time make them stick, the new village can never have access to all the information necessary to take important decisions in all key sectors. Important decisions are now often made on the fly. Someone in the court catches the prime minister's ear with an idea that starts the ball rolling. The minister of finance is brought onside to ensure that money is set aside to pursue the initiative. A discussion, limited to a handful of politicians and officials, is held to review how and when to make the announcement. PowerPoint presentations are now the instrument of choice to move ideas to resolution. Gone are elaborate cabinet documents, discussion papers, and broad interdepartmental consultations.[63]

In brief, catching the prime minister's ear, that of his chief of staff, and the minister of finance is what has come to matter to launch a new initiative. The competition is intense and the number of proposed initiatives never-ending. Few of those involved are members of the village, but having access to them is critical. The same process applies when a decision is made to cut spending. The new village will decide that an across-the-board cut of, say, 5, 10, or 15 percent is required, an announcement is made, and the machinery of government is then called upon to come up with ideas on how to do it. But while the prime minister and his courtiers can make decisions on the fly when they concern new spending commitments, things are not that simple when considering cuts in spending. This requires a level of knowledge that the prime minister's court can never acquire. When cuts become necessary, it will rely on reviews, based on an across-the-board cut that applies to everyone.

Recent Program Review Exercises

We have seen in recent years many ongoing program reviews. They are variously labelled "strategic reviews" and "strategic and operational reviews," but the approaches resemble previous reviews. They remain in their essence across-the-board cuts, and the prime minister and his courtiers still retain the final say on all the cuts. Shortly after coming to power, the Harper government announced that it would carry out "strategic reviews." Their purpose, Harper explained, was to generate one-time cuts to enable the government to reallocate resources to fund emerging priorities. All departments and agencies were subjected to a strategic review over a four-year cycle, all with a view to achieving a 5 percent reduction in departmental spending. In 2011 the government reported that 98 percent of direct program spending had been reviewed and the departments had been able to identify 5 percent spending cuts from their low-priority programs.[64]

Departments were free to put forward low-priority activities for consideration so long as they met the 5 percent target. However, borrowing a page from the principal-agent theory, all departments were instructed to retain the services of an "outside adviser" to their strategic review exercise. I served as the external adviser to one such exercise, meeting on a regular basis with senior departmental and Treasury Board Secretariat officials. The necessary information was freely shared and we did review all programs and activities, however briefly in some instances.[65] Throughout the exercise, I was free to challenge any and all activities. There was an unwritten rule, however, that to the extent possible, the review would protect the department's organization and staff. We relied on the senior departmental officials, in some cases on Treasury Board staff and on our roundtable discussions to arrive at our recommendations. These focused on eliminating overhead positions at head office (cuts were to be largely made through attrition) and on a program operating at the regional level where it was felt that other government programs were competing with one another, creating an oversupply of similar programs.

I accompanied the minister and deputy minister to the Treasury Board meeting that considered our review findings. Treasury Board ministers posed a series of questions that focused on the "politics" of the situation and how the proposed cuts could be sold in the regions. They did not inform us of their decisions, however, making it clear that their recommendations would now be put before the prime minister and his office for consideration. It also was made clear to me that the prime minister and his advisers would have the final say.

The Harper government, fresh with a majority mandate, decided to launch in 2011 another review – this time, a comprehensive strategic and operation review – to find $5.2 billion in annual savings by 2014. As already noted, departments and agencies were asked to bring forward to Treasury Board ministers two possible expenditure reductions – one at 5 percent and the other at 10 percent. Later, the minister of finance declared that some departments and agencies would face cuts of more than 10 percent. All in all, some seventy departments and agencies were required to submit scenarios for a 5 and 10 percent reduction to their budgets. The cuts are to be implemented over a two-year timeline, well ahead of the next general election.[66]

The review was part of the government's decision to eliminate the more than $30 billion deficit by 2014 by – in the words of Prime Minister Harper – finding "billions in fat."[67] The departments were free to identify low-priority activities, but the Treasury Board suggested that the review should focus on both programs and operating expenses – notably, salaries, professional services consultants, and grants and contributions programs.[68] The process, like that of earlier strategic reviews, was designed to produce recommendations for Treasury Board ministers to review, and as before, the final say on spending cuts remained with the prime minister and his senior advisers. Both of the Harper government reviews have a clear message: public servants and their program evaluation work are not to be fully trusted. Borrowing a page from the principal-agent theory, the purpose of the outside adviser in the first review was to provide an independent assessment of the work of departmental officials and of their recommendations.

The second review (circa 2011–12) continues to involve outside advisers. The review was led by a special Treasury Board committee which included experts from "outside" government. The Treasury Board president and the minister of finance agreed to a $20 million contract with Deloitte Touche to provide "private sector advice to find billions in government fat." Finance Minister Flaherty explained, "It isn't good quite frankly for a government to just look at itself."[69] The message to both central agency and line department officials could not be clearer: they could not be fully trusted and it was best to look elsewhere, to private sector consultants, for advice. It was akin to putting the fox among the chickens. One senior government official observed, "For the first time ever, I saw Department of Finance officials saying 'hold it – these guys (i.e., Deloitte Touche) are going too far, too fast on spending cuts.'"[70]

Several weeks before the finance minister tabled the March 2012 budget, rumours swirled in the media and in Ottawa that the government was planning major cuts to its operations, cuts that could in some cases far exceed the 5 or 10 percent targets. Some public sector union leaders expected job losses of up to 50,000, the same number as in the Chrétien-Martin 1994–97 review.[71] Treasury Board President Tony Clement told the media two months before budget day that the government could cut $4 to $8 billion in spending in 2012–13 alone, while Finance Minister Jim Flaherty said that some departments could well be "facing cuts of 10 percent or more."[72] To be sure, if spending cuts are to be made, the first year of a majority mandate is, politically at least, the best time to make them.

All proposed spending cuts were sent to the prime minister for decision. The 2012 budget included not only $5.2 billion in cuts but the elimination of 19,200 public servants from the payroll. Flaherty explained, "We will implement moderate restraint in government spending. The vast majority of savings will come from eliminating waste in the internal operations of government, making it leaner and more efficient."[73] The cuts are to be implemented over a three-year period and at least 7,000 of the job losses will be handled by attrition. It should be noted that the Harper government has added 30,000 positions to the public service since it took power. The government earmarked $900 million to cover salary costs, buyouts, waived pension penalties, and education and training allowances for laid-off employees.[74]

The cuts to departments varied from 1.1 percent in Veterans Affairs to 8.7 percent in regional agencies and to 16.8 percent in Finance.[75] Only a handful of small programs and agencies were eliminated, including the National Round Table on the Environment and the Economy, the Public Appointments Commission, and Katimavik. Comparing the 1994–97 Chrétien-Martin review and the 2012 Harper-led review, Jeffrey Simpson wrote, "The Chrétien government took hard decisions to stop doing things … [In the Harper review] the savings remained impossible to identify, hidden as they were behind the budget's verbal thickets of rationalize, consolidate, integrate, streamline, refocus, reconfigure, modernize, realign."[76]

Looking Back

There is no graduate program or professional development program to prepare one to become prime minister. Prime ministers learn by doing. Few
people ever occupy the position – Canada has had six in the past thirty-two
years, from two different parties. Prime ministers have come to dominate
their governments to the point that any decision of any consequence con-
cerning either new spending or spending cuts invariably flows from them.
They operate with limited information: briefing notes from their own office
and central agencies or what a minister with standing in the prime minister's court may argue.

The more important problem is that prime ministers always operate
from an overloaded agenda. Leaving aside a handful of priorities or pet
projects, they are left to react to events and proposals from a variety of
sources while having to deal with the media and the demands of the day.
Prime ministers and their courtiers can have a hand in all policy areas and
virtually all facets of government operations if they so decide. The individual responsible for managing the prime minister's agenda has considerable
influence in Ottawa. Prime ministers and their courtiers have a choice – to
keep a tight control on things and concentrate decision making in a few
hands or delegate more authority to ministers to shape the expenditure
budget. At least since the 1970s, they have consistently opted for keeping
tight control.

We know that the Government of Canada has run a deficit in twenty-
nine of the past forty years.[77] We also know that it has taken on new
responsibilities and has grown substantially since the early 1970s. In 1973
the Canadian government employed 201,888 public servants.[78] In 2010,
it employed 283,000.[79] With some notable exceptions, year after year the
government adds new activities and new positions. The efforts of various
central agencies to reduce government spending since the early 1970s have
met with little success. Only when the government is forced to act (a recognition that government deficits need to be addressed or an outside event
brings the government's difficult fiscal situation into focus) and only when
the prime minister makes it a key priority will the expenditure budget be
pruned back.

Trudeau's Bonn-inspired spending cuts had some immediate effect but did
little to deal with the growing annual deficits of the late 1970s and early
1980s. Chrétien's 1994–97 program review exercise broke a long string of
government deficits and laid the groundwork for eleven annual budget sur-

pluses. Chrétien and Martin were the architects of the review exercise, and Chrétien's firm hand was an important reason for its success.[80] It will be recalled that the review came on the heels of Chrétien's winning a majority mandate.

Harper launched his 2011–12 strategic and operational review after his government ran four annual deficits while projecting at least another three.[81] In 2009–10 the Harper government ran a $55 billion deficit and in three years added $94 billion to the government's debt.[82] Harper's review came on the heels of winning a majority mandate. There is every indication that the review will have a major impact on the government's expenditure budget equal to Chrétien's 1994–97 review. More is said later about Harper's review. Suffice it to note here that all departments had to implement a 5, 10 percent or, in some cases, more cuts in their budgets. Some two months before the 2012 budget was tabled, the government announced that it had already eliminated 4,700 public service positions.[83]

All of which is to say that the prime minister and his courtiers have to drive cuts in the expenditure budget, relying on across-the-board cuts to guide the review. Line departments and agencies have to identify possible spending cuts, but the prime minister always retains the authority to sign off on all final decisions. The prime minister is both the catalyst and the referee, the ultimate guardian.

When the prime minister takes his eye off the ball, when he attends to other priority issues, and when a general election is only a year or so away, the expenditure is turned over to the machinery of government to manage. This is not without implications. Government operations grow by stealth, and head office bureaucracies quietly expand. Ottawa's machinery of government consists of central agencies, line departments, crown corporations, and arm's-length agencies. The next chapter explores how the machinery of government operates and how it tries to keep things running on their tracks.

5

The Machinery: Running on Its Tracks

When political and bureaucratic elites meet to talk about the expenditure budget, across-the-board cuts make sense. This largely explains why the majority of spending cuts in Ottawa in recent years have been across-the-board and often have been announced by the prime minister like bolts of lightning from a clear sky. The machinery of government is then left to pick up the pieces.

The machinery of government is made up mostly of spenders, not guardians, and it is a field of specialization in its own right.[1] It is a vast machine, performing a wide variety of tasks. The Government of Canada website lists 350 different departments, agencies, crown corporations, and entities of various types. Some collect taxes, others provide assistance to the private sector, others to artists, yet others to Canada's Aboriginal population, and still others provide a regional perspective ... and the list goes on. There are also crown corporations that look after the government's surplus land and operate the CN Tower, deliver postal services, provide ferry services, and perform many other services. In addition, there are various museums, cultural agencies, and regulatory agencies.[2] In brief, the machinery of government is a hodgepodge of entities, with mandates and responsibilities tied directly or indirectly to Parliament and to Ottawa's expenditure budget. Some have to manoeuvre to secure support for new funding or to protect their "A" base. Others are tied to a formula or operate at arm's length from the government's expenditure budget process.

The prime minister holds the key to the machinery, and his prerogative is jealously guarded, presumably by him and certainly by the Privy Council Office. PCO's organizational chart has a deputy secretary to the cabinet who is responsible for "Legislation, House Planning and Machinery of Government" and an assistant secretary to the cabinet whose sole responsibility is the machinery of government. The assistant secretary's title is a misnomer because neither the cabinet nor individual cabinet ministers have any say on how to structure the machinery or the organization of government. The prime minister alone decides whether a government department should be established, scrapped, or merged with another department. This is made clear to ministers and public servants in many ways, including PCO's 2011–12 Report on Plans and Priorities, which explains that it is the prime minister's responsibility and his responsibility alone to establish "the machinery of government, including matters such as the structure and organization of government, Cabinet decision-making processes and machinery of government changes."[3]

PCO's argument that it must keep tight control of machinery of government issues is tied to the requirement that it operate above the fray. PCO officials believe that every minister and every government organization would have an interest to protect or promote if they had a say in shaping the machinery of government, and this would lead to endless competition to expand one's turf. PCO officials also maintain that the machinery of government belongs to the prime minister because it is his government, and therefore he should be free to structure its policy-making processes and organize its capacity to deliver public services as he sees fit.[4] The machinery has only a handful of guardians – the prime minister and several PCO officials – who make the decisions. PCO's machinery of government secretariat delivers no program or public service; its sole purpose is to advise the prime minister on machinery issues.

The machinery of government is highly path-dependent. Responsibilities with specific mandates are still assigned to sectoral departments and agencies. The bulk of the machinery still operates in vertical top-down organizations that are relatively independent from one another. This somehow has to square with the reality that public policies and even government programs no longer recognize organizational boundaries, and virtually all policy issues now require a horizontal perspective. This has wide implications for the expenditure budget and for accountability in public spending, as will be seen in this chapter, which looks at recent changes to the machinery of government in Ottawa.

Everything in Government Is Now Horizontal

John Stuart Mill argued over 150 years ago in his *Representative Government* that responsibility is best provided and the work best done if all functions of similar subjects are allocated to single departments.[5] This notion has guided the development of our machinery of government from the very beginning. For example, the Department of Agriculture was established in 1867, at the time of Canada's birth. To be sure, the department was small, employing only twenty-seven people, but it had a clear responsibility for the sector. In this sense, the government defined an organizational space, labelled it "agriculture," and housed in one department all responsibilities for the sector. It provided for a neat and tidy organizational model where accountability requirements were straightforward.

Government departments have continued to be organized along these lines. They remain hierarchical, and they have some units responsible for program delivery, others for financial management, and so on. Units and officials in the department are in turn organized hierarchically, with clear boxes laid out on an organizational chart and with a chain of command running from the minister through the deputy head to the lowest-level employee.[6] In this sense, the machinery of government still defines a specific space for every unit and for every public servant. Departmental units are assigned responsibilities in the organizational charts, as are public servants through job descriptions.

As in the military (which provided the model for government bureaucracy), hierarchy establishes lines of authority for the transmission of commands and allows a "calculability of results for those in positions of authority." It also provides the "governed" a clear line for appealing "the decision of a lower office to the corresponding superior authority" and, as Mill argued, enables a variety of activities to be brought together in one organization.[7] It comes as no surprise, then, that the government has simply added new activities and new offices to existing departmental structures as well as creating new agencies and departments. Finally, hierarchy enables a minister, who is "blameable" or at least "answerable" for both policy and administration under the principle of ministerial responsibility, to reach down into the bureaucracy to secure an explanation for any problems that arise and to find solutions to them. This system has served the Anglo-American democracies very well for more than a hundred years with a remarkable degree of stability.

J.R. Hodgetts maintained that a "coherent description of programme allocation" could best be achieved by "adopting broad functional categories for the basic responsibilities of government."[8] He listed several and traced the evolution of federal departments through these lenses. Departments, even as recently as forty years ago, had fairly clear mandates and a distinct turf to protect. In addition, the ability to define clear departmental mandates was supported in the public administration literature. Luther Gulick had a simple question to guide policy makers: Is there "bleeding" between organizations?[9] Although departments were hardly ever watertight and self-contained, they could go about their work with limited concern for the work of other departments. Departments protected their turf because they occupied a fairly well-articulated space.

Things are vastly different today. Indeed, departments "bleed" profusely, and government policies and programs are increasingly linked. Several years ago, for example, it took no less than twenty federal departments to plan new measures to promote development in Canada's North. It took nearly two years for the process to run its course, and it involved extensive consultations with stakeholders and a number of consultants' reports. This is how many policy issues are now handled in Ottawa. Any proposed policy not co-opted by the prime minister and perhaps the minister of finance invariably brings together a number of federal departments or agencies, along with provincial departments, interest groups, consultants, lobbyists, think-tanks, and pollsters.[10]

As issues became more complex and interconnected, it became apparent that no single department had all the necessary policy tools and program instruments. In response, central agencies were strengthened, but line departments and agencies continued to function as before. The result is that departments now come to the table with only part of the answer in hand, unable on their own to impose a comprehensive solution. In brief, though the machinery of government still respects organizational boundaries, policy issues no longer do, and policy making has consequently become horizontal, consultative, and porous.

The result is that unless the prime minister decides to take charge of a policy issue, the machinery takes over and holds a never-ending series of meetings. This ensures a minimum of controversy and media attention, which in turn serves the interest of the prime minister and his courtiers. It enables them to keep a lid on things that are of limited interest to them. However, it makes work challenging for policy analysts in government – unless, of course, they are assigned to work on an initiative that has caught the prime minister's interest.

Two well-known practitioners have recently voiced concern over Ottawa's policy-making process. David Dodge, former deputy minister of finance and head of the Bank of Canada, laments the fact that public servants are now "hidden a bit" from the long-standing tradition of speaking their minds in public hearings or committee sessions.[11] Don Drummond, a highly respected senior official with the Department of Finance, argues that Ottawa is moving away from evidence-based policy analysis. He writes, "I think that the state of policy analysis in the federal government is dismal." It is worth quoting Drummond at length on the issue. "My sense of a dismal state of policy analysis is largely based on discussions with former and current civil servants and a monitoring of published work." He adds, "We are living in a time of unprecedental divide between the political and bureaucratic in Ottawa."[12] He makes the point that it is very difficult for public servants to speak policy truth to politicians when there is no market for it. The implications for the expenditure budget are obvious: if policy is either the product of many hands or, as is now often the case, the product of only a few hands that ignore evidence-based policy advice, then the expenditure budget will support new initiatives that are based, more often than not, on the politics of the situation or on political ideology.

The senior public service has had to adjust to this new reality. Marcel Massé, who could speak from the perspective of both a senior career official and a senior cabinet minister, concluded that "this means that those who traditionally simply make decisions will have to spend much more of their time explaining situations, setting out the various options and trade-offs, and persuading those involved, before proposed solutions become acceptable. A good part of the present unpopularity of both politicians and public servants is due to our insufficient adaptation to these new requirements of our jobs." He saw a new role for career officials, which has yet to be defined.[13]

What about the government's expenditure budget? How can the government reconcile the horizontal nature of policy development with a machinery of government that remains largely vertical? Prime ministers and their advisers are the main architects of the horizontal policy and decision-making process. The problem is that line ministers must still assume responsibility for departmental policies and programs in accordance with the doctrine of ministerial responsibility. However, this is becoming increasingly difficult, especially in the spending of public money.

The machinery of government in some ways now also extends beyond the government. Government officials have been busy of late searching for ways to form new partnerships with the private sector. Many have bought into David Osborne and Ted Gaebler's argument that governments should "steer," not "row."[14] This has been part of the movement calling for a cultural shift away from bureaucratic government towards entrepreneurial government. To do this, Osborne, Gaebler, and others argue that governments should establish broad policy frameworks and either turn over government operations to agencies with a high degree of management autonomy or set up partnership agreements with private firms to deliver the services. This poses new challenges for the concept of accountability in public spending in that blame avoidance becomes easier when accountability is shared by several or a multitude of actors. Osborne and Gaebler never answered how one could separate those who "steer" from those who "row" and then hold both responsible for their decisions to spend public funds, either collectively or individually.

To manage public-private agreements is not without cost. It serves to make government operations thicker and more expensive because staff is required to manage the partnerships and the transactions. Officials in one government department, reporting on how they were able to make a public-private partnership work, put it well when they wrote, "Individuals, organizations and governments must relinquish their control mentality when trying to manage resources."[15] To relinquish control also means, to some extent, relinquishing responsibility for managing financial resources assigned to them. In a detailed study of a public-private partnership involving the Government of Canada and a private firm, Jennifer Berardi concluded that "the direct lines of accountability and responsibility that are typically enjoyed in traditional public sector organizations are not always applicable in a partnership arrangement."[16] Again, under partnership agreements, it is extremely difficult to pinpoint who is ultimately responsible for what. The favoured solution has been to create still more government units to assess, monitor, and evaluate performance.

It is becoming clear that we are moving away from Max Weber's classical model in which the individual bureaucrat is not allowed to "squirm out of the apparatus in which he was harnessed ... He is chained to his activity by his entire material and ideal existence."[17] Governing without boundaries now allows public servants to squirm out of the apparatus because there are different harnesses available to them, and they are strongly encouraged to establish new partnerships with non-government groups. An ability to squirm out of one's harness makes it more difficult to hold someone accountable for program spending. It also adds still more fuel to J.E. Hodgetts's "doctrine of mutual deniability."[18]

A Fault Line in the Machinery

The attenuation of boundaries between departments has also given rise to a fault line in the machinery of government, separating senior and policy-oriented officials from program managers, and especially from front-line workers.[19] The latter increasingly report that they are accountable to a variety of actors: their immediate supervisors, their clients, public-private partnerships, and Canadians generally. Senior officials, in contrast, tend to look up to the political and policy process for accountability. Alan Williams, a retired senior public servant, summed up the view of most of his counterparts in Ottawa when he wrote, "I always believed that one of our prime objectives was to keep our ministers out of trouble."[20]

The federal Task Force on Public Service Values and Ethics referred to the existence of a fault line: "Our dialogue with public servants revealed to us a certain divide between levels in the public service, perhaps especially where public service values are concerned. Many at the middle and lower levels of the public service no longer feel connected to the senior levels, and they are not sure whether they necessarily share the same values as those at higher levels." The task force report added that one "source of this fault line appears to be the confusion about accountability, and the tension between customer accountability and political accountability. Those closest to the front line of accountability feel their primary accountability to citizen/customers while those farther up may feel primary accountability to citizen voters and taxpayers, as mediated by the political process."[21]

What the above suggests is that the difference between managing up and managing down in the public sector has become substantial and probably overshadows the differences between managing in production, procedural, craft, and coping organizations of the kind described by James Q. Wilson in his influential book, *Bureaucracy*.[22] Program managers and front-line workers in departments such as the Correctional Services, Taxation, Industry, and Human Resources Development have more in common with one another than with their own senior people. There appears to be two distinct spaces emerging within the public service. One is occupied by career officials who manage up and are preoccupied with the prime minister's courtiers and keeping their ministers out of trouble: the horizontal policy process. The other is occupied by career officials who deal with program implementation and look down to the front-line workers providing services to Canadians, the music-teacher type.

The above also suggests that institutional structure matters, because it provides specific roles for political and administrative actors and between senior and front-line public servants. When you draw boundaries, you not only establish space within which people can operate, but you also draw a visible understanding of how things work. When you remove boundaries, you remove this understanding, and without boundaries in government we end up with "a big conceptual mess."[23] When a fault line emerges between senior and front-line public servants, it leads to uncertainty and confusion about the proper role of the institution within which one operates.

Because public policies and even many program decisions are now the product of many hands, we are told to think in terms of shared accountability. As James March and Johan Olsen argue, "Organized interests are accountable to policy makers even as policy makers are accountable to organized interests. Policy makers are accountable to bureaucrats, even as bureaucrats are accountable to policy makers."[24] How this can work in managing the expenditure budget and how we can hold relevant officials to account is not at all clear. The machinery of government has not been adjusted to reflect this new reality.

No Surprises Please

Paul Tellier, former clerk of the privy council and secretary to the cabinet, told deputy ministers at one of their weekly breakfast meetings that he and the prime minister did not want "any surprises."[25] One can appreciate that from the prime minister's perspective, the requirements of horizontal government, access to information legislation, permanent election campaigns tied to a multitude of government entities, and a disconnect between frontline workers and senior managers would place a premium on having the machinery of government run quietly on its tracks, generating no or very few surprises for the prime minister and his courtiers to manage.

The potential for controversy or surprises is always present, with 30 cabinet ministers and 350 organizations always operating under the watchful eye of the national and regional media and opposition parties in Parliament. Sitting at the top and constantly battling an overloaded agenda, one can easily appreciate why the prime minister and the clerk of the privy council would want the run-of-the-mill machinery of government to cough up no surprises. In fact, the machinery of government is generally able to run on its tracks, provided that it is not buffeted about by uncertainty. Bureaucracy never reacts well when it feels threatened or when it has to function in an uncertain environment. More to the point, it can run quietly on its tracks if it is allowed to do so. Bolts of lightning from above, threats to its survival, and constant questioning about its level of resources can unnerve a department and, in the process, cough up surprises.

There is a tacit understanding between the centre of government and the rest of the machinery that agencies will run on their tracks, avoid controversies, and generate reports for the centre, provided they sense that they are being treated fairly or that an equilibrium is maintained between the political leadership they are asked to serve and themselves. All bets are off if an agency considers that it has been cut loose by the prime minister's court. This is when the media and opposition MPs receive brown paper envelopes and the responsible minister no longer enjoys the full support of departmental or agency officials. Line department officials can down tools but go through the motions, giving the appearance of action while actually standing still. The minister of defence and his political staff, as well as the chief of defence staff, likely knew that brown envelopes reporting their frequent use of government jets would find their way to the media after it was leaked that the department was looking at cutting back its number of employees.[26]

It will be recalled that the chief of defence staff, General Walter Natynczyk, defended his use of the government's private aircraft, explaining that the Challenger squadron was not getting enough use: "So aircraft are flying around empty because we have to maintain the proficiency of the pilots and indeed the crew. The aircraft costs for the crew, for the flying, it's all been prepaid."[27] He never explained why the government had six Challenger jets if some had to sit idle. In Question Period, the prime minister insisted that Natynczyk was on "government business" when he made use of the department's aircraft. The controversy erupted after copies of emails inside the department surfaced in public.[28]

Feeding the Beast

The prime minister's court has plenty of help and no shortage of processes to ensure that the machinery of government runs quietly on its tracks. Central agencies – the Prime Minister's Office, the Privy Council Office, the Treasury Board Secretariat, and Finance – exist in large measure to keep the machinery running smoothly.

I consulted a senior deputy minister of a line department on 20 October 2011 to test my thinking in researching this book. I wanted his perspective on the various reporting requirements designed by central agencies: Reports on Plans and Priorities (RPPs), Departmental Performance Reports (DPRs), and Management Accountability Framework (MAF). He replied, "I prepare for the exams by feeding the beast ... Do you really think that I take seriously the Board's [i.e., Treasury Board Secretariat's] Management Accountability Framework, which is managed by a bunch of people that have never managed anything?"[29] Feeding the beast, whether one takes it seriously or not, requires a lot of effort, a lot of resources, and a lot of paper, as we will see in the next chapter.

The 3,000-plus officials in central agencies have no program or public services to deliver to Canadians. They exist to coordinate, assess, monitor, control, and at times lead on issues. The size, role, and requirements of central agencies have created yet another fault line inside government – there are those who manage information, deal with the media, and fall on hand grenades to protect the government, and then there are those on the front line delivering services. The former hold the upper hand and consume a great deal of human and financial resources. They not only create, adjust, manage, and essentially call the shots in the machinery, but they also advise those who decide who gets financial resources. Front-line public sector workers – the music teacher type – share one common frustration: the constant demand for information from central agencies and departmental headquarters. Public servants report that the demand for information on policy and administrative issues has increased "exponentially" in recent years and now "eats up a lot of resources."[30]

Central agencies have not only grown, but people who work in them have more senior classifications and higher pay than those occupying similar positions in line departments. They also decide in large measure who makes it to the deputy minister and associate deputy levels. In addition, there are many in the Privy Council Office who enjoy a deputy-minister-level classification, though they do not have the responsibility of managing a government department. It simply comes with being in the Privy Council Office. Given that central agency officials have no programs to manage and deliver, they can spend all their time on policy issues, working on briefing material, micromanaging specific files whenever a crisis flares up, and demanding more and more information from front-line managers and their employees in order to monitor their programs and performance.[31]

To be sure, central agencies have a much stronger policy capacity than they had forty years ago. They have strategic planning capacities and, if need be, can have a direct hand in the day-to-day work of departments. At times, they can be heavily involved in transactions or specific departmental files; at other times, not at all. It depends. If it involves the prime minister's interest or if the government's political standing may be in jeopardy, central agency officials will be present – even, if necessary, physically in the department, directing things.[32] If they require new money to deal with the issue, it will quickly be found.

Still, officials in central agencies need to rely on data provided by line departments, which partly explains the constant stream of requests for information. It should surprise no one that if you add positions in central agencies, this gives rise to more requests for information to line departments and agencies. This is their bread and butter. But that is not all. Ministers need to be briefed on proposed new initiatives and on anticipated questions, both in Parliament and from the media. Just responding to access to information requests and any difficulties they may create for the minister and the department can consume a great deal of ministerial time. A number of new requirements, from access to information to whistle-blowing legislation, only add to briefing requirements.

It is difficult to determine the amount of time the machinery of government spends on "feeding the beast," on briefing its ministers, and dealing with the public. Consultations with front-line employees suggest that they spend more time providing briefing material for the system than in dealing with taxpayers.[33] Feeding the beast requires a great deal of time, effort, and resources in Canada, where there are more central agencies than in any other Anglo-American democracy, where access to information legislation has been in place for about thirty years, where federal-provincial relations generate a great many policy papers and briefing materials, and where there are more oversight bodies than, for example, in Britain or Australia.

A government survey of 221,434 positions was carried out in the late 1980s to identify all jobs that had at least some responsibility for dealing with the general public, even if it amounted to only 10 percent. The survey found 92,481 such positions, or 41.8 percent of the total number of positions.[34] When carrying out research for this book, I asked Treasury Board officials and an official with the Commissioner of Official Languages whether the 1980s study had been updated. The answer was no. However, they agreed that one could easily speculate that in the federal public service there are fewer jobs that have at least 10 percent of their responsibility dealing directly with Canadians than there were in the late 1980s. One reason is the hugely increased reporting requirements and the growth of oversight bodies.[35] They added that this explains the significant rise in the number of federal public servants in Ottawa, compared with those in the regions. Some thirty years ago, 65 percent of senior positions were located in Ottawa; today, the number is closer to 75 percent. Thirty years ago, 70 percent of federal public servants were in the regions; today the number is about 58 percent.[36]

Like ministers, line managers have come to rely on the staff in their departments to get things done, which explains why there are more staff positions to feed the machinery than there are positions delivering services to Canadians. Indeed, knowing how the system operates and how to navigate in it has become a much-valued attribute, even inside the federal public service, as one regional line manager explained: "I simply do not have the time to deal with all the nonsense central agencies keep throwing at us. That is what our staff people in Ottawa are paid to do. When there is a problem with the Treasury Board Secretariat, Finance, or PCO, they take over. I attend some of the meetings when I have to or when I am in Ottawa. Frankly, it is just another world. It is so far removed from what I do, it is unbelievable. Sometimes I think that they speak in tongues." But he adds, "You need these people around if you want to get things done and to protect your back."[37] Another manager reported that he "tries to avoid involving head office or central agencies" as much as possible. He said that it is important "in a line operation to keep your head down, keep things under control here, and don't involve Ottawa people unless you absolutely have to. They will leave you alone if you don't give them a reason to call you. My measure of success is how often that phone rings and someone in Ottawa is on the line. If it rings often, we are doing something wrong. If it doesn't ring, we are doing fine. From time to time, you get head office people introducing a new approach. You know they have to keep busy so that they come around with a new Treasury Board approach in this or that area. We just go along filling their forms while we deliver the programs."[38]

In their detailed study of "service in the field," Barbara Carroll and David Siegel quote a government official's claim that people working in regional offices "value the ability to work one-on-one with clients. That starts to break down immediately when you get into layers in Ottawa."[39] Front-line managers and workers doubt that they dominate their deputy minister's agenda as much as they did thirty years ago. They have every reason to think so, and they can point to a body of literature to prove their case.[40]

Deputy Ministers: Looking to the Centre, to Their Ministers, and to One Another

Although their mandate is not always clear, deputy ministers are very busy people. According to a detailed study of their workload, on average they work eleven hours and twenty-eight minutes a day, or fifty-seven hours a week, spending one hour out of every three on interdepartmental issues. It is interesting to note that deputy ministers typically allocate nearly twice as much time to meetings with their peers as to matters involving their own minister.[41] On average, they allocate more of their time to crisis management (16 percent) than to human resources management (15 percent); they are at the very centre of departmental activities, and they try as best they can to accommodate the "urgent," the "important," and the "unforeseen" in their daily agenda."[42]

Governments everywhere in Canada have recently attached a great deal of importance to improving services to the public. Many front-line public servants are puzzled by the sudden emphasis on service to customers. After all, a good number of them have spent most of their careers trying to convince senior departmental and central agency officials that service to citizens is important. In their exhaustive study on service in the field, Carroll and Siegel report on Canadian field workers' frustration with head office because over the years it has been "tirelessly inserting as many obstacles as possible to prevent them from providing good customer service. After this history," the authors note, "it is easy to imagine how field staff feel when they see large amounts of scarce funds spent on expensive consultants and glossy publications to convey to them exactly the same message they have been struggling in vain to convey to head office for years." As Carroll and Siegel point out, "Despite 'empowerment,' 'decentralization,' 'TQM,' and a myriad of other buzz words, acronyms, and improvements in communication technology, the gulf between head office and the field remains."[43]

Deputy ministers, most of whom earned their promotion in central agencies, understand well how the prime minister's court operates and what it values. To avoid political controversies and to keep their ministers out of trouble are what matters. This and an ability to position their departments in the Ottawa system are highly valued. Within the department, the ability to secure new funding and protect departmental budgets make for strong deputy ministers in the eyes of their peers and of senior departmental officials.[44]

A Thicker Government

The current machinery of government has grown partly because of the need to manage blame-avoidance strategies, and this in turn has led to thicker government. Christopher Hood writes that politicians and public servants have become increasingly concerned with blame-avoidance in response to the new media and the emphasis on transparency.[45] We now have many more "blame generators" – among others, officers of Parliament – than we had thirty years ago. As R. Kent Weaver argues, blame generating and blame avoiding in parliamentary systems are centred on party, reflecting strong party discipline. Parliamentary systems "make blame-generating much easier than in a Presidential system."[46] In a majority government in a parliamentary system, opposition parties can do little more than generate blame.

Blame avoidance can be expensive to manage. Weaver maintains that because of the principle of collective cabinet responsibility, which calls on the government to share blame for failed policies, the government is "likely to throw good money after bad to prop up failed policies."[47] Blame avoidance can add substantial costs to government operations because it requires a large staff.[48] The machinery now houses hundreds of units in Ottawa with mandates to coordinate, assess, promote liaison between departments and with central agencies, encourage interprovincial coordination, evaluate, control, and review.

The Gomery Commission's review of the sponsorship scandal revealed the extent to which both political and public service actors engaged in blame-avoidance strategies. It is hardly the only case.[49] It will be recalled that in his testimony before Justice Gomery, Prime Minister Chrétien accepted full responsibility for the sponsorship program but insisted that he "knew nothing about specific sponsorship contracts, their values or the amount of commissions paid to Liberal-friendly firms."[50] He joined others in pursuing a strategy of "I take responsibility but am not to blame," promoting consequence-free accountability. The machinery of government is designed to support strategies of plausible deniability.

The machinery has central agencies that oversee the work of line departments and at times direct it. The doctrine of ministerial responsibility, meanwhile, ties the political world to the bureaucratic machinery, and it too facilitates blame-avoidance strategies. The doctrine, for the most part, now asks ministers to answer only in Parliament for departments and agencies and for their public servants. It is this, more than anything else, that prompted J.E. Hodgetts to write about the doctrine of mutual deniability.

The doctrine, which underpins in several important ways the machinery of government, is being challenged as never before. Rooted in military history and in Weber's hierarchy, it requires that the individual in charge of the organization should answer publicly for the actions of both the organization and its employees; in other words, whoever is at the top should take responsibility. In the Westminster-Whitehall model, public servants have traditionally been expected to respect hierarchical accountability, refrain from any public profile, and remain anonymous; if they have to speak out, they must do so under the minister's authority. Ministers are in charge of departments, answer in Parliament and in public, and speak to the media on behalf of their departments. Consequently, they expect loyalty from their public servants, from the deputy minister all the way down to the front-line workers. This is another reason why the prime minister and his courtiers attach a great deal of importance to ensuring that the machinery of government runs quietly.

Critics of the doctrine maintain that it is no longer appropriate to hold ministers responsible for the department while public servants, who may have committed the errors, are allowed to go unpunished, at least publicly.[51] They believe that the doctrine of ministerial responsibility acts as a cloak for a lot of murkiness in departments and agencies.[52] Some observers, including practitioners, argue that attempts to draw a distinction between accountability and responsibility have been unconvincing.[53] They have a point. While Jocelyne Bourgon insists that "where authority resides, so resides accountability," Alex Himelfarb, another former clerk of the privy council, insists that "authority can be delegated, but accountability can't."[54] If two former clerks cannot agree on what the doctrine actually entails, then what are MPs, let alone the general public, to make of it? The PCO has introduced the notion of "answerability" into the mix, and this complicates matters further. One can easily appreciate that the distinction between answerability, responsibility, and accountability was lost on the senior public servants who came under attack before parliamentary committees for their role in the Al-Mashat affair or the sponsorship scandal.[55]

Some observers argue that accountability in government under the doctrine breaks down because, on the one hand, public servants are constrained from being critical of their ministers while, on the other, they are shielded from direct public scrutiny. The doctrine makes ministers accountable, responsible, and answerable for administrative matters. It is for this reason that both elected politicians and public servants can serve up a menu of plausible deniability whenever errors occur.

In the sponsorship scandal, Chrétien and Alfonso Gagliano, the minister, blamed the bureaucrats for not assuming their responsibilities, while Chuck Guité, the senior public servant in charge of the program, blamed Chrétien's political staff and the minister for getting involved in administrative issues, such as the selection and location of projects and the advertising firms.[56] Guité had to testify under oath before a commission of inquiry and in a court of law. Justice Gomery, who conducted the inquiry, asked, "How can we have responsible government, but no one is prepared to take responsibility when things go wrong?" What was remarkable from the testimony before Justice Gomery was that neither elected politicians nor public servants evinced any sense of guilt or acceptance of responsibility. Instead, they pointed the finger at one another, from Jean Chrétien and his office to the minister responsible, right down to Chuck Guité.

A fundamental element of the doctrine of ministerial responsibility is the anonymity of public servants, which senior public servants continue to endorse. Public servants do not want to be dragged into partisan political debates, and they know full well that even purely administrative matters can be turned into highly charged partisan political issues. But anonymity is being challenged from all sides. Ministers are no longer willing to accept responsibility when things go wrong in their departments.[57] Access to information legislation, public-private partnerships, the horizontal nature of policy making, and the new media have all served to expose public servants to public scrutiny.

After several aborted attempts, the federal government finally enacted legislation to establish the "accounting officer" concept, a potentially important development in Ottawa's machinery of government, particularly when it comes to the management of public funds. In 2003, Chrétien declared that he would introduce the concept, although nothing came of it.[58] In riding the sponsorship scandal to power, Harper made a commitment to establish the concept, patterned on the British model, and within months of coming to power in 2006, he unveiled a legislative package designed to strengthen accountability.[59] The package provided for the introduction of the accounting officer concept to Canada "within the framework of ministerial responsibility."[60] Accounting officers occupy a key position in the system of financial control and accountability in Britain; they hold responsibility in their own right and are the responsible witnesses before the Public Accounts Committee. As the Treasury explains, "The essence of an Accounting Officer's role is a personal responsibility for the propriety and regularity of the public finances for which he or she is answerable. The responsibilities of an Accounting Officer are laid down in a memorandum which is sent to every new Accounting Officer on appointment. The memorandum establishes the procedure to be followed when a minister overrules an Accounting Officer's advice on an issue of propriety and regularity. It also makes it clear that the Accounting Officer is responsible for delivering departmental objectives in the most economic, efficient, and effective manner."[61] This should go some distance towards acknowledging that the public service has a distinct persona in the machinery of government, at least in Britain. That said, Harper later watered down his proposal from what he had to say in his 2006 election campaign platform. It is interesting to note that he endorsed the traditional PCO review in his *Accountable Government: A Guide for Ministers*, a document that he issued as his government assumed office.[62]

There is every indication that the Privy Council Office had serious reservations about Harper's proposal, and this may well explain his decision to change his position once in power. For instance, the PCO produced a document for the use of deputy ministers that did not square with Harper's original position. The document, *Guidance for Deputy Ministers*, which remains on the PCO's website, goes beyond the argument that the public service has no "constitutional personality" and argues that public servants "do not have a public voice, or identity, distinct from that of the Minister, nor do they share in their Minister's political accountability." It adds, "In supporting the Minister's accountability, a Deputy Minister may find himself or herself before a parliamentary committee to explain what went wrong. He or she might say, for example, yes, an error was made. I am accountable to the Minister of the department and, with the support of the Minister, I have fixed the problem – this could include informing a committee that disciplinary action has been taken, but it would not extend to naming those concerned even if their identity had somehow been disclosed through the media or otherwise."[63]

The Privy Council Office did not revise this document after Harper's accountability package made it through Parliament, but in March 2007 it produced a document, *Guidance for Accounting Officers*, that further attenuates the concept. This documents argues that, for accounting officers, accountability before parliamentary committees means supporting their ministers' accountability before Parliament. This suggests that accounting officers are not accountable in their own right, independent of their departmental ministers.[64] It does not deal with the fact that deputy ministers are delegated authority directly by Parliament under various statutes, including the Public Service Employment Act and the Financial Administration Act. These acts do not allow powers to be delegated to ministers. Parliament turned specific power over to deputy ministers to protect the neutrality of the public service and the public purse from abuse by politicians.

Ralph Heintzman believes that the Canadian version of the accounting officer concept "has none of the key features of its British model and several unfortunate innovations." He argues that the Canadian version may have made accountability in government even murkier. He goes to the heart of the matter when he writes, "The accounting officer principle, properly understood, does even more than clarify who is accountable for what, important though that is. It does not simply allow the public service to draw a line for ministers; it requires the public service to draw a line for itself. It requires the public service, in its own actions and advice, to stay on the side of the line that is demarcated by public service values and not to venture onto terrains with other values and norms."[65] The point is that good management practice requires that a line in the sand be drawn.

Heintzman traces the root of the problem to the highly inappropriate "mental models" that are now in fashion, notably "the mental model of the private sector."[66] He says that too many, including many public sector leaders, have concluded that the public service, like a private corporation, must have a CEO and that the prime minister and the clerk of the privy council are expected to play a CEO role and should have all the power and tools of a private sector CEO. This, he maintains, led to the designation of the clerk as "Head of the Public Service" in the Public Service Reform Act of 1992. It explains why "it is entirely natural for deputy ministers to regard the Clerk – not their ministers – as their real boss, explicitly and implicitly, because that is what he or she is."[67] The Public Service Reform Act, it will be recalled, was influenced by the rise of New Public Management reform measures, which borrowed heavily from private sector management practices.

Attacking Red Tape

New Public Management (NPM) sought to empower managers by removing red tape. Red tape, it is argued, belongs to a different era, not to a modern machinery of government that looks to the private sector for inspiration. If the private sector can run operations efficiently with a minimum of red tape, why not the public sector? The Public Service 2000 exercise, which squared nicely with NPM, urged departments to launch reviews to identify "useless" red tape.[68] It produced a table that compared NPM with "old" public administration (see table 1).

The table speaks to what is wrong with public administration in a fast-changing global economy. In the eyes of the political leadership, the public sector had to shed its risk-averse culture and the heavy bureaucratic hand that inhibited creativity. The public sector had to learn from the private sector to become more task based and results oriented and to instill in its managers a bias for action. By the 1990s, red tape became the symbol of bureaucratic inefficiencies and had to be attacked.

Red tape is not without some value, however, at least in the public sector; there was a time when career officials saw a great deal of merit in it and in due process. Given recent developments, it is worth quoting how a former deputy minister saw things in 1961: "The Civil Service Commission may be slow and meticulous in the recruitment of staff, but this is because parliament rightly insists upon every citizen having an equal right to try for a job. Appropriation and allotment controls may impose on field workers certain delays, but parliamentary control over expenditures is much more important than these minor inconveniences. The same applies to controls over individual expenditures: these must be reported in the Public Accounts in order that parliament might review them, and a good deal of book-work is justified in making this possible."[69] The former deputy minister pointed out that government "supervisors" have no profit motive to encourage them to

TABLE 1: COMPARISON OF PUBLIC ADMINISTRATION AND NEW PUBLIC MANAGEMENT

Public Administration *Old culture*	*New Public Management* *New culture*
Controlling	Empowering
Rigid	Flexible
Suspicious	Trusting
Administrative	Managerial
Secret	Open
Power based	Task based
Input/process oriented	Results oriented
Preprogrammed and repetitive	Capable of purposeful action
Risk averse	Willing to take intelligent risks
Mandatory	Optional
Communicating poorly	Communicating well
Centralized	Decentralized
Uniform	Diverse
Stifling creativity	Encouraging innovation
Reactive	Proactive

Source: Public Service 2000 Secretariat, Ottawa

streamline work, simplify performance standards, and so on; nor should they.[70] No deputy minister would make such a statement today.

To remove red tape at the same time that organizational boundaries are collapsing is not without implications for the machinery of government, particularly for accountability in managing the expenditure budget. Red tape had served several purposes, including a check against political and bureaucratic miscues and abuses, as well as numerous checks in the spending of public money.

Looking Back

The machinery of government has expanded in size, adding a variety of new mandates, and is increasingly being asked to view the world from a horizontal perspective. Yet its basic form – central agencies overlooking the work of line departments and agencies – remains largely intact.

As governments grew and politicians and voters became impatient with government bureaucracies, politicians and their advisers looked to the private sector for solutions. They considered that the private sector has far superior management practices, has a bias for action, and can focus better on objectives. As far back as the early 1960s, Grant Glassco argued that, as in the private sector, it is possible to empower managers in the public sector. His call, "Let the manager manage," resonated inside government and has echoed ever since.

NPM first took root in Britain and then in the Anglo-American democracies. It was designed to make the public sector look like the private sector. However, it soon ran against the political realities of the public sector, even though front-line managers and employees applauded efforts to empower their work and liked the new emphasis on improving services to the public. Many had little difficulty in seeing citizens as customers and saw merit in the flexibility of allocating or reallocating financial resources to different tasks. However, fault lines soon appeared. Senior-level officials looked up to the prime minister's courtiers, to the clerk of the privy council, at the same time as front-line program managers and their staff looked to their customers – as they were told they should do by various NPM measures.

The search was on to reconcile the attributes of the private sector with the political and bureaucratic realities of the public sector. In the absence of incentives that exist in the private sector, efforts to design a process were launched that, it was thought, would somehow enable the public sector to operate like the private sector. The notion that private sector management practices were superior and could apply to government became ingrained in the machinery of government. It became the new status quo. Public sector managers saw considerable merit in the flexibility and other benefits of the new approach to management, while politicians were in no mood to tell their constituents that the public sector could not be run as efficiently as the private sector. They wanted to be on the side of taxpayers and commit the public sector to change in the name of more efficient operations.

How, then, could the centre of government, the prime minister's courtiers, ensure that the machinery of government could run on its tracks and also ensure that private-sector management techniques could take root? The goal, more than ever, was to let managers manage, like their counterparts in the public sector, and hold them to account. The next chapter explores how this was to be done.

6

Let the Manager Manage So Long as It Squares with RPPs, DPRs, MAF, OCG, PCO, TBS, OAG, OLA, IBP, PSC, ATIP, CIEC, OPSICC, DAGs, QFR and That It Does Not Create Problems for the Minister and Deputy Minister or Draw the Attention of the Prime Minister and His Advisers

A senior official with Natural Resources Canada asked me why the government can never deliver on the promise to "let the manager manage." He added that his father, Raoul Grenier, had been secretary to the Glassco Commission that first gave life to the expression in 1962. It has been some fifty years, he added, and the same message has been restated many times. Yet "somehow we can never get it done. Why is that?"[1] The Glassco Commission sought to overhaul government operations and bring a new culture to management, one inspired by the business world. It is worth reminding the reader of one of Glassco's key findings: "All told, the structure of control built up between 1918 and 1951 was impressive – and unique. Measured against the most narrow objectives, it was also unquestionably effective: the standards of probity reached by the Government of Canada in its use of people and money are high. But good management consists in more than the avoidance of sin, and this Calvinistic approach to public administration, while well designed to discomfit bad managers, was bound to prove most frustrating to good ones."[2]

Glassco's call to "let managers manage" has been repeated time and again since 1962. The Lambert Commission, the Increased Management Authority and Accountability (IMAA) initiative of the 1980s, Public Service 2000, and several other government initiatives have all sung the same song.[3] Consequently, a number of attempts have been made to let the manager manage since the Glassco report, including New Public Management, which took flight in the 1980s.

J. Grant Glassco, a prominent businessman, brought a strong private perspective to his five-volume report.[4] The report made the case that like the private sector, government departments and agencies should be allowed to define management practices that suit their line of work.[5] He found that the government's financial controls were much too cumbersome and that there was a wide variety of checks, counterchecks, and duplication, and blind adherence to regulations. He saw no reason why government could not incorporate best management practices from the private sector into its operations.

The commission made a series of sweeping recommendations: it urged the government to replace its line-item budgeting approach and adopt a program- and performance-based budget system, and it recommended the establishment of a new central agency to promote human, financial, and material resources management. This is not to suggest that Glassco wanted to see a heavy management hand from the centre imposed on line departments and agencies. Indeed, he wanted the opposite. Borrowing a page from the private sector, he envisioned the new central agency as providing the leadership, the know-how, and an ability to set standards.[6] The Diefenbaker Conservative government endorsed the commission's findings and immediately appointed a minister responsible for the implementation of its recommendations. A new government bureau headed by a senior deputy minister was established to act as a "ginger group" to ensure that the recommendations would not fall by the wayside.[7]

In 1963, a year after the Glassco report was tabled, there was a change of government. However, this did not signal the end of Glassco. Lester B. Pearson's new Liberal government announced its support very early on in its mandate. The bureau overseeing Glassco's implementation was moved to the Department of Finance, and its director was appointed secretary to the Treasury Board. The Treasury Board staff, as Glassco recommended, was realigned around three broad functions: programs, personnel, and administrative practices and procedures. The Treasury Board was organized as a separate ministry, reporting to a new minister rather than through the Department of Finance. In addition, the government's financial management system was completely overhauled. The line-budgeting approach was abandoned for a program-based budgetary system, and many of the centrally imposed financial controls on line departments were discarded. Some five years after Glassco submitted his report, the president of the Treasury Board reported, "If I were to read the forty-eight recommendations in the first volume, I would be able to insert after thirty-six of them, the response: we have implemented that."[8]

While the government of the day was still implementing the Glassco recommendations, the auditor general shocked the nation when he wrote, "Parliament – and indeed the government – has lost or is close to losing effective control of the public purse." Some critics blamed Glassco for the crisis. One suggested that "Glassco failed to address itself to the operation of Cabinet and Parliament." Others argued that while Glassco wrote about the need to delegate authority down the line and to make spending decisions closer to where programs were actually being implemented, he failed to provide a clear direction for how managers in the public sector would be held accountable for their decisions.[9]

The Canadian government responded to the criticism by establishing in 2004 a royal commission on financial management and accountability, the Lambert Commission. The president of the Treasury Board explained that "the difficulties that have been encountered in attempting to develop, in the post-Glassco era, the concept of managerial accountability in the government environment are accordingly, one of the factors which have prompted the initiative." The commission came forward with numerous recommendations to "rediscover a sense of frugality" in government, including a substantial reorganization of central agencies. It also called for a strong emphasis on management rather than on policy and presented a series of recommendations on how to hold officials more accountable for their decisions. Although some recommendations were accepted, the Lambert Report has had very little impact on government operations.[10]

The search for ways to strengthen managerial accountability in government has intensified over the years, though with limited success. It is simply not possible to duplicate incentives that exist in the private sector, and we have not been able to define a managerial discipline that corresponds to market forces or the bottom line, as defined in the private sector. The rise of neoconservatism in Anglo-American democracies in the early 1980s saw governments strengthen their resolve to bring a private sector perspective to managing government operations – to let, if not force, managers to manage. As we have already noted, the accepted wisdom of the political leadership of the past thirty years or so – and this applies to both the political right and the left – is that private sector management is far superior to that found in government. Government bureaucracy was the villain, and weak management practices were the problem. Jean Chrétien in Canada, Bill Clinton in the United States, and Tony Blair in Britain all echoed the views of their predecessors – right-of-centre politicians Brian Mulroney,

Ronald Reagan, and Margaret Thatcher – in singing the praises of private sector management practices. For example, Tony Blair tabled a major statement on modernizing government, lamenting the fact that "some parts of the public sector were not as efficient, dynamic and effective" as the private sector.[11]

The desire to look to the private sector for inspiration now permeates the political and bureaucratic worlds in Ottawa. Indeed, a former senior federal public servant thinks that things have become out of hand. It is worth quoting him at length: "Without blushing or even without a second thought, we now talk about our 'customers' or 'clients' in a way that would not have occurred to public servants three or four decades ago. And this is just the tip of the iceberg ... Sometimes the results of this attempt to reinvent the public sector into the private sector are quite bizarre. I recently visited a well-meaning colleague who proudly presented to me the organizational renewal efforts of a high-priced foreign consultant that consisted in, among other things, the translation of all terms of public administration and parliamentary democracy into private sector equivalents, including the reinvention of members of Parliament as the shareholders of the corporation and Cabinet as the Board of Directors." In the early 1990s, when NPM came into vogue, a deputy minister waxed expansive about what he believed to be the renewal and transformation of his department. "This is really serious stuff," he exclaimed proudly. "It's just like the private sector."[12]

Vernon Bogdanor reports on the declining influence of the mandarins in Whitehall as the model to emulate. He writes that the "claims of the market are now held to trump the claims of the public domain and the state has been a widely acknowledged disappointment."[13] The public sector, he adds, has become a new kind of marketplace, where citizens are being transformed into consumers. If citizens are to become consumers, then government organizations must manage operations like the private sector.

However, the public sector can never operate like the private sector – it cannot duplicate market forces, and public servants cannot be motivated by the profit motive. Competition in the public sector can never be made to look like competition in the private sector, and accountability in the public sector is as different from that in the private sector as night and day. One can appreciate why Glassco, as a private sector executive, would think that "good management consists in more than the 'avoidance of sin' and the government's 'high standards of probity.'" Private sector firms need to have a bias for action and a high tolerance for risks if they are to prosper. Private sector managers are allowed to sin if, in the process, they can expand the firm's market share and increase its profits. Not so for the public sector, which operates in a highly charged political environment in which sins are not easily tolerated.

There is hardly any agreement on how to measure the performance of public servants, while it is relatively straightforward to measure performance in the private sector: turn a profit, capture a larger share of the market, and out-compete the competition. Although governments have produced numerous papers on the attributes of competent career officials, there is hardly any consensus on how to measure competence. One senior official in Ottawa spoke to this problem when he pointed out that for every ten people who will approve the work of any deputy minister, it is easy to find ten others who will claim that the same person ought never to have been promoted to that level.[14] Unlike in business, sports, law, and entertainment – or in academe, with its publish or perish criteria – there are no hard criteria to judge the success of the work of senior public servants. There are so many variables that have an impact on the success of a policy, a policy proposal, or a government program that it is difficult to single out one or even several officials responsible for its success or failure. The arrival of horizontal government has only made things more difficult.

Senior government officials usually operate in a competition-free environment, in that there is no one across the street producing similar products, so levels of competence cannot be compared. The chief executive officer of a private firm is judged on the basis of his firm's earnings – the bottom line. The head of a government department or agency is often judged on the appearance or perception of success. James Q. Wilson explains that success in government "can mean reputation, influence, charm, the absence of criticism, personal ideology or victory in policy debates." He adds that many government employees "often produce nothing that can be measured after the fact." Michael Blumenthal is much more blunt. He argues that, in government, "you can be successful if you appear to be successful ... Appearance is as important as reality."[15]

In short, the main difference between the public and private sectors is that the private sector manages to the bottom line, while the public sector manages to the top line.[16] Government agencies – to a far greater degree than private businesses – must serve goals or purposes that are not always the preferences of the agency's senior administrators. As Wilson explains, "Control over revenues, productive factors and agency goals are all vested to an important degree in entities external to the organization – legislatures, courts, politicians, and interest groups."[17] The result is that government officials often look to the demands of the "external entities" rather than down the organization. It is for this reason, Wilson argues, that government managers are driven by the constraints on the organization, not by its tasks, and that public sector managers invariably manage to the top line.

Gérard Veilleux, a former senior deputy minister and later a senior executive with Power Corporation, summed up the difference in this fashion: "In the private sector, you pursue a few unambiguous goals and you manage privately. In the public sector, you have to accommodate many goals, at times conflicting ones, and you manage publicly." Put differently, it does not much matter in the private sector if you only get it right 10 percent of the time so long as the 10 percent turns a handsome profit for the firm. In the public sector, it does not matter much if you get it right 99 percent of the time if the 1 percent will cast you and your department in a negative light in the media for a long period of time. Veilleux added, "In the private sector, you manage privately, in the public sector you manage publicly."[18] This explains why avoiding sins plays a central role in public administration and for government managers.

Looking to the Private Sector to Establish Salary Levels

The desire to emulate private sector management and to empower managers led to a number of changes in government operations. The Public Service Commission has delegated staffing authority to departments and has essentially been transformed into an audit agency or an oversight body. Similarly, the Treasury Board has moved more management decision-making authority to line departments and agencies. Today, departments and agencies submit less than a thousand submissions a year to the Treasury Board to secure authority for financial or human resources transactions, compared with more than six thousand some thirty years ago. Departments have greater authority to classify and reclassify positions and to initiate financial transactions than they did.[19]

Meanwhile, the Treasury Board Secretariat's language has changed to promote a private sector perspective. When the secretary to the board described how the government was able to address its deficit in the mid-1990s, he said that the board did not focus only on "the costs of inputs" because that would "not lead to a rethinking of our business and business processes."[20] He did not specify who would now deal with "the costs of inputs," perhaps thinking that somehow the language of private sector management would take care of things. Nor did he explain how or when the government and public administration had been transformed into a business guided by business practices. It should be noted that strategic plans in government had been relabelled "business plans" and that pay-for-performance schemes had been introduced.

The challenge, then, was to make pay for performance work in the public sector, where performing is all too often in the eye of the beholder, and to insert the new private sector management-inspired language into practice.[21] Pay for performance has never been made to work properly in Ottawa or, for that matter, in other public jurisdictions. Efforts to anchor private sector management language into government vocabulary have placed a multitude of shadows on the shoulders of government managers and have, in the words of a mid-level manager, "created a big whale that can't swim."[22]

It bears repeating that advocates of NPM cannot point to a single jurisdiction where pay-for-performance schemes have been a success. The efforts have been described as senior public servants writing letters to themselves, or public servants marking their own exams.[23] In Canada, there was a time when the clerk of the Privy Council Office, the secretary to the Treasury Board, and the chair of the Public Service Commission would get together and discuss compensation levels. Then the clerk would meet with the prime minister, and they would agree to new salary levels. No more.

Ottawa now looks to the private sector for answers through the Advisory Committee on Senior Level Retention and Compensation, chaired by a senior private sector executive. Although the committee reports that the pay of senior government officials is lower than that of their private sector counterparts, compensation levels in business are used to determine the pay of government executives.[24] While comparing pay is relatively simple, it is not at all clear how one can compare with any degree of accuracy the work of a senior official in the public and the private sectors.

Career officials in the federal government now receive base salary and performance pay. The advisory committee has called for more attention "to identifying and managing marginal or poor performers." It explained that "there is little more demoralizing and detrimental to superior performance than ignoring situations where performance is weak or inadequate."[25] However, it offered little by way of advice or solutions. We know that senior public servants in one year used up the entire budget allocation to reward themselves for strong performance. The chair of the advisory committee observed that the committee "will refrain from recommending further increases to the at risk pay program until the government shows a commitment to ensuring the program does not reward poor performers."[26]

The Privy Council Office reports that performance pay has two distinct elements: a variable amount of at-risk pay, which needs to be re-earned every year, and a bonus for performance that surpasses expectations. It adds, "As in the private sector, it would be expected that most senior personnel would receive at-risk pay." It does not, however, explain why the public sector executives should receive at-risk pay "as in the private sector" or how the risks differ in the two sectors. It is significant that the performance review process has consistently "surpassed" the 20 percent benchmark at the high end and consistently missed the low end – that is, more than 20 percent of senior public servants exceeded performance expectations, while less than 5 percent failed to meet expectations.[27]

To establish performance is essentially an in-house process, conducted under the watchful eye of the clerk of the privy council. In the case of deputy ministers, they are expected to produce a self-evaluation of their performance for the previous year. The Privy Council Office then retains the services of a "recently retired" deputy minister on contract to review the self-evaluation and "gather further assessments."[28] The process involves a committee of senior officials to review the findings, but it is the clerk who decides who receives what and which public servants will make it to the deputy minister level.

As part of its strategic and operations review in 2011–12, designed to identify spending cuts of 5 to 10 percent, or in some cases more, the Harper government decided to tie performance bonuses for its senior officials to their ability to cut spending, including staff. Under this new approach, 40 percent of an executive-performance bonus is to be tied to the official's ability to cut his or her budget. This suggests that efforts to incorporate private sector management practices over the past thirty years or so have failed, or at least have fallen short of expectations. One would have assumed that senior public servants, like their counterparts in the private sector, would have been able to identify waste in their budgets over the past three decades or so. It also raises the question of whether senior public servants working under the parsimonious culture of the old public administration, with its emphasis on integrity, would have needed performance bonuses to deliver programs as efficiently and effectively as possible, since they saw it as their duty as servants of the state to do so.

A Shadow on My Shoulder

I once asked a government official, who had held a number of senior positions in the private sector before joining the federal government, to compare the two sectors. His response: "I always feel that there is a shadow on everybody's shoulder working in government."[29] That is, someone, somewhere, is constantly looking, monitoring, and assessing one's work, always on the lookout for a misstep. In the eyes of some, shadows on the shoulders of public sector managers have become a substitute – albeit a poor one – for the discipline of the market in the private sector.

It was not long after Glassco coined the phrase "Let the managers manage" that the avoidance of sin became all too often the measure of success in government, and the shadows on the shoulders of public sector managers became more and more present. Political crises or controversies in Ottawa are rarely fuelled by complex policy issues or by reviewing the government's expenditure budget. To catch someone "in sin," whether a minister or a public servant, is what so often fuels political debates or Question Period and reaches the front pages of daily newspapers.

One can hardly overstate the fact that public servants now operate in a highly politicized atmosphere. Government managers do not enjoy the same kind of privacy or private space that their private sector counterparts do. Any decision can become the subject of public debate, a question in Parliament, or a ten-second clip on the television news. The managers who decided, for example, to replace windows at the Department of External Affairs never expected that their action would receive intense media coverage, give rise to questions in Parliament, and move the minister of government services to declare that the decision was "stupid" and that he "wanted a full explanation," since he had never been made aware of the file.[30]

Ten years after the introduction of PS 2000 and nearly twenty years after NPM first surfaced, Human Resources Development Canada (HRDC) found itself mired in a full-blown political crisis. Senior officials became concerned in 1998 that one program was not performing as well as they had hoped, so they held an internal audit. The results began to emerge in mid-1999 and triggered a political firestorm that dominated the media for several months. The crisis, according to a former senior official at HRDC, became a "significant preoccupation for the Prime Minister and dominated the entire department and its minister."[31] The matter gave rise to 800 questions to the minister in Question Period, 17,000 pages of information on the department's website, 100,000 pages of material released to the media under Access to Information, numerous reviews and task forces, and a special examination by the auditor general.[32] The crisis ended with the release of the auditor general's review in October the next year.

The media and the opposition had pounced on the 34-page internal audit to declare that there was a "billion-dollar boondoggle" at HRDC involving the Transitional Jobs Fund. The document in question was not a financial audit but a "paper review" to establish the extent of documentation on file in a random sample of projects sponsored under the program. Paperwork on some projects was incomplete (for example, lacking cash flow forecasts and a description of activities to be financed), and there was little follow-up on some of the projects that had been approved.

The minister in a media scrum declared that there was "sloppy administration and we need to do a better job of ensuring that our files are complete."[33] That night the item got top billing on the TV news, with reports of stunning revelations about government mismanagement.[34] The next day the print media got into the act, led by the *Globe and Mail*'s front-page story headlined "Bureaucrats Mismanaged $3 Billion." *La Presse*'s headline read "Un monumental fouillis administratif," and the *Vancouver Sun*'s was "Sloppy Records Keep Public from Knowing if $1 Billion in Federal Grants Wrongly Spent."[35] The *Globe* suggested that the minister, Jane Stewart, was not to blame because she was not in charge when the grants were awarded and that the then-deputy minister, Mel Cappe, should accept some of the responsibility. The *Globe* noted, however, that Cappe had since become clerk of the privy council and "heads the entire Civil Service."[36]

Opposition MPs called on Stewart to resign, citing the doctrine of ministerial responsibility. Others soon joined in. The federal information commissioner declared publicly that "the file management system within the government has collapsed and continues to collapse."[37] The media began to ask questions about "who knew what, where and when, and whose head should roll [of the Watergate variety]"[38] and questioned the neutrality of the public service. Career officials were asked to testify before the House of Commons Standing Committee about what, how, and why things had gone wrong. They also appeared in the media, losing their traditional anonymity in order to answer questions and to report on new measures to strengthen the department's grants and contributions.[39] When Mel Cappe agreed to answer the committee's questions about his old department, some observers remarked that "the days of the faceless public servant entrenched in the Westminster system are over."[40]

The controversy lingered on for months in Parliament and in the media. Jane Stewart's year in hell saw the media cast her in an extremely negative light almost daily. The *Globe and Mail* reported on its front page on 2 August 2000 that she was "expected to be named Canada's ambassador to the Netherlands … because of the controversy surrounding the way officials in her department administered a job grants program."[41] The media, including the *Globe*, were always quick to add, however, that the criticism directed at her was unfair because it was Pierre Pettigrew who had been minister when the grants were handed out.

The controversy ended only when the auditor general's office reported that the audit of the one- or three-billion dollar "boondoggle" had centred on 459 projects selected at random from 10,000 projects, that the total amount of money involved in the 459 projects was about $200 million, that less than a dozen of the projects were "problematic," and that there was hardly any missing money.[42] Jane Stewart tabled a detailed report to the Standing Committee on Human Resources Development on the department's 16,971 active files on grants and contributions. The total value of these files amounted to $1.58 billion, and, of this, the only outstanding debt to the government was $65,000.[43] The media quickly lost interest in the story, as did the opposition parties. Both had paid precious little attention to the actual facts as they were being made public. But the first impressions had taken root, and to this day one still hears references to the $1 billion boondoggle at HRDC. One would be extremely hard-pressed to find a comparable story in the private sector.

It will be recalled that before the sponsorship scandal erupted in the Canadian media, Chuck Guité had been the poster boy for government efforts to introduce private sector management to government operations. Here was an individual who could get things done. He was an entrepreneur working in government, the kind that politicians and NPM promoted. He was told to cut red tape and to make things happen. This he did, and he was rewarded with several promotions over a relatively short period of time while being highly praised: "A man of action, a man of decisions, it did not take him 50 years to reach a decision. In terms of client services, there were few who could beat him."[44] The Prime Minister's Office and the minister responsible for the sponsorship initiatives all supported Guité's rapid promotions. He had done what he believed was expected of him, or what would be expected in the private sector. But when Canada's sponsorship scandal began to hit the front pages of the country's newspapers, the politicians and senior public servants ran for cover: the doctrine of ministerial responsibility and a resort to the traditional politics-administration dichotomy came in handy for all of them.

Hardly a month goes by without a scandal, a front-page story of an administrative miscue, or a political or administrative gaffe. The sins take various forms, but they dominate the political debates and overshadow the federal government's $250 billion expenditure budget. The following is one example among many. While the Ottawa system was working on preparing the 2012–13 budget, Environment Minister Peter Kent, with input from the prime minister's court, had to plan a response to the media story that his department had turned down recycling equipment when purchasing several hundred new workstations. This, after the department had spent more than $140,000 to store equipment for a year before deciding to auction it off and buy new furniture.[45] One strongly doubts that the media would be interested in a private sector executive making a decision to buy new furniture.

Speaking in Tongues: The Public Sector's Version of How the Private Sector Decides

At the risk of sounding repetitive, private sector incentives and market forces simply do not and cannot apply to the public sector. To empower managers and to introduce other private sector practices to government implies a loosening of bureaucratic and political control over managers. Since there is no "bottom line" in government, a process has to be established to judge how well managers are doing and whether they are "achieving results."

What to do? Governments have, since the mid-1980s, introduced one measure after another in an attempt to assess performance, strengthen accountability, and promote greater transparency. Without wishing to engage the reader in a lengthy descriptive review of the various accountability and performance review processes in government, it is important to provide an appreciation of what line departments and their managers have to cope with daily. Central agency officials and officers of Parliament insist that these measures are necessary to "preserve public trust, enhance economy, efficiency and effectiveness and ensure transparency and accountability."[46] Necessary or not, the measures have added layer after layer of reporting requirements and imposed a paper burden that would be unthinkable in the private sector.

MAF Appears to Be Riddled with Game Playing

The centrepiece of Treasury Board's new accountability regime is labelled Management Accountability Framework (MAF). Introduced in 2003, MAF continues to evolve to assess good management in line departments. In 2008–09, good management consisted of ten elements: public service values; governance and strategic direction; policy and programs; people; citizen-focused services; learning innovation and change management; risk management; stewardship; accountability; and results and performance. By 2011–12, good management under MAF consisted of fourteen elements:

values and ethics; management for results; citizen-focused services; internal audit; evaluation; financial management and control; management of security; integrated risk management; people management; procurement; information management; information technology (put on hold for 2011–12); assets management and investment planning; and management of products. The reader may wish to consult the Government of Canada's Treasury Board Secretariat website to gain a full appreciation of MAF's workings, criteria, means of evaluation, and results by departments for previous years.

Treasury Board Secretariat officials initiate two-way discussions with departments, but all rankings are a Treasury Board decision. The rankings are made public on the board's website and tell departments whether their performance is "strong," has "opportunities for improvement," is "acceptable" or is "attention required." The narrative accompanying the rankings is extensive, and a considerable amount of time is spent by both central agency and line-department officials in establishing levels of performance. These vary by department and by the elements of good management. One line department's deputy minister reported, "You figure what it is Treasury Board is after and you give it to them. At one point, my department received an 'opportunity for improvement' and we decided to hire a consultant to produce a report for us on the issue. The purpose here was to send a message to the board that we took their concerns seriously. That was good enough to move us to the 'acceptable' level the next year."[47]

MAF assessments are taken seriously by central agencies – the clerk of the privy council turns to them to assess the performance of deputy ministers, and the Treasury Board Secretariat uses them to assess the performance of departments and agencies. Deputy ministers in line departments and agencies also take MAF assessments seriously, if only because the Privy Council Office looks to them to establish their performance pay. Central agency officials sing the praises of MAF, but not so line departments. The former see it as a valuable accountability mechanism, whereas a good number of senior line department officials see it as little more than an "exercise in feeding the beast."[48] One line department deputy minister explained, "MAF is not really connected to my work. I come to work in the morning and here is what's on my mind: I need to think about what my minister is thinking, I need to look at what the prime minister and the clerk are worried about, I need to look at what the media are saying. I need to understand how stakeholders view my department. I need to focus on what my assistant deputy ministers are doing. Is MAF an important part of that equation? No."[49]

Central agency officials readily admit that assessing MAF is subject to "methodological limitations," though they insist that there are signs of improved management performance in government.[50] They also report that MAFs are a mix of "quantitative and qualitative measures" and that the process remains the one instrument available to assess how well departments are doing. A senior Treasury Board official said, "We know what line department people are saying about MAF. But what would they prefer? No reporting process, no way to assess how well they are doing? It may not be perfect, but it is what we have and, frankly, we see improvements year after year. Departments cannot have it both ways – less and less financial central control and no reporting requirements."[51]

Still, a former Treasury Board secretary and a former line department deputy minister teamed up to write about "utopian frameworks" in government and offered the following advice to public servants: "Novelty does not last ... it would be prudent to wait for the next new initiative that will inevitably shift the focus off the last one."[52] Thus, unlike in the private sector, the bottom line for government managers is a moving target. The process may be reinvented under a different name, but the objective remains: feed the beast in the hope that somehow levels of performance can be established and that somehow this can correspond in some way to how the private sector determines performance. Another former senior public servant sees little evidence that senior departmental officials look to MAF as a genuine management framework. He suggests that they see it as just one more requirement which they need to comply with for the purpose of reporting to central agencies.[53]

MAFs are hardly the only process that ties line departments to central agencies in search of a bottom line. The Treasury Board, as part of the estimate process, requires departments to prepare a number of documents, including Reports on Plans and Priorities (RPPs), which are individual expenditure plans for each department and agency providing "details on net program costs and human resources requirements," and Departmental Performance Reports (DPRs), which give an account of "results achieved against planned performance expectations."[54]

RPPs and DPRs are part of the budget process and are tabled in Parliament. They are yet another process to which managers at all levels must contribute. It is not at all clear who takes the reports seriously. We saw earlier that MPs pay scant attention to them. Treasury Board Secretariat officials take them seriously in the sense that they have to coordinate the efforts to produce them and may point to them in their discussions and negotiations with departments. Some line departmental officials take them seriously; others do not. One director general at Industry Canada said that he lets his staff do the work, knowing that they will get the numbers right and that the narrative will not get him or the department in trouble. He simply signs off on the material, often without giving it a second thought. He explained that he "had better things to worry about."[55]

In yet another attempt to borrow a page from the private sector, departments are expected to produce an "Integrated Business Plan" that outlines the department's mission, its priorities and challenges.[56] The Integrated Business Plan was introduced by the clerk of the privy council in the hope that it would bring together the various reporting requirements in one comprehensive report. In preparing their "integrated plans," departments "are well advised to define their business goals."[57] In 2008 the clerk asked an outside panel of experts (six members, four of whom came from the private sector) to review the Integrated Business Plan process. The panel made a number of recommendations, insisting that "integrating business planning ... is fundamental to delivering on business goals in tough times, much more than it is in good times." It added, however, that the process would only be effective if the clerk of the privy council "continues to emphasize the fundamental importance of integrated planning," and it urged the "Treasury Board Secretariat to meet or exceed its target of a 25 percent reduction in the reporting burden by 2010–11."[58] The target has not been met. Some line department officials maintain that the burden is greater today than it was in 2008. The panel never explained what "business goals" in government would actually look like.

More Shadows on Shoulders

In addition to the Privy Council Office and Treasury Board Secretariat, managers have to deal with the work of the Office of the Comptroller General, the Human Resources Officer, the Chief Information Officer, and the Public Service Commission. These agencies, too, do not provide direct services to Canadians; they exist to oversee the work of departments, to issue directives, and to hold departments to account.

The government has recently added still more new oversight bodies – new shadows on the shoulders of their managers. In 2004, the auditor general, in one of her reports, pointed to what she regarded as serious weaknesses in the government's internal audit community.[59] This report came on the heels of the sponsorship scandal. The Office of the Comptroller General responded by outlining a new Policy on Internal Audit, designed to address the concerns. The new policy provided for the establishment of

Department Audit Committees (DACs), with a majority of their members recruited from outside the federal government. The policy also called for a direct reporting relationship between the Chief Audit Executive (CAE) and the deputy minister. In the interest of full disclosure, it should be noted that I was an adviser to the Treasury Board, as the Simon Reisman Visiting Fellow, during the development and early stages of the policy. I also sat on two DACs, one as a member of the Atlantic Canada Opportunities Agency (ACOA) committee and the other as chair of the Canadian Heritage Department (PCH) committee.

The new policy added at least $40 million a year in spending to the internal audit function in large departments and saw staff increases from 359 full-time equivalents in 2005–06 to 602 in 2009–10 in the government's internal audit committee. The policy urged departments to appoint three outside members to their DACs, preferably one with financial, accounting, and auditing skills, one with private sector experience, and the third with public sector skills. Initially the thinking was that the DACs should report directly to the minister rather than to the deputy minister. The reaction from the deputy minister community was mostly negative on the creation of external audit committees and was outright hostile to the idea that DACs should report directly to their ministers. The Treasury Board pushed ahead with the policy but, in the end, relented and agreed that DACs would report to deputy ministers.

An assessment of DACs was conducted in 2011 and like in so many other matters in the public sector, reported that it was "difficult to quantify some benefits." It noted simply that DACs were able to achieve "some benefits, including improved risk management, improved efficiency and effectiveness and averted risks." These findings, however, were based not on specific cases but mostly on interviews and focus group sessions with DAC members and senior government officials. The consultants reported that they interviewed fifteen deputy ministers and thirty external members who chaired departmental DAC committees. The review concluded with a recommendation that the "Office of the Comptroller General limit the number of former public servants that are external members of DACs."[60] Another review of DACs concluded: "As is the case with most management innovations, it is difficult, at this early stage, to determine whether the recent DAC initiative has resulted in more benefits to the federal government than costs."[61] The review added that ministers "have shown little interest" in the work of DACs.[62]

When I was the Simon Reisman fellow at Treasury Board in 2005–06, I observed firsthand that most deputy ministers saw little merit in establishing new DACs. They believed that it, together with the other measures, was "overkill" – a response to the sponsorship scandal. However, things are different today. My conversations with deputy ministers, together with the 2011 DAC assessment prepared by a Vancouver-based consulting firm, reveal that most deputy ministers now support DACs. The DACs are now part of their organization and essentially act as advisers to deputy ministers. Many are staffed by former deputy ministers who are not about to challenge the status quo. Indeed, as in many other cases in government, once an organization is able to survive for a few years, it becomes the new status quo. If it does no harm, why not protect it?

Government managers have had to incorporate several other private sector management measures in their work. One can see the hand of the Office of the Auditor General (OAG) in these measures. The Treasury Board literature and policies on risk management talk about incorporating risk management in departmental business models and the need for senior departmental managers to be aware of risks in all business processes. Risk management, the Treasury Board Secretariat explains, is important in departmental "business activities" and in achieving "business objectives."[63]

Borrowing yet another page from the private sector – this time from the Sarbanes-Oxley Act – the Treasury Board secretariat introduced a policy on Internal Control on 1 April 2009.[64] The policy requires line deputy ministers to sign an annual "Statement of Management Responsibility including Internal Control over Financial Reporting." It is designed to ensure the "establishment, maintenance, monitoring and review of departmental system of internal control." The policy gives the Office of the Comptroller of Canada responsibility for monitoring "government-wide compliance" and "recommending corrective action when a department has not complied with the requirements of the policy."[65]

In addition, since 2009, line departments and agencies have been required to produce Quarterly Financial Reports (QFRs) to compare planned and actual expenditures. One departmental Finance officer insists that the exercise contributes nothing to better administration and only adds to the departmental reporting burden.[66] He maintains that the idea originated with a Conservative senator who sits on boards of directors and decided that it should apply in government.[67] The government bought the idea and included it in its revisions of the Financial Administration Act.

Following the lead from the private sector and the Office of the Auditor General, the government decided in the late 1990s to move away from expenditure-based accounting to accrual accounting.[68] The thinking was that there ought to be little difference in accounting for business and accounting for government. But there are major differences. Governments are elected; they operate with a public service; resources are raised through the confiscatory powers of taxation and distributed through an expenditure budget; many government assets are not employed to generate revenues; and governments have a much wider accountability regime to a much broader variety of stakeholders than businesses do.[69]

Officers of Parliament

Managers in the federal government have to deal with twelve more shadows on their shoulders in the form of officers of Parliament. The following can claim some status as officers of Parliament: Office of the Auditor General; Office of the Commissioner of Official Languages; Office of the Information Commissioner; Office of the Privacy Commissioner; Office of the Public Sector Integrity Commissioner; Public Service Commission of Canada (one can, however, debate whether the commission is an agency of government); the Conflict of Interest and Ethics Commissioner; the Office of the Procurement Ombudsman; the Parliamentary Budget Officer (albeit part of the Library of Parliament); the Commissioner of Lobbying; the Director of Public Prosecutions; and the Chief Electoral Officer.

Canada has more officers or agents of Parliament than the other Westminster-inspired parliamentary systems of government, and they have increased their staff considerably and expanded their mandates in recent years. The seven officers who have a direct impact on managers now (i.e., in 2011–12) employ more than 2,000 persons and spend over $250 million.[70] The 2,000 employees with officers of Parliament, as well as some of the 3,000 employees in central agencies and the thousands who carry out "oversight" work and prepare documents in line departments and agencies (1,457 employees out of a total of 5,682 in Industry Canada alone) go to work every morning looking for administrative miscues; they seek to put in place processes to prevent such miscues and to monitor and evaluate the performance of individual public servants, departments, and programs.[71] In May 2010 the ACOA had 286 of its 700 employees working on various accountability reports.[72] This explains why officers of Parliament are very often viewed – in the words of a senior line department official – as "the enemy in the room."[73] Like central agencies within the government (some 4,000 employees) and staff units in line departments and agencies, they do not deliver programs to Canadians.

Their measure of success centres on what measures or processes they can claim to have championed and implemented. Officers of Parliament, such as the auditor general, have sought to break out of the traditional boundaries to establish new turf for themselves, but not necessarily at the urging of Parliament. Indeed, in some ways, they now appear to function as free agents, accountable to no one but themselves. Of course, they cannot be subordinate or accountable to the government of the day, because that in itself would compromise their *raison d'être*. But once established, agents of Parliament, like other bureaucratic organizations, want to expand their sphere of influence, and Parliament has not been very effective in its dealings with them. Predictably, opposition parties and the media support an expanded role for officers of Parliament, while those on the government side of the House do not. Political parties that supported agents of Parliament while in opposition can very quickly turn sour on them once they themselves are in power.[74]

The Office of the Auditor General once had clear boundaries defining its role and responsibilities. Its purpose was to assist the Public Accounts Committee of the House of Commons and report to the committee the results of its investigations of financial probity and compliance with appropriation authority. Today, nearly 60 percent of its budget goes to "qualitative" or "soft reviews" that "bear little apparent relationship to efficiency or economy in the use of funds, human resources, or material."[75] A good number of reports published by the office now have little to do with financial probity. They are essentially political documents, in that they stake out policy positions or explore issues that have nothing to do with financial audits. Yet the office continues to insist on its non-political nature, even though it regularly engages in policy debates. Neither it nor the media bothers to explain that qualitative or soft reviews can never be as certain or conclusive as financial audits. Yet the office has become particularly adroit at attracting media attention, and it now reports its findings to the media as much as to Parliament.

The Canadian auditor general, it will be recalled, became a media star during the sponsorship scandal. There was talk on a number of open-line shows of "Sheila Fraser for prime minister," and she was described as a "folk hero with the electorate."[76] The office has successfully created its own distinct voice and essentially views Parliament as just another consumer of its reports. Its activities are no longer based on the exact work of accountants but increasingly on comprehensive policy work. The voice may not be partisan, but it is political. It is sufficiently influential that the prime minister, ministers, and senior public servants must invest time and effort to deal with it. In fact, it has become an important policy actor in its own right, a far cry from its original mandate.

In 2010, for example, it published a report on managing animal diseases. In 2009 it argued that Public Safety Canada had no pandemic management plan in place to oversee national disasters; the government responded that it had such a plan but it was the responsibility of Health Canada to manage and coordinate with other agencies.[77] In 2008 it published a report examining whether the Canadian government successfully manages risks associated with invasive alien plants, seeds, and pest and plant diseases that might enter the country. In 2007 it published a report that examined Canada's ability to keep its borders "open and secure." In this report. Sheila Fraser underlined "the need for effective targeting methods so that low-risk people can enter while appropriate action is taken for those who are high-risk." In the same annual report, the office published a report that was highly critical of the ability of the Department of Foreign Affairs and International Trade to manage human resources. In 2005 it published a report criticizing the government's ability to manage horizontal issues, claiming that central agencies "do not provide enough leadership or guidance to various federal organizations."[78]

The above-noted reports, which are chapters in the annual reports, are mixed in with financial audits and are given the same legitimacy as the financial audits. Yet they read like consulting reports, containing many points that could be challenged or are open to interpretation. In the eyes of the media and of Canadians in general, the auditor general speaks with an authority and influence that consultants do not enjoy. This credibility, however, is based on straightforward financial audits.

The officers of Parliament all speak from a narrow viewpoint, according to their particular mandates or interests, and no one is charged with bringing a broad overarching perspective. Consequently, those in government have several independent officers looking over their shoulders from different and at times conflicting perspectives (for example, privacy versus access to information). Opposition parties view officers of Parliament as their natural allies and do not want to challenge them, let alone hold them to account, preferring to let them wander wherever they want in the hope that they will uncover a situation embarrassing to the government.

An excellent case in point is the parliamentary budget officer, a position established by the Harper government as part of its Federal Accountability Act. The government's insistence that the office was created to "ensure truth in budgeting" could not have been lost on the minister of finance and his officials, who apparently are not as credible as a parliamentary budget officer. It was not long before the budget officer was embroiled in a political controversy. He began to challenge the government's spending estimates, its economic forecasts, and its projected revenues. He questioned whether the government's 2009 economic stimulus package would actually create the 189,000 jobs it projected,[79] and he said it would "push the country to the brink of a persistent deficit."[80] Somehow, he was able to arrive at this and other conclusions with a handful of employees, while the 800-strong Department of Finance could not.

The media gave the budget officer wide coverage, and overnight he made the transition from an obscure bureaucrat to someone in high demand by journalists. In some ways, he is playing the role that the leader of the opposition once played; also, he enables the media to challenge the government without having to do the legwork. Veteran MP Carolyn Bennett went to the bottom of the matter when she observed that the parliamentary budget officer should "work for parliamentarians, not the public." She took exception to his "habit of releasing reports to the public at the same time as he gave them to the MPs requesting the information, or tabled them in the Commons and Senate."[81]

The Harper government, in establishing the position of a parliamentary budget officer, sought to help MPs understand the government's budget process. But the first incumbent saw his role as less about helping MPs understand it and more as providing a second set of numbers to the Department of Finance's short- and mid-term budget forecast.[82] He has made it clear on several occasions that his mandate is to tell the "truth in budgeting" and that his $2.8 million annual budget is not sufficient to allow him to do so.[83] Like other officers of Parliament, his reporting relationship has been geared more to the media than to parliamentarians. Officers of Parliament, it seems, are able to tell the truth in a way distinct from everyone else in government.[84]

Senior public sector managers whom I have consulted over the years argue that the piling on of processes and evaluation schemes, one on top of the other, has made government operations thicker, has complicated decision making, and has let in far too many actors with little or no management experience, who impose processes that may or may not make sense but collectively serve to weigh down managers. We know that officers of Parliament work independently of one another and have limited interest in working with central agencies. Their many employees and most senior officials report to the media more than to Parliament. Public sector managers are left to manoeuvre as best they can in responding to the many demands for information that in consequence come their way – no easy task when at the same time they are making every effort to avoid creating problems for their ministers, their departments, and the government of the day.

Looking Back

The government, inspired by political leaders and the Office of the Auditor General, concluded that a combination of performance evaluation reports and bringing individuals with private sector experience from time to time to oversee the work of public servants would somehow create a private sector bottom line for public servants.

Oversight bodies and agents of Parliament are often regarded as standing up for taxpayers. Their work is rarely challenged by the media or the opposition parties. Government ministers may do so, but their criticism is often viewed as self-serving. Still, officers of Parliament and their 2000-plus employees represent a significant cost to Canadian taxpayers. But this tells only part of the story: they generate a heavy workload in all government departments and agencies because officials are constantly having to feed material to both central agencies and to officers of Parliament.

The public and private sectors, despite the plethora of private sector management measures, remain as different as night from day. Yet this does not appear to deter either politicians or, ironically, officers of Parliament in their attempt to define a bottom line for government managers. The next chapter considers still more attempts to duplicate the private sector's ability through market forces to determine winners.

7

Program Evaluation: Turning a Crank That's Not Attached to Anything

H.L. Laframboise predicted in 1978 that a new industry, the evaluation industry, would rise in Ottawa.[1] In my book *The Politics of Public Spending in Canada*, published in 1990, I was able to write that Laframboise's prediction had come to pass and that, except for those who were part of the industry, there were few in Ottawa who had any enthusiasm for program evaluation.[2] It was apparent that these evaluations were very costly and that their contribution to the government's policy making and decision making was negligible. I reported then that even central agency officials directly involved in the venture acknowledged that it had serious shortcomings and that much work was still required to identify and refine performance indicators in government.

There were other critics too. The Nielsen Task Force, established by Brian Mulroney to review programs and identify cuts in spending, concluded that "government program evaluations were generally useless and inadequate. Yet guided and inspired by the Office of the Comptroller General, departments have put in place significant evaluation groups over the past year."[3] Rod Dobell and Allan Maslove urged program evaluators to put more "realism" into the work and went on to pronounce that program evaluation had had no impact on the expenditure budget.[4]

Little has changed over the past twenty years, apart from the fact that more money and staff are now being dedicated to the evaluation industry. It will be recalled that program evaluation was born when the federal government replaced line-item budgeting with program budgeting. Program budgeting, too, was thought to hold considerable promise in its day. The thinking was that if information were provided on simple administrative details (i.e., line-item budgeting), then decisions would be made on details; similarly, if information were given on policies and programs, then policy decisions would be made. The extent to which program budgeting was highly regarded in Ottawa is best exemplified by the minister of finance's statement at the time. He declared it "a major budget breakthrough."[5] The approach was to be such a powerful instrument that many actually believed that it could remove politics from the budgeting process – that it would provide such clear and rational answers that the government would be compelled to embrace it. In fact, this was so widely believed in some quarters in government that senior public servants felt the need to reassure politicians that they would continue to make the key program decisions and that politics would still weigh heavily in the decision-making process. Al Johnson wrote that program budgeting "must not seek to substitute science for politics in the decision-making process."[6]

The purpose of this chapter is to review the program evaluation function and its role in the expenditure budget process. Program evaluation is part of the government's effort to create a bottom line in the public sector that compares with that found in the private sector. If market forces cannot evaluate performance, other means must be found to do so.

The Crank Keeps Turning

The Office of the Auditor General (OAG) and central agencies, especially the Office of the Comptroller General (OCG) and the Treasury Board Secretariat (TBS), continue to attach a great deal of importance to program evaluation. Two other central agencies, the ones with most clout in government – the Privy Council Office and Finance – have less interest in it. They are too busy, it seems, with more important issues.[7] The function's three champions, in particular the OAG, are constantly pushing for more resources to be allocated to program evaluation. In response to this internal pressure, the government enacted a "new policy on evaluation" on 1 April 2009, which sought, among other things, to:

- establish evaluation as a deputy head function;
- establish quality standards for individual evaluations;
- introduce new requirements for program managers to develop and implement ongoing performance measurement strategies.[8]

The policy committed the government to evaluating on average 20 percent of direct program spending every year, beginning in April 2013. The thinking was that after a four-year transition period to give departments time to "revamp up" the evaluation capacity, the government would be able to have all its programs evaluated on an ongoing five-year cycle.

New resources have been committed to program evaluation in recent years. When I published *The Politics of Public Spending in Canada* two decades ago, program evaluation activities were supported by about $50 million and employed 300 persons. Today the government spends about $80 million every year and employs about 500 full-time equivalents. In addition, most departments hire outside consultants to carry out their evaluations. In 2009–10, for example, about 93 percent of evaluations involved outside consultants do at least part of the work.[9]

The OAG rendered its verdict on the government's program evaluation efforts in 2008, and it was not complimentary. It argued that the government was ill prepared to evaluate all of its programs over a five-year period as the 2006 Federal Accountability Act (and later the 2009 government policy) required. The office was not impressed with the quality of the evaluation, pointing out that "often departments had not gathered the performance information needed to evaluate whether programs are effective." It added that of the 23 evaluation reports the office reviewed, "17 noted that the analysis was hampered by inadequate data, limiting the assessment of program effectiveness." The OAG criticized the TBS, claiming that "it did not provide sustained support for effectiveness evaluation – it made little progress on developing tools to assist departments with the long-standing problem of a lack of sufficient data for evaluating program effectiveness."[10] One might pause to note that an assistant auditor general, a principal, a lead director, two directors, five other OAG officials, and some outside consultants all worked on the OAG report, *Evaluating the Effectiveness of Programs*. It would have been interesting if someone had similarly evaluated the cost and value of the 39-page report, which became chapter 1 of the 2009 *Fall Report of the Auditor General*.

It was not the first attempt by the OAG to promote program evaluation. In 1978 it reviewed the procedures followed by eighteen departments and found "few successful attempts." In 1983 it conducted another review and concluded that "few high-quality evaluations were being done"; in 1993 it carried out yet another review and reported that "the system's results are often disappointing. Program evaluations frequently were not timely or relevant," and in a 1996 follow-up to the 1993 audit, the office found that "little progress had been made to address effectiveness issues." By 2000 things had gone from bad to worse, with the OAG reporting that "the evaluation function has actually regressed."[11]

The OAG is not in the habit of offering advice to government managers on how to evaluate program effectiveness. Its officials do not see this as part of their role. They purposely avoid action, preferring to count the dead after the war. They sit in judgment, time after time reporting that not enough is being done, that information-gathering processes are not up to par, and that performance indicators require a great deal more effort. The role of the TBS and the OCG, meanwhile, is to establish the program evaluation policy, provide direction, issue directives and guidelines, and provide oversight and support. The TBS has consistently urged line departments and agencies to embed program evaluations into program management, but with little success.[12]

The onus is on line department managers to square the circle, to make program evaluation relevant and worthwhile. However, they know all too well that there is a near complete disconnect between program evaluation policy, front-line program managers, and the expenditure budget. Peter Aucoin wrote a paper in support of program evaluation for the TBS, arguing that it can constitute an important part of modern government. His verdict on the efforts, however, was hardly positive. He pointed out that the "TBS do not figure prominently" in the budget process, since the Department of Finance now dominates it. He added that the expenditure budget process has become "essentially an administrative process with no review and reallocation. The new management board roles of TB/TBS do not compensate for its loss of influence." Aucoin recognized that program evaluation has never been "embedded" in the expenditure budget's decision-making process.[13]

There is also a disconnect between program evaluation and the political world. Jack Harris, the MP for Saint John's East, did not have to wait for a program evaluation report to jump to the defence of the search-and-rescue team in Newfoundland, asserting that the $1 million that the chief of defence staff spent on twenty-one flights he took on the government's VIP jet to pro-sports and fundraising events and for a family holiday in St Martin would have saved the unit for several months.[14] One would be hard-pressed to find anyone interested in a comparable case in the private sector.

Government policy claims that program evaluation is somehow tied to expenditure management, that it "plays an increasingly important role in the effective management of public spending."[15] Yet the policy goes on to say that program evaluation efforts have been hindered by "the unavailability or low quality of performance measurement data."[16] It failed, however, to show a link between program evaluation and the expenditure budget process. The authors of the Treasury Board policy on program evaluation consulted with senior government officials and reported that "deputy ministers acknowledged that evaluations are used in many, often untraceable ways."[17] This is the best they could report, hardly an impressive conclusion coming from TBS officials, traditionally one of the champions inside government of program evaluation.

The above also attests to the disconnect between the auditor general, some central agencies, and line departments. The OAG's 633 employees, all far removed from the delivery of government services, view program evaluations as key to understanding how well government departments and their programs perform. The TBS, meanwhile, turned to program evaluation some forty years ago to ensure that it would still retain control over spending departments as it moved away from line-item budgeting. Program evaluation, the thinking went, would inform Treasury Board officials and ministers on how well departments, their managers, and programs were performing. At the risk of sounding repetitive, there is now a widely held consensus that program evaluation has never lived up to expectations.[18]

Yet program evaluation was given a new lease on life when the auditor general and politicians turned to private sector management practices to improve government operations and program delivery. To empower government managers required a capacity to evaluate performance, to find somehow a semblance of a bottom line for the public sector – and, *faute de mieux*, program evaluation once again became the solution. Its success in contributing to better management and to the expenditure process remains as elusive as ever.

Going through the Motions

Line departments and agencies consider program evaluation to be a burden that holds little advantage for them. Government managers in line departments know better than anyone else that they operate in a highly charged political environment. Moreover, the fact that evaluation results are now subject to disclosure under access to information legislation makes them less frank than they might otherwise be.[19] The line managers also know that program evaluation is fraught with conceptual problems. There is now a whole body of literature decrying program evaluation techniques as lacking on several fronts.[20] Indeed, it doesn't take much thought to recognize the challenges involved in evaluating public sector programs.[21] How can one possibly isolate reasons for, say, the success or failure of an economic development program? How does one deal with currency fluctuations in an increasingly global economy? What about interest rates, what about unwarranted political interference, what about the state of the local economy, and what about the impact of other government policies and programs (e.g., fiscal policy)? How can one possibly evaluate a Government of Canada program on climate change?

There are many questions that have never been answered by the OAG, the TBS, or in fact, by anyone. How do you measure the value of a defence program or a diplomatic initiative, let alone the role of the deputy minister in charge? How can government departments and agencies know if they are doing a good job? How can Parliament possibly decide whether departments and deputy ministers are effective? How can one possibly isolate a deputy minister's contribution to a government-wide initiative?

Three students of management summed up the problems with program evaluation when they wrote: "Despite a quarter of a century of performance management within the public sector, there are still major problems and the expected improvements in performance, accountability, transparency, quality of service and value for money have not materialized."[22] Few observers still sing the praises of program evaluation, and the few who do can point only to pockets of success that do not apply to an entire organization.[23]

Unless a department dislikes a program (a rare occurrence indeed), no deputy ministers would want to present to ministers, Parliament, and the media a negative program evaluation. Why would a deputy minister possibly want to draw negative attention to the department? Departments have simply learned to cope with program evaluations and a stream of outside consultants; they still regard program evaluation as a kind of "gotcha" tool for the auditor general and the TBS.[24] The OAG acknowledged as much in its annual report when it wrote, "It is too often as though departmental managers are saying – if central agencies want us to provide financial and program information and measurements of our efficiency and effectiveness, we will of course provide them. But we don't see that information as being at all relevant to the day-to-day job we are being asked to do. So, providing it is a tiresome task, we will perform it in a desultory manner."[25] Again, the problem is that many managers regard evaluation as a means to generate information for someone outside the department, including the media, giving them ammunition to come back and point out where they have failed. Doug Hartle put his finger on the issue when he wrote almost forty years ago, "It is a strange dog that willingly carries the stick with which it is beaten."[26]

If program evaluation made a significant contribution to the expenditure budget process, one could assume that there would have been no need for Treasury Board ministers to sign a $19.8 million contract to provide advice on finding savings in government operations and "on public and private sector best practices in improving productivity and achieving operational efficiencies." This contract was on top of a $2.5 million contract to Price-Waterhouse Coopers for advice on how to reduce the size of the government's data centre.[27]

Ruth Hubbard, former chair of the Public Service Commission, and Gilles Paquet wrote about the "cult of quantification" evident throughout the federal government. They argue that "quantophrenia has become a security blanket for public servants under surveillance. Consequently, even if such exercises are regarded as mostly futile, and rather costly in terms of resources required, junior executives simply have bowed to the edicts from above, and developed the habit of filling the required forms 'creatively' so as to keep the 'beast' satisfied."[28] They are hardly alone in questioning the relevance of the cult of quantification.

Ian Clark, former Treasury Board secretary, and Harry Swain, a former senior deputy minister in Ottawa, wrote a practitioner's perspective on program evaluation. They looked at the government's *Guidance for Deputy Ministers*, which says that "information on results should be gathered and used to make departmental decisions" and then to look at "what happens in reality." They reported, for example, that Industry Canada's 2003–04 departmental performance report (DPR) was "highly informative" but that they "could not find a single confession of failure."[29] It is difficult to imagine that departments with 5,649 employees, a budget of $1.4 billion, and a multitude of policy and program units do not have at least one confession of failure.[30] The Nielsen Task Force on program review went to the heart of the matter when it observed, "Routine evaluations conducted by departmental officials are undertaken for the department's deputy minister. By definition, therefore, they tend to be self-serving."[31]

No less revealing is the "highly respected manager" quoted by Clark and Swain, who told them that having to respond to the accountability framework, to change management initiatives and provide new paperwork meant that the manager and the departmental staff "were spending less than 45 percent of our time on actually delivering the various programs for which we were responsible."[32] Ironically, the OAG in one of its audits of the evaluation function in Environment Canada, discovered that officials in the unit spent "about 40 percent" of their time on tasks other than evaluation, without reporting what the other tasks may have been.[33] The point is that those charged with actually delivering public services spent less than 45 percent of their time doing so, while those charged with evaluating programs spent 60 percent of their time doing something else.

As already noted, the OAG is far removed from the political realities of the day and central agency officials are two or three steps removed from the delivery of front-line program services (the music teachers). Line department officials in the field manage programs, deliver services, meet with clients every day, and report up the line to ministers who answer for them in Parliament. They know that assessment of their performance and that of their programs are inherently subjective, that partisan politics is never far from the surface, that government programs often pursue multiple goals, and that performance measurement in government is not only inherently political but varies over time.[34]

The market for program evaluation reports is thus limited largely to officials in the TBS, OCG, OAG, and the Ottawa-based evaluation community. What matters to the evaluation community is how many program evaluation reports are completed in a given year and whether the number squares with what was envisaged. How the reports were received and what impact they may have had on programs are not important. Parliament, as we saw earlier, has little interest in these reports. Keith Martin, a widely respected former MP, observed that "studies, when they are done, cost the taxpayers hundreds of thousands of dollars and yet are complex and thrown onto a shelf to collect dust."[35] A review of some program evaluation reports explains this observation. There are striking similarities between the reports, no matter which programs are being evaluated or which departments produced them.

Industry Canada carried out in the fall of 2009 a "final" evaluation of its Community Access Program. It launched this program in 1994 to provide affordable Internet access and skills training in public locations in rural areas to stimulate economic development. Funding varied from $20 to $64 million a year. The evaluation was managed by the Evaluation and Audit Unit in the department, with the assistance of outside consultants, and the process was guided by a steering committee. Early in the report, its authors state that the evaluation is "limited by a lack of recent client outcome data, a lack of time series data showing attribution of client outcomes to program outputs, the inherent bias of key informant opinions and the evolving nature of the program."[36] The verdict? The program is said to have had "some" success at providing access (surely, between $20 to $64 million over a fifteen-year period will do that) but while "use of internet has continued to increase," attribution to the program "could not be fully established."[37]

Canadian Heritage carried out an evaluation of its Canadian Studies Program in July 2010. The evaluation was undertaken by the department's Evaluation Unit with the help of some outside consultants (i.e., EKOS Research Associates), the same firm employed by Industry Canada in its evaluation. The process was guided by a working group made up of representatives of the evaluation units, as well as the Canadian Studies Program, which met on a regular basis.

The Canadian Studies Program was established in 1984 with the goal of encouraging "Canadians to learn about Canada." The program was revised in 2005 to focus on Canada's youth rather than the general population. Its budget amounts to $1.2 million a year, and it allocates $200,000 a year in grants and $265,000 in contributions, while $752,000 a year is set aside for salaries and operating expenses. There is a substantial difference between a "grant" and a "contribution." An individual or an organization that meets the eligibility criteria for a grant will receive payment without meeting further requirements. In the case of a contribution, the individuals or organizations receiving it must demonstrate that they meet conditions over the life of the agreement. The government can audit a recipient's use of a contribution but cannot do so with a grant.[38]

Predictably, the evaluation's first recommendation urges the program's management "to identify realistic and measurable expected results that are aligned with the program's objectives and would support effectively the demonstration of the program's attribution to the changes by its intervention on the target population," while the third recommendation reads that the "program management should improve its performance measurement strategy and ensure that adequate collection data and analysis are performed to allow an effective program monitoring and support future evaluations." The fourth and final recommendation suggests that management "should explore ways to improve the efficiency of the program, especially with regard to its administrative cost ratio."[39] One hardly needs an evaluation report and outside consultants to conclude that something was not right when the cost of managing the program amounted to well over half of the total program spending.

These evaluation reports are typical of the hundreds produced every year in the Government of Canada. Readers are invited to look at some of them – they are easily accessible online. Those of all departments follow the same pattern. All are couched in cautious, bureaucratic language so as not to draw the attention of the media or opposition MPs. What I find most remarkable is that today's evaluation reports read much like the ones I consulted when carrying out research over twenty years ago for my study, *The Politics of Public Spending in Canada*. Today's evaluation reports, like those from twenty or thirty years ago, invariably point to a lack of relevant performance indicators, lack of relevant data, difficulty in defining outcomes, and difficulty in tying outcomes to the programs.

Program evaluation reports have had no visible impact, even when government decides from time to time to review its expenditure budget. This was true in the ambitious Chrétien-Martin program review of 1994–97, in Harper's first strategic review exercise of 2006–10, and in the strategic and operational reviews unveiled on 7 June 2011. I do not recall the department looking at a single program evaluation when I acted as the outside adviser to the ACOA strategic review exercise.[40]

The 1994–97 Chrétien-Martin exercise was guided by six criteria against which government programs were assigned. The criteria were sent to all departments and agencies with a directive that they test their programs against them. The questions were:

1 Does the program area or activity continue to serve a public interest?
2 Is there a legitimate and necessary role for government in this program or activity?
3 Is the current role of the federal government appropriate, or is the program a candidate for realignment with the provinces?
4 What activities or programs should or could be transferred in whole or in part to the private or voluntary sector?
5 If the program or activity continues, how could its efficiency be improved?
6 Is the resultant package of programs and activities affordable within the fiscal restraint? If not, what programs or activities should be abandoned?[41]

The Chrétien-Martin review generated a number of studies, both inside and outside government, to capture lessons learned.[42] Precious little is said in these studies about the role of program evaluation reports in generating potential spending cuts.

As already noted, Harper's strategic and operating review – designed, initially at least, to eliminate the government's deficit by 2014–15 – relied on outside consultants to identify potential spending cuts.[43] In addition, senior public servants were told that a good part of the annual performance would be tied to their ability to find potential spending cuts within their own jurisdiction. There is no indication that either the consultants or senior government officials, including the prime minister's courtiers, turned to program evaluation reports for assistance. The criteria to guide how to identify spending cuts, assuming they exist, were never made public.

It will be recalled that when he was Treasury Board minister, Stockwell Day wrote to all Treasury Board employees asking for suggestions on how to get the government's fiscal house in order. One would have assumed that after over thirty years of program evaluation efforts someone would have generated some suggestions. He received no reply or, in the words of journalist Daniel LeBlanc, "all he got in return was a big nothing."[44]

So Why Is This So?

There are fundamental conceptual problems with program evaluation that have never been resolved, and prospects for their resolution are dim. This is not limited to Canada. A recent review in Australia reveals that government departments there "continue to find it challenging to develop and implement performance indicators, in particular effectiveness indicators that provide quantitative and measureable information, allowing for an informed and comprehensive assessment and reporting of achievements against stated objectives."[45]

When one combines fundamental conceptual problems that have never been addressed in program evaluation with the conviction that public servants cannot be fully trusted when it comes to establishing expenditure budgets (again, witness the recent government decision to contract-out advice on the strategic and operating review), one sees why politicians have given up on the ability of public servants to generate ideas for cutting spending. Indeed, evidence-based policy making appears to have taken a back seat in Ottawa to policy making based on political ideology, on political commitments made during election campaigns, and, at times, on the whims and wishes of the prime minister (see, for example, Chrétien and the Millennium Scholarship Fund).[46] The Harper government's crime legislation and its inability to support it through evidence or to provide a proper costing speaks to how new spending commitments are decided today.

New spending is only the tip of the iceberg. The problem with public sector budgeting is not so much what government spends on new measures but its apparent inability to stop spending on measures that have long passed their "best by" date. This is where public servants and their outside consultants, producing reams of program evaluation reports and various performance review assessments, have been kept busy turning a crank that is not attached to anything.

Why is this so? Which of the theories outlined earlier explain the fact that senior public servants would happily continue to turn cranks not attached to anything? Does public choice theory explain this behaviour? What about path dependency and new institutionalism? The theories – especially path dependency, tied as it is to the study of institutions – certainly hold merit in understanding the continuing efforts at program evaluation, with little to show in terms of rethinking or financing ongoing programs.

I decided to consult decision makers in line departments for their thoughts. Most put up a lukewarm defence of program evaluation, making the point that one ought not to look at it from the narrow perspective of seeing which programs died or were enriched because of it. They admitted that program evaluation has been useful on occasion. Some asked, What do you suggest – that we do not evaluate programs? But they acknowledged its weaknesses as a management tool and had precious few concrete examples to show that it had made a positive contribution.[47] There was also the sense that someone else is responsible for program evaluation, and there is little that line department officials can do about it. One senior deputy minister summed it up well when he observed, "You have to pick your battles and what to do about program evaluation is never even near the top of my list."[48] Anyone wishing to take up the issue would have to deal with vested interests in the OAG, OCG, and TBS.

There are only two individuals in Ottawa who can do this – the prime minister and the clerk of the privy council. They, too, must pick their battles, and there is little to be gained for them in picking this one. As we saw earlier, there is never a shortage of potential problems, crises, and looming battles on their overloaded agenda. Certainly, there is no political advantage for the prime minister taking on the auditor general in the era of permanent election campaigns. The prime minister would quickly be on the defensive in Parliament and in the media, and when you are on the defensive in politics, you are losing. Meanwhile, the clerk of the privy council would, with the prime minister's blessing, have to engage the auditor general in a public debate, which would quickly become a politically charged debate. Clerks of the privy council intuitively shy away from such debates.

The overload problem is all too often overlooked when it comes to understanding how and why government decides.[49] Since too many of the key decisions in modern government are concentrated in the hands of only a handful of individuals, many activities are left to roll along on their tracks, provided they do not draw negative attention to the government. Program evaluation is one of many issues that is crowded out by more urgent and political imperatives. One would be hard-pressed to find a comparable situation in the private sector.

What about the Treasury Board Secretariat?

The TBS and its 2,000-plus full-time equivalents are responsible for financial and human resources policies. On the financial side, the board's role is rooted in oversight of the government's A-base budget, or continuing programs. While PMO-PCO and the Department of Finance look after new spending and the development of the annual budget, TBS is responsible for reviewing departmental spending plans, establishing the government's expenditure plan, and monitoring it through the spending estimates that are tabled in Parliament every spring. In brief, Treasury Board acts – or should act – as the government's budget office.[50] In theory, if the Treasury Board played its budget office role to the full, there would be little need for the prime minister's across-the-board cuts or for the strategic and operating reviews in search of 5 to 10 percent spending reductions, or to pay $20 million to outside consultants to assist in identifying spending cuts.

The TBS is not what it was when it comes to playing its budget office role. Indeed, since the arrival of NPM and initiatives such as PS 2000, which are designed to make public sector management look like private sector management, TBS has been searching for a new role in the expenditure budget process, with little to show for.[51] Previously, centrally prescribed rules and regulations, together with a thorough knowledge of line department programs, gave TBS both a carrot and a stick with which to gain the attention of departments. When TBS decided to rely on evaluation and performance reports prepared by the departments, it lost the stick, since the departments essentially became self-governing management entities. When asked to implement across-the-board cuts, departments and agencies are now left on their own to identify where the cuts could be made. In the past, departments often looked to program and capital budgets for cuts while protecting their own organizations. This explains why political actors have decided, in more recent years, to invite outside advisers to carry out strategic reviews in line departments and have turned to a $20 million consultant contract to assist in carrying out the reviews.

Treasury Board's role in reviewing new funding has been taken over by the Department of Finance and the Prime Minister's Office. Departments, in turn, are frequently under great political pressure to implement new spending initiatives as soon as they are announced by the prime minister. This all too often leaves TBS officials scrambling to pick up the pieces after departments have started spending. This would have been unthinkable thirty years or so ago when the Treasury Board was de facto the government's budget office.[52]

The fundamental issue here is that TBS became uncertain about its role when NPM-type measures were being introduced. TBS sought to become "softer and more gentle" as it began to rely on evaluation and performance reports of one kind or another when managing the government's expenditure budget and to rely less on "hard edge" questions.[53]

In embracing a private sector management model, TBS decided to provide more decision-making authority to line departments and agencies. Line departments today have considerable more authority in financial decisions (more discretion) and human resources (staffing and classification) than in years past. As noted earlier, in 1983 Treasury Board processed 6,000 transactions from departments, while today it is less than 1,000.[54] The Treasury Board's program branch, the one branch in government that reviewed in detail departmental expenditure budgets, was disbanded as part of an ambitious reorganization to signal a shift of emphasis away from expenditure review and towards management issues.[55]

Traditional Treasury Board functions, however, have suffered. On the expenditure side, TBS officials moved away from playing a "guardian" role towards a more "facilitator" role, in efforts to let managers manage, thinking that this was in line with private sector management practices. In the process, at least from a Department of Finance perspective, the system lost a guardian. Indeed, some Finance officials feel that the TBS had become less of a guardian and more of a claimant on behalf of the spending departments. The Privy Council Office and Finance, staffed with some 2,000 public servants, have since developed a comparative advantage in developing a knowledge of departmental programs. In time, Finance stopped sharing information with TBS staff, fearing that the information might make its way to line departments and assist them in making claims for more funds.[56]

We saw in an earlier chapter that institutionalists attach a great deal of importance to the "socializing" process that transforms individuals into institutional members so that they embrace the logic of appropriateness of their institutions. TBS officials witnessed such a sea change as the Treasury Board began to promote private sector management measures and to distance itself from its traditional guardian role. New positions accompanied the new efforts to let managers manage and to support public sector managers by decentralizing decisions on financial and human resources issues, but at the same time requiring managers to produce one performance report after another. Officials at TBS who wished to focus on centrally prescribed procedures and on keeping a tight rein on how government spent public funds lost influence and were overlooked for promotion.[57] A new logic of appropriateness took root, and when the time came for TBS to play its traditional guardian role, it fell short of the mark. The other guardians had to look elsewhere, to outside advisers and to those who stayed the course in pursuing guardian-type activities, most notably the Department of Finance.

A Production Line of Reports

The Department of Finance and the Privy Council Office are primarily concerned with macroeconomic policy, with the broad parameters of budget making. They have no capacity to get into the nitty-gritty of departmental spending plans. That responsibility falls, or at least should fall, to the Treasury Board Secretariat. As we have seen, TBS staff lost sight of their traditional responsibility of managing expenditure, opting instead to manage the assembly line producing a variety of reports in order to implement "Results Based Budgeting and Parliamentary Reporting." TBS officials also report that they pursued private sector accounting practices that did not square fully with government requirements.[58] In consequence, there has been a lack of discipline and regularity in managing the government's expenditure budget. In time, departmental budgets became padded to the point that they could no longer serve as a proper baseline on which to establish future years' funding levels.

In the interest of giving government managers greater freedom to manage, departments were allowed to transfer money from program funding (typically vote 5) to administrative costs, such as salaries, training, and travel (typically vote 1). The result is that in the early 2000s a considerable amount of money flowed out of vote 5 to vote 1.[59] When departments ran short of program money, they went to the Treasury Board to increase program funding levels. Treasury Board ministers found it a great deal easier in a minority government situation – where there was always the prospect of a general election a few months down the road – to fund programs rather than the overhead cost of government.

The TBS operates at two levels: within government with line departments working on performance and accountability, and between government and Parliament to submit accountability reports. The TBS is now at the centre of a veritable assembly line of performance reports: an annual report to Parliament on Canada's Performance, as part of the Estimates, and a series of other reports – notably, Reports on Plans and Priorities (RPPs) and DPRs, while managing numerous activities under MAFs.

The assembly-line approach of producing reports tilted TBS's role towards supporting senior departmental managers. This in turn served to make its role in the expenditure budget process unfocused and fragmented. Again, the Department of Finance moved in to occupy more of the expenditure management territory, but with a focus on the broad picture and not on the details of departmental spending patterns.

The price that departments had to pay to gain management authority on financial and human resources was to spend a great deal of time and effort on performance evaluation and accountability reports. New resources, both financial and human, were required to work on these reports, but this was bearable because the centre allocated new resources to departments for this purpose. In return, departments had a relatively free hand to look after input costs – creating new positions, adding to the travel budget, reclassifying positions to higher levels, and adding funding to staff development and training. In brief, senior line department managers were free to reallocate money to areas they thought important – and they did.

The government decided in 2007 that departments would no longer be allowed to transfer funds from vote 5 (program funding) to vote 1 (operations) without Treasury Board approval. TBS officials had finally come to the conclusion that departments and agencies had been padding vote 1 budgets and that evaluation reports were of little help in assessing the merit of the transfers.

It became clear, however, that the cost of government operations had gone up in relation to other activities. In 2010–11, operating expenses of departments and agencies (excluding National Defence) accounted for 18.4 percent of total government spending. Public debt charges accounted for 11.4 percent, transfers to persons 25.2 percent, transfers to governments 19.6 percent, other transfer payments 13.6 percent, crown corporations 3.9 percent, and National Defence 7.9 percent.[60] In contrast, in 1998–99 both the operating and the capital category had accounted for only 13 percent of total government spending, while transfers to persons had accounted for 23 percent; to governments, 17 percent; and to other transfers, 12 percent.[61] I note that public debt charges had amounted to 27 percent of total spending in 1998–99, but represented only 11.4 percent in 2010–11. Total federal government spending in 1998–99 had been $164.6 billion, while it amounted to $270.5 billion in 2010–11. An increase of 4.4 percent in operating costs over an eleven-year period, particularly when "capital" spending within departments was included in 1998–99, is substantial, outstripping the rate of inflation.

Public Accounts provides a more detailed record of actual spending than the estimates do. It combines operating and departmental capital expenses and includes National Defence. For 2010–11, Public Accounts reported that the largest component of federal government spending in that fiscal year was "operating expenses," which accounted for 26.3 percent of total expenses. This was followed by transfers to persons, 25.2 percent; transfers to other levels of government, 19.6 percent; transfers to other individuals, businesses, and organizations, 13.6 percent; funding for crown corporations, 3.9 percent; and public services charges, 11.4 percent.[62] In 2010 the government spent $3.1 billion in travel expenses and $8.1 billion in professional services.[63]

In contrast, Public Accounts for 2001–02 operating expenses amounted to 16.1 percent. Total transfer payments to persons, government, organizations, and businesses amounted to 52.1 percent; public debt charges, 22.9 percent; and crown corporations, 2.5 percent. In that fiscal year, the government spent $2.2 billion on transportation and communication expenses and $5.1 billion on professional and special services.[64] If one goes back in history to review Public Accounts in the 1960s, 1970s, and 1980s, spending patterns were that much different again, with operating expenses much lower in relation to other expenses.[65]

Shifting Priorities by Stealth

The shift from centrally prescribed rules, regulations, and processes (the old public administration) to program and performance evaluations (private sector inspired) led to new spending on staff, travel expenses, staff development, higher classification creep, and new positions at head offices in order to work on program evaluation and performance requests and to deal with the demands of parliamentary officers. It is highly unlikely that the politicians who championed NPM in the hope that it would introduce private sector management measures to government are pleased with the results and the new spending patterns.

Even a cursory comparison of a department's management structure from the one that existed before NPM came into fashion speaks directly to the above. A government department in the mid-1970s typically had a deputy minister, an assistant deputy minister responsible for administration and finance, another for planning, and from two to four program assistant deputy ministers. Today, Public Works and Government Services Canada has one deputy minister, one associate deputy minister, eight assistant deputy ministers, including one responsible for departmental oversight, three associate deputy ministers, and three chief executive officers.[66] It was not long after associate deputy minister positions came into fashion that the new associate assistant deputy minister position was also created.

In March 2011 there were more than 6,000 public servants in the executive group, the senior management group that lies between the deputy minister and associate deputy minister levels and the mid-level managers and the working levels.[67] In 2000, there were 3,293 in the executive group.[68] It will be recalled that the Treasury Board, once again borrowing a page from the private sector, announced with great fanfare in 1989 that it was launching a new initiative to "cut executive-level jobs in a bid to improve morale and operations." It was concerned that the executive group had grown to 2,562 members and argued that "if you take a whole layer out of the management pyramid, then the managers below automatically gain greater control over operations."[69] The initiative failed badly, but its failure has never been mentioned in the numerous performance evaluation reports submitted annually to Parliament.

Officials in central agencies and line departments readily recognize that classification creep is widespread in the federal government. It has mostly benefited Ottawa-based officials, rather than front-line program managers and workers – the music teacher type.[70] It is now relatively easy for an incumbent to rationalize his or her qualification to a higher level. As one official observed, the "personnel system has been transformed into a personal system." He argued that the government-wide wage freeze imposed during the mid-1990s forced deputy ministers to find other ways to award their more senior officials with pay increases, and reclassification was one way of doing so. He added, "We did what we had to do to manage the organization, and reclassifying some senior positions was the price to pay to keep things going and to get things done."[71] Job reclassifications are now relatively easy to secure by having departments hire the right consultant to do the necessary paperwork.

It is also a great deal easier for a deputy minister to agree to a reclassification than to deny it. The deputy minister can no longer blame the Treasury Board for turning down a reclassification request, given that authority now lies in his or her own hands. No market discipline influences the decision, and there is little advantage in saying no. But there are plenty of reasons for saying yes – not least, keeping senior officials happy. Deputy ministers are very busy individuals, and they would much sooner spend their energy on more pressing and difficult issues than saying no to a reclassification request. Saying yes means that someone else will look after the paperwork – again, likely an outside consultant – and a happier management team will result; saying no could mean an unhappy senior manager and possibly a need to initiate staffing action if the disgruntled official decides to go elsewhere.

With less control from the Treasury Board, we now know that travel, professional services contracts (consultants), and professional development and training budgets increased at a much faster rate than program spending. Ralph Heintzman, who had a direct hand in shaping and drafting the Tait Report on public service values and ethics, published in 1996, was deeply concerned when the Treasury Board decided in the mid-1980s to let public servants collect frequent flyer points and loyalty points from hotels when on official travel.[72] He argued that public servants should never be placed in a position to be able to promote their self-interest as government employees. However, letting the manager manage and the fact that private sector employees could collect points won the day for public servants.

Management coaching came into fashion in the private sector in the 1980s and has since grown in scope. Management coaching, it is argued, helps both the individual manager and the organization to cope better with today's volatile marketplace and fast-changing global economy. It is now a $2 billion per annum industry and even has spawned a new international journal.[73] Before long, "coaching and mentoring" also came into fashion in the federal public service. Management consultants, many of them former senior federal public servants, charge between $1,800 and $2,000 a day to coach public servants in the executive group on their career prospects and management style.[74]

It is easy to appreciate that a private firm has a much better chance of assessing the impact of coaching on the individual manager and on the firm's bottom line than it is on a government department. It should be relatively simple to establish, after the fact, the input cost of coaching in the federal government through the financial information system. But how could one possibly determine whether coaching had improved a department, a unit, or even a manager's performance, given that so many variables determine output and performance in the public sector? No report has been submitted to Parliament on the cost of management coaching and its impact.

The Crank Does Not Measure Up

Program and performance evaluation have never measured up to expectations. Looking back, it is hard to understand why a senior deputy minister felt the need to reassure politicians that they would still be making key political and program decisions after program budgeting had replaced line-item budgeting. Some forty years after program budgeting took over, even its fans are on the defensive. In a report to the World Bank on Canada's experiences with program evaluation, Robert Lahey concluded, "There is sometimes a tendency to adopt unrealistic expectations when considering what evaluation and performance monitoring can deliver on, for example, in satisfying a political need. While monitoring and evaluation (M and E) should serve an important place in public sector management, the expectations about how and when M and E can be used and what it can initially deliver on need to be tempered by reality, and generally remain modest."[75] Yet at the urging of the Office of the Auditor General, the Treasury Board Secretariat continues to promote program evaluation activities in departments and to earmark more resources to them. An increasing number of program evaluations are produced every year with little visible effect on program spending. One is reminded here of a line from the operetta *Iolanthe*: "They did nothing in particular, and did it very well."

The shift from line-item budgeting (with its emphasis on input costs) to program budgeting (with its emphasis on program evaluation), combined with the move to make public sector management look like that in the private sector, has come at an important cost to taxpayers. Importing private sector management vocabulary to government is the easy part. The much more difficult part is to generate inside government the kind of market discipline that the private sector has to operate in. The findings of a McKinsey and Company survey comparing the public sector to the private sector, carried out in the United States, sounds familiar in Ottawa. The survey reports that only 40 percent of public sector respondents agree that the government has a robust performance management system (compared with 64 percent in the private sector) and only 38 percent of public sector respondents agree or strongly agree that their agencies hold challenging reviews to evaluate performance against plans (compared with 56 percent in the private sector).[76]

Why, then, is a veritable army of consultants kept busy turning cranks that are not attached to anything and are tied to the expenditure budget only by adding to its cost? As noted, two individuals in Ottawa have the power or influence to challenge the usefulness of program evaluation: the prime minister and the clerk of the privy council. And as already noted on numerous occasions, they are extremely busy people with demanding agendas; they see little merit in doing battle with the auditor general or in meddling with program evaluation activities. The prime minister and the clerk always have ninety-nine problems on their plate, and as columnist Stephen Maher wrote, "money isn't one of them," whereas private sector managers have to keep a constant eye on revenues, expenditures, and the bottom line.[77]

Turning over more and more management authority to departmental deputy ministers and their senior officials was not without a cost, as we have seen. How are they held accountable? The answer: they have their departments produce more and more performance reports while making certain that their departmental actions do not draw negative media attention to them or their ministers. Does public choice theory provide an explanation? To be sure, public servants in evaluation units and their consultants will happily keep busy because it is in their economic interest to do so. But it does not tell the whole story. Institutionalism and path dependency provide an equally convincing explanation. The failure of New Public Management and the notion that it is possible to make the public sector look like the private sector provides yet another answer.

What about the Herman Finer/Carl Friedrich debate on accountability as outlined in chapter 1? That chapter suggested that Finer had it right – accountability in the public sector is best assured by putting in place detailed rules, controls, regulations, and sanctions. As we have shown in the preceding pages, government is unlike the private sector in a great many ways, and one must therefore rely on controls and hierarchy to promote accountability and a parsimonious culture in government operations.

In the next chapter, we look at the public service as an institution, how public servants fare in relations to others, including the private sector.

8

The Public Service: The Ambivalent Institution

A former employee of the Public Service Commission told me that when he worked there in the 1970s, one of the roles of the public service was to be a model for private sector firms and other organizations on how to deal with employees.[1] Indeed, a number of Treasury Board documents attest that the goal was for the federal public service to "set an example as an enlightened employer."[2] The objective was to establish high standards in employee benefits so that others would strive to follow suit. Things are different today. For one thing, the global economy has forced the private sector to heed competition in other countries rather than just in its own, let alone in the public sector, for guidance on dealing with employees. As a result, many private sector employees are asking why public servants should enjoy more generous benefits than themselves. As well, since governments throughout the Western world are struggling with stubborn deficits, some observers as well as politicians are looking to the public service to generate savings.[3]

The purpose of this chapter is to look at the state of the Canadian public service, its costs, and its role in the government's expenditure budget. One of many recent reviews of the public service reports that "the Canadian public often thinks of government as too complicated and worries that it has become politicized, self-interested and process-oriented."[4] Some thirty years after New Public Management came into vogue, government bureaucracies throughout the Western world are still under attack as too expensive and too lethargic.[5] Things look different from inside government. Peter DeVries, one-time director of fiscal policy in the Department of Finance, maintains that there is not "a lot of slush money sitting in the system because departments' budgets have been strained over the years."[6] Who has it right? This chapter seeks to answer this question and to understand what motivates public servants and their decisions.

Size Matters

There are various sources (e.g., Statistics Canada, the Treasury Board Secretariat, and the Public Service Commission) that report on the size of the Canadian public service. There is also more than one way to establish size. First, there is the core public administration, including separate employees for which the Treasury Board is the employer; second is the broader public service that includes crown corporations, military personnel, the RCMP, and other entities not included in schedules 1, 4, and 5 of the Financial Administration Act.[7] Under the latter, employment in 2010 stood at 420,685, an increase of 5,288 from the previous year. Close to one in three employees in this category works in the Ottawa-Gatineau area. Statistics Canada reports that this proportion has been on the increase since the 1990s, when it was roughly one in four. The federal government employs nearly 20 percent of the total Ottawa-Gatineau workforce.[8]

Under the core public administration category, the federal government employs 283,000 public servants, 6,784 in the executive category, 45 deputy ministers, and 32 associate deputy ministers.[9] This information is provided by the clerk of the privy council in his annual report to the prime minister on the public service, as well as by the Public Service Commission in its annual report. The reports provide a fairly complete demographic breakdown of the federal public service in terms of the number of employees, average age, years of experience, mobility, employee types (i.e., intermediate and term), official languages, visible minorities, and gender. The clerk's annual report says nothing, however, about employment in Ottawa-Gatineau versus the regions, nor does it report on the number of public servants employed in oversight functions or in the preparation of various evaluation and performance reports. It also makes no reference to Ottawa-based staff hired on contract, which represents lucrative business opportunities for local consulting firms. One firm "secured more than $124 million in billings in 2011 – easily triple the firm's federal business since the late 1990s."[10]

The Public Service Commission does provide a regional breakdown. In March 2011, it counted 216,709 public servants in its universe, an increase of 664 from the previous year. Of these, 94,478 were in the Ottawa-Gatineau or the National Capital Region (NCR), an increase of 1,476 from the previous year. This suggests that the other regions lost public servants to the NCR. It also reveals that 43.6 percent of federal public servants work in the NCR, a substantial increase over the past thirty years.[11] The Harper 2012 budget pledged to look more to Ottawa-Gatineau than other regions in eliminating 19,200 federal public service jobs, though early indications are not promising.[12]

It is interesting to note that in the early 1980s, before New Public Management (NPM) came into fashion, only about 30 percent of federal public servants worked in the NCR.[13] Most front-line managers and workers (music teacher types) work in the region, not in Ottawa itself. It is also interesting to note that the Department of Finance saw an increase of five employees from the previous year (from 797 to 802), that the Privy Council Office had an increase of 19 (from 867 to 886), and the Treasury Board Secretariat an increase of 79 (from 2,066 to 2,145).[14]

To sum up, since the arrival of NPM and the consequent push for the public sector to emulate the private sector, central agencies have grown, more public servants work in the Ottawa-Gatineau region, management layers have been added to line departments, including such positions as associate deputy ministers, and officers of Parliament have also grown in number and their offices have grown in size. One would be hard-pressed to see how all this could have been the result of adopting private sector management practices.

What Does It Do?

The Canadian public service performs a wide variety of activities. For the most senior public servants, their institution's most important responsibility is to provide policy advice to the prime minister and to ministers. They are expected to offer frank advice to politicians, free of fear or favour. They assist or support ministers in their dealings with Parliament, the media, and the public. They manage and deliver a wide range of services and manage a regulatory regime. Finally, public servants act as a check against political abuse; they should always ensure that ministers act within the statutes – and some statutes delegate decision authority directly to public servants. In addition, deputy ministers can now be called before parliamentary committees to answer for their decisions as accounting officers.[15]

When senior public servants speak out about their institution, they invariably highlight its role in delivering services to the public.[16] Kevin Lynch urged readers to "think" about the "concept of service excellence" in the Passport Office in his 2009 annual report to the prime minister.[17] In the first annual report, in 1992, Paul Tellier wrote about doing "business" differently, "to refocus efforts on service" and the "thousands of different programs and services provided by the federal government."[18] Mel Cappe, in the 2002 seventh annual report to the prime minister, wrote about how "fortunate" Canadians "are to have a federal public service to deliver service of the highest quality."[19] Senior government officials stress the importance of delivering "direct services to citizens such as veterans' benefits, unemployment insurance, passports, parks, ports and small craft harbours, navigational aids, search and rescue, regional and industrial and old age pensions."[20] Similarly, public sector unions, when opposing cuts in the public service, invariably refer to food inspectors, public health specialists, search and rescue workers, and the employees who deliver pension cheques to senior citizens.[21] These are all front-line service-delivery activities.

Senior public servants, from the clerk to deputy ministers, make every effort to brand the public service as a service-delivery institution. In their annual reports, they do not deal with the substantial shift of human resources away from the front lines to Ottawa, and away from actually delivering services to the management of oversight functions. Nor do they explain the rise in the number of management layers in Ottawa and the number of policy coordination and liaison units, or the level of financial resources earmarked to the various evaluation units, or the contributions that new oversight units make to service delivery. As Wayne Wouters recently wrote, "We have lost momentum ... Our vertical department-by-department approach to service delivery is more than just inefficient – it is failing to meet Canadians' expectations."[22]

Classification creep and the establishment of new "associate" positions are an Ottawa head-office phenomenon. But that is not all. A survey carried out by the Public Sector Commission reveals that 60 percent of the respondents from the National Capital Region reported that they had been promoted during the past five years, compared with only 48 percent for "all other regions."[23] Front-line managers and workers (the music teacher type) do not enjoy the same opportunities for promotions as their Ottawa-based counterparts. The evaluation and performance evaluation industry is also an Ottawa head-office function. Little has changed for front-line managers and their staff at the point of program delivery – other than having to respond to an increasing number of requests for information.

The Public Service: Still Showing the Way?

Despite sustained measures to introduce private sector management practices to government, the public service continues to strive to show the way as an ideal employer. It still leads in a number of areas, and both senior government officials and public sector unions take great pride in underlining this fact. The Treasury Board Secretariat makes it clear that "employment equity contributes to a strong and sustainable Public Service of Canada by ensuring that the workforce reflects the rich diversity of Canada's population. The achievement of employment equity continues to be an objective of the Public Service."[24] The federal public service outperforms the private sector in all areas of employment equity. Kevin Lynch, the clerk of the privy council, stressed its importance in 2009 – hardly the first clerk to do so – by making it a key component of the 2009–10 Public Service Renewal Plan. He insisted that managers had to produce strategies to address the concerns of employment equity groups and added that "overall levels of visible minority group representation among post-secondary recruits "were to exceed workforce availability (WFA)."[25]

The Employment Equity Act requires the Public Service to monitor and promote the "representativeness" of its workforce and provides for compliance audits.[26] The legislation identifies four groups: women, Aboriginal peoples, persons with disabilities, and visible minorities. The government reported that as of 31 March 2010, women comprised 54.8 percent of the core public administration, a marginal increase from the previous year at 54.7 percent. This representation level was above the WFA for women (52.3 percent). Aboriginal peoples made up 4.6 percent of the core public administration, a marginal increase from the previous year, at 4.5 percent; this representation level was above the WFA for Aboriginal peoples (3.0 percent). The representation of persons with disabilities was at 5.7 percent, a slight decrease from the previous year, at 5.9 percent, but still above the WFA for this group (4.9 percent). The representation of visible minorities remained below the WFA of 12.4 percent for this group, though it experienced the largest gain of the four designated groups, an increase from 9.8 percent in 2008–09 to 10.7 percent in 2009–10.[27]

Senior public servants also take pride in the public service's ability to attract both francophones and anglophones and to serve Canadians in both official languages. In its annual report on official languages for 2009–10, the Treasury Board reported that 31.4 percent of employees in the "core public administration" were francophones, while 68.6 percent were anglophones, and that 23.8 percent of francophones were employed in federal government institutions which were not part of the core public administration, compared with 76.2 percent for anglophones. In 1978, 24.7 percent of positions in the core public administration had a bilingual requirement, compared with 41 percent in 2010. This is not to suggest that all incumbents in bilingual-designated positions meet language requirements (some

92 percent of incumbents met language requirements in 2010).[28] The merit principle had to be adjusted over the years to accommodate both employment equity objectives and the Official Languages Act.

The Employment Equity Act also applies to federally regulated private sector employers, which include crown corporations, the Canadian Forces, and the Royal Canadian Mounted Police, as well as federal contractors with over 100 employees. It is estimated that about 10 percent of the Canadian workforce is covered by the legislation.[29] The legislation does not apply to the great majority of retailers and manufacturing firms. In addition, when it applies to private sector firms, the requirements are not as demanding as they are for federal government departments and agencies. The legislation requires designated employers to identify and eliminate barriers for targeted employment groups. However, private sector firms do not have to contend with a proactive Treasury Board Secretariat or with the clerk of the privy council who issues directives, establishes objectives, and monitors performance.

Emulating the Private Sector: Up to a Point

It is a rare document indeed in which the Privy Council Office or the Treasury Board Secretariat does not employ a business-inspired vocabulary when dealing with management practices in government. Like deputy ministers, they refer to their "lines of business," their "business plans," and their "bottom line." Starting at the very top, with the clerk of the privy council, we increasingly hear about the "business of government" and "integrated business plans."[30] They are not alone. In its fifth annual report, the Prime Minister's Advisory Committee on the Public Service, co-chaired by former clerk Paul Tellier and former cabinet minister David Emerson, employed the word "business" on fourteen occasions in their eleven-page report. Among other things, the committee urged the public service to "transform the way it does business," arguing that the "current business model of fragmented administrative services is inefficient and costly" and that government operates in "a long-cycle business."[31] In its sixth annual report, the committee urged the government to pursue "a new business model."[32]

What about pay, compensation, and other employee benefits? How do public sector employees compare with their private sector counterparts? Much has been written in recent years about the benefits that government employees enjoy. Some politicians, even on the government side, have raised concerns about generous pension plans, while public sector unions report that their members are increasingly worried about government intentions and the apparent desire to direct its "deficit-fighting plan" directly at public servants.[33]

Private sector lobby groups and organizations such as the Canadian Federation of Independent Business and the Chamber of Commerce continue to make the case that their members are finding it difficult to attract employees because of overly generous benefits in the public sector.[34] Senior public servants, meanwhile, continue to insist that public servants join the institution to serve their country, not to make money.[35] Frank Graves, head of EKOS which has carried numerous public opinion surveys for federal government departments and central agencies, disagrees. He maintains that "the public service attracts those looking for a safe harbour and the government has provided the ultimate secure job if you can get it."[36]

In 2004, the Treasury Board launched an ambitious review of federal government "public sector compensation and comparability."[37] The purpose, at least in part, was to respond to "recent external studies about the comparability of federal compensation to that paid for similar work in the Canadian private sector" and claims that "there was a significant and growing premium in favour of the federal public sector."[38] The study was completed in 2007 and was only made public after requests were made for it under the access to information legislation.[39] On releasing the study, the Treasury Board stressed that it did not represent either the policy or the views of the Treasury Board, adding in bold letters: "This report is in no way a statement of Treasury Board or Government views on federal public sector compensation."[40] The government never explained why it wished to distance itself from a report that provides factual information on pay and compensation.

The study begins by reminding the reader that public servants carry out a diversity of activities, "from operating icebreakers in the high Arctic to inspecting aircraft, from protecting our borders, from delivering employment insurance and pension cheques to issuing passports, from geological research in the field to preserving historic sites."[41] Reminiscent of speeches and reports by senior public servants, nothing is said about the public servants who work in Ottawa in policy, coordination, liaison, and coordination units; and like other federal government reports dealing with management, it refers on a number of occasions to government departments and public servants "achieving their business purposes."[42]

The report is ambitious in that it looks at the core public service and at separate employers or departments that have legal authority to manage their own human resources regime: the Canadian Forces, the RCMP, and such groups as federally appointed judges, parliamentarians, employees of Parliament, and ministerial staff. The report's scope was detailed. It reviewed salaries and wages, performance pay, recruitment and retention allowances, other allowances and premiums, overtime, retroactive payments, pensions, employees' life and disability insurance premiums, employee payments for health and dental plans, and employee contributions to statutory programs (Canadian Pension Plan, Quebec Pension Plan, and Employment Insurance; severance pay; leave usage and cash-outs of unused leave entitlements).[43]

The point of reference is 2002–03, and it provides a cost breakdown of the following: employer contributions to pensions plans, which amounted to $1.79 billion in that year for the core public service; for the separate employer category, $470 million, of which the employer paid 74 percent of the costs and employees 26 percent (I note that the employee percentage has gone up since 2002–03). The government, meanwhile, contributed 84 percent of costs related to the pension plans for parliamentarians and federally appointed judges. Life and disability insurance plans cost taxpayers $200 million for both the core public service and separate employers. The government also bears the full cost for health (for costs not covered by Medicare) and dental plans for current employees and their dependents; the costs for 2002–03 amounted to $280 million. Retired public servants and their dependents also participate in the Public Service Dental Care Plan and in a separate Pensioners' Dental Plans; the government contributed $185 million on behalf of pensioners for health and dental coverage, while pensioners paid about $115 million.

The report reveals that public servants in the core public service used a total of 7.74 million days of leave in 2002–03, which included statutory holidays. This amounted to 41.2 leave days per employee, consisting of 17.3 vacation leave per employee, 8.3 sick leave, and 1.6 family-related leave. Payments for severance amounted to $88 million, while for separate employees, severance was $33 million. The government, as we have seen, offers performance pay for managers. Performance pay in the core public service for managers amounted to $32 million. Over 90 percent of the managers received performance pay in 2002–03. In the same year, about 6,700 employees in the core public service alone were reclassified to a higher position, with higher pay.[44]

The introduction of collective bargaining had a profound impact on pay and other compensations in the federal public service, as can be imagined. Public service salaries, at the turn of the last century, rose by about only half of the national cost-of-living increases. The guiding principle was that salaries for public servants should be fair and allow for "the maintenance of a standard of living that would make for the good of society" and be fair to taxpayers in that "compensation should not materially exceed that paid for similar services by enlightened employees in the general industrial and commercial world." In 1932, before the arrival of public sector unions, salaries for public servants had been reduced by 10 percent "generally," in view of the Great Depression and the loss of jobs and salaries in the private sector.[45]

Things changed in the aftermath of the Second World War. The public service grew in response to the war effort and a more interventionist public sector in the economy. In 1946 a royal commission – the Gordon Commission – was established to look at administrative classifications in the public service, and a year later the government set up the Pay Research Bureau to provide "objective information on compensation and working conditions in government, business and industry."[46]

Collective bargaining reached the public sector in the 1960s. In March 1967, labour-management relations in the Canadian government entered a new era with the passing of the Public Service Staff Relations Act, which established for federal public servants collective bargaining that sought to duplicate employer-employee relations in the private sector.[47] A capacity to compare with other sectors was therefore needed in order to establish salary levels and compensation packages. A background paper, prepared for the implementation of collective bargaining, made the case that one can "envisage a need for government leadership in areas such as working conditions, employee relations, or non-wage benefits."[48] But, the document went on to argue that, under collective bargaining, the "federal government, as an employer, would not be a pace-setter – would not lead the private sector on the total value of all elements of compensation for comparable work."[49]

The concept of "comparability" ran into problems from the very beginning. TBS officials wrote, ten years after collective bargaining was introduced, that "there have never been settlements or arbitral awards that have not provided increases to rates of pay regardless of the comparability situation."[50] A 2007 review added, "With the failure of the Government either to enlist the unions' cooperation in implementing the total compensation comparability approach, or to give itself the legislative tools to apply it directly, the state of affairs in the real world of salary determination" described above would persist.[51] The Pay Research Bureau was cut in 1992 after thirty-five years of operations. It was felt that the bureau did not incorporate a sufficiently broad sample of non-government organizations –

focusing only on large unionized firms – to provide an accurate comparison of the public and private sectors.[52]

The Treasury Board report makes the point that there are only three ways to determine compensation: one party decides unilaterally; the parties agree; or a third party decides. Prior to collective bargaining, the government determined compensation, with some input from employees' associations. Today, compensation is determined through bargaining with certified unions. Governments of all stripes have been reluctant to resort to legislation to settle disputes, leaving it essentially to trial by combat to determine compensation.[53]

The Treasury Board report argues that trial by combat may suit the private sector, but it is less certain about the public sector. It points out that "excessive compensation outcomes can threaten the size or even the survival of a private company, necessarily placing a constraint on union demands. In the public sector there is no such economic brake on compensation outcomes, at least not in the short term, especially for relatively small groups of employees. One may ask whether it is reasonable to pay public employees relatively high compensation simply because they may be able to translate their privileged role in providing essential services to the public into a means to force generous collective agreements."[54] Yvon Tarte, chairperson of the Public Service Staff Relations Board, had a similar view. In a speech to the 1999 National Joint Council Seminar, he argued, "The strike method of dispute resolution in the public sector does not have the same foundation as it does in the private sector. In 1967, Jake Finkelman, the father of labour relations in the federal public service, thought long and hard and hesitated before being convinced to accept and recommend conciliation/strike as a method of dispute resolution for the federal Public Service. Several years later he expressed the view that, given the opportunity, he would not go down that road again."[55]

The Treasury Board reports that some observers have a simplistic notion of compensation in claiming that the government should "simply pay" public servants "what the private sector pays for the same work. The argument for this position is that the private sector salaries and wages are subject to the discipline of the market. Pay too much, and your business may not last." The problem, the report explained, is that "many government jobs have few direct analogues in the private sector and policy and other considerations can drive the federal government away from the market norms." It adds that "most salaries and other compensation terms are determined directly or indirectly through collective bargaining" and, further, "many see the federal Government's ability to pay as virtually unlimited."[56]

As already noted, the Treasury Board Secretariat and senior public servants have transformed the management vocabulary in government from that of public administration to one inspired by the private sector. Yet they readily admit that many government jobs have few direct equals in the private sector and that the discipline of the marketplace belongs only to the private sector.

Collective bargaining in the public sector is unlike bargaining in the private sector because the push and pull in government depends not on the bottom line – on how well the firm and its employees are doing in a competitive environment – but on political and policy considerations and on the state of public finances. There is a world of difference between the two situations. For one thing, the great majority of public servants work in a non-competitive field. For another, public sector managers and employees do not have financial incentives, as found in the private sector, to minimize labour costs. Then again, public sector managers have no incentive, no interest in moving their operations to jurisdictions with lower labour costs, as happens in the private sector. Public sector managers, from deputy ministers down to executive officer level 1 (typically at the director level), do not belong to a union and are not part of the collective bargaining process. However, they benefit from the process in that it is understood that managers should enjoy the same or better employee benefits than unionized public servants and that over time their salary levels need to be higher.

This is not to suggest that the employer is completely helpless. The employer has, on occasion, imposed wage controls (circa 1975) in the government's attempt to deal with inflation. In the mid-1990s, the employer went further and froze the salaries of public servants (a freeze in 1991, a two-year freeze in 1995). In 1996 the employer simply suspended collective bargaining. Public sector unions, for their part, maintain that it is unfair for the employer to have a dual role – as employer and legislator.[57] They argue that the government as employer can override the collective bargaining process when confronting difficult economic issues or a substantial drop in revenues. However, when the employer limits its role to the "employer" role, the process is one of push and pull, with public sector unions able to push against political and policy considerations, not against a bottom line or market forces or a competitive firm.[58]

Even when the employer turns to its legislative role and declares a freeze on salaries, it is still possible for public sector unions to secure other concessions. During the wage restraint period (circa 1992–99), public servants were able to gain better pension benefits while paying less of the cost. The Public Service Superannuation Act was amended in 1999 to reduce the salary-averaging period from six to five years. In addition, the Pensioners' Dental Services Plan was introduced in 2001. The Treasury Board's *Expenditure Review of Federal Public Sector Compensation* concluded that federal public employees "have done well relative to the Canadian private sector since the introduction of collective bargaining, even if there have been periods of arbitrary restraints, especially in the early and mid-1990s."[59]

Comparing Apples and Oranges

Collective bargaining influences salary levels for EX1, the first-level executive in government.[60] EX1 salary levels in turn influence those from EX2 to EX5 and also from DM1s (deputy minister level 1) to DM4s. By policy, there is a difference of 12 percent in the maximum of two adjacent levels, except between EX3 and EX4 and DM1 and DM2. The difference here is 15 percent each, because of the important moves or transitions into the assistant deputy minister level and to the rank of a full deputy minister in charge of a department or agency.[61]

Comparing public and private salaries is not without challenges and caveats, but there are studies that have sought to provide answers. The Treasury Board's *Expenditure Review of Federal Public Sector Compensation* looks at several attempts and provides its own comprehensive assessment. Some of the reviews – one by the Canadian Federation of Independent Business (CFIB) – argue that federal public servants earn considerably more than their private sector counterparts. The CFIB study, for instance, maintains that "federal employees in public administration enjoy a 15.1 percent wage premium over their private sector counterparts – 23.3 percent when non-wage benefits are included."[62] However, the Treasury Board study points to a number of flaws in the CFIB study, including the assumption that the "skill and experience requirements for the various occupations" in the two sectors are the same, which "is unlikely to be true."[63]

Morley Gunderson produced a report for the Treasury Board in 2003 which stated that public sector employees "invariably earn more than do employees in the private sector who have the same endowment of other wage-determining characteristics." The study looked to such characteristics as education, age, gender, length of tenure, and concluded that the federal government paid a "premium in 2003 ranging from 12.4 percent when controlling for collective bargaining coverage in 46 occupations to

23 percent when not controlling for collective agreement coverage or any occupation groups."[64]

The Treasury Board ended its review of these studies with this observation: "Our own analysis in this report confirms a relatively rapid and unprecedented rate of increase in real average salaries in the federal public sector. If federal public sector salaries continue to grow faster than salaries in the private sector or elsewhere in the economy, a substantial wage premium will certainly open up in favour of the public sector."[65] The review also made the point that it is difficult to compare salaries between the two sectors for a variety of reasons. Still, it argued that on salaries, positions at more junior levels up to the first executive level (EX1) in the federal government are superior to their counterparts in the private sector, but that executives at the more senior levels receive lower compensation than their peers in the private sector.[66] The study did not explain how one could establish a parallel between, say, the work of an assistant deputy minister in Aboriginal Affairs and Northern Development Canada with that of a vice-president at a major Canadian financial or manufacturing firm. It did, however, observe that a move towards "greater comparability for executives" between the public and private sectors requires "greater rigour in defining what are executives in the public sector. The essence of being an executive in the private sector is to be accountable for substantial results." It also reported that the government has met with little success in assessing performance.[67]

The Battle of Pensions

The media have in recent years taken a strong interest in Ottawa's pension plans for public servants, MPs, and judges, suggesting that the government is much more generous with its own employees than the private sector could ever be. The *Globe and Mail* summed up the issue: "There are 17.6 million Canadians in the work force, 11 million are without pension plans, 4 millions of these have registered retirement saving plans, 4.5 millions have defined benefit plans that guarantee pension income of retirees until they die and 55 percent of these are held by public sector employees."[68] In another article, the *Globe and Mail* reported that "84 percent of public service employees have pensions, 78 percent of these plans are gold plated defined benefit pensions, 25 percent of private sector workers have a pension plan, while 11 million workers or 60 percent of Canada's workers have no pension at all."[69]

Critics of the federal government's pension plans maintain that they are not sustainable and that taxpayers had to pick up the pieces when the 2008 financial meltdown pushed some private pension plans to the verge of collapse.[70] Malcolm Hamilton, a pension expert, argued in 2010 that the government had "a few options" to deal with the rising costs of federal pension plans: raise the retirement age; reduce indexing, which was pegged to inflation; and ask public servants to share half of the cost rather than paying 32 percent.[71] The C.D. Howe Institute recently claimed that the federal government's unfunded liabilities for its pension plans totalled $227 billion, or $70 billion more than reported in the Public Accounts.[72]

The Treasury Board study went straight to the point on pensions. It reported that the various public sector pension plans are "among the best in the country in terms of both their security and the value they provide to plan members. The features that offer retirement without penalty as early as age 55 with 30 years of service, or in some cases at an earlier age or with less service, are particularly attractive, especially when combined with full protection against inflation."[73]

There are several key issues with federal pension plans, one of which is employer contributions, which was addressed in part in 2005. The proportion of pension costs paid by public servants stood at only 25 percent in 2002–03, with the taxpayers picking up the rest. The government announced in July 2005 that it would phase in contribution increases so that in time employees would contribute 40 percent of the cost.[74] In March 2012 the government declared that employees would "eventually" contribute 50 percent of pension costs and that, starting in 2013, it would increase normal retirement age to 65 from 60. Other features were left intact, including pensions being fully indexed to inflation.[75] John Gordon, head of the Public Service Alliance of Canada, was quick to serve notice that public sector unions would challenge any government decision to move to a 50-50 employer-employee contribution ratio.[76] The federal public service pension is now portable, allowing public servants to transfer their entitlements to many external plans or to take out the cash. However, because the federal plan is so generous in relation to other plans, it is hardly possible to bring individuals with their entitlements into government "without subsidizing recruits."[77]

The public service pension plan holds a number of significant advantages. First, it allows for early retirement at age 55 for those with 30 years of service, or at age 60 with at least two years of service and, starting in 2013, at age 65. Second, the plan provides for 100 percent automatic full indexation of "all" benefits every year to compensate for inflation, as measured by the Consumer Price Index. This measure dates back to 1974 when the 2 percent cap introduced in 1970 was removed so that the plan would be fully indexed to inflation. Again, the goal is to move over time to a 50 percent employer/50 percent employee contribution ratio. Typically, private firms that actually support employee pension plans have a 50-50 cost-sharing ratio. Deputy ministers can earn pension credits up to 90 percent of their fully indexed pension for life after ten years of service in that position. In addition, they and associate deputy ministers who leave the public service before age 60 can continue contributing to their public service pension up to age 60.[78]

The Treasury Board study concluded that "it is evident the federal Public Service Pension Plan compares favourably to *major* public and private pension plans in Canada." It added that "the current service benefits are costing Treasury Board in real dollars expressed as a percentage of payroll much more than those earned under the vast majority of other defined benefit plans in the country."[79] It is important to stress that the comparison is only between the federal public service pension plan and pension plans from other large public sector organizations and large private firms – in other words, with 4.5 million Canadian workers out of 17.6 million in the workforce. Parliamentarians and federally appointed judges enjoy an even more generous pension plan.[80]

Federal public servants also enjoy a number of employee benefits that compare favourably with those found in other large organizations, though there are precious few studies that compare them with private firms. Benefits include the provision of vision and dental care, health practitioners such as physiotherapists, hospital room coverage, prescribed drugs, and life and disability insurance. These benefits are, for the most part, cost-shared with the employee, though financed mainly by the employer. In some cases, such as life and disability insurance for managers, the programs are entirely financed by the employer. For some of the benefits, the employee has to pay a deductible to access them. When the Public Service Dental Care Plan was implemented in 1987, contributions to the plan were set at 50/50 employer-employee. However, soon afterwards, an out-of-court settlement led the employer to assume 100 percent of the plan's costs.[81]

Still other employee benefits for federal public servants are generous from a comparative perspective. The federal public service has the following leave entitlements: 11 statutory holidays; new employees have 15 days annual leave, an entitlement that increases with years of service to a maximum of 30 days (six weeks) after 28 years; sick leave at 15 days per year, which one can accumulate; up to 5 days of family-related leave; and most unionized employees can take one day of personal leave and one day of voluntary service each year. Maternity and paternity leaves are granted in line with the Employment Insurance Act, with tops to 93 percent of regular earnings for a combined maximization duration of one year with no prior service requirement.[82] Until recently, parking was provided free for public service managers. However, the government announced that effective 1 July 2010, it would no longer "subsidize parking for employees." The change did not affect deputy ministers, who are given cars, drivers, and a parking spot.[83]

By comparison, in the finance and insurance sector, annual leave for salaried employees amounts to 11.5 days annually and goes up to 24.8 days after 20 years. About three-quarters of employees in the sector top up Employment Insurance payments for maternity leave (only 12 percent provided a top-up for parental leave), but half of them require a minimum of 36 weeks of prior service or employment with the firm.[84] The federal public service, meanwhile, tops up both maternity and parental leave to 93 percent of an employee's salary for a combined duration of up to one year, with no prior service required.[85]

Some employee benefits continue for public servants in retirement for both core public administration and separate employers. The Public Service Health Care Plan (PSHCP) and Public Service Dental Care Plan are made available to pensioners. The PSHCP supplements provide health care insurance in the areas of prescription drugs, hospital charges, health practitioner costs, and vision care. Some 45 percent of those covered by the program are pensioners. The employer contributed $163 million, while pensioners paid $73.8 million towards the costs of PSHCP for pensioners and their dependents in 2002–03.[86]

The Pensioners' Dental Services Plan (PDSP), meanwhile, is a voluntary plan established by the Treasury Board to provide public service pensioners and their eligible dependents with a plan for dental coverage. The plan was introduced in 2001 as one of several benefit improvements affecting pension, life insurance, and the death-benefit plans. PDSP is contributory; pensioners' benefits are paid on the same basis as those paid under the Public Service Dental Care Plan. The employer agreed at the outset to pay 60 percent of the cost of the plan.[87] It is not possible to compare pensioners' benefits between the federal public service and the private sector because the benefits are unique to the public sector. Very few employers outside the federal government provide the same level of health and dental care to retired employees as they do to their full-time staff.[88]

Until recently, all federal public servants were eligible for severance pay when they left the public service or retired. This amounted to between one half to a full week's pay for every year of service, up to a maximum of thirty weeks. An employee who is terminated for incompetence is also entitled to severance pay, after at least ten years of continuous employment. Payments for severance pay in 2002–03 amounted to nearly $90 million, of which $68 million were paid into a Registered Retirement Savings Plan. Severance pay, in the words of the Treasury Board study, is "mainly a public sector phenomenon"; accordingly, providing a comparative perspective between the public and private sectors is not possible.[89]

The government sought to eliminate severance pay in 2009–10. The Public Service Alliance of Canada (PSAC, the public sector union) has 172,000 members, the majority employed with the federal government, and it was the first union to agree to eliminate severance pay.[90] It agreed to do so in return for a 5.3 percent wage increase over three years. Under the agreement, existing public servants were paid for the severance they had already accumulated (they had a choice to get paid out at the time of the agreement or when they left the public service), but this was eliminated for new employees. Laid-off employees will still get severance, and PSAC negotiated increased payments for them. The government then imposed the same deal on its managers and other non-unionized workers. Treasury Board agreed to assume the full cost of severance payouts, rather than making departments find the money from their own budgets. PSAC told its members that it was able to limit job losses, secure a 1.5 percent increase in each of the next three years, and obtain other concessions in return for agreeing to eliminate severance pay at a time when the economy was "rocky."[91] The ratification vote among members was close, with only 52 percent of the clerical and administrative workers voting in favour.[92]

Another union, the Professional Institute of the Public Service of Canada (PIPSC), made it clear that it would oppose any government initiative to cut severance pay for its members. PIPSC's president declared, "My members aren't willing to sell the future for a wage increase now."[93] The head of the Association of Financial Officers declared, "They offered it and we considered it for all of 20 seconds. We're not interested, it is a really bad deal and to be honest, it's insulting."[94] In November 2011, PIPSC declared that it fully intended to "fight to keep our Severance Pay."[95]

One of the authors of the Treasury Board's *Expenditure Review of Federal Public Sector Compensation* updated some of the data in 2011. He reports that total personnel costs grew by 60 percent, from $23.2 billion in 2001–02 to $37.1 billion in 2009–10. Total per capita compensation for federal public servants stood at $92,000 in 2009–10. This does not include costs for office space, travel, computers, and training. He writes, "The main component shaping compensation spending are: budgetary allocations for salaries, transfers from non-salary to salary budgets, collective bargaining, salary determination directly by the Treasury Board, benefits negotiations, and policy decisions regarding the pension plan."[96] He concludes with the observation that "the scale of growth in the eleven years from 1998–99 to 2009–10 has been remarkable: forty percent more employees, more than a doubling of the total salary mass (+ 110 %), and a 52 % increase in the average salary invite questions about the rationale for these increases."[97]

The fastest-growing classification groups between 1995–96 and 2006–07 included the executive category (up 51 percent), financial management (46 percent), and economists and social scientists (98 percent). The groups that shrank the most included general services (a drop of 39 percent), ships' crew (minus 20 percent), and clerical and regulatory (minus 16 percent).

Shifting More Priorities by Stealth

The shift in classification groups in recent years has taken away employees from front-line offices and at the operational level but has added to the management, policy, and administrative categories.[98] The shift led to a slew of reclassifications, the highest proportion being in the secretarial and clerical groups. Stenographers (ST) were reclassified from the secretarial group to the clerical (CR) group, and those in the clerical group were reclassified to the administrative category (AS).

There have also been numerous reclassifications within occupational categories. In the personnel administration (PE) group, the lower levels (i.e., level 2) fell between 19 and 12 percent between 1991 and 2003, and level 3 fell from 42 percent to 29 percent. Levels 4 and 5 simply increased in proportion. In the case of the executive category, there was a decline at the EX1 level (from 65 percent of the group to 53 percent) but an increase at the EX2 level (from 18 to 25 percent) and at EX3 level (from 10 to 16 percent). It will be recalled that the Treasury Board delegated authority on classification to deputy ministers in line departments.

Staffing authority has also been delegated to line departments, with the Public Service Commission now essentially performing an audit function. Promotions can be awarded with or without competition. An individual can be reclassified or promoted if senior departmental officials decide that the incumbent's work has changed enough to warrant a reclassification. In brief, staffing and classification authorities have been delegated to deputy ministers and, in turn, to other senior departmental managers. Promotions in the form of reclassifications are now fairly common in the federal public service (over 35 percent of promotions are from reclassification).[99] No data is available on the number of positions that were declassified, or classified downwards. Anecdotal evidence suggests that this is rare.[100]

All of the above has increased spending, especially the wage bill. It has increased in recent years because new positions have been created in both the core public administration and the separate employer agencies. As we saw earlier, the number of senior managers (i.e., the executive category) jumped from 4,121 in 2007 to some 6,000 in 2011. The number of public servants under the Public Sector Employment Act went from 167,309 in 2002 to 216,709 in 2011.[101] The impact on the wage bill is considerable, given the reclassifications and the fact that the shift away from lower-paying categories to higher-salaried ones has been substantial. The number of federal public servants making, for example, $100,000 nearly doubled between 2007 and 2010.[102]

Finding the Money

Reclassifications, the establishment of more positions in the senior executive category, new positions, and the provision of employee benefits require new funding. There are two ways to fund overhead costs: political approval for new spending on new initiatives that require new positions; and public service managers transferring funds from non-salary to salary expenditures.

The Treasury Board study produced a detailed assessment of how increases in the public service salary mass were financed over a five-year period. Salaries in the core public service and separate employers increased by $4.2 billion over the five years, 1997–98 to 2002–03, from $8.2 billion to $12.4 billion. The funds came from three sources: an amount approved by the Treasury Board for implementing new policies or workload increases; Treasury Board transfers to departments to cover salary increases from collective bargaining; and other salary increases and internal transfers by departments from non-salary activities to salaries.[103] The study revealed that Treasury Board transfers for implementing new policies or workload increases amounted to between $1.3 and $1.6 billion. Treasury Board transfers to finance salary increases from collective bargaining, changes to the structure of the pay bands and other developments, including settlements to implement equal pay for work of equal value, came to $2.4 billion. Transfers initiated by line departments into salaries from other approved budgets for non-salary activities amounted to $1.2 billion.[104]

Transfers within departments during the year to pay for salary increases and reclassifications hold a number of implications. For one thing, they amend what the government and Parliament approved in the spending estimates. While ministers and Parliament will be able to see the shift in the estimates the following year, it is both after the fact and lost in the thousands of pages submitted to Parliament in the budget and spending estimates. In addition, senior public servants know full well that it is considerably easier to sell new spending on programs or high-profile initiatives to the prime minister and his courtiers than it is to sell them overhead costs or the reclassification of public servants.

Up to the early 1990s, Treasury Board imposed some central controls on the number of employees in departments and had a process in place to monitor reclassifications. Prior to the early 1980s, departments wishing to reclassify positions had to justify the request before the Treasury Board. Again, the call for letting managers manage, the introduction of New Public Management, and the desire to emulate private sector management led the Treasury Board to delegate authority over staffing and financial management to senior department officials. The delegation of authority gave senior managers a free hand to manage budgets and to transfer funds between non-salary and salary allocations. This, in turn, led to a shift in priorities and financial allocations within government by stealth.

Looking Back

This chapter makes the point that when it comes to management, the public and private sectors are unalike in a wide variety of ways. For one thing, collective bargaining in the two sectors operates in different worlds. The Treasury Board study, *Expenditure Review of Federal Public Sector Compensation*, goes to the heart of the matter. "The legitimate demand for continuity in the provision of public services, coupled with the absence of a 'bottom line' or market test of appropriate compensation, often makes it difficult for governments to resist settlements that might be unwarranted."[105] No government wants to deal with public service strikes in the months leading up to a general election.

Public sector unions, for the most part, oppose efforts to link salary to performance and productivity. Their argument is that "performance pay for individuals creates unhealthy tensions in the workplace, as destructive competition may emerge and some employees may be tempted to claim credit for what is in fact a group result." Try that for size in the private sector. Public sector unions also hold a "mistrust of the objectivity and fairness of public service managers in assessing performance and awarding any pay for performance fairly."[106]

Private sector unions no longer have the presence or influence that they once had. Indeed, most unionized workers are now found in the public sector. The private sector has seen the number of unionized workers drop from 26 percent in 1984 to 18 percent in 2003.[107] By 2010, only 14.1 workers in the private sector belonged to a union, while over 71 percent of public sector employees were members of a union.[108] The goal of private sector unions is, of course, to increase labour's share of income and to secure employee benefits. Union leaders, however, must always keep an eye on economic circumstances and adjust their demands, sometimes downward, as was the case recently in the auto sector. Private sector union demands cannot stray too far from market forces and competition for fear that investments and jobs will move to a lower-cost jurisdiction.[109] The rise of the global economy has had a profound effect on private sector unions and their workers.

Public sector unions have a very different agenda. The role of the shareholder and management are played by elected and appointed officials, governed by political, public policy goals. It is not too much of an exaggeration to write that the goal of public sector union leaders is to transfer income from those who do not work in the public sector to those who do.[110] Public sector unions hold distinct advantages over their private-sector counterparts. One senior Treasury Board Secretariat official explained: "Union representatives often go to opposition Members of Parliament and provide both documents and arguments against the closure of an office, reducing staff in their constituencies. Union representatives do not see it as a partisan political activity, they claim that they do it to defend the interests of their members."[111] Senior cabinet minister John Baird played his role to the full as an MP from Ottawa when he declared that the "Public Service won't see major cuts in the months leading up to the 2011 general election."[112] However, he has had little to say on the topic since the government was able to secure a majority mandate in the election and after Harper launched his 2011–12 strategic and operational review.

Study after study, including the exhaustive Treasury Board review on compensation, make the case that federal public servants, up to and including the EX1 category, enjoy equal or better pay and substantially more employee benefits than their private sector counterparts. It is important to note that the comparison is with relatively large firms. Senior private sector executives earn considerably more than their public sector counterparts. But how is one to compare the work, responsibility, and accountability requirements of a CEO in a large manufacturing firm with those of a line deputy minister in Ottawa?

A recurring theme in the public sector literature, including government reports, is that it is difficult to evaluate performance and that it is virtually impossible to establish a link between productivity improvement and collective bargaining. The Treasury Board compensation review acknowledged as much when it wrote that "measuring productivity meaningfully and reliably is inherently difficult," and it added that even when measuring productivity is possible, for example, when processing cheques, "the bargaining relationship is one where either economic or political power prevails."[113] In the private sector, firms live or die by market share and productivity improvements. The above may well explain why university and college graduates look to the federal government as an employer of choice. The government has recently had a surge of applications for federal jobs. In 2009, nearly 35,000 graduates applied, with some applying to several different occupational groups.[114]

Something Is Wrong

Although federal public servants enjoy better pay, better employee benefits, and security of tenure relative to their private sector counterparts, there are signs that not all is well. Surveys reveal a stubborn morale problem that will not go away, and the federal public service has in the past few years been plagued by "soaring disability claims."[115] According to a report from the PSAC, nearly 4,000 public servants – a record – filed disability claims in 2010. Mental health disorders, led by depression and anxiety, accounted for nearly 50 percent of the claims. In 1991, only 23.7 percent of the claims were for mental health disorders. Bill Wilkerson, co-founder of the Global Business and Economic Roundtable on Addiction and Mental Health, described the federal government workplace as "an emotionally airless environment" and an "almost uninhabitable workplace."[116] Statistics Canada reported in 2009 that "low morale was prevalent among executives and knowledge workers" and that in the federal public service "many employees felt that workplace conditions were not conducive to confidence in management, job satisfaction and career advancement."[117] A number of observers also have written about a "serious morale challenge" in the federal public service.[118]

How, then, does one reconcile better salaries, generous benefits, and relatively secure employment with growing morale problems and soaring disability claims, nearly half of which are linked to depression and anxiety? The next chapter seeks to answer this question.

Many of the theories and the findings from chapter 1 resonate in the present chapter, which, once again, makes the case that no single theory can explain how government decides and why. Students of public and rational choice theories have seen in this chapter plenty of evidence to suggest that public servants are budget-maximizing bureaucrats. Proponents of the principal-agent theory will also see evidence that their perspective explains how public sector managers have been able to transfer money to support public service salaries which was earmarked for other activities. Students of guardians and spenders in public finance could make the case that guardians lost too much of their influence when they delegated staffing, classification, and financial decision making to line departments. Lastly, the findings of this chapter again spoke directly to the Herman Finer/Carl Friedrich debate on accountability.

9

Management with a Capital M Never Interested Me Very Much

Arthur Kroeger, the dean of deputy ministers in his day, who served as deputy in six departments, often made it clear that his interest was in solving important policy issues and that general management and management theory never interested him "very much."[1] Deputy ministers who make it to the top still do so with policy skills, with an ability to move the government's agenda, a capacity to work with central agencies, and a willingness to fall on hand grenades, despite the arrival of New Public Management and the various management accountability processes now in place in Ottawa. It is indeed very rare for a public servant working on the front line, delivering programs or services in a local or regional office, to achieve the rank of deputy minister.

I chose five large operational and program departments – Aboriginal Affairs and Northern Development, Human Resources and Skills, National Defence, Public Works and Government Services, and Transport Canada – in late November 2011 to look at the background of their deputy ministers. All five had served in a senior position in the Privy Council Office shortly before their current positions or before their appointment as deputy minister in another department. One of the five had been with a provincial government before joining the federal public service. None had served in a regional office delivering front-line programs and services with the federal government. All had worked in policy units for most of their careers, and two had been assistant deputy ministers (Policy) in line departments.[2] Not one had served as chief financial officer or head of administration, finance, and human resources before making it into the deputy minister's ranks.

Serving in the Privy Council Office, where one can work closely with the clerk of the privy council and other members of the prime minister's court, has become the rite of passage to becoming a deputy minister.

The picture in the private sector is very different. The president-CEO of Scotiabank, Richard E. Waugh, began his career as a branch employee in Winnipeg in 1970.[3] Gerald McCaughey, president-CEO at the Canadian Imperial Bank of Commerce (CIBC), started his banking career as an account executive.[4] The same is true in the manufacturing sector. Dianne Craig, president-CEO of Ford Canada, started her career with Ford in an entry-level position in sales and marketing.[5] Paul L. Rooney, president-CEO of Manulife Financial, began his career with the firm as an actuarial student and worked his way up in sales, marketing, and was chief financial officer for Manulife before his CEO appointment.[6] Randy Eresman worked in several positions on the operational side of the business – more specifically in natural exploration, production, and the development of storage facility – before being appointed president-CEO of Encana.[7]

Old habits die hard in government, as students of institutionalism and path dependency have often observed. As already noted, introducing a private sector management vocabulary to government is the easy part. Changing a mind-set anchored in years of tradition and in a firmly entrenched bureaucratic culture is quite another matter. Public servants who wish to make it to the top know that the ability to avoid controversy and negative attention to their ministers and their departments, combined with a capacity to promote the policy preferences of the prime minister's court and to defend their department's interest – or, more often, that of central agencies in interdepartmental committee meetings – are what truly matters. In brief, the ability to work the "thick" process-oriented Ottawa system is what counts for the ambitious public servant. Management is still left to the less gifted, to those not able to make it to the top.[8]

General Lewis MacKenzie claims that the ability to work the Ottawa system has now become a major factor for promotion, even within the military: "Regrettably, the mastery of the Ottawa game became one of the criteria, if not the key criterion, for selection as the Chief of Defence Staff. This reinforced the opinion of field soldiers that senior field command was not the route to follow if one aspired to be CDS – a most unfortunate and uniquely Canadian development."[9] Working well with the centre of government and other departments requires wide experience in the system and an ability to think in political (albeit not necessarily partisan) terms and to navigate the upper echelons of the political-bureaucratic world.

Understanding Management in the Government of Canada

There are two management cultures at play in the federal government, and they view the world from vastly different perspectives. One looks up and is concerned primarily with the policy process, with ministers, central agencies, Question Period, and the senior public service. The other looks down and out – to citizens, clients, programs, program delivery, levels of services, and the managing of staff and financial resources. The *Discussion Paper on Values and Ethics in the Public Service* pointed to the differences between "managing up" and "managing down." It argued that managing up has as its focus "ministers and their needs or purposes" and constitutes "an essential element of our democratic system of government." But "it has its side effects. One of them is a preoccupation with managing up ... [which] ... obscures the importance of managing down." The problem is that "many senior public servants have made their careers because of their skills in managing up. They have been valued and promoted because they were adept at providing superiors with what they needed, in a timely fashion."[10]

The managing-up culture is preoccupied with process, with protecting the prime minister and ministers, and with managing the media and their gotcha bias. Its emphasis is on blame avoidance. The managing-up culture is the one that matters most, and it is expensive to operate. The managing-down culture has little choice but to tolerate the managing-up culture and try to work around it. To challenge the managing-up culture by pointing to its flaws, even internally, is a sure way for public servants to stunt their careers.

The Auditor General Made Me Do It

The Office of the Auditor General (OAG), together with the notion that one can import private sector practices to the public service, is responsible for many management practices introduced to government over the past thirty years or so. Revisions to the Auditor General Act in 1977 turned out to be a seminal development in the management of federal government operations. The revisions considerably expanded the role and responsibilities of the auditor general and the OAG. They would continue to look at the financial statements and to assess how public funds are spent but now would also have the mandate to examine "how well the government managed its affairs" and "how policies are implemented."[11]

Sharon Sutherland writes that the "shift lifted the Office of the Auditor General (OAG) from its position at the centre of a small control bureaucracy in the late 1970s to its contemporary position alongside and sometimes apparently above government, where it regulates government's management processes. This seismic shift that created the modern OAG gave the organization more money and ubiquity – it brought with it political power."[12] The OAG produces all manner of reports, labels them audits, and as Sutherland argues, "the media confer the status of revealed truth on all it writes." She adds that the "lion's share of the OAG budget, 60 percent ... is spent on discretionary–Value for Money studies that can be on literally any organizational or policy topic, past or future, conducted by any method."[13] The OAG and the country's large private sector accounting and consulting firms have, over the years, redefined the government's management agenda.

Pick any management measure introduced by the federal government since the 1980s and one can trace its origin either to the OAG or to private sector management thinking – more often than not, a combination of both. The idea that the internal audit function needed to be strengthened and showered with new funding came from the OAG. The idea that more and more resources needed to be earmarked for program evaluation continues to come from the OAG. The OAG, borrowing a page from the private sector, stressed the importance of integrated risk management. The Treasury Board Secretariat responded with a risk-management policy, and now line departments have units or an official at head office with a mandate to promote risk management.[14] The OAG has been a strong advocate of all manner of accountability requirements, including the Management Accountability Framework (MAF), and it monitors how well line departments and agencies are implementing them.

Neither the OAG nor the media ever bother to explain to Canadians that the above activities can never be as certain or as conclusive as financial audits. However, the activities do enable the OAG to contribute to policy debates and to participate in the making of public policy. The OAG has become a political actor, which may explain why it often informs the media of its findings first, rather than Parliament.[15]

Some observers doubt whether accountants have the capacity to carry out such tasks, since many government programs are the result of political judgment alone; others question whether it is appropriate for accountants to undertake value-for-money audits in government.[16] Certainly, the auditor general has made some sweeping statements that have raised the eyebrows of many in government, as in a recently expressed doubt as to whether the Department of Defence could successfully engage in a war effort. Defence specialists have to wonder how the auditor general and the "hordes" of accountants are in a position to make such an assertion. Moreover, they question whether it is the proper role of an auditor to make such a judgment. I recall reading a chapter on regional economic development programs that was lacking in both substance and insight.[17] It reads like the many typical consulting reports on regional development that federal departments have produced over the years. If one were to carry out a value-for-money audit of the work, one would conclude that it was not public money well spent.

It will be recalled that Sheila Fraser, when auditor general, became a media star after she reported on the sponsorship scandal in 2004; there was talk on a number of open-line shows of "Sheila Fraser for Prime Minister," and she was described as a "folk hero with the electorate."[18] The office has successfully created its own distinct voice to carry out its work, and in many ways it views Parliament as just another consumer of its reports. Let me note again an ironic fact that it was a *Globe and Mail* journalist, Daniel LeBlanc, who first exposed the sponsorship scandal. The OAG, with a staff of over 600, was not even aware of the financial improperties and maladministration until a journalist brought the fact to light.

By focusing its attention and resources on value-for-money audits and management reform, the OAG has, inadvertently or not, created a number of positions in government – all in the head offices of departments and agencies – and added considerably to the government's expenditure budget. There is now a well-staffed industry of officials working on various reporting requirements, new management processes, and program evaluations. Deputy ministers had found it necessary to put in place the human and financial resources needed to respond to the new reporting demands of the OAG, Treasury Board, and Office of the Comptroller General. This is not to suggest that senior public servants were enthusiastic about the new approach. Deputy ministers simply created new units, handing the steering wheel over to them with the message "Now, you drive; you respond to whatever information is being asked for, but make certain that you do not draw negative attention to the minister or the department."

Deputy ministers still prefer to focus on broad policy issues and on positioning their departments to gain more support from the centre of government. The market for such activities may not be as strong as it once was – evidenced-based policy advice is no longer as convincing to politicians as it used to be. The government's decision to go to outside consultants for advice on identifying spending cuts and – according to some sources – its decision to spend $2 billion to build new prisons, against the advice of current and former senior officials with Corrections Canada, speak to the new political realities in Ottawa.[19]

This of course follows on the political agenda that politicians had in mind in the 1980s when they considered that public servants had gained too much influence on policy and had neglected management for too long. This, in turn, led to the introduction of New Public Management measures in government. Some thirty years later, politicians continue to press for better management practices and for a greater control in setting the policy agenda.

Senior public servants, meanwhile, have been left to square the circle. They have had to adjust their contribution to policy making and, in the process, to transform public sector management so that it will increasingly look like private sector management, or at least give the appearance of doing so. On policy, they have demonstrated greater enthusiasm for the government's policy agenda than in years past. Peter Aucoin went to the heart of the matter in 2004, when he spoke about senior public servants' practice of "demonstrating enthusiasm for the government's agenda either as a tactic to advance their own personal career or in the mistaken notion that neutral public servants should all be, as one British scholar put it, 'promiscuously partisan,' that is, partisan to the government-of-the-day, but willing to change when a different party takes over."[20] Aucoin went on to argue that the pressures that have produced the politicization of government and public administration are "not likely to abate, let alone be reversed."[21] Colin Campbell also writes about the recent tendency of senior public servants to "resolutely associate" themselves with political leaders and their agenda to advance their careers.[22] They are more likely to support a government's agenda if they have served in various central agencies and departments than if they have served only in a single department or on the front line, delivering programs and services. A director-level official has this to say when I carried out consultations while working on this book: "The first day our deputy minister arrived in the department, he had this message for us: I am on very good terms with the prime minister and I fully intend on keeping it this way."[23]

The desire to have senior public servants wholeheartedly endorse a political agenda may well explain why the Harper government included a clause in its accountability bill to appoint "special advisers" to deputy ministers or place authority in the hands of the government of the day through an order-in-council, rather than through the Public Service Commission. Maria Barrados, former president of the Public Service Commission, estimates "that there are about 200 such advisers in government," which she finds unacceptable. She maintains that "it gives the government access to the bureaucracy that is inappropriate to me and violates the spirit and core of what the Public Service Commission is all about and supposed to do." She feared the further politicization of the public service, not in a politically partisan sense, but "in the sense of civil servants being too accommodating to their political masters."[24] This concern now appears to belong to a different era.

On management, senior public servants concluded that producing more evaluation and performance reports and responding to the OAG's latest fashion would somehow be seen as making public sector management look like that in the private sector. The result is that government departments are top heavy with overhead units producing all manner of reports, from risk management to evaluation and performance-pay schemes. One suspects, however, that many senior public servants would agree with the findings of Julian LeGrand on motivation in the public sector when he concluded that it is "difficult, if not impossible" to construct a viable measuring and monitoring system to indicate better performance.[25] No matter, it is in their interest to produce such reports and to respond to the wishes of the OAG and central agencies. No one in line departments is in a position to stand up and say that these costly initiatives are leading nowhere and that the notion that one can transform public sector management to look like that of the private sector is misguided.

Life in a Line Department

The Department of National Defence recently provided a revealing view of contemporary management in a government department. Lieutenant General Andrew Leslie led an exercise to review departmental operations to identify potential cost savings, which, he pointed out, entailed "an unprecedented level" of research.[26] Looking at the growing government deficit and the need to address it, he predicted that the government would expect DND to make significant savings. In brief, he saw no new money coming in for his department and anticipated that there would be strategic and operational reviews to reduce spending.

Leslie's "transformation" exercise looked at spending "trends" from 31 March 2004 to 31 March 2010. He determined that the department's "tail" (i.e., personnel in head office and in non-operational jobs) had grown by about 40 percent, while the "tooth" (i.e., personnel in operational and/or deployable jobs) had increased by 10 percent. In addition, he reported that consultants – some 5,000 people, many in Ottawa – had consumed about $2.7 billion annually and the number was growing. The executive or senior manager category had increased at a higher rate than lower-ranking personnel.[27]

Leslie's report speaks to management in a government department some twenty-five years after NPM came into fashion and after efforts had been introduced to implement private sector management. He points out that the guiding force and "most of the energy" in efforts to manage operations and to cut spending were focused on "keeping as much of the status quo as possible." He adds, "Everybody was treated the same way, and every subordinate organization within the layer collectively showed an equal amount of pain." He labels this as a flat tax approach and maintains that it results "in overhead staying much the same, while support to front-line deployable units is cut far more than originally forecasted."[28]

Leslie documents where growth in the department took place from 2004 to 2010. It did so mostly outside the front-line operational units. The number of people employed at headquarters grew four times faster than in front-line units, and the number of public servants employed in the National Capital Region "surged by 61 percent." He goes on to note that the "number of military and civilian personnel performing overhead functions … has increased disproportionately, even when allowances were made for new operational demand for manning the new organizational constructs established in 2005." The growth fed what Leslie described as "many layers of complex, bureaucratic processes that are counter-productive to efficiency and effectiveness."[29] Leslie reports that the 5,000 consultants mentioned above are employed on an ongoing basis, but that there is no clear "picture of the disposition of these people." He insists that the costs of the consultants should be reported as personnel costs.[30] Leslie urged the department to cut its travel budget by $22 million a year, which would serve to increase productivity. He pointed out that "domestic and international travels are both expanding and neither are managed in a coherent manner."[31] One would be hard-pressed to identify many private firms that would manage operations along the lines DND does.

Leslie experienced difficulty in producing his report. It was leaked by DND that he was meeting stiff resistance, and he was asked to stop examining the bureaucratic side of DND. Leslie said, "We have been told that this will be addressed in the future by development of institutional alignment options." He added that "even before the report was released, internal resistance to his recommendations was already crystallizing."[32]

The surge in employment at DND is not an isolated case. The Royal Canadian Mounted Police, for example, has seen staff at its head office in Ottawa doubled over the past ten years. It was revealed in November 2011 that there are now 4,569 people at the head office, compared with 2,247 in 2000, a 100 percent increase. The overall number of RCMP personnel has grown substantially in that period, but only by 50 percent. Head office staff now account for 15 percent of total RCMP personnel, up from 11 percent in 2000. Gaëtan Delisle, a retired staff sergeant, speaking on behalf of front-line police officers, put it very well when he said that "you have less people to do the work, and more people to report to."[33]

The Bigger Picture

The Public Service Commission tables annual reports that provide information on staffing. The commission's 2010–11 annual report reveals that the number of senior managers (the executive group) went from 4,121 in March 2007 to 5,102 in March 2011.[34] A Treasury Board official reported in the fall 2011 that the number was around 6,000, while a Treasury Board report in 2008–09 put the number at 5,364.[35]

The regions had substantially fewer promotions to the EX group than the Ottawa-Gatineau region did. Overall, the trend to locating more and more public servants at head offices in Ottawa continued. Though hiring into the public service declined in most parts of the country in 2010–11, the drop was much more pronounced in the regions (down over 17 percent) than in the National Capital Region (10 percent).[36] The Library of Parliament sought to update the percentage of jobs in the National Capital Region compared with the regions. It reported that in 2010, some 42 percent of federal public servants were located in the Ottawa-Gatineau region and that this proportion had shot up since the 1990s, when it was about 26 percent. By contrast, only 16 percent of federal public servants in the United States are in Washington; in the United Kingdom only 16.6 percent of public servants are in London, while 21.6 percent of France's public servants are located in the Île-de-France region of Paris.[37]

The Treasury Board Secretariat provides a breakdown of reclassifications for every department and agency from 2004 to today. I looked at five departments, ranging from a large department, Human Resources and Skills Development, to a small agency, the Atlantic Canada Opportunities Agency; the other three were Health, Fisheries and Oceans, and Agriculture and Agri-Food Canada. All five had a strong program and operations focus. I also looked at position reclassifications for two central agencies, the Privy Council Office and the Treasury Board Secretariat. In all cases, I looked at a twelve-month period, depending on the availability of the data, either from 1 April 2010 to 31 March 2011 or from 1 October 2010 to 30 September 2011.

Two reasons were given for the reclassifications – changes in duties and grievances. The Atlantic Canada Opportunities Agency had three reclassifications, all resulting from a change of duties: two in head offices and one in the Nova Scotia office. Agriculture and Agri-Food Canada reclassified 64 positions over the twelve-month period, all because of changes in duties. The majority of the reclassifications were in overhead functions – corporate services, information systems and 25 were in research. Fisheries and Oceans Canada, which has a strong regional presence and delivers a number of programs, reclassified 59 positions – 6 resulting from a grievance, one from departmental audit or monitoring, 18 from "incumbent oriented occupational group," and the rest from changes in duties; 20 of the 59 positions performed an overhead function – executive secretariat and financial, administration, or human resources functions.

Health Canada reclassified 122 positions over a twelve-month period, one due to a grievance, another for training development, and the rest because of changes in duties. Some 51 of the positions were performing overhead functions – evaluation, corporate services, a risk management official, policy coordination. Human Resources and Skills Development Canada, a large department with a strong regional presence, had, relatively speaking, a limited number of reclassifications over the twelve-month period from 1 October 2010 to the end of September 2011. The department reclassified only 13 positions, 2 as a result of grievances and the rest because of changes in duties; 4 of the positions performed overhead functions.

The Privy Council Office reclassified 12 positions from the first of July 2010 to 30 June 2011, all as a result of changes in duties of the incumbent. It is interesting to note that 3 of the reclassifications were in the senior executive category (EX), 2 of them to the category and one within the category but to a higher classification. The Treasury Board Secretariat reclassified 59 positions (a high number compared to the large operational departments noted above). The reasons for the reclassifications were unclear.[38]

The bulk of the reclassifications were for Ottawa-based officials and many are performing overhead-type functions. Few of the reclassifications were for front-line managers and their staff delivering programs and services. I could not find a single reclassification as a result of a change of duties at the regional level.

As already noted, deputy ministers now hold authority to reclassify positions and to hire consultants to prepare the paperwork to produce the reclassification. Until a few years ago, deputy ministers and senior departmental officials also had the authority to move funds from vote 5 (program resources) to vote 1 (operating expenses) to meet funding demands for reclassifications or establishing new positions.

Sense of Frugality

Gordon Robertson, a widely respected former clerk of the privy council and cabinet secretary, laments the loss of frugality in the federal government.[39] It is worth repeating J.L. Granatstein's point that senior public servants seventy years ago served "wearing suits that were shiny with use" in an era when a parsimonious culture permeated the public service.[40] Public servants then had to deal with a wide range of centrally prescribed rules and controls on staffing and financial resources. This was also a time when public servants had full confidence in their institution, and no one felt the need to borrow private sector management practices to improve government operations. As Granatstein said, public servants "of course wanted a comfortable salary, but almost all would have remained at their posts without it … They felt a duty to serve their country and its people. If that sounds trite and pious today, it is only because our age is more cynical."[41]

With a myriad of centrally prescribed rules and controls, senior public servants were free to focus on policy, to promote a major initiative, and to leave administrative matters to an administrative class. Central controls enabled them to tell their subordinates that they had the power only to recommend a reclassification or a staffing action and had no authority to move funds from a program vote to support overhead expenses from salaries, to hire consultants, or to fund international travel.

Delegation of authority since then has been accompanied with a requirement to produce one evaluation and performance assessment report after another. Managers have never been able to make results-based accountability work. Year after year, the auditor general points out that the capacity to measure performance in government departments is inadequate and urges that more resources and greater efforts be earmarked to that end. Year after year, the Treasury Board Secretariat makes the case that line departments need to do better at program evaluation. The Treasury Board now produces an annual report on the "Health of the Evaluation Function," and it introduced in 2007–08 a central funding initiative worth $10.7 million a year to increase government-wide allocation to evaluation functions. Its 2010 annual report pointed to several weaknesses, including the need to emphasize "the use of evaluations to support a broader range of decisions."[42] Yet year after year, the efforts still come up short. Other than the Treasury Board Secretariat and the Office of the Auditor General – which has done a very poor job at assessing its own performance or having independent, arm's-length evaluation of its performance carried out – it is not at all clear that there is a market for such performance evaluation reports.[43]

Members of Parliament have shown precious little interest in the reports. The former chair of the Public Accounts Committee explains that they are "lacking in credibility and objectivity and are basically self-serving and congratulatory fluff."[44] If there is one parliamentary committee that should have some interest in these reports, it is the Public Accounts Committee. The media, MPs, and voters also pay scant, if any, attention to the volumes and volumes of reports submitted to Parliament every year.

Management in Government Is about Blame Avoidance

Al Johnson, former deputy minister of health and secretary to the Treasury Board, described management in government as the "ability to expect the unexpected, to know that something, somewhere in the department, however small, can suddenly become a major problem that consumes your energy and that of your minister. The big issue will never get you, the small ones will. You go to work in the morning, thinking what could blow up today."[45] Notwithstanding the plethora of NPM measures introduced in recent years, deputy ministers still define their main responsibility as keeping their ministers out of political trouble and not bringing negative attention to the department. In brief, deputy ministers are in the business of not goofing up.

"Goofing up" can mean any number of things. If a deputy minister demonstrates a continuing inability to work with ministers, he or she is unlikely to remain as deputy for very long. But here, too, deputy ministers must learn to walk a fine line: they must "make their ministers look good" but also must make sure that their "ministers keep to the government's agenda."[46] Long-serving and successful deputy ministers know where to draw the line and when to ring the alarm bell and to whom. They inform the clerk of the privy council, with whom they work out a game plan to deal with "a rogue minister."[47]

Successful deputy ministers can manage accident-prone ministers or even turn around an error-prone department. The prime minister and the clerk always keep a watchful eye on ministers and make changes when necessary. If a minister and deputy are associated with ongoing problems highlighted in the media and raised in Question Period, one of them will go. In short, successful deputy ministers do not have the habit of losing ministers.

Today, the management of communications permeates every aspect of governance, from unveiling new policy initiatives to the most trivial of administrative matters. No issue, however small, can be wrapped in a communications strategy. Access to information legislation has inhibited the ability of deputy ministers to manage goof-ups.[48] This explains why I cannot recall seeing a single DPR, RPP, or MAF scorecard making the front pages of the *Globe and Mail* or *La Presse*. These are managed so that any potential negative attention has been removed.

Extravagant or wasteful spending does, however, grab the media's attention. The *Globe and Mail*, for example, reported that "Canadian taxpayers forked out almost $2 million, including more than $1,600 to remove a bed – to spruce up a luxury Muskoka resort for last year's G8 summit. The renovation included $500 to remove a small light fixture."[49] The information was obtained under access to information legislation. Taxpayers understand this, and so do politicians. A few months earlier, the *Globe and Mail* had reported that the Canadian Revenue Agency (CRA) had already spent $42,900 to help a dyslexic worker learn French. The article explained that CRA has 40,000 employees, but the agency's pursuit of second-language training for the individual could cost up to $171,600, with no assurance of success.[50] The department had a choice: support the individual's second-language training and deal with the media fallout or deny the training and deal with charges that it was unwilling to accommodate employees with learning disabilities. Private sector managers do not have to deal with such issues, nor do these issues ever appear in DPR, RPP, or MAF reports.

The media are constantly on the lookout for wasteful spending. The *Ottawa Citizen* reported in late 2009 that the Department of National Defence spends about $2 million a year on taxis for its employees in Ottawa.[51] A few months later, the *Citizen* ran an article reporting that the Department of Public Works paid $1,000 to remove a light switch and $2,000 to purchase two potted plants.[52] The *Globe and Mail* ran an article that federal public servants "are routinely filing millions of dollars in expenses including overtime and computers toward a construction project that doesn't exist."[53] The *Hill Times* ran a story reporting that the Privy Council Office had spent $1.6 million on a commission (the Public Appointments Commission) that did not exist.[54] It will be recalled that the government announced in March 2012 that it was doing away with the commission's secretariat.[55]

As every public sector manager knows full well, the above are not isolated cases. Robert Fonberg, the deputy minister of defence, had to make a decision when it was brought to his attention that renovations to the Nortel building, which the department had bought to house its personnel, would amount to over $600 million in addition to the $208 million the government paid to purchase it. DND had prepared a document that read: "Media, parliamentarians and Canadians will be focussed on the cost to taxpayers for the acquisition of the Campus and the subsequent retro-fit costs." In response, Fonberg emailed DND, "Why are we using the $623 million fit up cost? It is without context and a lightning rod." The cost was removed from all the public documents. When the story broke after an access to information request, Fonberg did not respond to an interview request.[56] By making sure that the costs were removed from the public documents, Fonberg was simply doing what deputy ministers do – he was trying to protect his minister and the department from public criticism. Fonberg had no way of knowing that an access to information request would follow. Removing the renovation cost had made sense. If nothing else, it would delay the problem to a day when perhaps his minister had moved on to another portfolio or when he himself had been assigned to another department.

Fonberg had to deal with the fallout of another access to information legislation when it was revealed in January 2012 that he had approved a $374,000 renovation to his executive suite of offices at a time when his department was dealing with Harper's strategic and operational reviews. Peter MacKay's office – MacKay was Fonberg's minister – sent an email to the media insisting that "the approval of these renovations rests with the Department of National Defence" and that the minister had nothing to add.[57]

Today's deputy ministers, unlike those under the old public administration when they usually stayed with the same department throughout their careers, now range through a "multiplicity" of departments before retirement. Indeed, some have up to five assignments as a deputy minister before leaving government. Gordon Osbaldeston, in his study of accountability in government, was highly critical of the short duration of deputy ministers in line departments, claiming that it made accountability more difficult.[58] The length of time a deputy minister stayed in one department between 1867 and 1967 was on average twelve years, but it fell to only three years between 1977 and 1987.[59]

C.E.S. Franks concluded that between 1996 and 2005 the length of time dropped still further, to 2.3 years. He reports that on 17 July 2006 (after thirteen years of uninterrupted Liberal rule), nine of the twenty-two serving deputy ministers had served six months or less in their current office.[60] More recently, two observers of government report that the "average length of time for current deputies is now only 19.4 months." They add that NHL coaches, "even under difficult leadership conditions they face, still have a longer average current tenure than deputy ministers."[61] Not only is this in contrast to the old public administration, but it is difficult to see how this practice could have been borrowed from best management practices in the private sector. Musical-chair management appears to be a federal government phenomenon, which leaves departments and agencies empty of institutional memory and with little capacity to mentor new recruits; and new recruits see their role models jumping from one opportunity to another.

Loyalty to Self

The Canadian literature reports that "a new breed of public servant has emerged with an ethos less oriented to public interest and frugality than towards career advancement and making a mark through bold plans and expenditures."[62] Public servants can no longer point to politicians to explain all problems of values and ethics in government. The Public Service Commission noted this development with deep concern. It reported that "public perceptions of the ethical standards of public servants are currently at their lowest point in seven years ... Many other professions were rated higher. For a public service striving for an exemplary reputation for integrity, these findings are troubling."[63] The clerk of the privy council wrote in the fourteenth annual report to the prime minister on the public service that "changing public attitudes toward government, coloured by high-profile cases, have tarnished the reputation of politicians and public servants alike."[64]

Introducing the business-management model did change some things in government, not always for the better. Greed may well have accompanied the model into government. Market forces, competition, and the bottom line can act as a check against greed in the private sector. But what about the public sector? Senior government officials now end their careers with extremely generous pensions. In Canada, as we saw, deputy ministers, after ten years in that position, enjoy an indexed pension set at 90 percent of their salaries, based on the average of their best five years. Under the special retirement allowance, deputy ministers are credited with two years of service for every year worked, to a maximum of ten years. The special allowance was introduced in 1988 because deputy ministers increasingly work in "a volatile environment" that does not "allow most of them to continue to normal retirement age." This view, however, has been challenged. The head of a civil service union, for example, recently argued that while deputy ministers may get shuffled around, "I don't know that I have ever heard of a deputy minister getting fired."[65] The emphasis is now on the individual and individual performance, however difficult this is to measure in the public sector. The result is that we have witnessed a shift to "self first, duty second" and away from "duty first, self second."

Deputy ministers no longer go quietly into retirement. Instead, they have opportunities to earn money – as consultants or lobbyists and on special government contracts – and a good number of them take these opportunities. Indeed, high-level experience in government has become a valuable qualification in the private sector, particularly with associations of various kinds and with government relations and lobbying offices in large national and multinational firms.[66]

The Office of the Auditor General identified a "values" problem in 1995. Far from a standard financial audit, the lead chapter in its 1996 report drew attention to "Ethics and Fraud Awareness in Government." The OAG based its findings on interviews with public servants and reported that "86 percent of public servants – 93 percent of senior managers – believe that their programs are administered ethically and 88 percent of public servants believe that their immediate supervisors are ethical."[67] No matter, the office saw things that needed fixing and called for an "Ethical Framework" and identified possible elements, including a statement of principles, leadership, and the role of individual public servants.[68] Government officials did what they usually do when challenged by the auditor general – they launched a review of their own, hired consultants to help, and introduced a process for departments and agencies to implement.[69]

In 1999 the government establish the Office of Values and Ethics in the Treasury Board Secretariat and appointed two deputy ministers as "co-champions" to promote them. Then, in 2003, the government issued a Statement of Public Service Values and Ethics, designed to "guide and support public servants in all their professional activities."[70] Three clerks of the privy council wrote about the importance of values and ethics in their annual reports to the prime minister on the public service.[71] All departments now have a unit or officials promoting values and ethics. However, the three clerks all went on to secure three of Canada's best ambassadorial appointments available: London, Paris, and Rome. None of them had any experience in foreign affairs, and all three were able to retain their senior deputy minister-level salaries while serving abroad. One former official at

Foreign Affairs observed that the appointment was a "classic case of do as I say, not as I do."[72]

Under the old public administration, there were no central agency offices and no units or officials in line departments promoting values and ethics. But there were role models showing the way. Long-serving public servants of that era included Clifford Clark, Robert Bryce, Escott Reid, Gordon Robertson, Norman Robertson, O.D. Skelton, and Graham Towers. They were widely respected, and no one would have believed that they needed a values and ethics framework to do the right thing and to think of duty first. There were also rigid rules to prevent administrative wrongdoing.

Public servants were career officials in the true sense, and they were there for the long haul. Long service was expected, and it provided a continuity in policy making that is not seen today. As Granatstein reports, "Robert Bryce's career extended from the end of the Depression into the 1980s, if one considers appointments and advisory roles."[73] Bryce was no exception.[74] Deputy ministers by and large retired quietly with their public service pension, happy in the knowledge that they had served their country away from the limelight. Trust in the government's ability to do the right thing was high.

It is more than ironic that since the government followed the auditor general's recommendation to establish a values and ethics program, we have witnessed a series of high-profile cases of wrongdoing in the government. Chuck Guité, the public servant at the heart of the sponsorship scandal, was awarded a performance bonus in the year that the auditor general accused him of "breaking every rule in the book."[75] But that is not all. A senior official at Health Canada was caught setting up a fraudulent scheme with Aboriginal leaders to defraud the government of millions of dollars. Paul Cochrane, an assistant deputy minister, was convicted of fraud and sentenced to one year in jail for accepting $200,000 in "gifts" between 1994 and 2000 after giving preferential treatment in granting about $70 million to a foundation that had "a history of highly questionable financial practices."[76] Another former Health Canada official, Patrick Nottingham, pleaded guilty in November 2005 to fraud for his role in funding an Aboriginal treatment centre.[77] Yet another official, Paul Champagne at National Defence, was submitting false invoices for information technologies and related services and was later charged with fraud and money laundering. The minister announced that Champagne was implicated in "a very sophisticated criminal scheme" and that steps had to be taken to recover "$160 million after discovering a massive fraud in computer contracts."

Champagne replied that he had simply followed private sector practices in getting the job done and compared himself to Wal-Mart, on the grounds that his style did not fit the bureaucratic culture."[78] However, he later "pleaded guilty to two breaches of trust and fraud charges."[79]

Five officials in the Department of Immigration in the Toronto regional office were operating a payback scheme for approving the applications of new Canadians. The officials, who included a senior manager, were charged in 2004 with "conspiracy to commit fraud, breach of trust, fraud upon the government and various charges" after it was learned that they had operated a scheme under which bribes, ranging from $4,000, to $25,000, were paid in exchange for helping applicants secure permanent resident status in Canada.[80] A former passport examination officer pleaded guilty in May 2007 to running a scam that allowed non-Canadians to obtain Canadian passports because of documents that he falsified between 2003 and 2004.[81]

An audit at the Department of Fisheries and Oceans in 2006 "uncovered rule-breaking by public servants," including "forbidden free travel for spouses." Public servants also habitually booked high-priced air fares, each costing on average $5,000 or more per flight. This enabled them to receive more air miles to secure free flights.[82] A federal public servant was sentenced to five and a half years in prison in 2005 for breach of trust and for dealing in blank Canadian passports. Some 246 blank Canadian passports had been stolen and then sold for $1,000 each.[83] A high-ranking Canadian diplomat was caught recruiting Canadians in Egypt to spy on a Saudi prince and princess. By the time Canadian security officials were informed of this, the diplomat had retired in Saudi Arabia "and could not be disciplined."[84]

The government was forced to cancel a contract with a moving and trucking firm after it was discovered that public servants who oversaw the review process received free golf games and that one who evaluated the bids had accepted a Caribbean cruise with a vice-president from the winning firm.[85] Officials in the Department of Public Works and Government Services (PWGS) were caught claiming too much overtime. A series of "unusual claims were processed without challenge," including one that claimed 61.5 overtime hours in one week, which meant that the employee would have worked 99 hours that week, or more than 14 hours a day for seven days. The government has a policy that limits the number of hours an employee may work each week to 48, unless there are exceptional circumstances, which should be documented. The claims were processed without explanation.[86]

The Canada Revenue Agency uncovered fraud committed by two of its employees in 2008. In one case, a veteran CRA employee routed $300,000 generated from illegitimate returns into his bank account. In an apparently unrelated matter, another employee racked up $100,000 using similar means of inducing the government into issuing refunds and payments to accounts the employee controlled. CRA has refused to reveal whether it fired or charged the person. Indeed, the department kept news of the fraud from going public, but it had to release the story when it received a request for information.[87] In 2010 the RCMP was called in to investigate the assistant deputy minister in charge of the government's real estate portfolio because of allegations that he had engaged in favouritism and was in conflict of interest with one of his supporters. The government department announced on its website that "disciplinary measures were involved and the employee is no longer employed with PWGSC."[88] In late 2011 it was revealed that the RCMP had begun a wide-ranging investigation of CRA employees who were said to have accepted bribes in exchange for a substantial reduction in the tax assessments of certain firms. The investigation also focused on retired public servants who are now well paid private sector consultants. The opposition asked for a country-wide investigation, and the parliamentary secretary to the revenue minister responded in a written statement that the alleged wrongdoings "go back at least a decade."[89]

It is important to note that, leaving aside the sponsorship scandal, politicians were not involved in the cases discussed above. Nor are politicians involved in the management of pay for performance. As mentioned, Chuck Guité, the official at the centre of the sponsorship scandal, consistently received performance bonuses from a scheme managed by senior public servants. Moreover, Paul Cochrane, the senior Health Canada official at the centre of the fraud case noted above, for which he was later found guilty, was awarded a $7,300 performance bonus in August 2000 for "meeting the expectations," of his job.[90]

It stands to reason that the shift favouring the attributes of individuals over those of the community should be felt in every corner of our political-administrative institution. Public servants do not operate in a vacuum. Society values individual accomplishments as much as it did forty years ago, but collective accomplishments are less valued, and "belief in the efficacy of state action has been cracked."[91] The fact that the public service in Canada is now less institutionalized is one of the reasons why individuals within it matter more.[92] And, of course, we have witnessed changes in motivation.[93] This should come as no surprise, given the sustained efforts to make the public sector look like the private sector.

The government's decision to earmark 40 percent of the "at risk" pay for performance for senior managers, based on how much they contribute to identifying permanent savings from the 2012 expenditure budget, speaks to this new reality.[94] This not only places the onus on individual managers to identify potential cuts, but it is based on the premise that unless an incentive carrot is dangled in front of managers, they will not, on their own initiative, volunteer where spending cuts can be made.

Knowing a Sow from a Cow

Managing in government is different not only from what it was forty years ago but also what it is in other sectors. Today it is about navigating in a horizontal world where, at the more senior levels, loyalty to the centre of government is as strong or stronger than loyalty to the department; despite New Public Management measures, managerial tasks give satisfaction to relatively few higher public servants.[95] A former minister of agriculture described the changes graphically when he told a Senate committee in 2006 that deputy ministers of agriculture no longer know "a sow from a cow" and that he longed for "the glory days of the public service" when the deputy minister of agriculture "lived and breathed farming and stayed in the job for 20 years." He added, "They would rather quit than be shuffled somewhere else. Some think that all you need now is a good education and you can run anything."[96] In horizontal government, a thorough knowledge of a sector or department is no longer central to one's work – the thinking goes that one can easily gain whatever knowledge is needed through briefing books.

Three things now dominate the agenda of a senior manager in Ottawa: the interdepartmental process; communications, as politics and governing have merged; and dealing with crises. Mobility in the senior ranks of the public service in Ottawa is now highly valued and, for many, is an important measure of success. To be sure, mobility has its advantages. It offers a broader perspective than a career in a single department would do. It enables the public servant to see things from different perspectives and thus become a stronger participant in horizontal government. At the same time, however, it promotes a disconnect between senior management and frontline program managers, who tend to have less mobility, particularly those in regional and field offices.

Deputy ministers now spend one hour out of every three on interdepartmental issues. It is interesting to note that they typically allocate nearly twice as much time to meetings with their peers as to matters involving their own ministers.[97] Avoidance of embarrassing disclosures and the ability to manage a controversy have ramped up spin operations to the point that spin is now central to government operations and management. Spin is about survival, and surviving in government is of course highly valued in both the political and the bureaucratic worlds.[98]

Cyberspace, the social media, twenty-four-hour news channels, gotcha journalism, the never-ending call for greater transparency, and the work of officers of Parliament (the blame generators) all make it extremely difficult, if not impossible, to have centralized control of sensitive or embarrassing information.[99] The solution: beef up the government's spin operations to deal with any fallout.

Today, there are an estimated 3,824 spin specialists or communications staffers in the federal government, including about 100 in the Prime Minister's Office and the Privy Council Office. Growth in the number of communications specialists began in earnest in the early 1980s and has shot up in recent years. There has been an increase of over 700 positions in the last six years alone.[100] Scott Reid, former director of communications to Prime Minister Paul Martin, explains: "At the political level, there really were no formal positions known as director of communications in the early '90s. By 2003, every minister had both a communications director and a press secretary ... you saw changes of that kind happen, all of which are clear indications that the emphasis on communications was increasing at both the political and bureaucratic level."[101]

No issue is too trivial for senior government officials to ignore in managing blame avoidance. Some observers, including Ralph Heintzman, have pointed to the "growing involvement of public servants in communications," suggesting that they are crossing the line at the highest level, putting "loyalty to the government of the day above loyalty to the public interest, and far above loyalty to the values of the very institution they were charged with leading."[102]

Management in government now takes a back seat to crisis management, to communications, to spin, to blame avoidance, to policy issues, and to interdepartmental processes, the big picture, as defined by the centre of government. Management has brought benefits to senior public servants; it has enabled them to do things that would have been impossible thirty years ago: staffing, the reclassification of subordinates, hiring consultants, and, for a period, transferring funds that Parliament had earmarked for programs to operations and overhead costs. However, for senior managers, the price has been quite bearable: adding more and more staff at head office to produce more and more evaluations and performance reports, while dealing with never-ending requests for information from the officers of Parliament.

Management: It's Someone Else's Business

As previously mentioned, in 2004 I was the Simon Reisman Visiting Fellow in the Treasury Board Secretariat in Ottawa. I am in the habit at my university of turning off lights in my own and surrounding offices and classrooms on my way out of the building at the end of the day – it is my way of saving on the university's electricity bill and, however modestly, helping the environment. The Treasury Board Secretariat is housed in a large sprawling office complex, L'Esplanade Laurier, in downtown Ottawa. I often worked there late into the evening, and the lights were always on. In my early days there, I searched for the light switch on my way out of the door, but with no success. One day I asked a public servant on my floor to show me where the light switch was. He had "no idea" and asked, "Why would you want to know?" When I explained, he said, "That really has nothing to do with you. Someone else is responsible for turning the lights on and off."

My experience in this respect is not unlike the work of public servants. It is exceedingly difficult for front-line workers and their managers to have a sense of responsibility in their place of work. It is true that their work was once guided by fairly rigid administrative rules, but it is also true that a number of these administrative rules have been done away with. In their stead, the work of front-line managers and workers is subject to many voices, many hands, and many oversight bodies.

Ministerial offices have more staff occupying more senior positions than at any time in the past. Their purpose is to make their ministers look good, an increasingly difficult task, given access to information legislation, the role of the media, and the prime minister's dominating presence. Access to information legislation and other developments have served to open up the world of front-line managers and workers to outside scrutiny and, by ricochet, to scrutiny from ministerial offices. This, of course, presents different challenges for front-line workers, who traditionally look to citizens rather than to ministers and their partisan staff in their day-to-day work. Contact between ministerial staff and front-line workers is now more frequent than in years past, as the political class tries to exert greater control over communications. This happens, at least in part, because there are times when a political crisis can start from a transaction between disgruntled citizens and front-line workers. But that is not all. Front-line managers must now also look down to their employees (and the consequences of whistleblowing legislation) and to public sector unions as they go about their work.

All of this has made it easier to engage in "buck passing" or shifting blame to others when things go wrong.[103] It also robs front-line managers of a sense of ownership and responsibility for their programs and resources. The establishment of Service Canada takes horizontal government a step further with its goal of providing one-stop, personalized service to Canadians.[104] The risk is that it will further disconnect citizens from government departments and separate service delivery from service and policy reforms. It could also inhibit the kind of incremental policy change and adaptation that is crucial to any organization that responds, learns, and adjusts to problems.

Managers have had to learn to deal with collective bargaining, public service unions, and the courts. As already noted, the public sector in Canada remains largely unionized. From a dead start in the mid-1960s, government workers now have collective bargaining and union membership. We compared earlier union membership between the public and private sectors and saw that in 2010 only 14.1 percent of private sector workers belonged to a union compared with over 71 percent for public sector workers.

The courts have been drawn into management issues. My consultations with public servants indicate that many government managers have simply given up trying to dismiss employees on the basis of non-performance, fearing that they will have to defend their action in court. As Jeffrey Simpson writes, rights are "fundamentally about me and responsibility is mostly about us."[105] Table 2 reveals that 451 public servants were released for "misconduct" over a six-year period and only 453 for "incompetence or incapacity" over the same period (about 75 employees on an annual basis).

The pattern of employee dismissal for misconduct or incompetence has not changed in recent years. In 2007–08, 49 employees were terminated for misconduct and another 84 for incompetence, while in 2010–11 the numbers were 54 and 99, respectively.[106] The above may explain why the great majority of front-line managers and workers do not take annual performance evaluations seriously. Carroll and Siegel write that "virtually everyone" laughed when they asked public servants in the field about the performance appraisal system. They report that performance appraisal is largely a matter of going through the motions and that neither supervisor nor subordinates take it very seriously. They quote one front-line worker as follows: "There hasn't been anyone in the last seven years come and tell me I've ever done anything wrong. Nobody ever comes to look ... They don't tell you you've done something right; and they don't tell you you've done something wrong. There's no review of the operation."[107] A review of the Public Service Modernization Act also recently served a negative verdict on the ability of government managers to deal with non-performers. Some 65 percent of respondents recorded a "not at all" or "to a moderate

TABLE 2: PUBLIC SERVANTS TERMINATED, CANADA

Year	Discharge for misconduct	Release for incompetence and incapacity	Total
2000	63	67	130
2001	107	81	188
2002	93	104	197
2003	77	92	169
2004	90	89	179
2005	21	20	41
Total	451	453	904

Source: Data provided by the Government of Canada to the Commission of Inquiry into the Sponsorship Program and Advertising Activities, Ottawa, 31 May 2005. See also http://www.pwgsc.gc.ca/compensation/ppim/ppim-3-5-3-3.html, which provides for a general categorization of the reasons for Public Service of Canada employee departures.

extent" answer when asked about the capacity of managers to deal with their employees, including non-performers.[108]

Even senior public servants have turned to the courts to challenge the government – their employer. The Supreme Court ruled that the government had to release parts of documents classified as cabinet secrets to its own lawyers, who were suing the Treasury Board for a pay increase. The material in question explained why government lawyers in Vancouver were excluded from salary increases that were given to their Toronto-based colleagues.[109]

Certainly, it has never been easy to deal with non-performers in government. It is even more difficult today, given collective bargaining and the possibility that employees and their union representatives will go to court if management initiates any action to remove anyone for non-performance. To avoid the hassles, managers focus on things over which they have more control. In any event, they have little incentive to engage in what would likely be a two-year process to terminate an employee for non-performance. Even if they think they have a solid case, there is no guarantee of success. For example, an arbitrator instructed a government department to rehire six public servants in Ontario who had been fired for exchanging pornographic emails at work that included images of bestiality, nude obese and elderly women, and degrading and violent sexual activity. The arbitrator ruled that the government lacked cause to dismiss the men, and his decision made it to the front pages of Canada's national newspapers. To be sure, the message was not lost on government managers.[110]

It is also revealing that "no sponsorship-related discipline" came to the attention of the "major government unions." Union representatives were quick to argue that the problem was at the political level, not with public servants.[111] Former cabinet ministers who met with Justice Gomery at five roundtables stressed the point that public servants lacked the ability to impose sanctions or to replace incompetent staff. They also spoke about what they labelled widespread "institutional inertia" in government departments.[112] Though staff are very rarely penalized for incompetence or mismanagement, public servants can still be dismissed if they bring negative attention to the department. Three Health Canada employees were fired in June 2004 for speaking out against departmental policies. The three scientists had publicly voiced their concern over the use of bovine growth hormone to enhance milk production in cows.[113]

There is also evidence to suggest that federal public servants are underemployed. A senior analyst in the Department of Citizenship and Immigration spent more than half his working day looking at news, sports, and porn websites from his desk while working at head office. The department took the unusual step of firing him for committing "time theft" by claiming that he was accepting pay for surfing the Internet. The employee appealed to the Public Service Labour Relations Board (PSLRB). He argued that he wasn't given enough work to keep him busy, and made the point that he had met every deadline and received positive performance appraisals. PSLRB ruled in favour of the employee and ordered the department to reinstate him immediately. The board argued in its ruling that it was surprised "that an employee could spend the amount of time that he did on non-work-related activities for months without his supervisors noting a lack of production or engagement."[114] Again, this ruling was not lost on other public sector managers: Why bother trying to discipline or fire an employee? It explains why the Treasury Board study on compensation concluded that "it is relatively rare for public servants to be fired, with the greatest number of involuntary departures resulting from dismissal while on probation." The study pointed out that of the 4,883 separations of indeterminate employees that took place in 2002–03, only 22 were released for incompetence or incapacity.[115]

I wish to note that I wrote to both the Public Service Commission and the Treasury Board Secretariat in January 2010 to update the data on the number of public servants terminated for incompetence. The Public Service Commission responded by pointing out that it is not responsible for this information. The Treasury Board Secretariat reported on 15 February 2012 that 45 public servants were released for incompetence in 2010–11.

Government departments have ombudsmen to which employees are invited to meet if they have "concerns or challenging situations in the workplace."[116] One ombudsman reported that she told the deputy minister that "young public servants are telling me that they have nothing to do."[117] However, when senior managers are asked to take on new responsibilities or deal with an increased demand to respond to oversight bodies, they automatically ask for new resources. They claim that their departments are stretched to the limit. The thinking is that it is someone else's responsibility to come up with the resources. The senior managers prefer to have things at rest, not to challenge the status quo, and to add rather than subtract when it comes to resources.

Looking Back

Jocelyne Bourgon, a former clerk of the privy council had this advice for public servants in her report to the prime minister on the state of the public service: "I want people to stop thinking that solutions in organizations cost thousands of dollars and needs somebody from out there. I believe the real change happens at a much more fundamental level. The only response to real change is – is it working, does it change my life, does it make me more effective, does it get the job done? All of those old fashioned questions – common sense."[118] Easy for her to write this. Clerks have the power to change things far more than front-line managers. A phone call to a minister, a deputy minister or, better yet, an aspiring deputy minister is often all that is needed to set in motion a new initiative or to bring about change.

However, there are limits even for the clerk. One is time. Ian Clark made the point very well when he wrote, "Tellier [the clerk of the privy council at the time] devoted considerable time to PS 2000 in its early days. But I would also submit that it would have been inappropriate for the Clerk to have continued this level of time commitment to public service management issues when the Charlottetown constitutional process gathered steam and the fiscal situation was approaching crisis proportions. The duty of the Clerk as the Prime Minister's Deputy Minister and Secretary to the Cabinet to advise and assist the Prime Minister and Cabinet on the government's policy agenda will almost always take precedence over managerial initiatives associated with the Clerk's role as Head of the Public Service."[119] There is never a shortage of crises for the clerk to attend to. But there are not many clerks who, even though they have the authority to do so, are in the habit of challenging the resource levels of line departments. That is someone else's responsibility.

The Treasury Board Secretariat has that responsibility. But it has largely abdicated its budget office role to concentrate on reviewing the various performance, evaluation, and accountability reports that it requires from line departments and agencies. It also oversees the allocation of new resources to departments so that they can respond to new oversight requirements. The various performance reports simply do not integrate the need to identify cost reductions in operations or programs.

Viewed from the outside, government operations are seen as unnecessarily complicated, process-oriented, and self-interested.[120] Senior public servants still wish to make the federal public service a "model employer" while at the same time making public sector management look like private sector management. Yet the public sector is dominated by politics, by the pervasive influence of the media, by blame avoidance in the era of permanent election campaigns, by frequent changes in priorities, by the inability to define measures of success and different accountability requirements. The private sector has had no choice but to adjust to the competitive nature of the global economy and initiate ambitious restructuring efforts. There has been, for example, a sharply declining rate of unionization in the private sector, but it has been on the rise in the public sector.[121]

The Government of Canada has restructured its operations by looking inward, by strengthening head offices at the expense of front-line managers and workers, by looking to the Office of the Auditor General to define the management reform agenda, and by piling evaluation, performance, and accountability reports one on top of another. This somehow is what it takes to make public sector management resemble that found in the private sector.

10

You Can Fudge Reports but You Cannot Fudge Rules

As we have seen, during the past thirty years, public administration became public management, and government administrators became managers in Canada and in much of the Western world. The private sector was the inspiration for this development and the source of many new measures as governments sought to transform bureaucrats into efficient, if not entrepreneurial, managers. The shift has been part of a broad political agenda in Anglo-American countries to make government operations more business-like and to put bureaucrats in their place while giving politicians the upper hand in shaping public policy.

The first sign of the transformation appeared some fifty years ago. We had the Glassco Commission in Canada and the introduction of Program Budgeting in the United States, which then spread to Canada and other Western countries. Traditional public administration soon became dated. It is worth repeating J. Grant Glassco's views on government operations. When he was asked to come forward with recommendations on how to improve management, he wrote, "Good management consists in more than the avoidance of sin, and this Calvinistic approach to public administration, while well designed to discomfit bad managers, was bound to prove most frustrating to good ones."[1] Drawing on his private sector experience, Glassco found it easy to distinguish good managers from bad ones and to pardon sins if the bottom line was healthy. He saw no reason why the same logic could not apply in the public sector.

Glassco's solution was to "entrust" departments and agencies with the "power of decision" in many areas previously controlled by Treasury Board and by centrally prescribed rules and administrative prescriptions. Treasury Board staff were to shift their work away from a detailed review of departmental budgets to reviewing programs from a broad perspective and to assessing how well government managers were meeting their objectives.[2]

As is so often the case in government, the transformation was slow and not without significant challenges. As the "new" Treasury Board started to take shape, the government came under attack in the Commons over sins committed by the Department of National Defence. In June 1970, the House of Commons held a special debate on the government's failure to protect the public treasury in refitting the aircraft carrier *Bonaventure*. The opening motion included accusations of "waste, extravagance, and other abuses in the spending of government money." During the debate, opposition members from all parties hurled accusations at the government and concluded with pleas to introduce "administrative integrity." Specific details were brought up, such as the awarding of two separate contracts – for different amounts – to remove fifty-two chairs from the *Bonaventure*'s briefing room.[3] The concept of "let the manager manage," was suddenly being put severely to the test, at least in the political arena.

It would not be the last time that the concept was tested. As we saw earlier, J.J. Macdonell shook things up in Ottawa when he wrote that "Parliament and indeed the Government has lost or is close to losing effective control of the public purse."[4] Macdonell set in motion a series of changes within the Treasury Board Secretariat that are still being felt to this day. He called for the establishment of the Office of the Comptroller General (Macdonell was shocked to hear that the federal government did not have a chief financial officer, as large firms did). The government responded by establishing a Royal Commission on Management.[5] The comptroller's office had originally been established in 1931, but it was merged with the Treasury Board Secretariat in the immediate post-Glassco period.[6] In addition, new centrally prescribed rules in financial and human resources management were introduced in response to Macdonell's call for action.

Macdonell had a direct hand in constructing a crisis in accountability in government, and he was able to exploit it to enlarge the mandate, scope, and size of the Office of the Auditor General. In his 1976 report, he concluded that "due to the highly unsatisfactory state of financial control throughout government to which I have directed the attention of Parliament in my 1975 Report and in this Report, I consider it my professional duty as a responsible servant of Parliament to increase still more substantially the professional resources of my Office in an effort to counterbalance to some extent the deficiencies and weaknesses that have been disclosed, discussed, reported to the House of Commons and acknowledged by the Government."[7] In the private sector, if a firm has poor financial controls, it either rectifies the situation immediately or it dies. In government, the solution to the crisis was to expand the OAG and introduce comprehensive audits. From a veritable dead stop in 1970 ($35,811), the OAG spent $8,817,966 in professional services in 1979.[8] The management consultant industry, with virtually no experience in the public sector, had found itself a new champion in the federal government. There was no better cover. Macdonell could hardly be accused of political patronage: he was not even part of the government bureaucracy, and he was on the side of virtue as he set out to eliminate waste in government spending.

Macdonell had built the management consulting practice of a large chartered accounting firm before becoming auditor general. He ended his career with the prediction that, in time, "comprehensive auditing with all of its implications for the government itself is almost inevitably going to restore effective control of the public purse to Parliament."[9] History has shown that he was badly mistaken.

The auditor general appears to be increasingly concerned about issues other than carrying out financial audits. Sharon Sutherland, who has published extensively on the role of the OAG, recently argued that officers of Parliament are working "in the wild west," reporting to committees that pay scant attention to them.[10] As already pointed out, comprehensive or value-for-money audits have enabled the OAG to stray far from its original mandate. Among many other examples, some of which we have already noted, the auditor general had a chapter in his November 2009 report addressing the government's immigration programs from a policy perspective. The chapter argued that under the Temporary Foreign Worker Program, foreign workers were vulnerable because they do not speak English and owe their status in Canada to their employer.[11] A public policy consultant in Ottawa could have easily written this report. It had little to do with a traditional financial audit.

In time, however, the Macdonell storm petered out. The Ottawa system battened down the hatches and, for the most part, simply ignored the recommendations of the Lambert Royal Commission. By the mid-1980s, Treasury Board Secretariat staff were quietly able to bring the Office of the Comptroller General back under their control. Things were back to normal. The media, in time, also lost interest in Macdonell's dramatic warning that both Parliament and the government were close to losing control of the public purse. Still, in the end, Macdonell got what he wanted: a substantial rewrite of the statutes, giving the OAG authority to carry out value-for-money audits and a considerable expansion of the office, both in terms of mandate and resources.

The politics of the 1980s centred on the patriation of the constitution, then on the Meech Lake Accord, and then on free trade negotiations with the United States. The media naturally focused largely on these issues and on political scandals, ignoring administrative miscues.[12] By 1980, as New Public Management came into view, Brian Mulroney, no less than Margaret Thatcher and Ronald Reagan, was firmly convinced that the public sector had a great deal to learn from the private sector. To the extent that he focused on fixing government operations, he looked to the private sector for solutions.[13]

The OAG, with more resources and a much broader mandate, also kept at it, pushing the government to commit more financial and human resources to program evaluation, risk management, ethics and values, and performance evaluation, along with whatever was in vogue in the private sector. It has never bothered, however, to explain the distinction between a financial and a comprehensive audit or how program evaluation or value-for-money audits could ever be as objective and definitive as financial audits.

As already noted, the market within government for what the OAG is selling is not very strong. It really comes down to the Treasury Board Secretariat and the off-and-on Office of the Comptroller General. Politicians on the opposition benches invariably applaud the work of the auditor general and other officers of Parliament because it makes political sense to do so. Officers of Parliament are not in the business of reporting what is right about government policies, programs, and operations. Opposition MPs are in the business of casting the government in a bad light, and the OAG and officers of Parliament are there to give them a helping hand.[14] They are the blame generators, pushing politicians on the government side and public servants to develop and manage blame-avoidance strategies.

There is ample evidence to suggest that opposition parties look to officers of Parliament for ammunition to attack the government. One well-known journalist recently explained that each officer of Parliament reports to a parliamentary committee, but the committees do not "even review the reports unless there are political points to score."[15] Seven agents of Parliament made an "unprecedented appeal" to the House of Commons committees to do "a better job of scrutinizing and overseeing" their work, but there was no response. They wrote in February and again in September 2011, with suggestions to strengthen their ties to Parliament, but never "heard a word."[16]

Politicians on the government side, meanwhile, are rarely, if ever, in the mood to take on the auditor general. There is no political advantage in doing so because the OAG has been successful in branding itself as the champion against government waste and inefficiency. The Trudeau government agreed to Macdonell's demands for new legislation, for comprehensive audits, and for new resources. The Harper government expanded the OAG's mandate by adding several crown corporations to its review mandate. Accordingly, there is a steep political price to pay should the prime minister make the case that the OAG has made government thicker and that year after year it has produced reports of questionable value.

In Government, It Is Better Not to Sin Than to Ask for Forgiveness

J. Grant Glassco, Allen Lambert, and J.J. Macdonell came to government to fix its operations, and they brought with them their private sector experience and perspective. NPM also looked to the private sector for inspiration, probably because those looking for change had nowhere else to look to for ideas. The minister of finance in Denmark echoed the views of many politicians when he argued in 2002 that "the public sector must learn to think, act, and be managed on the same terms as the private sector. The old bureaucrats must be smoked out."[17]

In Canada, after some thirty years of trying to make the public sector look like the private sector, there is little evidence to suggest that the efforts have borne fruit. Tom Jenkins, chairman of Open Text Corporation, led a review of Ottawa R&D spending, and in tabling his report in October 2011, he said he "was stunned at how little effort is spent figuring out what works." He added that "in business, our outcome is profits. We have to have that or the competitors in our markets will out-innovate us."[18] Some thirty years after sustained efforts to make management in government look like the private sector, a leading private sector executive, much like Glassco and Macdonell, was stunned to discover that there is no bottom line in the public sector and that public servants are not motivated by profit.

That said, the old bureaucrats have been smoked out in Canada and in many other Western countries. However, they have been replaced by a new breed of public servant who can scarcely be said to think, act, and manage on the same terms or in the same fashion as their private sector counterparts. Nor do they manage according to the values and processes of traditional public administration.

As we have seen, the old public administration was considered no longer up to the task. It involved bureaucrats having to deal with red tape, due process, administrative directives issued by central agencies, and having to go outside their departments to secure approval on a number of financial and human resources matters. The bureaucrats were risk-averse, and throughout their careers many of them stayed in their departments, where they gained a full appreciation of the sectors they worked in and where they learned to deal with the uniform application of administrative, financial, and human resources policies. The Public Service 2000 Secretariat, with a mandate to transform public sector management, argued that initiatives under the old public administration were all too often "preprogrammed and repetitive" and "input-process oriented."[19]

The old bureaucracy, however, held some distinct advantages. For one thing, it promoted a parsimonious culture. To repeat Lester Pearson's telling phrase, it was difficult to assist the government if you had "to spend two hours each day talking about the case of Désy's table linen or the salary of the newest stenographer."[20] The old bureaucracy served to minimize administrative and financial miscues and abuses. It would have been far more difficult, for example, for Chuck Guité to manipulate the sponsorship program the way he did. In brief, as Glassco discovered, the old bureaucracy was well designed for "avoiding sin."

It is not possible to overstate the point that politics is about avoiding sin or, in more recent parlance, managing blame avoidance. Politicians and taxpayers understand input costs, political patronage, financial abuses, and mismanagement. They have little interest, however, in program evaluation reports and in the numerous accountability exercises tied to performance assessments of one kind or another. If senior managers under the old bureaucracy spent too much time talking about the cost of Désy's table linen, managers under the new approach spend too much time responding to request after request for reports and data to feed the centre and the officers of Parliament. In the era of permanent election campaigns, access to information, and the new media, the avoidance of sin is even more important than in years past. Notwithstanding NPM, politics, politicians, and public servants remain joined at the hip. Any administrative matter, however trivial, can be turned into a hot political issue, casting the government in a negative light.

Ambitious public servants see a market for themselves in managing up and in protecting the government's political interest. They focus less on their department's ability to deliver programs and more on the prime minister's broad policy objectives and on keeping their ministers and their departments out of hot water. They are always at the ready to move the prime minister's agenda and to have the rest simply run on its tracks, as the centre prefers. Perhaps because government operations are much more transparent now, because the public service is much larger, and because the old bureaucrat has been transformed into a private-sector-type manager, we read more about wrongdoings. The literature reports that "a new breed of public servant has emerged with an ethos less oriented to public interest and frugality than towards career advancement and making a mark through bold plans and expenditures."[21] The press tells us that career officials now spend far too much time travelling, that too many receive a golden handshake, only to return to work on contract, and that too many have become spendthrift or have committed outright fraud. A Public Service Commission report stated, "Public perceptions of the ethical standards of public servants are currently at their lowest point in seven years ... Many other professions were rated higher. For a Public Service striving for an exemplary reputation for integrity, these findings are troubling."[22]

As we have seen in earlier chapters, hardly a week goes by without the media reporting that some politician or public servant has abused the public purse. A traditional financial audit, for example, revealed that the head of the Rights and Democracy group, which is tied to the Foreign Affairs department, had dined with employees at taxpayers' expense, spent forty-six nights in Paris (though the group has no program there), and failed to reimburse personal expenses incurred on his corporate audit card. The internal audit called for tighter financial control, yet the reports to Parliament were "mostly positive" and made "no mention of the questionable spending."[23] The government decided in 2012 to disband the group and move its activities to the Department of Foreign Affairs and Trade.[24]

In January 2012, the opposition called for a review of the government's training program for senior public servants. The Advanced Leadership Program in 2009 had several participants visiting thirty-five countries, including India, Mexico, and the United Arab Emirates. NDP MP Alexandre Boulerice told the media that the program cost $145 million a year to administer and commented, "I don't know why a Canadian bureaucrat needs to go to Mexico to find out how they do administration." The point is that MPs, the media, and taxpayers understand this information, which they would not be able to find by reading the thousands of pages of reports submitted to Parliament every year.[25]

The introduction of a business vocabulary does not change the simple, obvious, but powerful fact that public servants operate in a political context and that their activities have political implications. It is ministers, not career officials, who insist on error-free government, because they operate in a partisan political theatre, where even minor administrative miscues are fair game to opposition MPs. Ministers invariably want their departments to present the least possible target for attack and to avoid controversy.

Mark Jarvis and Paul Thomas summed up the challenge when they wrote that "life in the public sector is more subjective, value-laden, emotional, pluralistic, episodic, intense, and unpredictable."[26] Centrally prescribed rules, the promotion of a parsimonious culture, and traditional public administration values stand a much better chance of success in this environment than numerous performance and evaluation reports, which are written as communications tools in the hope of avoiding political controversy. The past thirty years are proof that in government it is better to avoid sin than to ask for forgiveness and that one can fudge reports but cannot fudge rules.

Where Is the Market for Policy Advice?

Successful firms produce a product, identify a market, define a marketing strategy, keep an eye on the competition, and pursue clients. Expenses are not an issue if the firm has a strong margin and turns a handsome return on investments. There is little need for program evaluation reports or sophisticated performance indicators. The firm's chief financial officer can easily speak to the bottom line. The market, and the market alone, for example, has been able to deliver a verdict on Canada's high-tech giants Nortel and Research in Motion.

What about the public sector? How does it compare? What is the market for senior public servants when generating policy advice and delivering programs and services? How can they establish success?

The market for policy advice in government in the post-positivism era is not nearly as clear as it was thirty to forty years ago.[27] At the risk of being repetitive, New Public Management had two objectives – to introduce a more rigorous private sector management structure in government and to give politicians the upper hand in shaping public policy. The market for policy analysis, where public policy problems could be reviewed scientifically (positivism) and where hypotheses could be prepared and tested through rigorous statistical analysis, has been on the defensive since the 1980s.

Public servants brought to government the knowledge they had acquired in the social sciences. They emphasized empirical research designs, the use of surveys and sampling techniques, proper data-gathering procedures; they produced input-output studies, cost benefit analyses, and developed socioeconomic models with predictive power.[28] If politicians and politics could not understand this, then politics itself was seen as the problem. The Thatcher era, the rise of neoconservatism, and the determination of politicians to grab the policy agenda and shape it to their wishes put senior public servants and their more formal policy-making processes on the defensive. Today, politicians, when developing public policy, take into consideration ideology, partisan concerns, the pressures of the day, and the ever-watchful media. One senior Industry Canada official explained, "We have reached the point where two plus two can now make five."[29]

The BBC's *Yes Minister* series, first broadcast in the 1980s, summed up how many politicians viewed the relationship between themselves and public servants. Although *Yes Minister* was a comedy, many came to see it as a documentary. Margaret Thatcher had each episode videotaped, and she apparently subscribed to the caricature of senior public servants which the series presented.[30] The series portrayed ministers as publicity-seeking dimwits, no match for the highly educated, unprincipled, and Machiavellian career officials. No matter the issue and however sensible the minister's position, Sir Humphrey, the senior official, usually had a position at odds with the minister's, and he nearly always won. Sir Humphrey's views were not rooted in an ideology that differed from the minister's or, for that matter, that stemmed from profound beliefs. Rather, he could be counted on to favour the status quo and, more important, to do whatever was needed to protect the interests of the department and the public service. Moreover, Sir Humphrey not only shaped all major policy decisions and ran the department, but he also managed political crises on behalf of his minister. Whatever the issue, the minister in the end had to rely on Sir Humphrey's considerable political and bureaucratic skills simply to survive.

In Ottawa, the policy advice function has been turned on its head. The Sir Humphreys are now often told by the prime minister and his courtiers which policies to pursue. Politicians in power know what they want and see no need to wait for advice from career officials, with their perceived tendency to cling to the status quo.

Senior public servants have adjusted. As we saw earlier, Peter Aucoin wrote about their habit of "demonstrating enthusiasm" for the government's agenda, either as a tactic to advance their own personal careers or in the mistaken notion that neutral public servants should all be, as one British scholar put it, "promiscuously partisan" – that is, partisan to the government of the day but willing to change when a different party takes over.[31] They are more likely to do this if they have served in various central agencies and departments rather than in a single department, where they are able to gain a thorough understanding of a sector or policy field. Don Drummond laments the loss of the "analytical discipline" in government that "combined rigour in theory and quantitative methods."[32] He maintains that important policy shifts in recent years on such policy issues as immigration and environment have not been accompanied by policy analyses of the kind produced for the Free Trade Agreement and the introduction of the goods and services tax.[33]

Munir Sheikh, the former chief statistician for Canada, fell on his sword over the government's decision to cancel the long-form census and replace it with a voluntary survey. Shortly after the government announced that the 2011 census would include only the short form, a chorus of protests erupted from 370 groups opposed to the decision. The government responded by arguing that it does not wish to secure information by threatening to send Canadians to jail for failing to fill out the census. The minister responsible for Statistics Canada explained that the government wanted to strike a proper balance in getting the needed data and the citizens' desire to maintain privacy.[34] Sheikh later pointed out that Statistics Canada had worked well with the Office of the Privacy Commissioner and there were no issues of violating privacy in gathering census data.[35]

Sheikh resigned after the minister announced that the quality of the voluntary survey data would be as good as that of the long-form census and that both he and Statistics Canada were behind this decision. Sheikh felt that media stories on the matter were damaging the reputation of Statistics Canada and that they cast doubt on his own integrity.[36] He later was adamant that a voluntary survey can never be a substitute for the mandatory census.[37]

Sheikh has recently asked a number of questions that remain unanswered. The questions go to the heart of post-positivism and the loss of influence of senior public servants in shaping public policy. They include: Did the government analyze carefully the consequences of a loss in data quality as a result of the voluntary survey? Did it consider how this loss in quality would affect the data needs of users? Did it examine the negative consequences of this on policy development, including that at the federal level? In undertaking such an analysis, why did the government not consult with data users? Did it compare these consequences from the loss of data quality against any privacy gains?[38] In a world where two plus two can equal five, there is little need to answer these questions.

Research institutes, think-tanks, and lobby groups have also had a profound impact on the policy work of public servants. Politicians can now turn to a host of research institutes to get the answers they are looking for on any policy issue. These cover the full political spectrum, from left to right. Should this tactic fail, politicians can turn to the 2,000 or so lobbyists in Ottawa who are always at the ready to promote their clients' perspective. There are even lobbyists working to promote the interests of the tobacco industry. If policy truths are not absolute, elected politicians now have any number of sources to consult to establish truths as they wish to hear them.[39]

The role of permanent career officials in policy making some thirty years ago was to search for relevant information, analyze it, and provide advice to politicians on the government side. Information and data were not then readily accessible.[40] Today, one can Google any policy issue and quickly obtain the relevant information. If policy making in a post-positivism world is a matter of opinion, where 2 + 2 can equal 5, Google searches may well provide the answer.[41]

Google search is a profoundly democratic instrument. It opens up the policy-making field to anyone who is interested. Allan Gregg put it very well when he wrote, "Feeling more knowledgeable, connected and in control of our personal lives has also directly reduced our reliance on authority. As a result, we have little incentive to uncritically swallow the claims of political leaders who don't seem to understand our concerns, share our experiences or speak in a way we find authentic. Our political leaders have not only failed to adjust to this new reality, they also avoid honestly and directly engaging on our most pressing issues."[42] He could have added that senior public servants have also failed to adjust.

Where Is the Market for Management?

Management in the Canadian government is now essentially about producing annually a large number of accountability and performance assessment reports, keeping things running on their tracks, and avoiding controversy and negative media attention. The notion that it was possible to duplicate private sector management in government has proved to be ill-conceived, misguided, and costly. It is worth repeating that the public and private sectors are fundamentally different in all important and unimportant ways.

The market for good management in government is also fundamentally different from that in the private sector. Unlike the private sector, it is mostly someone else's responsibility and if something goes wrong, it becomes someone else's fault. Letting the manager manage is one thing; making the manager manage is quite another. To be sure, senior government officials applauded Treasury Board's decision to delegate more and more authority to line departments and the government's move to transform the Public Service Commission essentially into an audit agency. But there has been a price to pay – the considerable expansion of units in head offices to generate reports to "feed the beast."

Good management is about hiring competent staff and managing human resources by rewarding your more productive employees and dealing with non-performers. It is also about allocating and reallocating scarce financial and human resources to high-priority areas and away from low-priority ones. As already noted, in government, collective bargaining sets the stage for managing human resources. Managers have little say in setting salaries, working conditions, and the process for declaring employees surplus. Even if collective bargaining does not inhibit a manager from taking a tough decision, it becomes a convenient cover to avoid doing so. It has never been easy to deal with non-performers in the public sector, but it is even more difficult today, given that employees and their union representatives can go to court to counter any action to remove someone for non-performance. No manager wants the ensuing hassle, preferring to focus on matters over which they have more control.

The above helps explain why there is little market for public servants to be strong managers. For one thing, a stay in the Privy Council Office, an ability to manage a political crisis, and to deliver what the prime minister and his courtiers would like to see remain the way to the top. A strong management pedigree, whatever it may look like in government, is not for the ambitious public servant. For another, there are many hands in the management soup, ranging from central agencies, officers of Parliament, public sector unions, and the media. Moreover, for all the talk about NPM and its accompanying measures, little has been said about what role politicians would now be expected to play in managing government operations. While politicians are prone to say that public sector managers must learn to think and act like private sector managers, they have little to say about how public servants should think and act under NPM.[43] If politicians continue to attach a premium on error-free government, they need to impose centrally prescribed rules on managers. The past thirty years have shown that it is not possible to have one without the other.

Reallocating Resources: It's Also Someone Else's Responsibility

Cuts in spending or reallocating resources are not generated by public sector management measures or by the hundreds of evaluation reports churned out every year by line departments and agencies. The federal government has a long history of failed reallocation initiatives.[44] Central agencies have not been able to make X budget exercises (or exercises in cutting spending) work over the years, if only because establishing a political consensus on the impact of the proposed cuts has often proved "impossible to achieve."[45] Cuts in spending, however, are possible, from time to time. Two conditions are required: an economic or a fiscal crisis and the prime minister driving the exercise. Think back to the Bonn cuts (Trudeau, circa 1978, the Bonn economic summit and inflation), the Chrétien-Martin program review (circa 1994–97, the *Wall Street Journal* editorial and Moody's decision to put Canada on a credit watch), and the Harper review (circa 2011–12 and the need to address a $30 billion annual deficit).[46]

Efforts to transform spending ministers into guardians have failed. It will be recalled, for example, that the Policy and Expenditure Management System (PEMS) was introduced to force ministers to enrich some programs while also identifying low-priority ones for reduction or termination. They had little difficulty in enriching programs but proved to be inept at cutting them. PEMS was short-lived. Introduced in 1979, it was put on life support in the mid-1980s and formally abandoned in 1989.[47]

The above suggests that the "lunch theory" to public spending still applies and that only the prime minister and his courtiers can establish a menu of spending cuts and make them stick. The argument, it will be recalled, goes like this. Ten people meet for lunch; they must decide whether to share one cheque or ask for ten separate ones. In theory, if they decide on one shared cheque, they will all choose the most expensive item. But if each is paying individually, they will probably chose differently.[48] There are several reasons why cabinet government has given way to governing from the centre. The apparent inability of spending ministers to put on a guardian hat is certainly one.[49]

The prime minister and his courtiers are always struggling to manage an overloaded agenda. When the politics of the day allow the prime minister to focus on expenditure reduction, the efforts work (both the Chrétien-Martin 1994–97 and the Harper 2011–12 reviews came on the heels of winning a majority mandate). However, when they take their eyes off the ball to focus on other priorities and on events leading up to the next general election, growth in expenditures re-emerges. This was the case for the Trudeau-Bonn cuts and the Chrétien-Martin review.[50] One can speculate that it will also be the case for the 2011–12 Harper review. As the Ottawa-based journalist James Bagnall wrote, this review may be yet another "pause in the upward trajectory of the civil service and the growing community of professionals who support them."[51]

Spenders will push and pull whatever levers are available in order to secure new funding. The political and bureaucratic culture in Ottawa is such that for policy and decision makers in government, responsibility for expenditure restraint always belongs to someone else.

Reallocating Resources within Departments: It, Too, Is Someone Else's Responsibility

Public sector managers have no interest in reallocating resources from their operations to programs. If given a choice, as this study has shown, they will shift resources away from programs to salaries, travel, and training, and from front-line offices to head office units.

Whenever government managers are asked to assume new responsibilities, they automatically ask for new resources. This behaviour is now well anchored in Ottawa's bureaucratic culture. In brief, the role of a government manager is to ask for new resources, not to reallocate the ones he or she has. In giving up its role as the government's budget office in pursuit of the management board concept, the Treasury Board Secretariat has essentially lost the ability to challenge line departmental managers to justify the financial and human resources under their supervision. James Lahey, the senior federal government official who led the 2004 ambitious compensation review, admitted as much when he observed that "compensation is the government's biggest operating cost, but no one takes overall responsibility for managing, tracking or even properly recording those costs."[52]

If resources have to be reallocated, then let someone else deal with the issue. It is no longer clear who that someone else is – hence, the need for the prime minister to announce spending cuts from above, like bolts of lightning. The various accountability and evaluation reports that line managers prepare are of no help.

There is no cost to government managers in retaining staff, even if the employees are non-performers. The cost is borne by taxpayers. Indeed, there are several reasons why government managers wish to retain or expand the number of their employees. As we have seen, dismissing non-performers is in itself a major challenge. In addition, managers are allocated a training budget for every staff member. Non-performers can sit in a corner and do nothing while the manager allocates the training funding to another employee or to another purpose.[53] Not only is there no cost to retaining non-performers on staff, but there is no process in place to reallocate human resources to higher priority areas. NPM measures have failed in this area. While they have, to some extent, "empowered" managers, they have had nothing to say about reallocating resources from low-priority to high-priority activities.[54]

In the spring of 2010, Nova Scotia government officials met with federal government officials in the Department of Agriculture to discuss programs for the sector. The apple industry in Nova Scotia is growing, but Agriculture Canada has no official to carry out applied research to resolve several issues in harvesting and processing apples. However, it has an official whose research interest is the hog industry. Nova Scotia's hog industry does not compare in importance with the province's apple industry. The problem: the hog researcher with Agriculture Canada is some twelve years away from retirement, and the province's apple industry will simply have to wait until then for Agriculture to hire a researcher with an interest in apples.[55] One can hardly imagine that the prime minister's courtiers would ever take an interest in a front-line employee such as the public servant monitoring the hog industry in Nova Scotia. Nor can one imagine a private business putting off a similar decision for twelve years.

The push to have all programs evaluated has also been misguided and costly. One federal official maintains that apart from some machine-like operations such as the passport office or Revenue Canada, where outcomes can be identified and measured (i.e., the number of passport applications or income tax returns processed by employee), no one has been able to identify "outcomes" in any of the hundreds of evaluation reports produced over the past thirty years or so.[56] That is, no one has been able to identify "outcomes" from programs designed to improve the social or economic well-being of individuals, and it is highly unlikely that anyone will, at least in the foreseeable future. Evaluation and performance assessment reports in the public sector invariably operate at a higher level of abstraction than a thorough review of input costs by a central budget office.[57] In any event, if only to avoid drawing negative media attention to the department, evaluation reports paint a rosy picture of any program's performance.

In the absence of a workable allocation or reallocation process, government managers are in the business of protecting turf – safeguarding and, if possible, expanding their level of resources. Director-level managers have no incentive to reallocate resources. They see the reallocating process going up through the organization to someone else. It is always someone else's responsibility, whether that person be the director general, the assistant deputy minister, the deputy minister, or officials in central agencies, in particular the Treasury Board. However, as we have seen, the Treasury Board no longer has the capacity to review in any detail the input costs of departmental programs and operations, having given up that ability.[58] The "someone else" ultimately has to be the prime minister and his courtiers.

One senior government official admitted as much when she observed that program, strategic, and operational reviews serve an important purpose in that "they enable us from time to time to take a look at the dead wood in the department."[59] The point she was making is that on their own, senior departmental managers do not have the capacity or the interest to deal with non-performers or dead wood. Given that their overloaded agenda allows the prime minister and his courtiers to focus on an issue only for a period of time, the result is that the government's expenditure process generates boom-and-bust cycles.[60]

That said, we have in recent years witnessed a reallocation of sorts, mostly by stealth, away from front-line offices. The delegation of more authority to managers to handle financial and human resources has strengthened the hand of departmental head offices at the expense of front-line offices and services. We saw earlier the substantial shift in resources from front-line offices to units based in the National Capital Region. Clearly, the need to feed the beast (the central agencies and officers of Parliament) has been a factor. The music teacher type of front-line worker is now too far removed from the key decision makers – the prime minister and his courtiers – to enjoy priority status either when cuts are being contemplated or when new spending plans are being formulated.

There may well be other factors at play. Deputy ministers are Ottawa-based, generally having worked in Ottawa for most of their careers and in central agencies, especially the Privy Council Office. The mind-set in Ottawa is that anything that truly matters must take place in Ottawa, especially, with the prime minister and his courtiers. Policy issues of any significance and the bringing of a horizontal perspective on things is somehow an Ottawa responsibility.[61]

Dominic LeBlanc, MP for Beauséjour, thinks that there are other factors at play. He explains: "Deputy ministers do not like to see any of the staff that were just laid off going up and down the elevator with them. It is easier for them to cut positions and staff, if necessary, in offices that they are unlikely to even visit."[62] To be sure, Ottawa-based public servants do not react well to even a hint that the decentralization program of government units that was introduced in the mid-1970s – but which died in the late 1970s – might be relaunched. The Ottawa real estate market matters to senior public servants in the National Capital Region, not those in Moose Jaw or Sydney.[63]

A thirty-nine-year veteran of the Canadian public service, who served both in a regional office and in Ottawa, reflected on his career when he retired in 2011. He was promoted to the managerial ranks early in his career in government after obtaining a graduate degree in economics and working for a few years in the private sector. His unit produced labour-market forecasts and promoted career information and development to students. He enjoyed the work, but he reports that things began to deteriorate in the 1990s when government "hooked its wagon to the adoption of private sector practices." Suddenly he "noticed classification creep beginning at all levels of the public service but, in particular, at the executive level." It is worth quoting him at length on his move from a regional office to Ottawa: "When I moved to the Nation's Capital – Ottawa – in 2000, I was in for a real eye-opener. After 17 years of working in an operational setting in a regional office, where you're connected to real citizens, I admit to being naïve with my surprise at how things worked at the 'Center.' I proved not to be particularly effective at this style of upside-down leadership. From the time I worked in the private sector in the late '70s to my arrival in Ottawa, I had always prided myself on being client-focused. Now I was a fish out of water. Serve the system, park your brain at the door (despite the espoused hype of being a learning organization), do what you're told, and all will be well."[64]

There are growing signs that the shift of resources from front-line offices to the National Capital Region is creating problems for front-line managers and their employees. For example, the queue of people waiting to have their employment insurance claims processed doubled between 2007 and late 2011. The growth in the waiting list for benefits paralleled a drop in staff in offices processing claims. The decline in staff amounts to 13 percent over the four-year period. The result "has been a system in turmoil," where "unemployed people" are not able to get through "even by telephone." The department, meanwhile, argues in its various evaluation and performance reports that all is well, insisting that it continues to strive to "maintain a flexible and sustainable workforce capacity comprising both permanent and temporary employees, working on a full-time or part-time basis."[65]

I interviewed an Ottawa-based mid-level manager for this study, asking her what she thought happened to the music teacher. She has since written several emails in search of the answer. She says that there are far too many federal public servants in Ottawa units who have too little to do or are engaged in "work-avoidance dodges." She, too, sees little merit in the hundreds of reports prepared every year for Parliament. In one of her emails, she wrote, "I called CRA with an income tax question and I was on hold for 45 minutes. I could not help but think that too many CRA employees were busy preparing reports saying that all is well at CRA."[66]

How Does One Explain Things?

This study makes it clear that the public administration discipline remains some distance from developing a comprehensive theory. One can discern a kernel of truth in all of the theories reviewed in chapter 1. Some are more relevant than others, but all have some relevance to the findings of this study. The study does demonstrate, however, that the theory suggesting that one can easily import private sector management measures to government simply does not work. It is worth repeating once more that the public and private sectors are fundamentally different in both important and unimportant ways. Efforts to import private sector management practices in government may well have had a negative impact – it may explain, at least in part, why the public service, as an institution, has lost prestige after thirty years or so of trying to implement NPM measures.[67]

Thomas Axworthy and Julie Burch report that almost half of all federal public servants have given serious consideration to leaving the job. They ask, Who can blame them? They explain that we have witnessed a "devaluation of the work of the public service and many public servants surveyed resent the fact that their hard work is perceived as not good enough for government work or that they themselves are seen as lazy bureaucrats."[68] Generous salaries, paternal and maternity leave, employee benefits, and extremely generous pension plans have not dispelled the low morale in the public service. Nor have attempts to import private sector management practices to government.

This study shows that there are tensions, if not outright contradictions, between the different intellectual streams that have fed into public sector reforms in recent years. As Christopher Pollitt and Geert Bouckaert point out, this is particularly evident between the "economistic, principal-and-agent theory of thinking, which is essentially low trust, and the more managerial way of thinking, which is more concerned with empowerment, innovation and motivation."[69]

Public choice and rational choice theories also resonate with the findings of this study. We know that consultants, agents of Parliament, academics, and many public servants have made quite a decent living producing reports, even "if little else happens in the long run."[70] Path dependency and the work of institutionists also resonate. The guardian-spender model still applies, though it has evolved to include new policy actors, and one important guardian – the Treasury Board Secretariat – has lost the ability to perform an effective budget-office role.[71]

This study also sheds light on the Herman Finer/Carl Friedrich debate on accountability. It makes the case that Finer has it right – that in the spending of public money, detailed processes, rules, controls, regulations, and sanctions work better than relying on the discretionary judgment of senior public servants. Relying on public servants' self-direction, self-regulation, judgment, and production of various performance assessment reports has serious limits – hence, the argument that while you can fudge reports, you cannot fudge rules.

Front-line workers – the music teacher types – have lost standing in the shift away from centrally prescribed processes, rules, and regulations and towards self-regulation and the more recent work of senior public servants in the head offices of government departments. It will be recalled that in chapter 1 we noted that the field of economics has had a profound effect on the study of public administration, and that the field is primarily concerned with formulating theories that explain what motivates decision makers in the public sector. The field of public administration, meanwhile, is primarily concerned with prescriptions to improve operations in the public sector. The next chapter explores further what happened to the music teacher and offers some prescriptions.

11

So What Happened to the Music Teacher?

New Public Management, New Public Governance, and recent public sector reforms have created new constituencies. In the process, front-line workers have become no one's constituency. Those who in the past would have spoken on their behalf – the local member of Parliament, the local media, and local community groups – have been shunted aside by more powerful forces. Misguided, costly, and ineffective accountability requirements, the work of agents of Parliament (the blame generators), the rise of permanent campaigns, and the need to control communications have reshaped how Ottawa decides, how it spends, and how it delivers public services. Governments operate in a vastly different world today than even thirty years ago. It is no exaggeration to say that we are witnessing at the same time the politicization of the public service and the bureaucratization of the body politic.[1] Jonathan Rose summed it up when he observed, "You've got bureaucrats who are doing the government's partisan work and also political staffers who are doing bureaucrats' work. So there's this blurring of lines between the two."[2]

Parliament, it seems, has simply given up and turned over its responsibilities to its agents. MPs have been left to pursue what they prefer to pursue – search for scandals, for administrative miscues, for the $10,000 spent on booze at a reception. The government has countered with report after report that serve little purpose other than enabling politicians on the government side and public servants to say to the media, "Look at these reports. You will see that all is fine." Policy making relies less and less on objective advice provided by public servants. It has become a matter of political opinion and has merged with communications.

Public servants have become sympathetic to the plight confronting politicians on the government side. Realizing that what their political bosses value is the ability to defuse politically dangerous issues, they have drawn on their experience to offer political advice. Yet politicians do not view their senior public servants in the same positive light as they did thirty years ago. Paul Tellier, former clerk of the privy council, argued in 2009 that "the trust between Canada's politicians and bureaucrats has never been more strained and steps must be taken to lower the temperature and rebuild frayed relations."[3] Another former senior federal official maintains that "we are living in a time of unprecedented divide between the political and bureaucratic in Ottawa."[4]

Policy units and units charged with responding to new accountability requirements secured the bulk of the new positions established as the prime minister and his courtiers shifted focus away from expenditure cuts to other issues in the years after the 1994–97 program review. The prime minister pursued his priorities – for example, the Millennium Scholarship Fund – and Jocelyne Bourgon, the clerk of the privy council, pursued her own priorities, which were to strengthen Ottawa-based policy, evaluation, and monitoring units. Don Drummond, for example, praised Bourgon for rebuilding the policy units in departments after they had been "weakened" in the 1994–97 program review exercise. The policy units, together with program evaluation and internal audit units, were indeed rebuilt between 2000 and 2010, when a substantial number of new positions were added to them. But this did not prevent Drummond in 2011 from writing about Ottawa's dismal policy capacity.[5]

It bears repeating that while these units were being rebuilt in Ottawa, the regional and local offices delivering front-line services were not rebuilt; in fact, they have been losing staff. Policy, planning, and monitoring units are much more "visible" to the clerk of the privy council than point-of-delivery offices are. In the process, the Ottawa system is losing sight of the music teacher types operating on the front lines of public service delivery. Front-line managers and their employees do not figure prominently in the work of central agencies or in the head offices of line departments and agencies, other than as producers of information. To answer Harold Lasswell's question – who gets what, when, how? – Ottawa's bureaucracy has been able to get more than in years past.

Attempts to make public sector management look like that of the private sector has made the Ottawa bureaucracy more expensive. Managers took advantage of their new-found authority to move funds between votes and activities to add to their salary and operations budgets. Consider the following: The core federal public service grew by 34 percent over the past ten years to 282,955 from 211,915 (2001–11). The bulk of the growth was in Ottawa-based units designed to serve the bureaucracy and accountability requirements, to generate policy advice, and to manage communications and media relations. The expansion of the federal government's bureaucracy outpaced population growth over the same decade at a rate of three to one.[6]

Harper's strategic and operations review in the summer of 2011 was set up in part to deal with this growth. It begs the question: Why, with all the ambitious public sector management reforms of the past thirty years, were all these public servants hired in the first place? It will be recalled that the federal government transferred a number of labour-intensive activities to provincial governments and third parties in the 1990s (for example, airports and ports). And this leads to a second question: Why did the Harper government see the need to spend $20 million on outside consultants to assist in identifying spending cuts? And a third: Why were all those new employees hired in policy evaluation and other head office units that are not up to the task? Yet another question: Are we to accept that significant cuts to the government's expenditure budget are possible only when the prime minister and his courtiers take charge and when the cuts are initiated in the immediate aftermath of the government winning a majority mandate? (e.g., the Chrétien-Martin 1994–97 program review and Harper's strategic and operational review 2011–12).

Public sector managers have benefited from attempts to emulate private sector management, but they have experienced few of the drawbacks. Salaries have increased in recent years, partly as a result of classification creep and collective bargaining. As we saw earlier, federal public servants still enjoy generous pension and other employee benefits when compared with other sectors.

Private sector employees, meanwhile, have had to adjust to the competitive requirements of the global economy. As this study points out, membership in unions in the private sector has dropped substantially, and fewer employees have defined-pension benefits. Because of the competitive nature of the global economy, some large firms with unionized workers have decided "unilaterally" to implement lower wages and benefits. Against the wishes of the union, Caterpillar simply declared that "any employee who works for EMC [in London, Ontario] after 11:59 of December 31, 2011 will be deemed to have accepted the wage and benefit terms of EMC's last offer."[7] The Royal Bank of Canada recently announced that it will place new hires into a defined-contribution pension plan, labelling the decision "responsible financial management."[8] No one inside government is suggesting that these measures should be introduced in the public sector.

As we saw in this study, senior public servants take great pride in speaking the language of the business community in their reports and speeches on the state of the federal public service and government operations. They did not, however, speak truth to their institution and to their fellow public servants when manufacturing plants closed during the severe economic downturn in 2008–09; when the pulp and paper industry – among other sectors – had to adjust to the competitive nature of the global economy, throwing thousands of Canadians out of work; and when many pension plans in the private sector melted away. Instead of calling for adjustments, federal deputy ministers pushed for adding more staff to their head office operations, and few in government called for a review of employee benefits to square with developments in the private sector – that was someone else's responsibility. Public servants, then, ought not to be surprised that this leads to boom-and-bust budgeting in government.

The reason public servants have been able to draw the benefits in borrowing practices from the private sector yet experience few of the drawbacks is, again, because the public and private sectors are different in every way. Collective bargaining in the public sector can ignore the global economy, can apply political pressure to secure benefits for its current and even retired employees, and can inhibit the ability to deal with non-performers. This study makes the point that attempts to create a "bottom line" in government operations that resembles that in the private sector have all failed badly. Not only have business-inspired reforms failed, they have made matters worse. Public sector morale has fallen, policy units are less certain about their role in a post-positivism world, and relations between politicians and public servants have deteriorated.[9] Evaluation units are busy turning cranks that are not attached to anything, and MPs and even cabinet ministers are left on the outside looking in, as the prime minister and his courtiers create policy and new initiatives.

Jane Jacobs identified a set of values that exist in each of the two sectors but are incompatible. The private sector, for example, values initiative and enterprise, invests for productive purposes, is thrifty, optimistic, and open to inventiveness. The public sector values obedience and discipline, adheres to tradition, respects hierarchy, and is exclusive.[10] Because these differences were ignored, there is no doubt that the public service as an institution has been knocked off its moorings. Attempts to make it manage like the private sector have played havoc with two distinct ethical standards and roles that both sectors have played successfully down the ages.[11] Public servants have lost their way, uncertain how they should now assess management performance, how they should generate policy advice, how they should work with their political masters, and how they should speak truth to political power and to their own institution.

The last thirty years have given us sufficient proof that public sector administration can never be made to look like private sector management in either substance or style. Efforts to overhaul the government's IT sector, its approach to employee classification, and its largely unread evaluation and performance assessments would simply not be acceptable in the private sector.[12] And while many private sector executives have, over the past thirty years, been shrinking their head offices, removing management layers, and sticking to their knitting,[13] senior federal public servants have been shrinking their regional and local offices, enlarging their head offices, and adding new "associate" positions at virtually every management level in their organization.

The various public sector reforms have also given life to the theories that borrow from the economic discipline. If they did not resonate before the reforms, they do now. The delegation of more authority over human and financial resources made it easier for budget-maximizing bureaucrats to pursue opportunities. Classification creep, the shifting of more and more positions to the National Capital Region, and the addition of new policy planning and evaluation units in Ottawa play into the hands of budget-maximizing bureaucrats. If nothing else, the reforms have given us still more government and in the process have shifted both concerns and resources away from the regional and local offices that deliver public services.[14] It takes the prime minister and his courtiers, from time to time, and when circumstances allow, to put on the brakes and introduce major spending cuts.

The principal-agent theory is also very much alive today. Attempts to shift emphasis from input costs to assessing outcomes have muddied the accountability waters. Politicians and taxpayers have little interest or knowledge in how best to assess the work of government units evaluating programs. More to the point, principals in the past had a better capacity than they do now to direct the work of agents and to hold them to account by looking at input costs, by carrying out a detailed review of proposed spending, and by identifying the parliamentary votes that funded activities.

It was a universe that they easily understood, unlike the obtuse and cautiously drafted reports we see now, designed to avoid tough questions and political controversies.

The guardian-spender model has also been transformed. The guardians now consist of the prime minister, his courtiers, and the minister and Department of Finance. They remain all-powerful within government. But they are also spenders whenever they want to be. They have to ask no one when deciding on new spending projects. Conversely, they can also launch spending cuts – mostly across-the-board ones – and are able to make them stick.

However, the cuts are ad hoc in nature and are struck in a period of fiscal crisis or, again, on the heels of a prime minister winning a majority mandate. As we saw earlier, spenders continue to look for opportunities and are often able to win some concessions, especially when a general election approaches or when the government's fiscal problems are no longer being discussed in the media.

Treasury Board Secretariat was the one guardian that had a capacity to keep a check on the spenders on a continuing basis. As we have seen, it has lost this capacity. Its new purpose is to relay management concerns to line departments and agencies and to identify ways to empower managers. Just as the short-lived Policy and Expenditure Management System could not transform spenders into guardians, the management board concept has not been able to turn spenders into guardians within line departments and agencies – one only has to consider classification creep to see evidence of this.

There is no need to repeat here what we saw in chapter 2 on Parliament's growing inability to review in a meaningful fashion the government's expenditure budget. Veteran MP Pat Martin summed up the problem when he observed: "A cursory overview of vague and confusing generalizations not only fails to give a clear picture of spending priorities, it provides the opportunity to hide a lot of spending that would never fly if given the light of day. Sunlight is a powerful disinfectant."[15] A review of input costs which members of Parliament can easily grasp provides sunlight. Thousands of pages of performance review and evaluation reports do not.

Students of public and rational choice theories and principal-agent theories can now say, "We told you so." However, students of traditional public administration can also say that the theories simply became self-fulfilling prophecies. Soon after they made their presence felt in the literature, and with the help of some high-profile politicians (such as Margaret Thatcher), the search was on for a new approach to managing government operations – hence the call to import private sector management practices and the implementation of New Public Management (such as PS 2000). Students of traditional public administration could make the case that Herman Finer would be entitled to say, "I told you so," based on his work published more than seventy years ago.[16]

What to Do?

Unless one is able to disconnect the work of public servants from a highly charged political environment – which is unlikely – one should look to the past for the way ahead. To rediscover roots offers promise because the basic contours of our political institutions and the relationship between our political and administrative institutions remain largely intact. The argument here is that public sector administration remains joined at the hip to the country's political institutions. Ambitious public service reforms are unlikely to have much success without correspondingly ambitious reforms to the political institutions. Waiting for such a development is like waiting for the Greek month of calends.

If anything, our political institutions are less tolerant of administrative miscues than they were forty years ago. Permanent election campaigns, tied to the rise of the new media and gotcha journalism, along with access to information legislation, had a profound impact on public sector management at about the same time that politicians decided to look to the private sector for inspiration on how to fix bureaucracy. Thus, precisely at the point when politicians, the media, and taxpayers sought more clarity on how government spends and looked for ways to ensure that public servants could not squirm out of their Weberian apparatus, centrally prescribed rules and processes were substantially reduced in a fruitless search for a bottom line in government operations. The verdict? We have witnessed in the last decade, in particular, a tremendous growth in the cost of government operations, and as Chris Pollitt and Geert Bouckaert argue in their widely read *Public Management Reform*, we have seen, after thirty years of public sector reform efforts, "falling civil service prestige."[17]

A former chair of the Public Service Commission of Canada teamed up with a well-known student of public policy to carry out an extensive survey of federal government executives. They discovered a public service that values "self censorship as a survival instinct in a world where critical thinking and sharp exchanges are no longer valued as they used to be." They also discovered a world where senior executives are not in charge, or even want to be. They write, "When faced with the hypothesis that they have to take charge, because nobody is truly and completely in charge, there was a forceful reaction of disbelief."[18] It may well be that Ottawa is now home to a very large bureaucratic machine in which no one is in charge and no one has power unless the prime minister decides to make it an issue.

Nowhere is this more evident than in shaping the expenditure budget. Although a crisis atmosphere helps (as in 1994–97 and 2011–12), recent history has shown that only the prime minister and his courtiers can generate substantial spending cuts. The machine will implement them, but then it will lie in wait for the good times to come again.[19] If history is a guide, they will.

What the machinery of government has learned to do well is to ensure that departments and agencies run on their tracks. The machinery is no longer capable of challenging the status quo from within or disputing others, such as the Office of the Auditor General, when it promotes measures that do not square with the values, requirements, and strengths of its institution. On policy, the machine has turned public servants into short-order cooks rather than sous-chefs when helping the government prepare a policy agenda.[20]

Returning to Roots

How, then, can we repair the relationship between politicians and public servants and rebuild the credibility of the Canadian public service? I believe that the answer lies in the pursuit of a Neo-Weberian state.[21] Indeed, a Weberian perspective on the state apparatus holds the most promise, given how our political institutions operate and the interests they wish to pursue. The first requirement is to recognize that the public and private sectors are very different. Year in, year out, we are informed that pay-for-performance schemes in Western governments report "mixed or downright disappointing results."[22] Canada is certainly no exception. Day after day, the media reminds us that the public sector can never be like the private sector.

We now need to promote the idea of a public service with a distinctive status, culture, terms, and conditions.[23] We need to reaffirm both the role of representative democracy and the central position of statutes in defining the role of policy makers and decision makers. The thinking here is that rediscovering roots will rescue the public administration from simple assumptions tied to economic self-interest and deductive models, and release it from the mantra that reforms inspired by the private sector can drive productive change in the public sector.

The thinking is also based on the reality that politicians are dealing with an accumulation of government departments, agencies, and organizations over which they have increasingly little control.[24] The shift away from public administration has only made things worse, with the public service essentially becoming a self-governing institution when it comes to administration. Too much administrative discretion has been turned over to senior public servants to establish new positions, salaries, and classifications and to deal with financial and human resources and other issues. It is only when operations become too costly, when a financial crisis looms, or when circumstances allow it that prime ministers will take a whack at the public service, cut it back to size, and show who is boss.[25]

A former senior federal public servant explained the problem as follows: "The recent experience of the federal public service demonstrates a tendency for employment and compensation to alternate between relatively rapid growth and freezes, imposed restraints or even reductions." This happens, he noted, "with surprisingly little rancour" because of early retirement incentives and generous compensation packages. Yet employees still feel "at risk and devalued," while those remaining feel "like victims."[26] It only takes a moment's reflection to appreciate that the private sector is very different on this front.[27]

Back to Basics

The goal is to place renewed emphasis on procedural controls and rules, on the distinctiveness of the public sector, and in rediscovering the public service's sense of frugality.[28] It calls for an overhaul of the work of agents of Parliament, the machinery of government, and rebuilding the relationship between politicians and public servants.

Officers of Parliament, most notably the Office of the Auditor General, have made government operations more complex, more expensive, and less accessible to politicians. J.J. Macdonell was wrong in his diagnosis of the problem, and taxpayers continue to pay a heavy price. He came to Ottawa convinced that public sector managers were not up to the task and that superior, private sector management could show the way to a better management. The Trudeau government felt that it had more important issues to deal with – a general election was looming – than to heed Macdonell's alarming cry that Parliament and the government had lost or were close to losing effective control of the public purse.[29] As we have seen, the government established a royal commission that had little lasting effect and agreed to expand the auditor general's responsibilities to include comprehensive or value-for-money audits, which have had a long-term negative effect.[30]

The OAG, as this study has shown, has pushed and pulled government departments into an ever-increasing amount of reporting requirements. Politicians on the government side have more important things to attend to than dealing with the auditor general, while those on the opposition benches invariably support an expanded role for the OAG in the hope that it will be able to produce ammunition they can use to embarrass the government. Senior public servants, meanwhile, are in no position to challenge, at least publicly, the work of the auditor general. They simply roll along with the new demands and add more resources to evaluation units, to risk management efforts, to values and ethics initiatives, to internal audits, and to financial management controls and information technology.

If the goal is to rediscover a parsimonious culture in government operations, politicians need to speak truth to the OAG. The office itself is not only expensive to operate, but it has forced departments to spend a substantial amount of public funds on highly questionable accountability requirements. The government should propose amendments to the Auditor General Act and return the office to what accountants do best – conducting financial audits. The proposed amendments should put an end to the OAG's tendency to run with the latest management fad found in the private sector and try it on for size on government departments.

Program evaluations in future should be limited to machine-like departments or programs – the number of public servants required to process passports, income-tax returns, and the like.[31] The evaluation of the work of policy units and a host of social and economic development programs have, as noted, kept too many public servants and consultants busy turning cranks that are not attached to anything.

Parliament – more specifically, one of its committees – should review the work of agents of Parliament. They are costly, and it is even more costly to respond to their requests for information. There are also far more agents of Parliament in Ottawa than in other Westminster-style parliamentary systems.[32] Parliament needs to review its relations with its agents with a view to strengthening accountability requirements. At the moment, officers of Parliament are free agents, answerable to no one, able to pursue their own purposes, always with an eye on the media. The work of the parliamentary budget officer, for example, is mostly about challenging the fiscal outlook and expenditure budget forecasts of the Department of Finance, rather than helping MPs understand the government's fiscal framework and expenditure budget process.[33] As we saw earlier, some officers of Parliament have acknowledged the problem and have tried to engage MPs on the issue, but without success. If MPs are truly serious about strengthening the capacity of their institution, they should start by reviewing the role of Parliament's own officers.

The Machinery

The government should accept that efforts to transform the Treasury Board Secretariat into a management board have failed at a considerable cost to taxpayers. The management-board concept was designed to bring a friendlier face to line departments and agencies. It did away with many centrally prescribed rules and processes, promoting a kind of blameless accountability and essentially abandoning its budget-office role. It now relies on a variety of soft evaluation and performance assessments in carrying out its work.

In the immediate aftermath of the sponsorship scandal, for example, the Treasury Board Secretariat produced a paper on the doctrine and practice of ministerial responsibility, arguing, "Accountability should not be directly equated with blame ... The challenge is to develop a capacity for capturing lessons learned."[34] Only among Ottawa-based public servants can "accountability" without "blame" hold any kind of currency. Try that on for size in the private sector. It is revealing to note that neither the OAG (with about 800 person years) nor the Treasury Board Secretariat (with about 2,000) had any inkling that the government was running a sponsorship program in which a senior public servant broke "just about every rule in the book."[35] It took the work of a tenacious journalist to uncover what has been described as the political and financial scandal of the decade.[36] The Treasury Board Secretariat's proper role is to be a guardian of the public purse and nothing less. The other traditional guardians – the Privy Council Office and the Department of Finance – do not have the mandate or the capacity to review in any detail departmental spending plans and their operations.

The government should eliminate most, if not all, associate positions in departments and agencies. Associate positions were at first limited to the associate deputy minister level. However, they are now common at virtually all management levels. There are some twenty associate deputy ministers and a growing number of senior associate deputy ministers, associate assistant deputy ministers, associate directors general, and associate directors. One can only imagine what Max Weber would make of this development.[37] He sought to define in specific terms how a bureaucratic organization should function. He insisted that officials should be organized in a clearly defined hierarchy of offices, that each office should have a clear, legally defined sphere of competence, that work in the office should constitute a career, and that officials be subject to strict and systematic descriptions and controls in the conduct of their offices. Weber saw distinct roles and responsibilities not only for government departments but also for each position, in that the incumbents would understand clearly what was expected of them and then be held to account for their activities. Weber's bureaucracy was designed to operate on the basis of office hierarchy, with clear lines of authority and subordination.

Hierarchy and technical skills are important for a host of reasons. To define the necessary technical skills not only ensures an efficient organization but insulates it from "dilution by influences from outside and corruption from within the organization."[38] Hierarchy provides clear lines of authority through which commands can be transmitted, and it allows "calculability of results" for those in positions of authority.[39] Moreover, a hierarchical division of responsibility and authority ensures that the higher office does not take over the work of the lower, and it gives the "governed" a clear line for appealing "the decision of a lower office to the corresponding superior authority."[40] The creation of new "associate positions" muddles the distinct spaces Weber envisaged for every box in departmental organizational charts.

While associate positions are common in the Ottawa bureaucracy, they are not common in regional and local offices. They make for thicker government, muddy effective accountability, and make it more difficult for front-line managers and workers to communicate up the hierarchy. They promote a head-office perspective and an unaccountable system. They also promote a disunity of command as each official tends to distort the information he or she passes upward in the hierarchy. In brief, associate positions enable officials to vary the degree of responsibility and risks in the performance of their duties, depending on circumstances and personal objectives.[41]

The Relationship

Sir Michael Bichard, former permanent secretary in Britain, maintains that effective public service reform is not possible without public servants being "genuinely committed to personal accountability."[42] We can only wish him well in pursuing this objective in his country, since there is little likelihood of such a development in Canada. One only needs to see how Canada implemented the accounting officer concept to see that personal accountability for public servants continues to be a non-starter. As we saw, Canada's version of the accounting officer is, at best, a continuation of the status quo. Some observers make the case that it has made matters worse.[43] The Government of Canada continues to insist that only politicians can be accountable to Parliament and to Canadians. Notwithstanding the introduction of the accounting officer concept, the Privy Council Office insists that "the accounting officer mechanism does not give accounting officers a sphere of accountability that is independent of that of their ministers."[44] PCO is essentially arguing that nothing has changed. It does not, however, explain why the concept was introduced if it changes nothing.

This study calls for simplicity in the machinery, a delayering and thinning exercise, and a clarification of the roles of both political and administrative actors. In turn, it calls for a renewed emphasis on the need to organize the machinery of government in a defined hierarchy of offices with clear lines of authority. And it calls for the preservation of a public service as an institution that has a distinctive status, culture, and terms of conditions of employment. There is a need for an ambitious reform agenda to reconnect public administration to its roots. The agenda should be enshrined in legislation and should define in statutes the role of the prime minister; and it should establish in statutes a distinct personality for the public service so that public servants have a legal basis for resisting instructions from elected politicians when asked to perform essentially political acts; and the agenda should stipulate that spending estimates be submitted to Parliament in a form that is easily understood by members of Parliament and taxpayers – a return to line-item budgeting.

The chain of accountability – from voter to MP, from MP to prime minister and cabinet ministers, from cabinet to line ministers, from line ministers to the heads of government departments and agencies, and from senior public servants to front-line managers and their employees – needs to be rebuilt. Transparency is the key to accountability in the public sector, just as market forces and the bottom line are in the private sector. This sums up the difference between the two sectors. The bottom line in the public sector is trust, and transparency fuels trust.[45]

If conflicts over an administrative decision between politicians and public servants become public, so be it. Surely it is not a sin against representative democracy for citizens to be informed that a minister has forced public servants to keep an office open in a high-unemployment region. It is far more democratic to have this done in the open for all to see than to have it hidden behind the doctrine of ministerial responsibility. The prime minister and ministers should have the final say on such issues, but when they meddle in administrative issues, it should be a matter for Parliament to debate – or at least to be informed of – and for citizens to be told.

I borrow a page from Ralph Heintzman in recommending a Charter of Public Service, a three-way moral contract between public servants, ministers, and Parliament. The purpose is to establish ground rules, guidelines, and boundaries which, as Heintzman explains "must be respected if the public service is to be a respected institution, trusted by ministers, by parliament and by Canadians." Heintzman calls for boundaries also for ministers and for members of Parliament. He explains that there must be "boundaries of language and behaviour beyond which they may not go if they are to keep their side of the bargain, in support of an ethical and professional public service dedicated to the public interest."[46]

Peter Aucoin, Mark Jarvis, and Lori Turnbull write that "the Canadian system of parliamentary government faces a fundamental problem that has been allowed to undermine Canadian democracy. The prime minister wields too much power over the operations of the House of Commons."[47] The prime minister also wields too much power over the machinery of government. We still do not have clear rules on the power of the prime minister and his main adviser, the clerk of the privy council. The prime minister acts as the chief executive officer while the clerk acts as chief operating officer. The thinking appears to be that if a corporation in the private sector can have a CEO and COO, so should government. It makes no more sense to have a CEO in government than it does to have a prime minister or a clerk of the privy council running a corporation. Government is government, with the clash of ideas during election campaigns and the need to advance "contestable public goods on behalf of a body of citizens who are bearers of rights and duties in a framework of a democratic community."[48] The private sector is the private sector and a private corporation pursues vastly different objectives than government.

Why attempt to make tough decisions when there is no good reason to do so, when there are no consequences for not doing so, and when everyone in the machinery of government knows that tough decisions are the responsibility of the prime minister, the clerk of the privy council, and other courtiers? Why be responsible when you know that responsibility somehow always belongs to someone else?

The goal now should be to alter substantially the internal logic of appropriateness, both at the elected level in government and in the bureaucracy. We need to define in statutes the role of the prime minister and that of the clerk of the privy council. Prime ministers and their ministers should retain full authority to make policy, to allocate financial resources, to establish how policy should be delivered, to decide on the size and shape of the public service, and to make appointments at the most senior levels in government departments, agencies, and corporations. They should have the authority to overrule public servants in all matters not covered by statutes, provided that such decisions are made public. Senior public servants should also remain accountable to the government, in the sense that only the prime minister and ministers should be able to impose sanctions and make appointments at the most senior levels.

But other things have to change. There is a need to give public servants an administrative space which they can occupy relatively free from political interference, a capacity to resist improper demands from elected politicians, and a sense of ownership, however tenuous, in their work. Paul Tellier, former cabinet secretary to the Mulroney government, told the media that senior public servants need to rediscover the capacity to "say no to ministers when required."[49] This will not happen just because we wish it to happen or because a former cabinet secretary suggests that it should. We need to give public servants a statutory capacity and duty to perform in this manner. If this is not possible, citizens will have to accept that their public service will never measure up to expectations. It will remain riddled with inefficiencies and will be far more costly to taxpayers than is needed. And retaining the best and the brightest in the public service will become increasingly difficult, despite generous salaries and highly attractive employment benefits.

How deputy ministers are appointed needs an overhaul. It is no longer appropriate for the prime minister and the clerk of the privy council to hand-pick appointees from a limited pool of candidates from central agencies who have little experience in actually delivering programs and services to Canadians. Other Westminster-style parliamentary systems and some provincial governments have opened up the appointment process to competition.[50] It is considerably easier to speak truth to power and to be fearless in providing advice when a public servant's appointment is supported by formal processes and structures, rather than leaving such officials on their own to deal with two powerful individuals – the prime minister and the clerk – who have all the power to decide who makes it to the top and who stays there.

Simplicity, formal rules, formal processes, a recognition that the public sector has its own intrinsic characteristics, along with the promotion of a parsimonious culture in government operations, a streamlined hierarchy, transparency, and a three-way moral contract, can rebuild the federal public service's credibility with Canadian taxpayers. This will assist members of Parliament and Canadians in general to gain a better understanding of government operations and a greater ability to determine "who gets the most of what there is to get."[51]

A practitioner who knows about public spending observed that "it seems absolutely human and understandable that if cuts are imposed, those who decide where the cuts should be implemented" will decide that they should fall on anybody but themselves.[52] Front-line managers, their employees, and the music teacher type of public servant would stand a better chance of being heard if public administrative and government operations returned to their roots.

NOTES

INTRODUCTION

1 Consultations with Marc Rochon, Ottawa, various dates. Mr Rochon is a former deputy minister at Canadian Heritage and head of the Canada Central Mortgage Corporation.

2 Consultations with Gérard Veilleux, Ottawa and Montreal, various dates. Mr Veilleux is a former deputy minister of federal-provincial relations, secretary to the Treasury Board, and president of the Canadian Broadcasting Corporation with the Government of Canada.

3 Lord Wilson of Dinton, "The Mandarin Myth," fourth lecture in a series on Tomorrow's Government, Ottawa, 1 March 2006, 7.

4 Consultations with former senior officials in the British government. See also Geoffrey K. Fry, "The Thatcher Government, the Financial Management Initiative and the New Civil Service," *Public Administration* 66, no. 2 (1988): 7.

5 Consultations with former senior British government officials, London and Oxford, various dates. See also Donald J. Savoie, *Thatcher, Reagan, Mulroney: In Search of a New Bureaucracy* (Pittsburgh: University of Pittsburgh Press, 1994).

6 See Donald J. Savoie, *Breaking the Bargain: Public Servants, Ministers, and Parliament* (Toronto: University of Toronto Press, 2003).

7 Alasdair Roberts, "Worrying about Misconduct: The Control Lobby and the PS 2000 Reforms," *Canadian Public Administration* 39, no. 4 (1997): 518.

8 We have seen, particularly since the 2008 financial meltdown, a slew of articles in the popular press about the cost of government operations. See, among many, many others, "Loose control, management blamed for costly PS," www.ottawacitizen.com, 5 December 2011.

9 See, for example, Tony Judt, *Ill Fares the Land* (New York: Penguin Press, 2010).

10 Michael Ignatieff, "9/11 and the age of sovereign failure," www.theglobeandmail.com, 9 September 2011.

11 Ibid.; *New York Review of Books*, www.mybooks.com/articles/archives, 29 April 2010.
12 See Jeffrey Simpson, "Income inequality: Deep, complex, and growing," www.theglobeandmail.com, 9 December 2011.
13 John Kenneth Galbraith, *Dimension* (Moncton: 1986), 13.
14 Tony Benn, "Manifestos and Mandates," in Tony Benn, Shirley Williams, et al., *Policy and Practice: The Experience of Governments* (London: Royal Institute of Public Administration, 1980), 68.
15 Shirley Willams, "The Decision Makers," ibid., 81.
16 See Donald J. Savoie, *Court Government and the Collapse of Accountability in Canada and the United Kingdom* (Toronto: University of Toronto Press, 2008), 74.
17 Quoted in Kathryn May, "As MP, he tried to reform public service," *Ottawa Citizen*, 15 October 2011, A3.
18 Ibid., A8.
19 John McEdowney and Colin Lee, "Parliament and Public Money," in Philip Giddings, ed, *The Future of Parliament: Issues for a New Century* (London: Palgrave Macmillan, 2005), 78.
20 Bev Deware made this observation in an interview with me as I was carrying out research for my book *Thatcher, Reagan, Mulroney*.
21 Quoted in "With an eye to the future, a watchdog departs," *Globe and Mail*, 13 May 2011, A4.
22 David A. Good, *The Politics of Public Money: Spenders, Guardians, Priority Setters, and Financial Watchdogs inside the Canadian Government* (Toronto: IPAC and University of Toronto Press, 2007), 36. See also G.W. Nutter, *The Growth of Government in the West* (Washington, DC: American Enterprise Institute, 1978).
23 "City hall starts to trim fat," *Times and Transcript* (Moncton), 13 August 2011, A1 and A3.
24 "Stephen Harper: Not the Conservative he once was," www.thestar.com, 1 October 2011.
25 See, among others, Pierre G. Bergeron, *Modern Management in Canada: Concepts and Practices* (Toronto: Methuen, 1987).
26 See, among others, Donald J. Savoie, *The Politics of Public Spending in Canada* (Toronto: University of Toronto Press, 1990); Good, *The Politics of Public Money*; and C. Hood and M. Wright, eds, *Big Governments in Hard Times* (Oxford: Martin Robertson, 1981).
27 Quoted in Good, *The Politics of Public Money*, 71.
28 J. Lynn and A. Jay, *Yes Minister: The Diaries of a Cabinet Minister*, vol. 1 (London: British Broadcasting Corporation, 1981), 57.
29 See, among others, Allen Schick, "Budgeting for Results: Recent Developments in Five Industrialized Countries," *Public Administration Review* 50, no. 1 (1990): 26–34.
30 See, among others, Martin Lodge and Derek Gill, "Toward a New Era of Administrative Reform? The Myth of Post-NPM in New Zealand," *Governance* 24, no. 1 (2011): 141–65.

31 See, among others, "IMF has one cure for debt crises: Public spending cuts and tax rises," www.guardian.co.uk, 9 May 2010.

32 "Make firm plans to cut deficits, Harper urges G20 ahead of summit," *Globe and Mail*, 17 May 2010, A1.

33 Andrew Dunsire and Christopher Hood, *Cutback Management in Public Bureaucracies: Popular Theories and Observed Outcomes in Whitehall* (Cambridge: Cambridge University Press, 1980), 42.

34 Quoted from Andrew Massey, "Mapping the Future: Research into Public Policy, Administration, and Management in Britain," workshop, University of Oxford, 19 and 20 April 2004, 2.

35 Christopher Pollitt and Geert Bouckaert, *Public Management Reform: A Comparative Analysis – New Public Management, Governance, and the Neo-Weberian State*, 3rd edn (Oxford: Oxford University Press, 2011), 219.

36 See, for example, Savoie, *Thatcher, Reagan, Mulroney* and *Court Government*.

37 Harold Lasswell, *Politics: Who Gets What, When, How* (New York: Meridan Books, 1958).

38 Edward Lazear, *Economic Imperialism* (Stanford University: Hoover Institution, 1999), 2 and 5 (mimeo).

39 See, among others, S.M. Amadae and Bruce Bueno de Mesquita, "The Rochester School: The Origins of Positive Political Theory," *American Review of Political Science* 93, no. 2 (1999): 269–95.

40 Donald F. Kettl, "The Future of Public Administration," www.net.org/pubadmin, undated, 4.

41 Lasswell, *Politics*, 295 and 443.

42 The two spaces are staffed by public servants with different preoccupations, incentives, behavioural norms, and criteria for success. See, for example, Henry Mintzberg and Jacques Bourgault, *Managing Publicly* (Toronto: Institute of Public Administration, 2000).

43 For a somewhat different perspective, see Hal G. Rainey, *Understanding and Managing Public Organizations* (San Francisco: Wiley, 2009).

44 Paul Thomas made a number of very insightful observations on this and other issues in a note to me in March 2012. See also James L. Perry, *Handbook of Public Administration* (San Francisco: Jossey-Bass, 1996).

45 See, among others, the work of the father of modern economics, Paul Samuelson, *Foundations of Economic Analysis*, enlarged edn (Harvard: Harvard University Press, 1983).

CHAPTER ONE

1 Hugh Heclo and Aaron Wildavsky, *The Private Government of Public Money*, 2nd edn (London: Macmillan, 1981).

2 See, among others, Christopher Pollitt and Geert Bouckaert, *Public Management Reform: A Comparative Analysis – New Public Management, Governance, and the Neo-Weberian State*, 3rd edn (Oxford: Oxford University Press, 2011).

3 Donald J. Savoie, *Breaking the Bargain: Public Servants, Ministers, and Parliament* (Toronto: University of Toronto Press, 2003).

4 B. Guy Peters, *Institutional Theory in Political Science: The New Institutionalism* (London: Continuum, 2005), 1.

5 See, among others, Bertrand Russell, *A History of Western Philosophy* (New York: Simon and Schuster, 1972).

6 R. MacGregor Dawson, *The Government of Canada* (Toronto: University of Toronto Press, 1963); *Democratic Government in Canada* (Toronto: University of Toronto Press, 1957); and *The Civil Service of Canada* (London: Oxford University Press, 1929).

7 J.E. Hodgetts, *The Canadian Public Service: A Physiology of Government, 1867–1970* (Toronto: University of Toronto Press, 1913).

8 James R. Mallory, *The Structure of Canadian Government* (Toronto: Macmillan, 1971).

9 See, for example, Kenneth Kernaghan, "Politics, Policy, and Public Servants: Political Neutrality Revisited," *Canadian Public Administration* 19 (1976): 446.

10 Woodrow Wilson, "The Study of Administration," *Political Science Quarterly* 2, no. 2 (1887): 198.

11 Robert A. Wardhaugh, *Behind the Scenes: The Life and Work of William Clifford Clark* (Toronto: University of Toronto Press, 2010).

12 Peters, *Institutional Theory in Political Science*, 12.

13 See James Buchanan, *Public Choice: The Origins and Development of a Research Program* (Fairfax, VA: Centre for Study of Public Choice, 2003); and by the same author, *Cost and Choice: An Inquiry into Economic Theory* (Chicago: University of Chicago Press, 1969). See also W.N. Niskanan, *Bureaucracy and Representative Government* (Chicago: Aldine-Atherton, 1971).

14 J.G. March and J.P. Olsen, *Rediscovering Institutions* (New York: Free Press, 1989), 23.

15 Amitia Etzioni, *A Comparative Analysis of Complex Organizations* (Glencoe, IL: Free Press, 1961). See also Michael Crozier, *The Bureaucratic Phenomenon* (Chicago: Chicago University Press, 1964).

16 See J.G. March and J.P. Olsen, "The New Institutionalism: Organizational Factors in Political Life," *American Political Review* 78, no. 4 (1984): 738–49.

17 See, among others, P. Pierson and T. Skoepol, "Historical Institutionalism in Contemporary Political Science," in I. Katznelson and H.V. Milner, eds, *Political Science: State of the Discipline* (New York: Norton, 2002).

18 See Bert A. Rockman, "The Changing Role of the State," in B. Guy Peters and Donald J. Savoie, eds, *Taking Stock: Assessing Public Sector Reforms* (Montreal & Kingston: McGill-Queen's University Press, 1998), 8–9.

19 See, among others, B.D. Jones, *Politics and the Architecture of Choice* (Chicago: University of Chicago Press, 2001).

20 Nils Brunsson and Johan Olsen, eds, *Organizing Organizations* (Copenhagen: Copenhagen Business School Press, 1998).

21 W.R. Scott, *Institutions and Organizations* (Thousand Oaks, CA: Sage, 2001). See also S. Stryker, *Symbolic Interactionism: A Social Structural Version* (Menlo Park, CA: Benjamin and Cummings, 1980s).

22 Peter Hennessy, *Whitehall* (London: Fontana, 1989).
23 Donald J. Savoie, *Court Government and the Collapse of Accountability in Canada and the United Kingdom* (Toronto: University of Toronto Press, 2008), 64.
24 See Hennessy, *Whitehall*.
25 See, among others, Savoie, *Court Government*.
26 J.L. Granatstein, *The Ottawa Men: The Civil Service Mandarins, 1935–37* (Toronto: University of Toronto Press, 1982), 12.
27 R.M. Punnett, *The Prime Minister in Canadian Government and Politics* (Toronto: Macmillan, 1977), 75.
28 Thomas S. Axworthy, "Of Secretaries to Princes," *Canadian Public Administration* 31, no. 2 (1998): 250.
29 Gordon Robertson, *Memoirs of a Very Civil Servant: Mackenzie King to Pierre Trudeau* (Toronto: University of Toronto Press, 2000), 87.
30 Paul G. Thomas, "Communications and Prime Ministerial Paper," paper presented in Bouctouche, NB, 8–10 June 2011, 34–5 (mimeo).
31 Granatstein, *The Ottawa Men*, 9–10.
32 Ibid.
33 Quoted in Steven Kelman, "Public Choice and Public Spirit," *Public Interest* 87 (1987): 81.
34 See, among others, Donald J. Savoie, *Thatcher, Reagan, Mulroney: In Search of A New Bureaucracy* (Pittsburgh: University of Pittsburgh Press, 1994).
35 Ibid.
36 Dennis Mueller, *Public Choice III* (New York: Cambridge University Press, 2003), 2.
37 Alasdair Roberts, *The Logic of Discipline: Global Capitalism and the Architecture of Government* (Oxford: Oxford University Press, 2010), 11.
38 Peters, *Institutional Theory in Political Science*, 47.
39 See, among others, S.M. Amadae, *Rationalizing Capitalist Democracy: The Cold War Origins of Rational Choice Liberalism* (Chicago: University of Chicago Press, 2003), and James Coleman, *The Mathematics of Collective Action* (London: Heinemann, 1973).
40 See, among others, Luc Leruth and Elisabeth Paul, "A Principal-Agent Theory Approach to Public Expenditure Management Systems in Developing Countries," *OECD Journal on Budgeting* 7, no. 3 (2007).
41 Richard Lipsey and Alec Chrystal, *Economics for Business and Management* (New York: Oxford University Press, 1997).
42 Richard W. Waterman and Kenneth J. Meier, "Principal-Agent Models: An Expansion," *Journal of Public Administration Research and Theory* 8, no. 2 (1998): 173–207.
43 See Donald J. Savoie, *The Politics of Public Spending in Canada* (Toronto: University of Toronto Press, 1990) and H. Helco and A. Wildavsky, *The Private Government of Public Money* (Berkeley: University of California Press, 1974).
44 Savoie, *The Politics of Public Spending in Canada*.
45 See, among others, Michael Jensen, *Foundations of Organizational Strategy* (Cambridge, MA: Harvard University Press, 1998).
46 Paul Thomas made this observation in an email to me on 10 March 2012.
47 Consultation with Gérard Veilleux, Montreal, 2007.

48 Kenneth Kernaghan, "Speaking Truth to Academics: The Wisdom of the Practitioners," *Canadian Public Administration* 54, no. 4 (2009): 503–4, and Ian Gow and Vince Wilson, "Speaking What Truth to Whom? Epistemological Difficulties in Public Administration," October 2011, 21 (mimeo, unpublished).

49 James Q. Wilson, *Bureaucracy: What Government Agencies Do and Why They Do It* (New York: Basic Books, 1989), i and x.

50 Barbara Carroll, "Is There a Gulf between Theory and Practice in Public Administration Journals? Can It Be Overcome?" in David Siegel and Ken Rasmussen, eds, *Professionalism and Public Service: Essays in Honour of Kenneth Kernaghan* (Toronto: Institute of Public Administration of Canada and University of Toronto Press, 2009), 288–303.

51 Donald F. Kettl, "The Future of Public Administration," in his *The Transformation of Governance* (Baltimore: Johns Hopkins University Press, 2002).

52 Aaron Wildavsky, *The Politics of the Budgetary Process* (Boston: Little, Brown, 1964).

53 Savoie, *The Politics of Public Spending in Canada*. See also Allen Schick, *The Changing Role of the Budget Office* (Paris: OECD, 1997).

54 Wildavsky, *The Politics of the Budgetary Process*, 43.

55 David A. Good, *The Politics of Public Money: Spenders, Guardians, Priority Setters, and Financial Watchdogs inside the Canadian Government* (Toronto: University of Toronto Press, 2007).

56 This is a play on words on Graham Allison. See Graham Allison, "Public and Private Management: Are They Fundamentally Alike in All Unimportant Respects?" in J.M. Shafritz and A.C. Hyde, eds, *Classics of Public Administration* (Chicago: Dorsey, 1987), 507–31.

57 C.J. Friedrich, *Constitutional Government and Politics: Nature and Development* (New York: Harper, 1937), and H. Finer, "Administrative Responsibility in Democratic Government," *Public Administration Review* 1, no. 4 (1940): 335–50.

58 Max Weber, *The Theory of Social and Economic Organization* (New York: Oxford University Press, 1947), 333–7.

59 Michael M. Harmon and Richard T. Mayer, *Organization Theory for Public Administration* (Boston: Little, Brown, 1986), 69.

60 Weber, *The Theory of Social and Economic Organization*, 337.

61 Quoted in Harmon and Mayer, *Organization Theory*, 72.

62 See Savoie, *Thatcher, Reagan, Mulroney*.

63 Max Weber, "Bureaucracy," in Hans Heinrich Gerth and C. Wright Mills, eds, *Max Weber: Essays in Sociology* (New York: Oxford University Press, 1946), 233.

64 Savoie, *Thatcher, Reagan, Mulroney*.

65 See, for example, Jonathan Boston, John Martin, June Pallott, and Pat Walsh, *The New Public Management: The New Zealand Model* (Auckland: Oxford University Press, 1996).

66 Christopher Pollitt and Geert Bouckaert, *Public Management Reform: A Comparative Analysis – New Public Management, Governance, and the Neo-Weberian State*, 3rd edn (Oxford: Oxford University Press, 2011).

67 See Michael Keating and Malcolm Holmes, "Reply to Aucoin and Hood," *Governance* 3, no. 2 (1990): 217–18.

68 See Savoie, *Thatcher, Reagan, Mulroney.*

69 Everyone was not of this view, however. See, for example, Don Tansley, *Confessions of a Bureaucrat*, Ottawa, 51, n.d. (mimeo). Don Tansley was appointed federal deputy minister of fisheries in 1978.

70 Gordon Robertson, *Memoirs of a Very Civil Servant*, 38.

71 A.W. Johnson, "The Role of the Deputy Minister," *Canadian Public Administration* 4, no. 4 (1961): 363.

72 John Hilliker, *Canada's Department of External Affairs*, vol. 1: *The Early Years, 1909–1946* (Montreal & Kingston: McGill-Queen's University Press, 1990), 243.

73 See Savoie, *Breaking the Bargain.*

74 See Gwyn Bevan and Christopher Hood, "Have Targets Improved Performance in the English NHS?" *British Medical Journal*, 332, 18 February 2006, 419–22.

75 "Senior civil servants use up entire budget for bonuses," *National Post*, 29 August 2002, A1 and A9.

76 See Savoie, *Breaking the Bargain*, 224.

77 See, for example, B. Guy Peters and Jon Pierre, "Governance without Government? Rethinking Public Administration," *Journal of Public Administration Research and Theory* 8, no. 4 (1998): 227–43.

78 Tony Blair, for example, observed while in office that "some parts of the public sector" were not "as efficient, dynamic and effective" as the private sector ("The Two Tonys," *New Yorker*, 6 October 1997).

79 See, for example, Peters and Pierre, "Governance without Government?

80 See Caroly J. Heenrich et al., *Governance and Performance: New Perspective* (Washington, DC: Georgetown University Press, 2000), and R.A.W. Rhodes, "Governance and Public Administration," in Jon Pierre, ed, *Debating Governance: Authority, Steering, and Democracy* (Oxford: University of Oxford Press, 2000), 54–90.

81 H. George Frederickson, "Whatever Happened to Public Administration? Governance, Governance Everywhere" (Queen's University, Belfast: Institute of Governance, Public Policy and Social Research, 2001), 11.

82 Peter Aucoin, "New Political Governance in Westminster Systems: Impartial Public Administration and Management Performance at Risk" (Halifax: Dalhousie University, 2010), 2 (mimeo).

83 Jon Pierre made this observation at the Festschrift conference, University of Pittsburgh, 19 November 2009.

84 See, among others, Ray Kuman Pruthi, *Theory of Public Administration* (New Delhi: Discovery Publishing House, 2005).

85 James G. Wilson, *Bureaucracy: What Government Agencies Do and Why They Do It* (New York: Basic Books, 1989).

86 Christopher Pollitt, "How Do We Know How Good Public Services Are?" in B. Guy Peters and Donald J. Savoie, eds, *Governance in the Twenty-First Century: Revitalizing the Public Service* (Montreal: McGill-Queen's University Press, 2000), 119–47.

87 John L. (Jack) Manion was a close friend. He made the observation in a private conversation while I was his deputy principal at the Canadian Centre for Management Development.

CHAPTER TWO

1 Canada, *Government Decisions Limited Parliament's Control of Public Spending* (Ottawa: Office of the Auditor General, May 2006), 2.

2 Consultations with Treasury Board Secretariat officials, Ottawa, 18–19 February 2009.

3 C.D. Yonge, *The Life and Administration of the Second Earl of Liverpool* (London, 1868), 3:340.

4 Canada, *Constitutional Documents: Consolidation of Constitution Acts 1867 to 1982*, www.laws.justice.gc.ca, n.d.

5 Vernon Bogdanor, *The New British Constitution* (Oxford: Hart Publishing, 2009), 15 and 288.

6 Adam Tomkins, *Public Law* (Oxford: Oxford University Press, 2003), 165.

7 C.E.S. Franks, *The Parliament of Canada* (Toronto: University of Toronto Press, 1987), 5.

8 Robert Marleau, quoted in the *Hill Times* (Ottawa), 18 February 2002.

9 Canada, Speech by the Hon. Lowell Murray: Souper hommage à Donald J. Savoie, Bouctouche, NB, 8 June 2011.

10 Norman Ward, *The Public Purse: A Study of Canadian Democracy* (Toronto: University of Toronto Press, 1962), 275.

11 See Begsey Stevenson and Justin Wolfers, *Trust in Public Institutions Over the Business Cycle* (Washington, DC: Brookings, 2011).

12 Lord Wilson of Dinton, "The Mandarin Myth," fourth lecture in a series on Tomorrow's Government, Ottawa, 1 March 2006, 7.

13 Neil Nevitte, *The Decline of Deference: Canadian Value Change in Cross National Perspective* (Peterborough: Broadview Press, 1996).

14 "Parliament's broke, MPs should fix it," *Hill Times*, 25 April 2011, 8.

15 "Facing up to our challenges," *Globe and Mail*, www.theglobeandmail.com, 28 April 2011.

16 See the work of the Institute for Research on Public Policy on Democratic Reform, at www.irpp.org.

17 Louis Balthazar, "Is the Decline of Parliament Irreversible?" *Canadian Parliamentary Review*, winter 2005, 17.

18 "How it happened: The events that led to the Harper government's downfall," www.ottawacitizen.com, 26 March 2011.

19 Carolyn Bennett et al., *The Parliament We Want: Parliamentarians' Views on Parliamentary Reform* (Ottawa: Library of Parliament, 2003), 7.

20 The reader can access the three reports, based on 65 interviews, at www.samaracanada.com.

21 Samara, *It's My Party: Parliamentary Dysfunction Reconsidered*, www.samaracanada.com, undated, ch. 2, p. 1.

22 Ibid.

23 See Donald J. Savoie, *Court Government and the Collapse of Accountability in Canada and the United Kingdom* (Toronto: University of Toronto Press, 2008).

24 The reader should consult the Department of Finance's website, which contains detailed information on the budget process and budget numbers. See also David A. Good, *The Politics of Public Money: Spenders, Guardians, Priority Setters, and Financial Watchdogs* (Toronto: University of Toronto Press, 2007).

25 See, for example, ibid., 52.

26 See Savoie, *Court Government*.

27 Canada, House of Commons, Standing Committee on Procedure and House Affairs, *The Business of Supply: Completing the Circle of Control*, December 1998, 15.

28 Jack Stilborn, *Committee Powers Relating to the Estimates* (Ottawa: Parliamentary Research Branch, 22 January 2003), 11.

29 Consultation with a former official with the Library of Parliament, Ottawa, 16 September 2011.

30 John A. Chenier, Michael Dewing, and Jack Stilborn, "Does Parliament Care? Parliamentary Committees and the Estimates," in G. Bruce Doern, ed, *How Ottawa Spends: Managing the Minority, 2005–2006* (Montreal & Kingston: McGill-Queen's University Press, 2005), 205.

31 Canada, *2011–12 Estimates – Part 1: The Government Expenditure Plans* (Ottawa: Treasury Board Secretariat, 2011), 7.

32 See Good, *The Politics of Public Money*, 48.

33 Canada, House of Commons, Special Committee on Procedure, *Third Report*, 6 December 1968, 429.

34 J.R. Mallory and Thomas, quoted in Canada, *The Business of Supply*, Sixty-Fourth Report, n.d., 21.

35 Canada, Report of the Liaison Committee on Committees' Effectiveness, *Parliamentary Government* 43 (June 1993): 4.

36 Canada, House of Commons, *Debates*, 7 February 1994, 962.

37 Robert Giroux made this point in the paper he presented to the IRPP and CIRRD conference, "Changing Nature of Power and Democracy," Montebello, QC, 12 October 2001, 2.

38 See, for example, Canada, *Committee Powers Relating to the Estimates* (Ottawa: Parliamentary Research Branch, 22 January 2003), 9.

39 Letter from John L. Manion to the author, 29 December 2001, and John L. Manion, *Information for Parliament on Government Finance*, report prepared for the Office of the Auditor General, 18 April 1992, 23–4.

40 See, among others, Donald J. Savoie, *The Politics of Public Spending in Canada* (Toronto: University of Toronto Press, 1990).

41 Whole of Government Framework, www.tbs-sct.gc.ca, n.d.

42 For an overview of the estimates process, see www.tbs-sct.gc.ca.

43 Whole of Government Framework, www.tbs-sct.gc.ca, n.d.

44 Manion, *Information for Parliament on Government Finance*, 26.

45 Ibid., 27.

46 R.B. Bryce, "Reflections on the Lambert Report," *Canadian Public Administration* 22, no. 4 (1979): 673.

47 Geoff Regan, quoted in "Conservative backbenchers, opposition MPs say they don't properly scrutinize $252-billion in annual spending," *Hill Times* (Ottawa), 5 December 2011, 41.

48 "Leadership," notes for an address by J.L. Manion to the Advanced Management Program, CCMD, Ottawa, 25 June 1993, 15.

49 My conversation with a government MP, Ottawa, 28 January 2002.

50 I owe this point to Evert Lindquist, who has dealt with this issue in his writings and who emphasized its importance in correspondence with me, October 2002.

51 Canada, *Report of the Auditor General of Canada to the House of Commons for Fiscal Year Ended 31 March 1976* (Ottawa: Supply and Services, 1975), 10.

52 Savoie, *The Politics of Public Spending in Canada*.

53 See Good, *The Politics of Public Money*, 48.

54 David Crane, "Federal government an extraordinarily secretive organization," *Hill Times* (Ottawa), 11 June 2011, 12.

55 Quoted as "Scrutinize spending estimates," *Hill Times* (Ottawa), 20 June 2011, 8.

56 Susan Riley, "The real scandal on Parliament Hill," www.ottawacitizen.com, 2 March 2012.

57 Alison Loot, co-founder of Samara, quoted in "What happened to political integrity and respect for Parliament?" *Postmedia*, 23 April 2011, www.montrealgazette.com.

58 Samara, *Welcome to Parliament: A Job with No Description*, Toronto: June 2010, 14.

59 "Andre Arthur: The MP who moonlights as a bus driver," *Globe and Mail*, 7 March 2011, A4.

60 Ibid., 3.

61 See, among others, Franks, *The Parliament of Canada*.

62 David Docherty, *Mr. Smith Goes to Ottawa: Life in the House of Commons* (Vancouver: UBC Press, 1997), 125.

63 Donald J. Savoie, *Breaking the Bargain: Public Servants, Ministers, and Parliament* (Toronto: University of Toronto Press, 2003), 183.

64 Both MPs quoted in "'You learn to be an MP by the seat of your pants,' say former MPs," *Hill Times* (Ottawa), 30 November 2010.

65 Samara, *Welcome to Parliament*, 18.

66 Ibid., 10.

67 Ibid.

68 See, for example, Savoie, *Court Government*.

69 "MPs say they don't have the time or resources to properly scrutinize bills, spending," *Hill Times* (Ottawa), 21 February 2011, 1 and 6.

70 Quoted in Samara, *Welcome to Parliament*, 10.

71 "Tories take Metro riding," www.timestranscript.canadaeast.com, 3 May 2011.

72 "Liberal: Steven Mackinnon," www.ottawacitizen.com, 17 April 2011.

73 "Subsidy news a relief for all," www.timestranscript.canadaeast.com, 25 October 2011.

74 Consultation with Hon. Dominic LeBlanc, Moncton, 6 August 2011.

75 See, among others, Docherty, *Mr. Smith Goes to Ottawa*.

76 Consultation with Hon. Dominic LeBlanc, Moncton, 6 August 2011.

77 "Saving of EI centres in Tory ridings draws fire," www.theglobeandmail.com, 1 September 2011.

78 "Critics say MPs' offices turning into de facto immigration offices," *Hill Times* (Ottawa), 4 October 2010, 1 and 15.

79 Canada, "On the Job with a Member of Parliament," www.parl.gc.ca, n.d.

80 Franks, *The Parliament of Canada*, 45.

81 "Mr. Manley on the move: Is the sky the limit?" *National Post*, 26 January 2002, B4.

82 Docherty, *Mr. Smith Goes to Ottawa*, 141.

83 See, among others, Peter C. Dobell, "Stress and the MP," *Parliamentary Government* 9 (November 1999): 5.

84 "A career marked by flair for drama," *Globe and Mail*, 15 January 2002, A5.

85 Docherty, *Mr. Smith Goes to Ottawa*, 131–2.

86 Franks, *The Parliament of Canada*, 97–8.

87 Docherty, *Mr. Smith Goes to Ottawa*, 9.

88 Franks, *The Parliament of Canada*, 23–4.

89 Quoted in Donald J. Savoie, *Governing from the Centre: The Concentration of Power in Canadian Politics* (Toronto: University of Toronto Press, 1999), 246.

90 Ibid.

91 Quoted in Edward Greenspon and Anthony Wilson-Smith, *Double Vision: The Inside Story of the Liberals in Power* (Toronto: Doubleday, 1996), 209.

92 See Savoie, *Governing from the Centre*.

93 "Young participera aux audiences publiques sur Via Rail et la loi sur l'assurance-chômage," *L'Acadie nouvelle* (Caraquet), 23 July 1989, A3.

94 See, for example, Herman Bakvis, "Transport Canada and Program Review," in Peter Aucoin and Donald J. Savoie, eds, *Managing Strategic Change: Program Review and Beyond* (Ottawa: Canadian Centre for Management Development, 1998).

95 The author of the letter, a former government MP under the Liberals, gave me a copy of the letter.

96 Exchange of material between a minister and his exempt staff and the deputy minister and senior departmental officials. The exchange consists of nine memoranda, and the material was given to me by a former minister.

97 See Savoie, *Breaking the Bargain*, 172.

98 Canada, Speech by the Hon. Lowell Murray: Souper hommage à Donald J. Savoie.

99 Paul Thomas, "Some Quick, Brief Thoughts on Reform to the Supply Process," University of Manitoba, 7 April 2012 (mimeo).

CHAPTER THREE

1 Donald J. Savoie, *The Politics of Public Spending in Canada* (Toronto: University of Toronto Press, 1990).

2 Speech by the Hon. Lowell Murray, 8 June 2011, Pays de la Sagouine, Bouctouche, NB (mimeo).

3 Defence Minister Peter MacKay, quoted in "MacKay not always in Afghan loop," www.thechronicleherald.ca, 3 October 2011.

4 See, among others, Donald J. Savoie, *Governing from the Centre: The Concentration of Power in Canadian Politics* (Toronto: University of Toronto Press, 1999).

5 Paul Martin, *Hell or High Water: My Life In and Out of Politics* (Toronto: McClelland & Stewart, 2008), 354.

6 Consultation with a deputy minister, Ottawa, 14 September 2011.

7 Consultation with Hon. Bernard Valcourt, Moncton, NB, 5 July 2011. The consultation was in French, and I have translated his points in the conversation.

8 David Heclo, Alex Swann, and Jennifer Espey, "Lessons learned in last election campaign? Polling commissioned by the media superficial," *Hill Times* (Ottawa), 11 July 2011, 14.

9 See, for example, Donald J. Savoie, *Visiting Grandchildren: Economic Development in the Maritimes* (Toronto: University of Toronto Press, 2006).

10 Ibid.

11 See, among others, "Integrity Commissioner Christine Ouimet gets $500K payout," www.thestar.com, 4 May 2011.

12 Savoie, *Visiting Grandchildren.*

13 Ibid.

14 Ibid.

15 David Alexander made this point in "New Notions of Happiness: Nationalism, Regionalism, and Atlantic Canada," *Journal of Canadian Studies* 15, no. 2 (1988): 41.

16 See, among others, Savoie, *Visiting Grandchildren.*

17 "Don't reform Senate, abolish it: Ontario premier," www.cbc.ca/news/canada/story, 31 May 2011.

18 Consultations with Dominic LeBlanc, MP for Beauséjour, various dates.

19 See Richard J. Van Loon and Michael S. Whittington, *The Canadian Political System: Environment, Structure, and Process* (Toronto: McGraw-Hill Ryerson, 1981).

20 "Political Football," *Toronto Star*, 5 December 1987, 2.

21 "Which federal party has the most career politicians?" www.theglobeandmail.com, 4 July 2011.

22 Savoie, *Governing from the Centre.*

23 Liane Benoit, "Ministerial Staff: The Life and Times of Parliament's Statutory Orphans," Commission of Inquiry into the Sponsorship Program and Advertising Activities, 2:146, Ottawa, 2004.

24 See "Dear Minister. A Letter to an Old Friend on Being a Successful Minister," notes for remarks by Gordon Osbaldeston to the Association of Professional Executives of the Public Service of Canada, 22 January 1988, 3.

25 Ibid., 4.

26 J. Stephen Dupré, "The Workability of Executive Federalism in Canada," in H. Bakvis and W. Chandler, eds, *Federalism and the Role of the State* (Toronto: University of Toronto Press, 1987).

27 Ian D. Clark, "Restraint, Renewal, and the Treasury Board Secretariat," *Canadian Public Administration* 37, no. 2 (1994): 209–48.

28 Peter Aucoin, "Administrative Reform in Public Management: Paradigms, Principles, Paradoxes, and Pendulums," *Governance* 3, no. 2 (1990): 115–37.

29 Allen Schick, "Micro-budgetary Adaptations to Fiscal Stress in the Industrialized Democracies," *Public Administration Review* 46, no. 2 (1988): 124–34.

30 Savoie, *The Politics of Public Spending in Canada*.

31 Donald Johnston, *Up the Hill* (Montreal: Optimum Publishing International, 1986).

32 Lloyd Axworthy, "Central of Policy," *Policy Options* 6, no. 3 (1985): 17–19.

33 "Spotted on CBC News.ca – the Harper Government 'Monika,'" www.cbc.ca/news, 6 March 2011.

34 The official is quoted in "Documents expose Harper's obsession with control," www.thestar.com, 6 June 2010.

35 Consultations with a senior Government of Canada official, Moncton, 7 January 2012.

36 "Spending millions to tell stimulus story," *Globe and Mail*, 25 February 2011, and "Tory government hiked ad spending to promote stimulus projects," www.theglobeandmail.com, 4 January 2012.

37 Ibid.

38 "E-mails cite directive to re-brand government in Harper's name," www.theglobeandmail.com, 7 September 2011.

39 David Taras, *Power and Betrayal in the Canadian Media* (Toronto: University of Toronto Press, 2008), 219.

40 Consultations with Jim Travers, Ottawa, 14 July 2009.

41 Consultations with Michel Cormier, Moncton, 31 July 2009. He had no objection to my reporting our conversation for the purpose of this book.

42 Kathy English, "Why the Star does not unpublish," www.thestar.com, 31 January 2009.

43 A minister in the Harper government made this point in a conversation with the author on 5 July 2011 in Moncton.

44 Maurice Lamontagne, "The Influence of the Politician," *Canadian Public Administration* 11, no. 3 (1968): 263.

45 Naomi Griffiths, *The Golden Age of Liberalism: A Portrait of Roméo LeBlanc* (Halifax: Lorimer, 2011), 42.

46 See Jonn Wanna, Lotte Jensen and Jouke de Vries, eds, *The Reality of Budgetary Reform in OECD Nations: Trajectories and Consequences* (Cheltenham, UK: Edward Elgar, 2010), 2.

47 Savoie, *The Politics of Public Spending in Canada*.

48 Jean Chrétien, *My Years as Prime Minister* (Toronto: Knopf Canada, 2008).

49 *The Outsiders' Manifesto: Serving and Thriving as a Member of Parliament* (Samara: Toronto, 2011), ch. 3, 1.

50 David A. Good, *The Politics of Public Money: Spenders, Guardians, Priority Setters, and Financial Watchdogs* (Toronto: University of Toronto Press, 2007), 73.

51 "Clement worked with mayors on G8 Legacy Fund," *Globe and Mail*, 16 August 2011, A5.

52 "Rules were broken over G8/G20 summit spending: Auditor General," www.nationalpost.com, 6 October 2011.

53 "It's not right: Auditor-General rips into Harper government over summit spending," www.ottawacitizen.com, 5 October 2011.

54 See, for example, "Tory ridings the winners from stimulus," www.ottawacitizen.com, 29 Octobet 2009.

55 Consultation with Hon. Andy Scott, Sussex, NB, 9 September 2006.

56 Quoted in Donald J. Savoie, "The Minister's Staff: The Need for Reform," *Canadian Public Administration* 26, no. 4 (1983): 523.

57 Canada, Treasury Board Secretariat, *Government Response to the Tenth Report of the Standing Committee on Public Accounts* (Ottawa, 17 August 2005), 7.

58 Canada, *Accounting Officers: Guidance on Roles, Responsibilities and Appearances before Parliamentary Committee* (Ottawa: Privy Council Office, 14 March 2007).

59 Savoie, "The Minister's Staff," 523.

60 Robert F. Adie and Paul Thomas, *Canadian Public Administration: Problematical Perspectives*, 2nd edn (Scarborough, ON: Prentice Hall Canada, 1987), 167.

61 Good, *The Politics of Public Money*, 75.

62 "Liberal MP shocked as Ottawa slashes 100 jobs in Shediac," *Telegraph Journal*, 26 July 2011. See also "Union protests Shediac job losses," www.cbc.ca/news, 18 August 2011.

63 Savoie, *The Politics of Public Spending in Canada*, 256.

64 See "PM seeks to tie NDP's name to Moncton demonstration," *Globe and Mail*, 9 May 1988, A1; see also "Angry crowd demand Cochrane's resignation," *Times-Transcript*, 24 June 1986, 1.

65 Savoie, *The Politics of Public Spending in Canada*, 297.

CHAPTER FOUR

1 The Right Honourable Tony Blair made this observation at Fox Harbour, NS, 22 July 2011. See also R.A.W. Rhodes and Patrick Dunleavy, *Prime Minister, Cabinet, and the Core Executive* (London: St. Martin's Press, 1999).

2 Senator Lowell Murray, quoting from B. Guy Peters, made this observation in Bouctouche, NB, 8 June 2011.

3 For a discussion on the distinction between power and influence, see Donald J. Savoie, *Power: Where Is It?* (Montreal & Kingston: McGill-Queen's University Press, 2010).

4 Carl Dahlström et al., *Steering from the Centre: Strengthening Political Control in Western Democracies* (Toronto: University of Toronto Press, 2011).

5 "Nik on the numbers – Canadians believe PMO has too much power," www.nanos@nanosresearch.com, 8 February 2011.

6 Consultation with a senior deputy minister, Ottawa, 15 September 2011.

7 Donald J. Savoie, *Governing from the Centre: The Concentration of Power in Canadian Politics* (Toronto: University of Toronto Press, 1999).

8 Paul G. Thomas, "Communications and Prime Ministerial Power," a paper presented in Bouctouche, NB, 8–10 June 2011, 12.

9 See, among others, Canada, *Fourth Report of the Prime Minister's Advisory Committee on the Public Service* (Ottawa: Privy Council Office, 2010).

10 See, among others, Savoie, *Power*, and R. Rose, *Understanding Big Government* (London: Sage, 1984).

11 Chief Justice Beverley McLachlin, "Unwritten Constitutional Principles: What Is Going On?" Remarks given at the 2005 Lord Cooke Lecture, Wellington, New Zealand, 1 December 2005, 11–12.

12 See Ricky Griffin, *Management* (Boston: Houghton Mifflin, 2005).

13 For insights on how these meetings unfold, see Lawrence Martin, *Harperland: The Politics of Control* (Toronto: Viking Canada, 2010).

14 See Jean Chrétien, *My Years as Prime Minister* (Toronto: Knopf Canada, 2007), and Paul Martin, *Hell or High Water: My Life In and Out of Politics* (Toronto: McClelland & Stewart, 2008).

15 Quoted in "Shootings empower Obama ammunition," www.telegraph.co.uk, 14 January 2011.

16 Jack Stagg made this observation in an interview I carried out for my book *Breaking the Bargain*.

17 Nick Sparrow and John Turner, "The Permanent Campaign: The Integration of Market Research Techniques in Developing Strategies in a More Uncertain Political Climate," *European Journal of Marketing* 35, no. 9/10 (2001): 904–1007.

18 Thomas, "Communications and Prime Ministerial Power," 7.

19 Savoie, *Governing from the Centre*.

20 See Donald J. Savoie, *Court Government and the Collapse of Accountability in Canada and the United Kingdom* (Toronto: University of Toronto Press, 2008).

21 Eddie Goldenberg, *The Way It Works: Inside Ottawa* (Toronto: McClelland & Stewart, 2006), 97–8.

22 Ibid.

23 Quoted in Savoie, *Governing from the Centre*, 155.

24 See Savoie, *Court Government*.

25 Harry Swain, *Oka: A Political Crisis and Its Legacy* (Toronto: Douglas & McIntyre, 2010).

26 Quoted from Donald J. Savoie, *The Politics of Public Spending in Canada* (Toronto: University of Toronto Press, 1990), 182.

27 Peter M. Blau and Marshall W. Meyer, *Bureaucracy in Modern Society* (New York: Random House, 1971).

28 "Industry lobbyists get most access to PM," *Times and Transcript* (Moncton), 2 October 2010, D1.

29 Jean Chrétien, *Straight from the Heart* (Toronto: Key Porter Books, 1985), 18.

30 Peter Aucoin and Donald J. Savoie, *Managing Strategic Change: Learning from Program Review* (Ottawa: Canadian Centre for Management Development, 1998).

31 Canada, Commission of Inquiry into the Sponsorship Program and Advertising Activities, Ottawa, 1 November 2005.

32 Savoie, *Court Government*, 336.

33 Paul Thomas, "Strategic Government Communications for the 21st Century," Galimberti Lecture, National Conference of the Institute of Public Administration of Canada, Victoria, BC, 30 August 2011, 3 (mimeo).

34 See David Suzuki, "Science must be free from politics," *Times and Transcript*, 22 August 2011, D4.

35 Savoie, *Court Government*, 310.

36 "Wright prepares for PM's chief of staff position, pressure cooker," *Hill Times* (Ottawa), 4 October 2010, 6.

37 Consultation with a director-level official with Industry Canada, Moncton, various dates, summer of 2011.

38 Quoted in "Inside the PMO: Harper's 'not the dictator's he's made out to be,'" *Hill Times* (Ottawa), 4 April 2011, 23.

39 See Stephen Goldsmith and William D. Eggers, *Governing by Network: The New Shape of the Public Sector* (Washington: Brookings Institution, 2004).

40 Quoted in Savoie, *Power: Where Is It?* 191.

41 Canada, Public Service 2000, *The Renewal of the Public Service of Canada* (Ottawa: Minister of Supply and Services, 1990), 95–6.

42 Quoted in "Inside the PMO: Harper's 'not the dictator's he's made out to be,'" *Hill Times* (Ottawa), 4 April 2011, 21.

43 David A. Good, *The Politics of Public Money* (Toronto: IPAC and University of Toronto Press, 2007), 76.

44 Ibid., 78.

45 Canada, Commission of Inquiry into the Sponsorship Program and Advertising Activities, Ottawa, 25 January 2005, 10,906.

46 Canada, *The Official Languages in Canada: Federal Policy* (Ottawa: Library of Parliament Political and Social Affairs Division, 27 April 2007).

47 Chrétien, *Straight from the Heart*, 117.

48 "Mr. Trudeau tries again," *Globe and Mail*, 3 August 1978, 6. See also "Fed-up: PM pledges postal shakeup," *Globe and Mail*, 2 August 1978, and Canada, Department of Finance, *Budget Speech*, 16 November 1978, 5.

49 See Savoie, *The Politics of Public Spending in Canada*.

50 Aucoin and Savoie, eds, *Managing Strategic Change*.

51 See Sandford Borins, "The Theory and Practice of Envelope Budgeting," York University, Toronto, Faculty of Administration Studies, January 1980, 3.

52 John Manley wrote that he identified himself with those in government "favouring fiscal responsibility" (Manley, "How Canada Slayed the Deficit Dragon and Created the Surplus," *Policy Options*, October 2005, 22).

53 Quoted in Ed Greenspon and Anthony Wilson-Smith, *Double Vision: The Inside Story of the Liberals in Power* (Toronto: Doubleday, 1996), 225.

54 Savoie, *Governing from the Centre*, 180.

55 Greenspon and Wilson-Smith, *Double Vision*, 221.

56 See, for example, Savoie, *Court Government*, 236.

57 Good, *The Politics of Public Money*, 87.
58 See, among others, Donald J. Savoie, *Breaking the Bargain: Public Servants, Ministers, and Parliament* (Toronto: University of Toronto Press, 2003).
59 Canada, *Budget Plan and Budget Speech* (Ottawa: Department of Finance, 29 March 2012).
60 Good, *The Politics of Public Money*.
61 Ibid., 39.
62 Hugh Heclo and Aaron Wildavsky, *The Private Government of Public Money* (London: Macmillan, 1974).
63 Savoie, *Court Government*.
64 See, for example, Canada, *Frequently Asked Questions or Strategic Reviews*, Treasury Board Secretariat, www.tbs-sct.gc.ca.
65 I served as the external adviser (2010) for the Atlantic Canada Opportunities Agency.
66 "Some departments face cuts of more than 10 %: Flaherty," www.ottawacitizen.com, 11 January 2012.
67 "Harper pledges to trim billions of fat in programs," www.ottawacitizen.com, 7 June 2011. See also Canada, "Treasury Board President reaffirms commitment to reduce government spending and return to a balanced budget" (Ottawa: Treasury Board Secretariat, 4 August 2011).
68 Canada, Address by Treasury Board President Tony Clement to Public Service Executives at the APEX Symposium, 8 June 2011, online at www.tbs-sct.gc.ca/June8, 2011.
69 Quoted in "Flaherty defends hiring consultant," *Times and Transcript* (Moncton), 21 September 2011, C3.
70 Consultation with a senior Government of Canada official, Ottawa, 25 March 2012.
71 See "Public service cuts could reach 50,000 according to union," www.ottawacitizen.com, 1 February 2012.
72 "Minister Clement says feds could cut between $4-billion and $8-billion this year alone." *Hill Times* (Ottawa), 30 January 2012, 1 and 40.
73 Quoted in "Budget: Public servants hit with job cuts, pension changes," www.ottawacitizen.com, 29 March 2012.
74 Ibid., and Andrew Coyne, "This is the terminus of Tory radicalism," www.nationalpost.com, 29 March 2012.
75 Canada, *Budget Plan and Budget Speech*.
76 Jeffrey Simpson, "Penny drops, Tory government balks," www.theglobeandmail.com, 30 March 2012.
77 See Canada, *Federal Deficit: Changing Trends*, www.publications.gc.ca, n.d.
78 See Canada, *Annual Report 1973: Public Service Canada* (Ottawa: Information Canada, 1974). Please note that I deducted from the 245,302 the 43,514 employees with the Post Office which has since been transformed into a crown corporation.
79 Canada, *Demographic Snapshot of the Federal Public Service* (Ottawa: Treasury Board Secretariat, n.d.), 4. The reader will note that there are various ways to establish the size of the public service. It depends on what one includes. For example,

the Public Service Commission reports that there were 216,709 public servants under the more narrowly defined Public Service Employment Act. See Canada, *2010–11 Annual Report* (Ottawa: Public Service Commission, 2011), ch. 2.

80 Savoie, *Court Government*.

81 "Flaherty retreats from pre-election deficit targets," www.cbc.ca, 8 November 2011.

82 Canada, *Fiscal Reference Tables: October 2011* (Ottawa: Department of Finance, 2011), 9, table 1.

83 "Public service jobs: The cuts are adding up," and "Federal government getting out of the language training business," www.ottawacitizen.com, 13 January 2012.

CHAPTER FIVE

1 See, for example, Audrey D. Doerr, *The Machinery of Government in Canada* (Toronto: Methuen, 1981).

2 Canada, www.gc.ca, undated.

3 Ibid.

4 I write from experience here. I worked with Steve Rosell, head of PCO's machinery of government secretariat in the early 1980s, when the prime minister decided to overhaul the government's economic development departments.

5 John Stuart Mill, *Considerations on Representative Government* (New York: Harper, 1869), 100.

6 J.R. Mallory, *The Structure of Canadian Government* (Toronto: Macmillan, 1971), 122.

7 Donald J. Savoie, *Thatcher, Reagan, Mulroney: In Search of a New Bureaucracy* (Pittsburgh: University of Pittsburgh Press, 1994), 26.

8 J.E. Hodgetts, *Pioneer Public Service: An Administrative History of the United Canadas 1841–1867* (Toronto: University of Toronto Press, 1969), and *The Canadian Public Service: A Physiology of Government, 1867–1970* (Toronto: University of Toronto Press, 1973), ch. 2.

9 Luther Gulick, "Notes on the Theory of Organization," in Luther Gulick and L. Urwick, eds, *Notes on the Theory of Organization* (New York: Institute of Public Administration, 1937).

10 Donald J. Savoie, "Searching for Accountability in a Government without Boundaries," *Canadian Public Administration* 47, no. 1 (2004): 1–26.

11 David Dodge, "Black coffee spiked with exasperation," *Globe and Mail*, 9 September 2011, A8.

12 Don Drummond, "Personal Reflections on the State of Public Policy Analysis in Canada," speaking notes for Queen's International Institution Public Policy, 3 December 2010, 342 and 346.

13 Marcel Massé, "Partners in the Management of Canada: The Changing Roles of Government and the Public Service," paper presented at the 1993 John L. Manion Lecture, Canadian Centre for Management Development, Ottawa, 5 and 8.

14 David Osborne and Ted Gaebler, *Reinventing Government: How the Entrepreneurial Spirit Is Transforming the Public Sector, from Schoolhouse to State House, City Hall to Pentagon* (Reading, MA: Addison-Wesley, 1992).

15 Canadian Wildlife Service of Environment Canada (Toronto: IPAC submission, January 1992), 9.

16 Jennifer Berardi, "The Niagara Casino Partnership: Game of Chance?" in David Siegel and Ken Rasmussen, eds, *Professionalism and Public Service: Essays in Honour of Kenneth Kernaghan* (Toronto: University of Toronto Press, 2008), 229.

17 Quoted in Louis C. Gawthrop, *Public Service and Democracy: Ethical Imperatives for the 21st Century* (New York: Chatham House Publishers, 1998), 11.

18 J.E. Hodgetts, "Royal Commissions and Public Service Reform: Personal Reflections," *Canadian Public Administration* 50, no. 4 (2007): 525–40.

19 See Savoie, *Thatcher, Reagan, Mulroney*, ch. 8. See also Barbara Wake Carroll and David Siegel, *Service in the Field: The World of Front-Line Public Servants*, Canadian Public Administration Series (Montreal & Kingston: McGill-Queen's University Press, 1999).

20 Alan Williams, "Erosion of Trust," *Canadian Defence Review*, August 2011, 60.

21 Canada, Task Force on Public Service Values and Ethics, *Discussion Paper* (Ottawa: Privy Council Office, 1996), 57.

22 James Q. Wilson, *Bureaucracy: What Government Agencies Do and Why They Do It* (New York: Basic Books, 1999).

23 Ibid.

24 James G. March and Johan Olsen, *Democratic Governance* (New York: Free Press, 1995), 59.

25 Various conversations with Marc Rochon, Gérard Veilleux, John L. Manion, and Bev Deware.

26 "MacKay racks up nearly $3 million in flights on VIP jets," www.theglobeandmail.com, 29 September 2011.

27 "Canada's top soldier scoffs at repaying jet expenses," www.theglobeandmail.com, 18 September 2011.

28 "Emails punch holes in MacKay's excuse for Cormorant flight from fishing holiday," www.vancouversun.com, 30 November 2011.

29 Consultation with a senior deputy minister, Ottawa, 20 October 2011.

30 Donald J. Savoie, *Court Government and the Collapse of Accountability in Canada and the United Kingdom* (Toronto: University of Toronto Press, 2008), 20.

31 See Donald J. Savoie, *Governing from the Centre: The Concentration of Power in Canadian Politics* (Toronto: University of Toronto Press, 1999).

32 Ibid., ch. 5.

33 See also Carroll and Siegel, *Service in the Field*.

34 Donald J. Savoie, *The Politics of Public Spending in Canada* (Toronto: University of Toronto Press, 1990), 213.

35 Consultations with a Treasury Board Secretariat official, Ottawa, 19 October 2011, and with an official with the Commission of Official Languages, Moncton, 14 August 2011.

36 Carroll and Siegel, *Service in the Field*. See also Canada, *Annual Report* (Ottawa: Public Service Commission 2010–11).

37 Quoted in Savoie, *Governing from the Centre*, 287.

38 Ibid.

39 Ibid.
40 Ibid. See also David Johnson, *Thinking Government: Public Administration and Politics in Canada* (Toronto: University of Toronto Press, 2011).
41 See Donald J. Savoie, *Breaking the Bargain: Public Servants, Ministers, and Parliament* (Toronto: University of Toronto Press, 2003), ch. 7.
42 Jacques Bourgault, "De Kafka au Net: la lutte incessante du sous-ministre pour contrôler son agenda," *Gestion* 22, no. 2 (1997): 21–2.
43 Carroll and Siegel, *Service in the Field*, 200–3.
44 See David A. Good, *The Politics of Public Money: Spenders, Guardians, Priority Setters, and Financial Watchdogs inside the Canadian Government* (Toronto: University of Toronto Press, 2007).
45 Christopher Hood, *The Blame Game: Spin, Bureaucracy, and Self-Preservation in Government* (Princeton: Princeton University Press, 2010).
46 R. Kent Weaver, "The Politics of Blame Avoidance," *Journal of Public Policy* 5, no. 4 (1985): 391.
47 Ibid., 392.
48 Paul C. Light, *Thickening Government: Federal Hierarchy and the Diffusion of Accountability* (Washington, DC: Brookings Institution, 1995).
49 Savoie, *Court Government*.
50 "Gomery inquiry: Jean Chrétien, a former PM testifies," www.cbc.ca/new, 8 February 2005.
51 See Christopher Kam, "Not Just Parliamentary 'Cowboys and Indians': Ministerial Responsibility and Bureaucratic Drift," *Governance* 13, no. 3 (2000): 380.
52 See, for example, Sir K.C. Wheare, *Maladministration and Its Remedies* (London: Stevens and Sons, 1973), 94.
53 See, among others, Barry K. Winetrobe, *The Accountability Debate: Ministerial Responsibility* (London: Home Affairs Section, Research Paper 9716, 28 January 1997), 9. See also Peter Aucoin and Mark D. Jarvis, *Modernizing Government Accountability: A Framework for Reform* (Ottawa: Canada School of Public Service, 2005), 67.
54 Alex Himelfarb, in testimony before House of Commons Public Accounts Committee, 3 May 2004.
55 Savoie, *Court Government*.
56 "Guité links PMO official to scandal," *Globe and Mail*, 16 May 2006, A6.
57 See Savoie, *Court Government*.
58 Ibid., ch. 11.
59 Ibid.
60 Canada, Office of the Prime Minister, *Federal Accountability Action Plan: Turning a New Leaf* (Ottawa, 11 April 2006), 30.
61 UK, Treasury, *Responsibilities of an Accounting Officer*, Memorandum (London, n.d.), 6.
62 Canada, Office of the Prime Minister, *Accountable Government: A Guide for Ministers* (Ottawa, 2006).
63 Canada, Privy Council Office, *Guidance for Deputy Ministers*, section 4, *Accountability for Addressing Errors in Administration* (Ottawa: n.d.), 4.

64 Canada, Privy Council Office, *Guidance for Accounting Officers* (Ottawa, March 2007).
65 Ralph Heintzman, "Establishing the Boundaries of the Public Service," paper prepared for a conference and festschrift in honour of Donald J. Savoie, Bouctouche, NB, 2–10 June 2011, 12 (mimeo).
66 Ibid., 23.
67 Ibid., 19 and 24.
68 Paul Tellier, "Public Service 2000: The Renewal of the Public Service," *Canadian Public Administration* 33, no. 2 (1990): 123–32.
69 Al Johnson, "The Role of the Deputy Minister: III," *Canadian Public Administration* 4, no. 4 (1961): 357.
70 Ibid.

CHAPTER SIX

1   Consultations with a senior NRCAN official, Ottawa, 14 September 2011.
2   Quoted in Canada, 2004 *March Report of the Auditor General of Canada* (Ottawa: Office of the Auditor General, 2004), ch. 7, exhibit 7.4.
3   See, among others, Donald J. Savoie, *Thatcher, Reagan, Mulroney: In Search of a New Bureaucracy* (Pittsburgh: University of Pittsburgh Press, 1994).
4   See, among others, "Government Organization, Royal Commission," www.thecanadianencyclopedia.com.
5   Canada, *The Royal Commission on Government Organization* (Ottawa: Queen's Printer, 1982).
6   Ibid., 91, 154, 156.
7   See, for example, Walter Baker, "Administrative Reform in the Federal Public Service: The First Faltering Steps," *Canadian Public Administration* 16, no. 3 (1973): 381–98.
8   E.J. Benson, "The New Dynamism," notes for an address to the Canadian Bar Association, Winnipeg, 29 March 1967, 14 (mimeo).
9   Canada, *Report of the Auditor General to the House of Commons for Fiscal Year Ended 31 March 1976* (Ottawa: Supply and Services, 1976), 10; J.R. Mallory, "The Lambert Report: Central Roles and Responsibilities," *Canadian Public Administration* 22, no. 4 (1979): 517. See also Savoie, *The Politics of Public Spending in Canada* (Toronto: University of Toronto Press, 1999), ch. 6.
10 Canada, Treasury Board, "Statement by the Honourable Robert Andras, President of the Treasury Board, on the Royal Commission of Inquiry on Financial Organization and Accountability in the Government of Canada," 22 November 1976, 4. See also Savoie, *The Politics of Public Spending in Canada*, ch. 6.
11 UK, "Modernizing Government," a document presented to Parliament by the prime minister and the minister for the Cabinet Office, 1999, 11.
12 Ralph Heintzman, "The Effects of Globalization on Management Practices: Should the Public Sector Operate on Different Parameters?" Paper presented to the Institute of Public Administration of Canada (IPAC) National Conference, Fredericton, NB, 31 August 1999, 7–9.

13 Vernon Bogdanor, "Oxford and the Mandarin Culture: The Past That Is Gone," *Oxford Review of Education* 32, no. 1 (2006): 162.

14 Quoted in Savoie, *Thatcher, Reagan, Mulroney*, 133.

15 James Q. Wilson, *Bureaucracy: What Government Agencies Do and Why They Do It* (New York: Basic Books, 1989), 197; Blumenthal, quoted on p. 155.

16 Ibid., chs. 7 and 11.

17 Ibid., 115.

18 Various conversations with Gérard Veilleux, Ottawa and Montreal.

19 See, among others, Donald J. Savoie, *Court Government and the Collapse of Accountability in Canada and the United Kingdom* (Toronto: University of Toronto Press, 2008).

20 V. Peter Harder, "The Public Service of Canada: A Key Partner in Productivity," presentation to the SUMMA Forum on Productivity, Ottawa, 15 March 1999, 3 (mimeo).

21 Antoinette Weibel, Katja Rost, Margit Osterloh, "Pay for Performance in the Public Sector: Benefits and Hidden Costs," *Journal of Public Administration Research and Theory* 20, no. 2 (2010): 387–412.

22 Quoted in Savoie, *Court Government*.

23 Guy Lodge and Ben Rogers, *Whitehall's Black Box: Accountability and Performance in the Senior Civil Service* (London: Institute for Public Policy Research, 2006), 48.

24 The committee labels this "external comparability" and draws its findings from a database of 300 organizations representing all sectors of the economy. See Canada, *Advisory Committee on Senior Level Retention and Compensation, Fourth Report, March 2002* (Ottawa: Treasury Board Secretariat, 2002), 1; and *Twelfth Report*, 23 April 2009 (Ottawa: Treasury Board Secretariat, 2009).

25 Ibid.

26 "Senior civil servants use up entire budget for bonuses," *National Post*, 29 August 2002, A1 and A9.

27 Canada, *Performance Management Program Guidelines: Deputy Ministers, Associate Deputy Ministers, and Individuals Paid in the GX Salary Range* (Ottawa: Privy Council Office, August 2011).

28 Ibid., 6.

29 Consultation with a Canadian government official, Toronto, 12 October 2006. The official was at the time employed with the Canada Lands Corporation.

30 "Public Works issuing more window dressing," *Ottawa Citizen*, 13 January 1995, A2.

31 David A. Good, "The Politics of Public Management: The HRDC Audit of Grants and Contributions" (Victoria: School of Public Administration, January 2002), 17 (mimeo).

32 Ibid.

33 Quoted in ibid., 10.

34 Ibid., 18.

35 Ibid., 19.

36 See Donald J. Savoie, *Breaking the Bargain: Public Servants, Ministers, and Parliament* (Toronto: University of Toronto Press, 2003), 148.

37   Quoted in ibid., 20.
38   See, among others, Savoie, *Court Government*.
39   See, among many others, "Job-grant reviews and accountant's nightmare," *National Post*, 8 February 2000, A9.
40   "Shovelgate demands full inquiry," *Ottawa Citizen*, 29 March 2000, A1.
41   "Embattled Stewart may go Dutch," *Globe and Mail*, 2 August 2000, A1.
42   See ibid.; and Hugh Winsor, "Jane Stewart lives," *Globe and Mail*, 20 January 2001, A13.
43   Canada, Human Resources Development Canada, news release: "Minister Stewart releases reports on grants and contributions action plan," 18 May 2000.
44   "Before you clamour for results-based management in the civil service, remember Chuck Guité could be its poster boy," www.theglobeandmail.com, 23 November 2005.
45   "Minister maintains silence on department's furniture," www.ottawacitizen.com, 28 July 2011.
46   Canada, 2004 *March Report of the Auditor General of Canada – Chapter 7*.
47   Consultation with a senior line department deputy minister, Ottawa, 15 September 2011.
48   See, among others, Savoie, *Court Government*.
49   Consultation with a senior line department deputy minister, Ottawa, 20 October 2011.
50   Consultation with Phil Charko, Ottawa, 14 September 2011.
51   Consultations with an assistant secretary, Treasury Board Secretariat, Ottawa, 17 October 2011. See also Joanne Kelly and Evert Lindquist, "Metamorphos in Kafka's Castle: The Changing Balance of Power among the Central Budget Agencies of Canada," in John Wanna, Lotte Jensen, and Jouke de Vries, eds, *Controlling Public Expenditure: The Changing Roles of Central Budget Agencies – Better Guardians?* (Cheltenham, UK: Edward Elgar, 2003).
52   Ian D. Clark and Harry Swain, "Distinguishing the Real from the Surreal in Management Reform: Suggestions for Beleaguered Administrators in the Government of Canada," *Canadian Public Administration* 48, no. 4 (2005): 459 and 472.
53   Ralph Heintzman, "Measurement in Public Management: The Case for the Defence," *Optimum* 39, no. 1 (2009): 71.
54   Canada, Reports on Plans and Priorities (RPPs) and Departmental Performance Reports (DPRs), *Treasury Board Secretariat*, www.tbs-sct.gc.ca, n.d.
55   Consultation with a director general official, Industry Canada, 20 October 2011.
56   See, for example, Canada, Department of Canadian Heritage, 2011–12 Integrated Business Plan.
57   Canada, *Report of the Expert Panel on Integrated Business and Human Resources Planning in the Federal Public Service*, www.pco-bcp.gc.ca, 15 December 2008.
58   Various consultations with central agency and line department officials (at Industry Canada, Natural Resources Canada, and Canadian Heritage), various dates in September and October 2011.
59   Canada, 2004 *November Report of the Auditor General of Canada – Chapter 1, Internal Audit in Departments and Agencies* (Ottawa: Office of the Auditor General, 2004).

60 *Five-Year Evaluation of the 2006 Policy on Internal Audit* (Vancouver: Ference, Weicker & Co., 15 April 2011).

61 Peter Larson and David Zussman, *Departmental Audit Committees in the Canadian Government* (Ottawa: Deloitte, n.d.), 20.

62 Ibid., 16.

63 Canada, *Risk Management*, www.tbs-sct.gc.ca.

64 The Sarbanes-Oxley Act was enacted in 2002 and is a United States initiative designed to establish standards for public companies. The act was in response to scandals in the business community that cost investors a great deal of money.

65 Canada, *Policy on Internal Control*, www.tbs-sct.gc.ca.

66 Canada, *Quarterly Financial Reporting*, www.tbs-sct.gc.ca.

67 Consultations with a senior public servant, Ottawa, 17 October 2011.

68 Canada, *1998 September Report of the Auditor General of Canada – Chapter 18* (Ottawa: Office of the Auditor General, 1998).

69 See Nola Buhr, "Accrual Accounting by Anglo-American Governments: Motivations, Developments, and Some Tensions over the Last 30 Years," paper presented to the Sixth Accounting History International Conference in Wellington, New Zealand, August 2010 (mimeo).

70 The information is drawn from the Treasury Board website – re the estimates. The seven are the Office of the Auditor General, the Official Languages Commissioner, the Access to Information Commissioner, the Public Service Commissioner, the Parliamentary Budget Officer, the Office of the Public Sector, the Integrity Commissioner of Canada, and the Privacy Commissioner.

71 The 1,457 employees at Industry Canada fall under "Internal Services" management and oversight services, audit and evaluation, public policy services, communication services, legal services, human resources management services, financial management services, information management services, information technology services, real property services, material services, requisition services and travel and other services" (Canada, Industry Canada, *Departmental Performance Report, 2009–10*, 12 and 44).

72 This information was provided to me as a member of the agency's Strategic Review Committee, Moncton, 18 May 2010.

73 Consultations with a senior department official, Ottawa, 20 October 2011.

74 An excellent case in point is the parliamentary budget office established by the Harper government following commitments made in an election campaign. Harper dismissed out of hand advice from Parliament's budget officer as "dumb," and his government has launched efforts to restrict the scope of the officer's work. See, among others, "Harper rejects dumb budget advice," www.nationalpost.com, 11 July 2009.

75 See Sharon Sutherland, "Parliament's Unregulated Control Bureaucracy," *Briefing Notes* (Kingston: Queen's University School of Policy Studies, 2002), 9. It should be noted, however, that the Office of the Auditor General has statutory authority to launch comprehensive or value-for-money audits.

76 "The woman who enraged voters," *Ottawa Citizen*, 9 June 2004, B1.

77 "Disaster agency itself a disaster," *Ottawa Citizen*, 4 November 2009, A1 and A2.

78 Canada, *Annual Reports*, selected chapters (Ottawa: Office of the Auditor General, 22 November 2005, May 2007, and 30 October 2007).

79 See "Week of heavy job losses puts pressure on Flaherty to open stimulus taps wider," *Globe and Mail*, 6 February 2009, A1.

80 "Why Canada's budget watchdog is so good at dropping the gloves," *Globe and Mail*, 31 January 2009, F3.

81 "Put tether on budget watchdog, MPs urge," www.thestar.com, 17 June 2009.

82 See, for example, "It's Finance Minister Flaherty versus Budget Officer Page," *Hill Times*, 24 October 2011, 1 and 20.

83 See, for example, "NDP, Liberals and Page to push for PBO's independence when the House of Commons resumes," www.hilltimes.com, 14 July 2011.

84 Neil Reynolds, "OOPS: Ottawa's mistake of grand proportions," www.theglobeandmail.com, 3 March 2010.

CHAPTER SEVEN

1 H.L. Laframboise, "The Future of Public Administration: Programs and Prospects," *Canadian Public Administration* 25, no. 4 (1982): 507.

2 Donald J. Savoie, *The Politics of Public Spending in Canada* (Toronto: University of Toronto Press, 1990), 116.

3 Canada, *An Introduction to the Process of Program Review* (Ottawa: Minister of Supply and Services, March 1986), 23.

4 Quoted in Savoie, *The Politics of Public Spending in Canada*, 115.

5 Edgar Benson, "The New Budget Process," *Canadian Tax Journal*, May 1968, 161.

6 Al Johnson, "Planning, Programming, and Budgeting in Canada," *Public Administration Review* 33, no. 1 (1973): 24.

7 This was also the case when I wrote *The Politics of Public Sending in Canada*; see ch. 4.

8 Canada, *Policy on Evaluation*, www.tbs-sct.gc.ca, April 2009.

9 Canada, *2010 Annual Report on the Health of the Evaluation Function* (Ottawa: Treasury Board of Canada Secretariat, 2010), 3 and 4.

10 Canada, *Evaluating the Effectiveness Program – Chapter 1, 2009 Fall Report of the Auditor General of Canada*, 3–5 (Ottawa: Office of the Auditor General of Canada, 2009).

11 Ibid., 4 and 5.

12 Ibid., 17.

13 Peter Aucoin, "Decision-Making in Government: The Role of Program Evaluation," a paper prepared for the Treasury Board Secretariat, 29 March 2005, 4, 5, 10. See also Christopher Hood et al., eds, *Controlling Modern Government: Variety, Commonality, and Change* (Cheltenham, UK: Edward Elgar, 2004).

14 "Top general vows to repay cost of using Ottawa's executive jet if he must," www.theglobeandmail.com, 19 September 2011, and news release: "NDP pass emergency resolution on search and rescue," www.jackharris.ndp.ca, 20 June 2011.

15 Canada, *Policy on Evaluation*, 5.
16 Ibid., 4.
17 Ibid., 5.
18 See, among others, Gene A. Brewer, "All Measures of Performance are Subjective: More Evidence on U.S. Federal Agencies," in G.A. Boyne et al., eds, *Public Service Performance: Perspectives on Measurement and Management* (Cambridge: Cambridge University Press, 2006); and Y.H. Chun and H.G. Rainey, "Goal Ambiguity and Organizational Performance in U.S. Federal Agencies," *Journal of Public Administration Research and Theory* 15, no. 4 (2005): 529–57.
19 See Canada, *An Introduction to the Process of Program Review*, 23.
20 See, among others, Carol Weiss, *Evaluation Research: Methods for Assessing Program Effectiveness* (Englewood Cliffs, NJ: Prentice-Hall, 1972); Aaron Wildavsky, "The Self-Evaluating Organization," *Public Administration Review* 32, no. 5 (1972): 509–20; James Q. Wilson, *Bureaucracy: What Government Agencies Do and Why They Do It* (New York: Basic Books, 1991); and Christopher Pollitt and Geert Bouckaert, *Public Management Reform: A Comparative Analysis – New Public Management Governance and the Neo-Weberian State*, 3rd edn (Oxford: Oxford University Press, 2011).
21 Rebecca M. Eddy and Tiffany Berry, "The Evaluator's Role in Recommending Program Closure: A Model for Decision Making and Professional Responsibility," *American Journal of Evaluation* 30, no. 3 (2009): 363–76. In Canada, see J. Mayne, "Audit and Evaluation in Public Management: Challenges, Reforms, and Different Roles," *Canadian Journal of Program Evaluation* 21, no. 1 (2006): 11–15; and James C. McDavid and Irene Huse, "Will Evaluation Prosper in the Future?" *Canadian Journal of Program Evaluation* 21, no. 3 (2006): 47–72.
22 Karen Fryer, Jigu Anthony, and Susan Ogden, "Performance Management in the Public Sector," *International Journal of Public Sector Management* 22, no. 6 (2009): 491.
23 See, for example, Christopher Pollitt, "Performance Management in Practice: A Comparative Study of Executive Agencies," *Journal of Public Administration and Theory* 16 (2005): 25–44.
24 Donald J. Savoie, *Governing from the Centre: The Concentration of Power in Canadian Politics* (Toronto: University of Toronto Press, 1999), 256.
25 Canada, Office of the Auditor General, *Annual Report* (Ottawa, 1986).
26 Douglas G. Hartle, "The Role of the Auditor General of Canada," *Canadian Tax Journal* 23, no. 3 (1975): 197.
27 See, among others, "Tories hire $90,000-a-day consultant to help cut spending," www.theglobeandmail.com, 20 September 2011.
28 Ruth Hubbard and Gilles Paquet, "Not in the Catbird Seat: Pathologies of Governance," *Optimum Online*, June 2009, 6.
29 Ian D. Clark and Harry Swain, "Distinguishing the Real from the Surreal in Management Reform: Suggestions for Beleaguered Administrators in the Government of Canada," *Canadian Public Administration* 48, no. 4 (2005): 458.
30 This information is based on Canada, *Treasury Board of Canada Secretariat–Industry Canada, Report, Estimates and Supply, 2011–12*, www.tbs-sct.gc.ca.

31 Canada, *Task Force on Program Review* (Ottawa: Supply and Services Canada, 1986), 23.

32 This information is based on Canada, *Treasury Board of Canada Secretariat–Industry Canada, Report, Estimates and Supply, 2011–12.*

33 Canada, *Evaluating the Effectiveness Program – Chapter 1*, 24.

34 See, for example, Hal Rainey, *Understanding and Managing Public Organization* (San Francisco: Jossey-Bass, 2003).

35 "Parliament is a colossal waste of money, says Grit MP Keith Martin," *Hill Times*, 29 November 2010, 6.

36 Canada, *Final Evaluation of the Community Access Program* (Ottawa: Industry Canada, 2009), 3 and 4.

37 Ibid.

38 For a more complete review of the differences between a contribution and a grant, the reader should consult the Auditor General's website, www.oag-bvg.gc.ca.

39 Canada, *Evaluation of the Canadian Studies Program* (Ottawa: Canadian Heritage, July 2010), 63.

40 I note, however, that one of the Treasury Board Secretariat officials assigned to work with us on ACOA's strategic review reported that some of her people did consult some evaluation reports.

41 See, for example, Arthur Kroeger, "The Central Agencies and Program Review," in Peter Aucoin and Donald J. Savoie, eds, *Managing Strategic Change: Learning from Program Review* (Ottawa: Canadian Centre for Management Development, 1998), 17.

42 Ibid., which brings together ten authors to review departmental cases. See also David Good, *Politics of Public Money: Spenders, Guardians, Priority Setters, and Financial Watchdogs inside the Canadian Government* (Toronto: University of Toronto Press, 2007), and Gilles Paquet and Robert Shepherd, "The Program Review Process: A Deconstruction," in Gene Swimmer, ed, *How Ottawa Spends, 1996–97: Life Under the Knife* (Ottawa: Carleton University Press, 1996).

43 "Faced with worsening economy, Ottawa delays its deficit target," www.theglobeandmail.com, 8 November 2011.

44 Daniel LeBlanc, "Stockwell Day tries again to make nice with his staff," www.theglobeandmail.com, 18 May 2010.

45 Australia, *Development and Implementation of Key Performance Indicators to Support the Outcomes and Program Framework* (Canberra: Australian National Audit Office, 2011), 12. See also R. Mulgan, "The Accountability Priorities of Australian Parliamentarians," *Australian Journal of Public Administration* 67, no. 4 (2008): 457–69.

46 See Savoie, *Governing from the Centre.*

47 Consultations with officials at Natural Resources Canada, Industry Canada, the Atlantic Canada Opportunities Agency, Canadian Heritage, and the Treasury Board Secretariat between March and November 2011, in Ottawa and Moncton.

48 Consultation with a senior deputy minister, November 2011, Ottawa.

49 For a classic essay on overload problems that resonates in the Canadian setting, see Samuel Beer, "Political Overload and Federalism," *Polity*, 1977, 8. See also

Anthony King, "Overload: Problems of Governing in the 1970s," *Political Studies,* 23, no. 2 (1975): 284–96.

50 See Canada, www.tbs-sct.gc.ca, and Good, *Politics of Public Money.*

51 E. Lindquist, "How Ottawa Assesses Department/Agency Performance: Treasury Board of Canada's Management Accountability Framework," in A. Maslove, ed, *How Ottawa Spends, 2009–2010: Economic Upheaval and Political Dysfunction* (Montreal & Kingston: McGill-Queen's University Press, 2009). See also Donald J. Savoie, *Court Government and the Collapse of Accountability in Canada and the United Kingdom* (Toronto: University of Toronto Press, 2008).

52 See, among others, Savoie, *The Politics of Public Spending in Canada.*

53 This is based on numerous conversations I had with senior TBS officials while I served as the Simon Reisman Visiting Fellow in 2004. See also Mulgan, "Accountability," 555–73.

54 Donald J. Savoie, *Breaking the Bargain: Public Servants, Ministers, and Parliament* (Toronto: University of Toronto Press, 2003), 224.

55 For a review of the organization of the Treasury Board Secretariat, see www.tbs-sct.gc.ca.

56 Treasury Board Secretariat officials acknowledged such concerns in discussions with them while I served as the Simon Reisman Visiting Fellow at the Treasury Board in 2004.

57 I base this observation on my experience as the Simon Reisman Visiting Fellow at the Treasury Board.

58 Here again, some TBS officials made this point in various conversations with them while I served as the Simon Reisman Visiting Fellow.

59 Ibid. One former senior Treasury Board official, when asked for an estimate of the amount, responded, "No one has added it up, but all told we are talking over one billion."

60 Canada, *Annual Financial Report of the Government of Canada, Fiscal Year 2010–11* (Ottawa: Department of Finance, n.d.), www.fin.gc.ca.

61 Ibid., for fiscal year 1998–99.

62 Canada, *Public Accounts of Canada, 2010–11,* www.tbs-sct.gc.ca, 1.7.

63 Ibid., 2.14.

64 Canada, *Public Accounts of Canada, 2001–02,* www.lac-bac.gc.ca, 3.10–3.13.

65 Public Accounts of Canada are available on the government website from 1995 to today. Earlier accounts are available in hard copy from public libraries, and – with some exceptions and revisions – they follow the same format.

66 Canada, www.tpsgc-pwgsc.gc.ca, organizational structure, text version.

67 Canada, www.psc-cfp.gc.ca, *Annual Report,* ch. 2.

68 Savoie, *Breaking the Bargain,* 216.

69 "Treasury hopes senior cuts will boost employee morale," *Ottawa Citizen,* 18 April 1989, A3.

70 Savoie, *Breaking the Bargain,* 225.

71 Quoted in ibid., 226.

72 Canada, *A Strong Foundation, Report of the Task Force on Public Service Values and Ethics* (Ottawa: Treasury Board Secretariat, 1996).

73 See *International Coaching Psychology Review*. See also S. Berglas,
    Real Dangers of Executive Coaching," *Harvard Business Review*, June
    86–92.
74 The Canada School of Public Service, a Government of Canada agency. See
    Canada, "Coaching for Effective Leadership" (Ottawa: Canada School of Public
    Service, 2011).
75 Robert Lahey, *The Canadian M & E System: Lessons Learned from 30 Years of
    Development* (Washington, DC: IEG World Bank, 30 November 2010), 31.
76 *Driving Federal Performance: Overview of Performance: Survey* (New York:
    McKinsey and Company, 1 October 2009), 5.
77 Stephen Maher, "Harper's inefficient route to government efficiency,"
    www.nationalpost.com, 11 November 2011.

CHAPTER EIGHT

1 Consultations with a former employee of the Public Service Commission, Sarasota,
   Fla, 29 March 2011.
2 See, among others, Canada, *Expenditure Review of Federal Public Sector Compensation Policy and Comparability* (Ottawa: Treasury Board Secretariat, 2007)
   1:15.
3 "Can Ottawa tame the beast?" *Globe and Mail*, 13 March 2010, F1.
4 "Canada's Public Service in the 21st Century," discussion paper (Ottawa: Public
   Policy Forum, April 2007), 2.
5 See, among others, Christopher Pollitt and Geert Bouckaert, *Public Management
   Reform: A Comparative Analysis* (Oxford: Oxford University Press, 2000), and R.
   Behn, *Rethinking Democratic Accountability* (Washington, DC: Brookings Institution, 2001).
6 Quoted in "Canada's Public Service in the 21st Century," 27.
7 Canada, *Demographic Snapshot of the Federal Public Service*, Treasury Board of
   Canada Secretariat, www.tbs-sct.gc.ca.
8 Canada, Statistics Canada, Government Publications 11-402-X, Canada Year
   Book, www.statscan.gc.ca, n.d.
9 Canada, *Eighteenth Annual Report to the Prime Minister on Public Service in
   Canada* (Ottawa: Privy Council Office, 31 March 2011), annex A, and Canada,
   www.psc-cfp.gc.ca (*Annual Report*, ch. 2).
10 "Why fat city's diet may not be," *Ottawa Citizen*, 24 March 2012, B1 and B3.
11 Canada, *Annual Report* (Ottawa: Public Service Commission, 2011), table 10. See
    also Katherine A.H. Graham and Gene Swimmer, "The Ottawa Syndrome: The
    Localization of Federal Public Servants in Canada," *Canadian Public Administra-
    tion* 52, no. 3 (2009): 417–37.
12 "Federal job cuts to hit Ottawa-Gatineau hardest," www.ottawacitizen.com, 29
    March 2012; "Hit list: PSC members affected by federal public service workforce
    adjustments," www.ottawacitizen.com, 12 April 2012; and "CBC, Health Canada,
    National Defence face Conservative cuts," www.theglobeandmail.com, 7 April
    2012.

13 See, among others, Donald J. Savoie, *Visiting Grandchildren: Economic Development in the Maritimes* (Toronto: University of Toronto Press, 2006).

14 Canada, *Annual Report*.

15 See Herman Bakvis, "Rebuilding Policy Capacity in the Era of the Fiscal Dividend," *Governance* 13, no. 1 (2001): 71–103, and Kenneth Kernaghan, *Bureaucracy in Canadian Government: Selected Readings* (Toronto: Methuen, 1969).

16 As an example, one can consult the clerk of the privy council's annual report to the prime minister. The reports are accessible on www.clerk.gc.ca.

17 Canada, *Sixteenth Annual Report to the Prime Minister on the Public Service of Canada* (Ottawa: Privy Council Office, 20 March 2009), www.clerk.gc.ca.

18 Canada, *First Annual Report to the Prime Minister on the Public Service of Canada* (Ottawa: Privy Council Office, 30 June 1992), www.clerk.gc.ca.

19 Canada, *Seventh Annual Report to the Prime Minister on the Public Service of Canada* (Ottawa: Privy Council Office, 31 March 2000), www.clerk.gc.ca.

20 See, for example, Canada, *Service Standards: A Guide to the Initiative* (Ottawa: Treasury Board of Canada Secretariat, n.d.), www.tbs-sct.gc.ca.

21 See, among others, "An absurd choice is no choice for Canadians," www.psac-afpc.com, n.d.

22 Canada, *Eighteenth Annual Report to the Prime Minister on the Public Service* (Ottawa: Privy Council Office, 2011), www.clerk.gc.ca. See section on program delivery.

23 *Survey on Bureaucratic Patronage in the Federal Public Service, Final Report* (Ottawa, 2005), www.psc-cfp.gc.ca.

24 Canada, *Reports: Employment Equity in the Public Service of Canada*, www.tbs-sct.gc.ca, n.d.

25 Ibid. See also, Canada, *2009–10 Public Service Renewal Action Plan*, www.clerk.gc.ca.

26 Ibid., and Canada, *Employment Equity Act*, SC 1995, c. 44, s. 22.

27 Canada, *Reports: Employment Equity in the Public Service of Canada*.

28 Canada, *Annual Report on Official Languages, 2009–10* (Canada: Treasury Board of Canada Secretariat, 2010); see statistical tables in Annex.

29 The most recent numbers available are to be found in Canada, *Employment Equity Act Review* (Ottawa: Human Resources and Social Development Canada, 2001), 13.

30 Canada, *Fourteenth Annual Report to the Prime Minister on the Public Service of Canada* (Ottawa: Privy Council Office, 30 March 2007), 4 and 9.

31 Canada, *Fifth Report to the Prime Minister: A Public Service for Challenging Times* (Ottawa: Prime Minister's Advisory Committee on the Public Service, March 2011).

32 Canada, *Sixth Report of the Prime Minister's Advisory Committee on the Public Service: Moving Ahead – Public Service Renewal in a Time of Change* (Ottawa: Privy Council Office, March 2012), 4.

33 See, among many others, "Day hints at two-tiered federal pensions," *Globe and Mail*, 23 March 2010, A8; "There's a lot of fear in public service, says NDP's Dewar," *Hill Times*, 28 March 2011, 37; "Can Ottawa tame its beast?" *Globe and*

Mail, 13 March 2010, F1 and F6–7; and "Fat City," *Maclean's*, 7 December 2009, 10.

34 See, for example, Catherine Swift, "Creating two classes of retirees," press release, Canadian Federation of Independent Business, n.d.

35 This theme runs in most of the clerk's annual reports to the prime minister on the public service, accessible at www.clerk.gc.ca.

36 Quoted in "Generational war brewing in PS, pollster says," www.ottawacitizen.com, 11 January 2010.

37 Canada, *Expenditure Review of Federal Public Sector Compensation.*

38 Ibid., 1:2.2.

39 I was one of the parties who made the request.

40 Canada, *Expenditure Review of Federal Public Sector Compensation*, 1:2.

41 Ibid., 1:2.3.

42 Ibid., 1:2.2.

43 Ibid., 1:2.3.

44 Ibid., 1:2.6 and 2.7–2.8.

45 Ibid., 1:2.4.

46 Ibid.; and Canada, *Report of the Royal Commission on Administrative Classification in the Public Service of Canada* (Ottawa: King's Printer, 1946), 15.

47 Canada, *Expenditure Review of Federal Public Sector Compensation*, 1:2.6.

48 Ibid., 1:2.9.

49 Ibid.

50 Quoted in ibid., 1:2.16.

51 Ibid.

52 "Federal workers have been losing ground for ten years," union update, PSAC (Ottawa, 19 June 2000).

53 Canada, *Expenditure Review of Federal Public Sector Compensation*, 1: 3.4.

54 Ibid.

55 "Notes for a Presentation by Yvon Tarte, chair of the Public Service Staff Relations Board, to the National Joint Council in Winnipeg," 15–17 September 1999, 7 (mimeo).

56 Canada, *Expenditure Review of Federal Public Sector Compensation*, 1:12.1 and 1:12.2.

57 See, for example, *Identifying the Issues: Final Report* (Ottawa: Advisory Committee on Labour Management Relations in the Federal Public Service, 2000).

58 For a different perspective, consult the work of Gene Swimmer, including *How Ottawa Spends: Seeing Red – A Liberal Report Card* (Ottawa: Carleton University, 1997).

59 Canada, *Expenditure Review of Federal Public Sector Compensation*, 1:5.15.

60 Blain Knapp and Christopher Studholme look at executive compensation in their "Improving Bureaucracy: Some Suggestions," *Optimum Online*, June 2011.

61 Canada, *Expenditure Review of Federal Public Sector Compensation*, 1:6.4.

62 Derek Picard, *Wage Watch: A Comparison of Public-Sector and Private-Sector Wages* (Toronto: Canadian Federation of Independent Business, October 2003), 15.

63 Canada, *Expenditure Review of Federal Public Sector Compensation*, 1:6.4.
64 Morley Gunderson, *Public-Private Sector Wage Differences with Emphasis on the Federal Government* (Ottawa: October 2003), 19 (mimeo).
65 Canada, *Expenditure Review of Federal Public Sector Compensation*, 1:6.12.
66 Ibid., 1:6.18.
67 Ibid., 1:6.19.
68 "Retirement lost," www.theglobeandmail.com, 19 October 2009.
69 Ibid., A16.
70 "Federal PS pensions a $58 billion debt time bomb: Think tank," www.ottawacitizen.com, 18 January 2010.
71 "Demands grow for civil service wages, pension reform," www.ottawacitizen.com, 23 February 2010.
72 "Ottawa's public sector pension bubble grows to $227 billion," (Toronto: C.D. Howe Institute, 13 December 2011).
73 Canada, *Expenditure Review of Federal Public Sector Compensation*, 1:14.1.
74 Ibid., 1:14.2.
75 "PSAC president lashes out at talk of changes to PS pensions," www.ottawacitizen.com, 17 January 2012.
76 See, among others, "Federal public servants who keep their jobs needn't fear cuts to their pensions," www.ottawacitizen.com, 29 March 2012.
77 Canada, *Expenditure Review of Federal Public Sector Compensation*, 1:14.3.
78 Ibid., 2:7.2.
79 Ibid., 1:14.9.
80 Ibid., 2:12.
81 Ibid., 2:8.
82 Ibid., 1:8.15.
83 "Time running out on PS parking perks," www.ottawacitizen.com, 31 March 2010.
84 Canada, *Expenditure Review of Federal Public Sector Compensation*, 1:8.16.
85 Ibid., 2:8; and Canada, *Maternity and Parental Benefits Guide*, www.tbs-sct.gc.ca.
86 Canada, *Expenditure Review of Federal Public Sector Compensation*, 2:8.
87 Ibid.
88 Ibid., 2:8.5.
89 Ibid, 2:6.15 and 1:8.14.
90 About the Public Service Alliance of Canada, consult www.psac-afpc.com.
91 See, among others, "PS unions fear battle over severance," www.ottawacitizen.com, 16 November 2010.
92 "PSAC accepts deal – barely," www.ottawacitizen.com, 2 December 2010.
93 "PIPSC cancels early contract talks with Tories over severance," www.ottawacitizen.com, 26 October 2010.
94 "PS unions vow not to surrender severance," www.ottawacitizen.com, 24 October 2010.
95 *Understanding Your Severance Pay*, www.pipsc.ca, 23 November 2011.
96 James Lahey, "Controlling Federal Compensation Costs: Towards a Fairer and More Sustainable System," in Christopher Stoney and G. Bruce Doern, eds, *How*

Ottawa Spends 2011–12 (Montreal & Kingston: McGill-Queen's University Press, 2012), 88.

97 Ibid., 92.

98 Canada, *Expenditure Review of Federal Public Sector Compensation*, 1:4.10.

99 Ibid., 1:4.11 and 4.12.

100 Ibid., 2:4.

101 Canada, *Annual Report 2010–2011* (Ottawa: Public Service Commission, 2011), ch. 2.

102 Mark Brownlee, "Public Service $400K club nearly doubles," www.montrealgazette.com, 15 November 2011.

103 Canada, *Expenditure Review of Federal Public Sector Compensation*, 2:5.9.

104 Ibid., 2:5.10.

105 Ibid., 1:6.8.

106 Ibid., 1:13.14.

107 Canada, *Perspectives* (Statistics Canada), 5, no. 8 (2008). See also "What does shift in union memberships mean for Canada?" www.theglobeandmail.com, 5 September 2011.

108 Ibid.

109 See, for example, Marcia Costa, "Labour Relations and the 1990s Employment Regimes in Canada and Brazil," *Just Labour* 9 (August 2006): 46. See also M. Gunderson, A. Ponak, and D.G. Taras, eds, *Union-Management Relations in Canada* (Toronto: Pearson Publishing, 2005).

110 "What does shift in union membership mean for Canada?" 44.

111 Consultations with a senior Treasury Board Secretariat official, Ottawa, 16 March 2010.

112 "Public service won't see major cuts, Baird says," www.ottawacitizen.com, 8 August 2010.

113 Canada, *Expenditure Review of Federal Public Sector Compensation*, 1:15.5.

114 "Record number of PS applications," www.ottawacitizen.com, 21 December 2009.

115 "PS disability claims soaring," www.ottawacitizen.com, 28 June 2011. See also "Depression in PS a public health crisis," www.ottawacitizen.com, 10 January 2010.

116 Quoted in "PS disability claims soaring."

117 Canada, *Public Service Employee Survey* (Ottawa: Statistics Canada, 12 May 2009).

118 See, among others, Hugh Winsor, "A New Style for the Public Service" (Kingston: Queen's University News Centre, 2010), 8.

CHAPTER NINE

1 See "Dean of Deputy Ministers – Arthur Kroeger dies," www.cbc.ca, 10 May 2008, and George Post, *Conversations with Canadian Public Service Leaders* (Ottawa: CCMD, March 1996), 13.

2 Biographical notes are available on deputy ministers on the Government of Canada website, www.canada.gc.ca.

3 www.investpoint.com, BNS-Bank, n.d.

4 www.cibc.com, Executive Team, n.d.

5 "Ford of Canada appoints veteran exec Dianne Craig as President and CEO," www.news.yahoo.com/Ford-Canada, 25 October 2011.

6 Company Management, www.manulife.com, n.d.

7 www.encana.com/aboutus/leadership.

8 Donald J. Savoie, *Thatcher, Reagan, Mulroney: In Search of a New Bureaucracy* (Toronto: University of Toronto Press, 1994), 175.

9 "Lewis MacKenzie: On choosing a chief of defence staff," *Globe and Mail*, 27 May 1996, A17.

10 Canada, *Discussion Paper on Values and Ethics in the Public Service* (Ottawa: Privy Council Office, 1996), 45.

11 Canada, *A Brief History* (Ottawa: Office of the Auditor General, n.d.), 1.

12 Sharon Sutherland, *The Office of the Auditor General: Government in Exile?* (Kingston: Queen's University, working paper 31, September 2002), 2.

13 Ibid.

14 Canada, *Risk Management: Policies and Publication* (Ottawa: Treasury Board Secretariat, n.d.).

15 Donald J. Savoie, *Breaking the Bargain: Public Servants, Ministers, and Parliament* (Toronto: University of Toronto Press, 2003), 248.

16 See, for example, Douglas Hartle, "Canada's watchdog growing too strong," *Globe and Mail*, 10 January 1979, A7.

17 Canada, *Overview of Regional Economic Development Programs*, ch. 17 (Ottawa: Office of the Auditor General, annual report 1995).

18 "The woman who enraged voters," *Ottawa Citizen*, 9 June 2004, B1.

19 See "Critics say Harper government throwing prison expansion money away," www.thestar.com, 10 January 2011.

20 Peter Aucoin, "Influencing Public Policy and Decision-Making: Power Shifts," notes for presentation to the 2004 APEX Symposium, "Parliament, the People, and the Public Service," Ottawa, 6–7 October 2004, 4.

21 Ibid.

22 Colin Campbell, *Executive Political Leadership in Canada* (Washington, DC: Association for Canadian Studies, 1989), 89.

23 Consultations with a director-level official with the Government of Canada, Ottawa, 8 January 2012.

24 "Accountability bill will saddle PS with political cronies," *Ottawa Citizen*, 10 October 2006, A1.

25 Julian LeGrand, *Motivation, Agency, and Public Policy: Of Knights and Knaves, Pawns and Queens* (Oxford: Oxford University Press, 2003), 47.

26 "DND report lays out plan to $1B," www.cbc.ca, 19 August 2011.

27 Canada, *Report on Transformation* (Ottawa: Department of National Defence, 2011), xii and xiii.

28 Ibid., 5–6.

29 Ibid., 31–2.

30 Ibid., 21. See also "General's report calls for dramatic cuts to bloated military staffing," www.theglobeandmail.com, 19 August 2011.

31 Lieutenant General Andrew Leslie, quoted in "Cutting military travel may boast productivity: Documents," www.ottawacitizen.com, 22 September 2011.

32 Lieutenant General Andrew Leslie, quoted in "Ottawa mandarins, general skirmish over bureaucratic cuts," www.ottawacitizen.com, 19 August 2011.

33 "Beleaguered RCMP wrestles with bloat at the centre," www.theglobeandmail.com, 28 November 2011.

34 Canada, *Annual Report, 2010–2011* (Ottawa: Public Service Commission, 2011).

35 Consultations with a Treasury Board Secretariat official, Ottawa, 17 October 2011, and Canada, *Annual Report to Parliament 2009–10: Human Resources Management* (Ottawa: Treasury Board Secretariat, 2010), appendix 2, figure 9.

36 Canada, *Annual Report, 2010–2011*, ch. 2.

37 Information provided by June Dewetering, Government Finance Section, Library of Parliament, in response to a request for the information from Dominic LeBlanc, MP, 15 November 2011.

38 The reader can review reclassification activities of government departments and agencies, some going back to 2004. See Canada, www.canada.gc.ca/depts/major/depind-eng.

39 See "Unnecessary government spending is no accident," *Globe and Mail*, 24 July 2009, B2.

40 J.L. Granatstein, *The Ottawa Men: The Civil Service Mandarins, 1935–37* (Toronto: University of Toronto Press, 1982), 9–10.

41 Ibid., 10.

42 Canada, *2010 Annual Report on the Health of the Evaluation Function*, www.tbs-sct.gc.ca/report.

43 The office argues that it has called for an international peer review of its performance. The most recent was conducted by a team of like-minded auditors from the Australian National Office in 2009. See Canada, *External Reviews* (Ottawa: Office of the Auditor General, 2010).

44 Shawn Murphy, quoted in "Annual departmental performance reports lack credibility, objectivity," *Hill Times*, 18 October 2010, 37.

45 From various conversations with Al Johnson. I invited Mr Johnson to join CCMD as a fellow when I served as its deputy principal in 1988–89.

46 Public Policy forum, *Managing Change: The Evolving Role of the Commonwealth's Top Public Servants* (Ottawa: Public Policy Forum, December 1998), 18.

47 Ibid., 13.

48 See, among others, Savoie, *Breaking the Bargain*.

49 "G8 spending includes $1,650 to remove bed, $3,500 to move light fixtures," www.theglobeandmail.com, 21 November 2011.

50 "CRA to spend $42,900 to help dyslexic worker learn French," www.theglobeandmail.com.

51 "DND's taxi bill nearly $2 million a year," www.ottawacitizen.com, 4 December 2009.

52 "Minister orders review of unacceptable invoices," www.ottawacitizen.com, 10 March 2010.

53 "Transport Canada factiously expensing millions," www.theglobeandmail.com, 13 September 2009.

54 "PCO 'waiting for Godot' on Public Appointments, spends $300,000 yearly anticipating," *Hill Times*, 28 November 2011, 1 and 7.

55 See, among others, "Harper axes his Public Appointments Commission," *Hill Times*, 9 April 2012, 15.

56 "Defence officials hid cost of Nortel campus renos," www.theglobeandmail.com, 28 November 2011.

57 "DND spends $374,000 to renovate offices of two top officials," www.ottawacitizen.com, 15 January 2012.

58 G.F. Osbaldeston, *Keeping Deputy Ministers Accountable* (Toronto: McGraw-Hill Ryerson, 1989), 167.

59 Jacques Bourgault, *Profile of Deputy Ministers in the Government of Canada* (Ottawa: Canada School of Public Service, 2005), 14.

60 C.E.S. Franks, "Tenure of Canadian Deputy Ministers, 1996–2005: Notes and Comments," Kingston, ON, unpublished paper, 29 June 2006, 7.

61 David Mitchell and Ryan Conway, "From the Deputy Shuffle to the Deputy Churn: Keeping the Best and Brightest in Ottawa," *Policy Options*, May 2011, 61.

62 C.E.S. Franks, *The Parliament of Canada* (Toronto: University of Toronto Press, 1987), 237.

63 EKOS conducted the survey in May 2001 for the Public Service Commission, *The Road Ahead: Perceptions of the Public Service* (Ottawa: Public Service Commission, 2002), 1.

64 Canada, *Fourteenth Annual Report to the Prime Minister on the Public Service of Canada* (Ottawa: Privy Council Office, 2007), 5.

65 "Supplements to ex-deputy ministers on the rise," *Globe and Mail*, 2 July 2007, A4.

66 See Frederick C. Mosher, *Democracy and the Public Service*, 2nd edn (New York: Oxford University Press, 1982), 154.

67 Canada, *1995 May Report of the Auditor General of Canada – Chapter 1* (Ottawa: Office of the Auditor General, 1995), 14.

68 Ibid., 21.

69 John W. Langford, "Acting on Values: An Ethical Dead End for Public Servants," *Canadian Public Administration* 47, no. 4 (2004): 432.

70 Canada, Treasury Board Secretariat, *Statement of Public Service Values and Ethics* (Ottawa: TBS, 2003); Canada, Office of Public Service Values and Ethics, *Values and Ethics Code for the Public Service* (Ottawa: Her Majesty the Queen in Right of Canada, 2003).

71 Jocelyne Bourgon, "Dedication," in Canada, Canadian Centre for Management Development, *A Strong Foundation*, 4–5; Canada, Privy Council Office, *Seventh Annual Report to the Prime Minister on the Public Service of Canada* (Ottawa: PCO, 31 March 2000), 2; Canada, Privy Council Office, *Ninth Annual Report*

to the Prime Minister on the Public Service of Canada (Ottawa: PCO, 29 March 2002), 11; Canada, Privy Council Office, *Tenth Annual Report to the Prime Minister on the Public Service of Canada* (Ottawa: PCO, 31 March 2003), 14.

72 Quoted in Savoie, *Court Government and the Collapse of Accountability in Canada and the United Kingdom* (Toronto: University of Toronto Press, 2008), 135.

73 See Granatstein, *The Ottawa Men*, and Gordon Robertson, *Memoirs of a Very Civil Servant* (Toronto: University of Toronto Press, 2000).

74 Granatstein, *The Ottawa Men*, 278.

75 See, among others, Savoie, *Court Government*, 132.

76 "Ex-Health bureaucrat jailed for fraud," www.canada.com, 12 March 2005.

77 "Former Health Canada director to plead guilty," *Ottawa Citizen*, 16 November 2005, A6.

78 "Ex-DND bureaucrat speaks out," *Globe and Mail*, 13 March 2004, A5.

79 "Former federal bureaucrat pleads guilty to fraud," *Globe and Mail*, 24 July 2007, A7.

80 "Charges laid in alleged immigration bribery plot," *Globe and Mail*, 17 December 2004, A7.

81 "Passport officer admits to document scam," www.canada.com, 16 May 2007.

82 "Fisheries audits find more abuses," *Globe and Mail*, 24 April 2006, A10.

83 "Ex-bureaucrat jailed for 5½ years in theft of blank passports," *Globe and Mail*, 18 April 2005, A9.

84 "Canadian envoy ran Saudi spy ring: Lawsuit," *National Post*, 14 May 2004, A1 and A22.

85 "400 million federal deal bungled twice, Auditor General," *Globe and Mail*, 8 November 2006, A4.

86 "Fed audit employee overtime," *Times and Transcript* (Moncton), 9 October 2006, B1.

87 This was made public by a former CRA employee on a blog, "Intoxicating," 17 September 2009. See also, "One CRA employee embezzlement case," www.theglobeandmail.com, 17 September 2009.

88 "Public Works under cloud over contracts," www.theglobeandmail.com, 2 February 2010.

89 "NDP demands Canada-wide probe of alleged corruption at tax agency," www.theglobeandmail.com, 4 November 2011.

90 These points were made by Jean-Guy Fleury, a senior Canadian government official in "Performance Management Program in the Canadian Federal Public Service," his presentation to the Governance for Performance in the Public Sector seminar, OECD, Berlin, 13–14 March 2002, 7.

91 Patrick Weller and R.A.W. Rhodes, "Introduction: Enter Centre Stage," in Weller and Rhodes, eds, *The Changing World of Top Officials* (Buckingham: Open University, 2001), 1.

92 B. Guy Peters, *Institutional Theory in Political Science* (New York: Continuum 2005), ch. 5.

93 See, among others, LeGrand, *Motivation, Agency, and Public Policy.*
94 "Senior bureaucrats' bonuses to be based on how much they cut," www.theglobeandmail.com, 11 October 2011.
95 The same is also the case in Britain. See Graham K. Wilson and Anthony Barker, "Bureaucrats and Politicians in Britain," *Governance*, 16, no. 3 (2003): 361.
96 Quoted in "The hole in accountability," *Ottawa Citizen*, 18 November 2006, B4.
97 Jacques Bourgault, "De Kafka au Net: la lutte incessante du sous-ministre pour contrôler son agenda," *Gestion* 22, no. 2 (1997): 21–2.
98 Ibid.
99 Christopher Hood," From FOIWorld to WikiLeaks World: A New Chapter in the Transparency Story?" *Governance* 24, no. 4 (2011): 635–8.
100 Based on information from the Treasury Board Secretariat, as reported in Steve Maher, "Harper's PR obsession fostering paranoia and paralysis in public service," www.canada.com, 30 November 2011.
101 Quoted in "PM Harper takes communications strategy to a whole new level," *Hill Times*, 21 November 2011, 33.
102 Ralph Heintzman, "Loyal to a Fault," *Optimum Online*, March 2010, 6.
103 Richard Mulgan, *Holding Power to Account: Accountability in Modern Democracy* (Basingstoke: Palgrave Macmillan, 2003), 197.
104 www.servicecanada.gc.ca.
105 Jeffrey Simpson, "In a world full of rights, we ignore our responsibility," www.theglobeandmail.com, 23 January 2009.
106 This information was provided to me by Treasury Board Secretariat officials on 15 February 2012. They informed me that the data came from the "Regional Pay System."
107 Barbara Wake Carroll and David Siegel, *Service in the Field: The World of Front-Line Public Servants* (Montreal & Kingston: McGill-Queen's University Press, 1999), 119.
108 See Canada, *Report of the Review of the Public Service Modernization Act, 2003*, www.tbs-sct.gc.ca, 22 December 2011, ch. 5.
109 "Cabinet cannot keep all its secrets," *National Post*, 12 July 2002, A1.
110 "Politician laments reversal of firings over emails porn," *Globe and Mail*, 13 July 2004, A1.
111 "Civil servants to be held accountable for ad scam: Brison," www.canada.com, 11 October 2005.
112 Jean-Jacques Blais made the case about the "bureaucratic inability to impose sanctions" at the Toronto roundtable (Commission of Inquiry into the Sponsorship Program and Advertising Activities, 5 October 2005). See also "NRCan's institutional inertia impedes renewable energy development in Canada: Advocates," *Hill Times*, 10 July 2006.
113 "Ottawa fires dissident scientists," www.theglobeandmail.com, 15 July 2004.
114 "But was it time theft?" *Globe and Mail*, 9 September 2010, A3.
115 Canada, *Expenditure Review of Federal Public Sector – volume 1* (Ottawa: Treasury Board Secretariat, 2007), 11.10, and fn. 166.

116 Canada, *Workplace Relationship: A Good Investment* (Ottawa: Canadian Heritage, Annual Report, 2009).

117 Consultation with a departmental ombudsman, Ottawa, various conversations in 2010–11.

118 Canada, *Sixth Annual Report to the Prime Minister on the Public Service of Canada, Theme 50, Putting People First* (Ottawa: Privy Council Office, 7 December 1998).

119 Ian D. Clark, *Distant Reflections on Federal Public Service Reform in the 1990s* (Ottawa: Office of the Auditor General, n.d.), 8.

120 *Canada's Public Service in the 21st Century* (Ottawa: Public Policy Forum, April 2007), 2.

121 Clark, *Distant Reflections on Federal Public Service Reform in the 1990s*, 6.

CHAPTER TEN

1 Quoted in Canada, *2004 March Report of the Auditor General of Canada* (Ottawa: Office of the Auditor General 2004), ch. 7, exhibit 7.4.

2 Ibid.

3 See Gérard Veilleux and Donald J. Savoie, "Kafka's Castle: The Treasury Board of Canada," *Canadian Public Administration* 31, no. 4 (1988): 524.

4 Canada, Office of the Auditor General, *Annual Report, Year Ended 1975* (Ottawa: Minister of Supply and Services, 1976), 9, and Donald J. Savoie, *The Politics of Public Spending in Canada* (Toronto: University of Toronto Press, 1990), 109–10.

5 Ibid.

6 Canada, Today's Office of the Comptroller General (OCG), www.tbs-sct.gc.ca, n.d.

7 Canada, *Report of the Auditor General for the Fiscal Year Ended March 31, 1976* (Ottawa: Office of the Auditor General and Information Canada, 1976), 19.

8 Denis Saint-Martin, *Building the New Managerialist State: Consultants and the Politics* (Oxford: Oxford University Press, 2000), ch. 4.

9 J.J. Macdonell, quoted in "Government regaining fiscal control," *Ottawa Journal*, 7 November 1979, A4. See also Sonja Sinclair, *Cordial but Not Cosy: A History of the Office of the Auditor General* (Toronto: McClelland & Stewart, 1979).

10 Sharon Sutherland, quoted in "Agents of Parliament are the wild west of accountability," www.ottawacitizen.com, 22 December 2011.

11 Canada, *2009 Fall Report of the Auditor General of Canada – Chapter 2, Selecting Foreign Workers under the Immigration Program* (Ottawa: Office of the Auditor General, 2009).

12 CBC ranked three Mulroney-era political scandals in the top ten in history: tunagate, airbus, and a combination of several others, including Robert Coates visiting a strip club in West Germany while minister of defence, Sinclair Stevens and Michel Côté on conflict-of-interest charges, and Roch La Salle for demanding a bribe. See "Up the skirt or in the till: Top ten scandals in Canadian political history," www.cbc.ca/news, 10 February 2005.

13 See Donald J. Savoie, *Thatcher, Reagan, Mulroney: In Search of a New Bureaucracy* (Toronto: University of Toronto Press, 1994).

14 Donald J. Savoie, *Court Government and the Collapse of Accountability in Canada and the United Kingdom* (Toronto: University of Toronto Press, 2008).

15 Kathryn May, "Parliamentary watchdogs still wait for reply on call for better accountability from MPs," www.ottawacitizen.com, 20 December 2011.

16 Ibid.

17 T. Pederson, quoted in Christopher Pollitt and Geert Bouckaert, *Public Management Reform: A Comparative Analysis* (Oxford: Oxford University Press, 2000), 44.

18 "Federal R&D Panel reports with six major recommendations," www.rd-review.ca, 17 October 2011, and "R&D tax scheme too rich, federal panel finds," *Globe and Mail*, 17 October 2011, A3.

19 Canada, *Changing Terms* (Ottawa: Public Service 2000 Secretariat, 1991).

20 John Hilliker, *Canada's Department of External Affairs: The Early Years*, vol. 1 (Montreal & Kingston: McGill-Queen's University Press, 1990), 243.

21 C.E.S. Franks, *The Parliament of Canada* (Toronto: University of Toronto Press, 1987), 237.

22 EKOS conducted the survey in May 2001 for Canada, *The Road Ahead: Perceptions of the Public Service* (Ottawa: Public Service Commission, 2002), 1.

23 "Lax spending disclosed," *National Post*, 5 September 2009, A8.

24 Canada, *Budget Plan, Budget in Brief,* and *Budget Speech* (Ottawa: Department of Finance, 29 March 2012).

25 "Bureaucrats $10,000 trips too expensive – NDP," www.nationalpost.com, 3 January 2012.

26 Mark D. Jarvis and Paul Thomas, "The Limits of Accountability: What Can and Cannot Be Accomplished in the Dialectics of Accountability," paper prepared for the Symposium Honouring Professor Peter C. Aucoin at Dalhousie University, Halifax, 11–13 November 2009, 42 (mimeo).

27 See, for example, Frank Fischer, *Reframing Public Policy: Discursive Politics and Deliberative Practices* (Oxford: Oxford University Press, 2003).

28 See, among others, Carol Weiss, "Policy Research Data, Ideas or Arguments?" in Peter Wagner et al., eds, *Social Sciences and Modern States* (Cambridge: Cambridge University Press, 1990).

29 Consultation with a senior Industry Canada official, Moncton, 23 December 2011.

30 Savoie, *Thatcher, Reagan, Mulroney,* 109.

31 Peter Aucoin, "Influencing Public Policy and Decision-Making: Power Shifts," notes for presentation to the 2004 APEX Symposium, "Parliament, the People, and Public Service," Ottawa, 6–7 October 2004, 4.

32 Don Drummond, "Personal Reflections on the State of Public Policy in Canada," in Fred Gorbet and Andrew Sharpe, eds, *New Directions for Intelligent Government in Canada: Papers in Honour of Ian Stewart* (Ottawa: Centre for the Study of Living Standards, 2011), 337.

33 Ibid., 338.

34 See, among others, "Tony Clement clears the air on census," www.theglobeand-mail.com, 21 July 2010.

35 Munir Sheikh, "Good Data and Intelligent Government," in Gorbet and Sharpe, *New Directions for Intelligent Government in Canada*, 305–35.

36 Ibid., 329.

37 "The inconvenient truth in Mr. Sheikh's resignation," www.theglobeandmail.com, 22 July 2010.

38 Sheikh, "Good Data and Intelligent Government," 327.

39 Savoie, *Court Government*, 156.

40 See, for example, Frank Fischer, "Beyond Empiricism: Policy Inquiry in Postpositivist Perspective," *Policy Studies* 26, no. 1 (1998): 129–46.

41 "Making Copyright Work Better Online: A Process Report," *Google Public Policy Blog-blogspot.com*, 2 September 2011.

42 Allan Gregg, "Telling the naked truth is good politics," www.theglobeandmail.com, 19 December 2011.

43 See, among others, Pollitt and Bouckaert, *Public Management Reform*.

44 For an excellent review of Ottawa's expenditure process, see Mike Joyce, "Prudent Budgeting and Budgetary Process Effectiveness in Canada's Federal Government Matters: Institute for Research on Public Policy," *Choices* 15, no. 6 (2009).

45 Ibid., 16.

46 See, among others, Peter Aucoin and D.J. Savoie, eds, *Managing Strategic Change: Learning from Program Review* (Ottawa: Canadian Centre for Management Development, 1998).

47 Canada, *Background Paper on the New Cabinet Decision-Making System* (Ottawa: Privy Council Office, n.d.); and "The new-look government: Set up to say no," *Ottawa Citizen*, 4 February 1989, 131.

48 Savoie, *The Politics of Public Spending in Canada*.

49 B. Guy Peters, Carl Dahlström, and Jon Pierre, eds, *Steering from the Centre* (Toronto: University of Toronto Press, 2011).

50 See David A. Good, *The Politics of Public Money: Spenders, Guardians, Priority Setters, and Financial Watchdogs inside the Canadian Government* (Toronto: University of Toronto Press, 2007).

51 James Bagnall, "Why fat city's diet may not be," *Ottawa Citizen*, 24 March 2012, B3.

52 Quoted in "Loose controls, management blamed for costly PS," www.ottawacitizen.com, 5 December 2011.

53 Consultation with an Industry Canada official, Moncton, 22 December 2011.

54 See, among others, Pollitt and Bouckaert, *Public Management Reform*.

55 Consultations with federal and provincial government officials during a roundtable meeting on economic development in Nova Scotia, Halifax, 26 May 2010.

56 Consultation with an Industry Canada official, Moncton, 22 December 2011.

57 J.C. McDavid and L. Hawthorn, *Program Evaluation and Performance Measurement: An Introduction to Practice* (Thousand Oaks, CA: Sage Publications, 2006).

58 See Donald J. Savoie, *Power: Where Is It?* (Montreal & Kingston: McGill-Queen's University Press, 2010).

59 Consultations with a senior Government of Canada official, 10 January 2002, Ottawa.

60 See, for example, James Lahey's observations in "Boom-bust PS carries cost," www.ottawacitizen.com, 5 December 2011.

61 Donald J. Savoie, *Visiting Grandchildren: Economic Development in the Maritimes* (Toronto: University of Toronto Press, 2006).

62 Dominic LeBlanc made these comments on *The House*, CBC, 30 August 2011.

63 See, among others, Donald J. Savoie, "Le programme fédéral de décentralisation: un réexamen," *Canadian Public Policy* 12, no. 3 (1986), and "La bureaucratie représentative: une perspective régionale," *Canadian Journal of Political Science* 20, no. 4 (1987).

64 "Leadership versus self-service in the public service: Why leading with integrity matters," www.open.salon.com, 10 January 2011.

65 "EI queue has ballooned since Service Canada staff cuts," *Globe and Mail*, 27 December 2011, A3.

66 An email from a middle-level federal government manager, 19 October 2010.

67 Pollitt and Bouckaert, *Public Management Reform*, 92.

68 Thomas S. Axworthy and Julie Burch, "Crisis in the Ontario and Federal Public Services," *Policy Options* 31, no. 3 (2010): 24.

69 Ibid., 10.

70 Ibid., 44.

71 See, for example, Good, *The Politics of Public Money*.

CHAPTER ELEVEN

1 See, for example, the work of Paul G. Thomas, "The Changing Nature of Accountability," in B. Guy Peters and Donald J. Savoie, eds, *Taking Stock: Assessing Public Sector Reforms* (Montreal & Kingston: McGill-Queen's University Press, 1998), 36, and Paul T. Hart, John Kane, and Haig Patapan, *Dispersed Democratic Leadership* (Oxford: Oxford University Press, 2009).

2 Jonathan Rose, quoted in "Documents expose Harper's obsession with control," www.thestar.com, 6 June 2010.

3 Quoted in "Firing poor performers will improve federal public service," www.theglobeandmail.com, 28 February 2008.

4 Don Drummond, "Personal Reflections on the State of Public Policy Analysis in Canada," in Fred Gorbet and Andrew Sharpe, eds, *New Directions for Intelligent Government in Canada: Papers in Honour of Ian Stewart* (Ottawa: Centre for the Study of Living Standards, 2011), 346.

5 Ibid., 344–5.

6 "Federal bureaucrats worry about jobs as cuts draw near," www.ottawacitizen.com, 1 January 2012.

7 "Caterpillar's Electro-Motive locks out union at London, Ont. plant," www.theglobeandmail.com, 2 January 2012.

8 "Look in the mirror, MPs, before reforming pensions," www.theglobeandmail.com, 3 January 2012.

9 Donald J. Savoie, *Breaking the Bargain: Public Servants, Ministers, and Parliament* (Toronto: University of Toronto Press, 2003).

10 Jane Jacobs, *Systems of Survival: A Dialogue on the Moral Foundations of Commerce and Politics* (New York: Random House, 1992), 66.

11 Ibid.

12 "Report cites costs, few immediate savings in federal plan to trim down centres," www.theglobeandmail.com, 11 September 2011.

13 See, for example, the work of Shoshana Zuboff, *In the Age of the Smart Machine: The Future of Work and Power* (New York: Basic Books, 1988).

14 For a review of the theories "about bureaucrats" and "programmes and bureaux" in the public spending context, see, among others, Andrew Dunsire and Christopher Hood, *Cutback Management in Public Bureaucracies: Popular Theories and Observed Outcomes in Whitehall* (Cambridge: Cambridge University Press, 2010), chs. 2 and 3, and John Alford and Janine O'Flynn, "Making Sense of Public Value," *International Journal of Public Administration* 32 (2009): 171–91.

15 Quoted in "Prime Minister's Office now rolled into Privy Council Office," *Ottawa Citizen*, 20 June 2011, 1.

16 Herman Finer, "Administrative Responsibility in Democratic Government," *Public Administration Review* 1, no. 4 (1940): 335–50.

17 Christopher Pollitt and Geert Bouckaert, *Public Management Reform: A Comparative Analysis* (Oxford: Oxford University Press, 2000), 92.

18 See Dunsire and Hood, *Cutback Management in Public Bureaucracies*, 170.

19 Ibid.

20 Jim Travers, "Branding Team Harper," www.thestar.com, 6 February 2007.

21 I note that the term Neo-Weberian has been employed in the literature since the 1970s. It gained new traction here.

22 See, among many others, J. Perry, T. Engbers, and S. Jun, "Back to the Future? Performance-Related Pay: Empirical Research and Perils of Persistence," *Public Administration Review* 69, no. 1 (2009): 39–51.

23 Lawrence E. Lynn, *Public Management: Old and New* (London: Portledge, 2006).

24 David E. Lewis makes a similar point in "The Adverse Consequences of the Politics of Agency Design for Presidential Management in the United States," *British Journal of Political Science* 34, no. 4 (2004): 377–404.

25 However, see E.A. Lindquist, "How Ottawa Reviews Spending: Moving Beyond Adhocracy?" in G.B. Doern, ed, *How Ottawa Spends, 2006–2007: In from the Cold, the Tory Rise and the Liberal Demise* (Montreal & Kingston: McGill-Queen's University Press, 2006), 185–207.

26 James Lahey, "Controlling Federal Compensation Costs: Towards a Fairer and More Sustainable System," in *How Ottawa Spends 2011–12*, 98.

27 One only has to look at layoffs in the auto sector in Canada in 2008–09 to see evidence of this. See, among many others, "Layoffs, losses seen for Canada auto parts – Conference Board sees 36,000 jobs cut in 2009," www.reuters.com, 18 June 2009.

28 Christopher Hood speaks to this point in *Explaining Economic Policy Reversals* (Buckingham: Open University, 1994).

29 See, among others, David A. Good, *The Politics of Public Management* (Toronto: University of Toronto Press, 2003).

30 The 1977 Auditor General Act gave the office a much broader mandate. See Canada, Office of the Auditor General, www.oag-bvg.gc.ca, n.d.

31 For insights on machine-like departments and programs, see James Q. Wilson, *Bureaucracy: What Government Agencies Do and Why They Do It* (Basic Books, 1991).

32 Donald J. Savoie, *Court Government and the Collapse of Accountability in Canada and the United Kingdom* (Toronto: University of Toronto Press, 2008).

33 See, for example, Library of Parliament, Parliamentary Budget Officer, *Recent Publications*, www.parl.gc.ca, n.d.

34 Canada, *Review of the Respective Responsibilities and Accountabilities of Ministers and Senior Officials* (Ottawa: Treasury Board Secretariat, 2005), 46.

35 "Sponsorship scandal: Breaking all the rules," www.cbc.ca/archives, 8 May 2002.

36 Desmond Martin situates the sponsorship scandal in Canadian Political History, in "Reflecting on Gomery: Political Scandals and the Canadian Memory," *Policy Options* 26, no. 5 (2005): 14–21.

37 Max Weber, *The Theory of Social and Economic Organization* (New York: Oxford University Press, 1947), 333–7.

38 Michael M. Harmon and Richard T. Mayer, *Organization Theory for Public Administration* (Boston: Little, Brown, 1986), 69.

39 Weber, *The Theory of Social and Economic Organization*, 337.

40 Quoted in Harmon and Mayer, *Organization Theory*, 72.

41 See, among others, Paul C. Light, *Thickening Government: Federal Hierarchy and the Diffusion of Accountability* (Washington, DC: Brookings Institution, 1995) and Anthony Downs, *Inside Bureaucracy* (New York: Little, Brown, 1967).

42 Sir Michael Bichard has been outspoken on this point. See his speaking notes at the Centre for Excellence in Leadership, London, 1 December 2006, 3 (mimeo).

43 See Ralph Heintzman, "Establishing the Boundaries of the Public Service: Toward a New Moral Contract," the Vanier Lecture, Institute of Public Administration in Canada, 2007.

44 Canada, "Accountable Government: A Guide for Ministers and Ministers of State – 2011," www.pco-bcp.gc.ca, undated.

45 See ibid.

46 Ibid., 27.

47 Peter Aucoin, Mark D. Jarvis, and Lori Turnbull, *Democratizing the Constitution: Reforming Responsible Government* (Toronto: Emond Montgomery Publications, 2011), 1.

48 Heintzman, "Establishing the Boundaries of the Public Service," 73.

49 "Mulroney's old top guns to fix PS for Harper," *Ottawa Citizen*, 22 November 2006, A1.

50 See, among others, Peter Aucoin and Mark D. Jarvis, *Modernizing Government Accountability: A Framework for Reform* (Ottawa: Canada School of the Public

Service, 2005), and Canada, Commission of Inquiry into the Sponsorship Program and Advertising Activities, Toronto roundtable, 5 October 2005.

51 Harold Lasswell, *Politics: Who Gets What, When, How*, new edn (Gloucester, MA: 1990).

52 Bernard Donoughee, quoted in C.C. Hood and M. Wright, eds, *Big Government in Hard Times* (Oxford: Martin Robertson, 1981), 201.

apple industry, 234; reclassification in, 201, 202

Alcock, Reg, 6

Al-Mashat affair, 121

Annual Reference Level Update (ARLU), 41

Aristotle, 17

Armstrong, Sir Robert, 4

associate positions, 173, 243, 249–50; associate deputy ministers, 116, 166, 171, 172, 184, 249–50; associate directors, 249

Atlantic Canada Opportunities Agency (ACOA): and number of accountability reports, 144; reclassification in, 201, 202

Aucoin, Peter, 17–18, 34, 152, 198, 228, 251

Auditor General, Office of the (OAG), 195–9; and accountability, 196, 248; accountability crisis and enlargement of, 221–3; Auditor General Act and, 195–6; avoidance of action in favour of sitting in judgment, 152; and campaign commitments, 54; effect on government operations, 247; effect on positions/costs in government, 197; "Ethics and Fraud Awareness in Government," 208; *Evaluating the Effectiveness of Programs,* 151; as financial watchdog, 28; government politicians and, 223–4; on HRDC crisis, 137; and internal auditing, 141–2, 196; and issues vs. financial audits, 222; Macdonell and, 221–3; and management practices, 195–6; Manion's report to, 46; and media, 196, 197; as officer of Parliament, 145; opposition and, 223, 248; on parliamentary control of public purse, 48–9; parsimonious culture and, 248; and performance assessment, 204; on performance measurement, 203; PM and, 160; and policy making, 196; as political/non-political, 145; and private sector management practices, 223; and

program evaluation, 150, 151–2, 153, 154, 155–6, 168, 196; purpose of, 145–6; reporting requirements, 197, 248; reviews/reports, 145–6; and risk management, 196; senior public servants and, 248; and sponsorship scandal, 145, 197; sweeping statements by, 196–7; value-for-money audits, 196, 197, 222, 223, 247, 278n75

Auditor General Act, 195

audits, internal, 141–4

Australia: National Office, 289n43; program evaluation in, 159; Senate in, 67

Axworthy, Lloyd, 6, 83, 98

Axworthy, Thomas, 237

Bagnall, James, 232

Baird, John, 190

Bakvis, Herman, 17–18

Barrados, Maria, 198–9

Beardsley, Keith, 96

benefits. *See* employee benefits

Benn, Tony, 5

Bennett, Carolyn, 71, 147

Benoit, Liane, 69

Berardi, Jennifer, 112

Bichard, Sir Michael, 250

bilingualism, 174–5

Blair, Tony: on PM's time to learn, 85; and private sector management practices, 129–30

Blais, Jean-Jacques, 292n112

blame avoidance: accountability and, 249; cost of, 119–20; effects on government, 119; management and, 204–7; politics and, 225; senior public servants and, 213; and sponsorship scandal, 120

Blumenthal, Michael, 131

Bogdanor, Vernon, 38, 130

Bonaventure (aircraft carrier), 221

bottom line: collective bargaining in private vs. public sectors and, 180; officers of Parliament and, 148; in private vs. public sectors, 14, 131,

224; program evaluation and, 150, 153; public sector management and, 129, 138; as trust, 251

Bouckaert, Geert, 237; *Public Management Reform*, 10, 245

Boulerice, Alexandre, 226

Bourgon, Jocelyne, 121, 218, 240

Britain. *See* United Kingdom

Brunsson, Nils, 21

Bryce, Robert, 48, 209

Buchanan, James, 19

budget maximization, 243

budgeting: guardians vs. spenders in, 28; line-item, 251; line-item vs. program-based, 128, 149–50, 168; principal-agent theory and, 26; spending on outdated measures, 159–60

budget(s), 41; cabinet and, 42; contents, 42; deficit vs. surplus, 105–6; and effective plan implementation, 7–8; factors affecting, 28–9; lockup, 42; March 2012, 100, 104; minister of finance and, 41–3; MPs and, 49–50; opposition and, 43, 45, 50; Parliament and, 48–50; PM and, 42; pressure regarding new initiatives, 42; speech, 41, 43

Burch, Julie, 237

bureaucracy: academics and, 35–6; attack upon, 16; identity crisis, 34–5; military and, 109; politicians and, 16; politics and, 111; public administration community and, 9–10; and reputation of government, 5

Bureaucracy (Wilson), 113

cabinet: and budget, 42; committees, 76; deputy ministers and, 32; and expenditure budget, 76; as focus group, 75–6; Harper and, 76; minister of finance and, 42; MPs and, 56, 67–8; and PCO, clerk of, 218; PM and, 67–8; as priority setter, 101; size of, 70; swearing in, 68

cabinet government: court government vs., 63, 89; governing from centre and, 85, 232

cabinet ministers. *See* ministers

Campbell, Colin, 198

Canada Revenue Agency (CRA): bribes, 211; fraud at, 210–11; second-language training, 205

Canada School of Public Service, 35

Canadian Association of Former Parliamentarians, 40

Canadian Centre for Management Development, 35

Canadian Council of Chief Executives, 92–3

Canadian Federation of Independent Business (CFIB), 176, 181

Canadian National Railways (CN), 83

Canadian Public Administration, 27

The Canadian Public Service: A Physiology of Government (Hodgetts), 17

Canadian Studies Program, 157

Cappe, Mel, 136, 173

Carroll, Barbara W., 27–8, 118, 119, 215

caucus: MPs and, 56; and spending, 50

CBC, on scandals, 293n12

C.D. Howe Institute, 183

census, long-form, 229

central agencies, 115–16; and communications, 72; demands on line managers, 117–18; and fault line, 116; and guardian-spender model, 244; information requests and, 116–17; and machinery running smoothly, 115; and MAFs, 139–40; and media relations, 72; and ministers, 116–17; officers of Parliament and, 147; and policy, 116; as priority setters of budget, 28; and program evaluation, 150, 156; and programs, 101; and spending cuts, 231–2; staff turnover in, 100; strengthening of, 110

centre, governing from: cabinet government and, 232; and departments, 94; and expenditure budget control, 76; and policy, 82; and protection of political interest, 93, 94; shift from cabinet government to, 85; as Western trend, 85

Champagne, Paul, 209–10

Charest, Jean, and Senate reform, 67

Charter of Public Service, 251

Charter of Rights and Freedoms, 41, 86

Chief Audit Executive (CAE), 142

chief information officer, 141

Chief of Defence Staff (CDS), 152, 194

Chrétien, Jean: and accounting officer concept, 122; and cabinet, 76; Dion and court of, 97; on election victory, 67; experience in government, 87; and gun control as matter of conscience, 56; on life of politician, 93; and Manley's protest regarding cuts to department, 99; and Millennium Scholarship Fund, 90, 159; not consulted as Trudeau's minister of finance, 98; policy preferences, 87; on prime minister as "le boss," 76; and private sector management practices, 129–30; program review (*see* program reviews); and Revenue Canada office for riding, 98; and sponsorship scandal, 6–7, 81, 93–4, 120, 121, 122

Citizenship and Immigration, Department of: payback schemes, 210; "time theft" at, 217

civil service (UK). *See* public service (UK)

The Civil Service of Canada (Dawson), 17

Clark, Clifford, 19, 209

Clark, Ian, 155, 218

classification creep, 33, 166–7, 173, 236, 241. *See also* reclassification(s)

Clement, Tony, 78, 98, 104

Clinton, Bill, 129–30

Coates, Robert, 293n12

Cochrane, Paul, 209, 211

collective bargaining: and comparability, 178; and human resource management, 231; impact on compensation, 177–8; and management,

15, 215; and non-performers, 216; in private vs. public sectors, 180, 242; productivity improvement and, 191; suspension of, 180

communications: increase in spin operations, 212–13; and labelling of initiatives as from "Harper government," 73; personnel, 72; PM's court and, 94. *See also* media

Community Access Program, 156–7

comparability: collective bargaining and, 178; compensation, 176–7, 178–9, 181–2; external, 276n24

compensation: classification creep and, 241; comparability of, 176–7, 178–9; cost of, 188–9, 233, 241; determination of, 179; history of, 177–8; market discipline and, 179; per capita, 186–7; private sector and, 133; of public servants, 23; in public vs. private sectors, 15, 181–2; risk and, 133–4; of senior officials, 133; traditional means of determining, 133; wage restraints, 180–1. *See also* performance pay

competition: and appointment of deputy ministers, 253; and private sector, 241; and private sector unions, 190; in private vs. public sectors, 130, 131

Comptroller General, Office of the (OCG): changes in, 49; establishment of, 221; and evaluation groups, 149; and internal control statements, 143; managers and, 141; Policy on Internal Audit, 141–2; and program evaluation, 150, 152, 156; reporting demands created by, 197; TBS and, 49, 221, 222

constituencies: government, 78–9; MPs and, 51, 53–5; new initiatives and, 78–9; process ministers and, 71; regional favouring and, 54; and spending, 65

Constitution Act, 1867, 38

consultants: cost of, 200; deputy ministers as, 208; management, 167, 222;

numbers of, 168–9; and program
evaluation, 151; and reclassifications, 203; retired public servants as,
211; and spending cuts, 197–8, 241;
and strategic and operating reviews,
103–4
Consumer Price Index, 184
contracting-out: deputy ministers and,
208; strategic and operating review
and, 159
controversies, 114–15; and blame
avoidance, 204–7; governing from
centre and, 93–4; intolerance of
political institutions for, 245;
ministers and, 226. *See also* crises;
scandals
Cormier, Michel, 73
Corrections Canada, 198
Côté, Michel, 293n12
court government: cabinet government
vs., 63, 89; and decision making, 63,
89, 90–1; and guardians vs. spenders, 90–1; and ministers, 62, 63,
71–2; and policy, 90–1; and power
vacuum, 91; and process participants, 75, 79; and scandals, 93
court of PM, 89; and across-the-board
cuts, 100; and cabinet ministers,
89, 90; and communications, 94;
courtiers, 63, 89; crises and, 91;
and departments, 95; and deputy
ministers, 92; and elites, 92–3; and
expenditure budget, 91, 96–8; and
government agenda, 89; and government by network, 95–6; and legacy
projects, 97–8; and machinery of
government, 114–15; managing up
to, 113; and media, 90–1; message
control, 94; and ministers, 95, 97;
and new spending, 97; as Ottawa-
based, 235; overloaded agenda of,
232; and partisanship, 89; PCO clerk
and, 89; and policy, 82; power of,
91–2; schizophrenic world of, 93–4;
and spending cuts, 98–9, 101–2, 232;
and spending priorities, 89; strong
vs. weak ministers and, 99; and tight

control vs. delegation of authority,
105
courts: and management, 215, 216;
power of, 86; public servants and,
216–17, 231
Craig, Dianne, 194
Crane, David, 49
crises: deputy ministers and, 118;
HRDC, 136, 137; management, 118;
and OAG, 221–2; PCO clerk and,
218; and spending cuts, 244, 246
crown corporations, 107

Davie shipyard, 97
Dawson, R. MacGregor, 17, 18
Day, Stockwell, 159
decision making: court government
and, 63, 89, 90–1; decentralization
of, 163; by departments/agencies vs.
Treasury Board, 132; forces/variables
affecting, 27; in government, 160–1;
by line departments, 162; minister
of finance and, 42; ministers and,
13; MPs and, 60; Prisoner's Dilemma
and, 26; public/rational choice and,
25; senior public servants and, 32
"Decline of Deference" (Nevitte), 39
deficits: and program reviews, 105–6;
and strategic and operating reviews,
103, 158
Delisle, Gaëtan, 201
Deloitte Touche, 103, 104
democracy: NPM and, 33–4; policy-
program separation and, 18; power
of PM and, 252; public service
reform and, 246
Democratic Government in Canada
(Dawson), 17
Denmark, public sector emulating
private sector in, 224
Departmental Performance Reports
(DPRs), 43, 47, 115, 140–1, 155, 164,
205
Department Audit Committees (DACs),
142–3
departments: ARLU, 41–2; associate
positions in, 249–50; "bleeding"

between, 110; and business goals, 141; central agency demands and, 117–18; and communications, 72; decision making, 132, 162; deputy ministers and, 197, 206; and DPRs, 140–1; duration of deputy ministers in, 206–7; and evaluation groups, 149; evolution of clarity of mandate, 109–10; and expenditure budget, 69–70; Finance and spending proposals from, 20–1; governing from centre and, 94; as hierarchical, 109; ideas for establishment/expansion of programs, 81–2; and Integrated Business Plans, 141; and MAFs, 139, 140; ministers and, 68–9, 76–9, 99, 100–1; new spending initiatives, 161–2; and new spending procurement, 77; NPM and management structure, 165–6; ombudsmen, 218; PM's court and, 95; and program evaluation, 153, 154, 160; and QFRs, 143; and reclassifications, 187–8; report production by, 199; resource reallocation within, 233–7; responsible government and, 108–9; and RPPs, 140–1; size of, 8; and spending cuts, 82, 98–9, 100; staffing authority, 187–8; strategic reviews and, 102–3; transfer of funds within, 164, 189

deputy ministers: accountability of, 172; appointment of, 81, 253; backgrounds of, 193–4; benefits, 185; and cabinet, 32; and Chief Audit Executive (CAE), 142; crisis management, 118; and DACs, 142–3; and departments, 197, 206; duration in line departments, 206–7; duties of, 81; front-line managers and, 193; and interdepartmental issues, 212–13; and internal control statements, 143; Johnson on role of, 32; and labelling of initiatives as from "Harper government," 73; and MAFs, 139; as managers of departments, 80, 81; and ministers,

32, 69, 80, 81, 204, 206; MPs and, 60; numbers of, 171; as Ottawa-based, 235; and PCO, clerks of, 124; PCO service and, 194; pensions, 184, 207–8; PM and, 81; PM's court and, 92; policy skills, 193; post-retirement work, 208; preference for policy issues, 197; and program evaluation, 154; and programs, 81–2; public administration and, 209; qualities/skills, 193, 194; and reclassifications, 166–7, 187–8, 203; role/responsibilities, 204; self-evaluations, 134; special advisers to, 198–9; special retirement allowance, 207–8; workload, 118

DeVries, Peter, 170
Deware, Bev, 6
Diefenbaker, John, 128
Dingwall, David, 97–8
Dion, Stéphane, 70–1, 97
Discussion Paper on Values and Ethics in the Public Service, 195
dismissals, 215–17
DND. *See* National Defence, Department of (DND)
Dobell, Rod, 149
Docherty, David, 51, 56, 57, 58
Dodge, David, 110
Drummond, Don, 110–11, 228–9, 240
Dupré, J. Stephen, 69

Eaton's, 82–3
Economic Action Plan, 72, 78–9
economics: changes in discipline of, 13; political science and, 11; and principal-agent theory, 25; and public administration, 34–5, 238; and public choice theory, 24; and scientific language, 13; theories, 9, 10, 238, 243
Edward III, King, 38
EKOS Research Associates, 157, 176
elections: MPs' campaigns, 53–4; permanent campaigns, 61, 88, 93, 245; promises/commitments, 65; regions and, 64; and spenders vs.

guardians, 65; and spending cuts, 65; spending on, 65

elites: and global economy, 93; PM's court and, 92–3

Emerson, David, 175

employee benefits: global economy and, 170; in private vs. public sectors, 170; in public sector, 184, 241; of public servants, 175–6, 177; retirement, 185. *See also* pensions

employment equity, in private vs. public sector, 174–5

Employment Equity Act, 174, 175

Employment Insurance Act, 185

Environment Canada, program evaluation in, 155–6

Eresman, Randy, 194

estimates. *See* spending estimates

"Ethics and Fraud Awareness in Government" (OAG), 208

ethics/values: *Discussion Paper on Values and Ethics in the Public Service,* 195; OAG's "Ethics and Fraud Awareness in Government," 208; in private vs. public sectors, 242–3; public administration and, 209; public opinion on public servants', 226; and scandals, 209–11; Statement of Public Service Values and Ethics, 208; Task Force on Public Service Values and Ethics, 113; TBS Office of Values and Ethics, 208

Etzioni, Amitia, 19–20

Evaluating the Effectiveness of Programs (OAG), 151

events. *See* controversies; crises

executive public servants. *See* senior public servants

expenditure. *See* spending

expenditure budget: cabinet and, 76; departments and, 69–70; evidence-based policy advice and, 111; government and, 61; government centralization and, 76; importance of, 8; machinery of government and, 107; ministers and, 69–70; MPs and,

54, 58–9, 76; Parliament and, 13, 61, 244; PEMS and, 69–70; PM and, 13; PM's court and, 91, 96–8; power vacuum and, 13–14; priority setters in, 28; program evaluation and, 152–3, 155, 158; regions and, 67

Expenditure Review of Federal Public Sector Compensation (Treasury Board), 181, 183, 184, 186–9, 191, 217

experts: PM's court and, 103–4; and strategic and operating reviews, 103–4. *See also* consultants

External Affairs, Department of, 23

Federal Accountability Act: and parliamentary budget officer, 146; and program evaluation, 151

Finance, Department of: and departmental programs, 162; and expenditure management, 164; and macroeconomic policy, 163; and parliamentary budget officer, 146–7; and spending proposals, 20–1; and TBS, 161, 162

finance, minister of, 13; and budget, 41–3; and cabinet, 42; decision-making powers, 42; in PM's court, 89, 90; and policy, 62; as priority setter, 101; and Standing Committee on Finance, 42

Financial Administration Act (FAA): and deputy ministers, 123; and ministers in management, 80; Quarterly Financial Reports (QFRs) in, 143

Finer, Herman, 29, 30, 169, 238, 245

Finkelman, Jake, 179

Fisheries and Oceans, Department of: reclassification in, 201, 202; rule breaking at, 210; and virus killing Fraser River salmon, 94

Flaherty, Jim, 103, 104

Fonberg, Robert, 206

Foreign Affairs and Trade, Department of, 208–9, 226

France, location of public servants in, 201

path dependency of, 108; PCO and, 107–8; and plausible deniability, 120; PM and, 107, 108, 252; and policy, 110, 111, 246; positions with responsibility for dealing with public, 117; private sector management practices and, 126; red tape and, 125; running on tracks, 87, 91–2, 114, 246; simplicity in, 251; as spenders vs. guardians, 107; and spending cuts, 246; time spent on, 117–18; uncertainty and, 114

MacKay, Elmer, 97
MacKay, Peter, 206
Mackenzie, Alexander, 23
MacKenzie, Lewis, 194
McKinsey and Company, 168
Macmillan, Harold, 87
Magna Carta, 38
Maher, Stephen, 169
Mallory, James, 18; *The Structure of Canadian Government,* 17
management: coaching, 167; consultants, 167, 222; good practices, 231. *See also* private sector management; public sector management; private vs. public sector management
Management Accountability Frameworks (MAFs), 115, 138–40, 164, 196, 205
Manion, John L., 35–6, 46–7
Manley, John, 99
March, James G., 20, 24, 114
market capitalism, and social inequality, 5
market discipline/forces: duplication in government operations, 33; in private sector, 180; and private sector unions, 190; public sector management and, 129
Marleau, Robert, 39
Martin, Keith, 156
Martin, Pat, 244
Martin, Paul, 6, 62–3, 71, 87, 106, 158
Maslove, Allan, 149
Massé, Marcel, 111

media: access to information legislation and, 73; centre, and relations with, 72; and controversy, 114–15; criticisms of public servants, 226; events, 72; OAG and, 196, 197; and officers of Parliament, 148; opposition and, 57; and oversight bodies, 148; and parliamentary budget officer, 147; PM and, 73, 74, 96; PM's court and, 90–1; and process participants, 79. *See also* communications; journalism/journalists
members of Parliament (MPs): and accountability, 58; accountability of, 55; and budget, 49–50; and cabinet, 56, 67–8; and constituencies, 51, 53–5; and decision making, 60; and departmental activities, 60; and deputy ministers, 60; election campaigns, 53–4; and expenditure budget, 54, 58–9, 76; in government vs. opposition parties, 55–6, 57; job description/expectations of, 50–1; ministers and, 59; newly elected, 52; and officers of Parliament, 248–9; ombudsman role, 55; opposition, 53, 57, 58; on Parliament, 40; parliamentary budget officer and, 147; on parliamentary committees, 51–2; party discipline and, 40–1, 51, 56–7; and performance evaluation reports, 204; PM and, 53, 56; and policy, 57–9; preparation for service, 51; and program evaluations, 48; promises/commitements, 53–5; public servants and, 52–3, 57–8, 59–61; reviewing of spending estimates, 13; and role of government, 54; role/functions of, 40–1, 56; from rural vs. urban constituencies, 55; as spenders vs. guardians, 55; and spending cuts, 54; and spending estimates, 43–6, 47; training/orientation for, 51; turnover of, 58; universities and, 53; variety of backgrounds of, 68
merit principle, 175

bureaucracies, 170; costs, 165–6; and democracy, 33–4; and deputy ministers, 193, 204; and employment in NCR, 172; failure of, 35, 169; as inappropriate for public sector, 12, 126; influence on policy, 198; and intradepartmental resource allocation, 233–4; lack of theory, 32–3; and letting managers manage, 14, 128; objectives of, 227; and pay-for-performance schemes, 133; and private sector, 224; private sector practices compared to, 130; public administration compared to, 30–4, 125; and Public Service Reform Act, 124; and public vs. private sector management, 223; removal of red tape, 124; and senior public servants' interest in management, 212; TBS and, 161; and Treasury Board delegation of authority to departments, 189

Nielsen Task Force, 30, 149, 155
Nortel, 227
Nottingham, Patrick, 209
Nova Scotia, apple industry in, 234
Nunziata, John, 57

OAG. *See* Auditor General, Office of the (OAG)
OCG. *See* Comptroller General, Office of the (OCG)
Office of Management and Budget (US), 23
Office of Values and Ethics (TBS), 208, 209
officers of Parliament, 144–7; cost of, 148; effect on government operations, 223, 247; MPs and, 248–9; OAG on, 222; opposition and, 223; as priority setters of budget, 28; review of, 248–9
official languages, 174–5
Official Languages Act (OLA), 80, 175
Oliver, Joe, 71
Olsen, Johan P., 20, 21, 24, 114

ombudsmen, 218
opposition: attacks on government, 223; and budget, 43, 45, 50; and controversy, 114–15; dissension within, 57; and media, 57; MPs, 53, 57, 58; and OAG, 223, 248; and officers of Parliament, 148, 223; and oversight bodies, 148; and spending estimates, 50; and training for senior public servants, 226
Osbaldeston, Gordon, 206
Osborne, David, 111–12
Ottawa Citizen, on wasteful spending, 205
Ottawa-Gatineau: employment in, vs. in regions, 171–2; percentage of public servants in, 201; senior public servants in, 201. *See also* National Capital Region (NCR)
Ouellet, André, 99
Ouimet, Christine, 65
oversight bodies, 33, 91, 93, 94, 117, 132, 141–4, 148, 214, 218

Paquet, Gilles, 155
parking, 185
Parliament: and accountability, 13, 37, 46; accounting officers and, 81; attitudes toward, 40; and budget, 48–50; budget officer, 278n74; Charter of Public Service and, 252; committees, 51–2; in constitutions, 38; control of public purse, 38, 48–9, 123, 129, 221, 222, 247; criticisms of, 39–40; culture of, 52; decline of, 39–40; documents submitted to, 13; and expenditure budget, 13, 61, 244; functions of, 39; MPs on, 40; omnipotence of, 38; and public money, 6; public servants and, 59; and responsible government, 37; role and spending of money, 13, 37–8; and spending estimates, 43–4, 49–50; and taxes, 38
parliamentary budget officer, 146–7
parsimonious culture, 32, 33, 134, 169, 203, 225, 247, 248

parties, political: discipline, 40–1, 56–7; government vs. opposition, 55–6; MPs and, 40–1, 51; party discipline and, 51; regions and, 64

partisanship: PM's court and, 89; promiscuous, 34, 198, 228; public servants and, 53, 73, 79, 121, 228, 239

path dependency, 21, 108, 160, 194, 237

Pay Research Bureau, 178–9

PCO, clerks of: as ambassadors, 208–9; appointment of deputy ministers, 253; and cabinet, 218; as CEO, 124; and change, 218; on changing public attitudes toward government, 207; as chief operating officer, 252; and crises, 218; definition of role of, 252–3; duties, 218; and ministers, 204–5; and PM, 95–6, 218; in PM's court, 89; and program evaluation, 160, 168–9; on values and ethics, 208–9

Pearson, Lester B., 32, 69, 128, 225

Pensioners' Dental Services Plan (PDSP), 177, 181, 185

pensions: cost of, 184; employer contributions, 177; employer vs. employee contributions, 181, 183, 184; portability, 183; private sector, 182, 242; in private vs. public sectors, 184; public sector, 175–6, 181, 182–7, 241; senior public servants, 207–8

performance: attitudes toward appraisals, 215–16; bonuses, 133–4; establishment of, 33, 134; evaluation reports, 148, 164; MAFs and, 139; and poor/non-performing personnel, 33, 215–17, 231, 233, 235; program evaluation and, 153; reports, 164; rewards for, 33

performance evaluation/measurement: accountability and, 169; difficulties in, 191; as not having expected results, 168; OAG and, 203, 204; in private vs. public sectors, 131; TBS and, 219

performance pay: amount of, 177; at-risk, 133, 211–12; bonuses, 133–4, 211; components of, 133–4; individual, 189–90; as not having expected results, 33; and politicians, 211

personnel administration (PE), 187

Peters, B. Guy, 24, 85

Pettigrew, Pierre, 136

Pierre, Jon, 35

Plato, 17

policy: central agencies and, 116; court government and, 90–1; deputy ministers and, 197; horizontality of, 113, 114; machinery of government and, 110, 111, 246; management vs., 129; minister of finance and, 62; ministers and, 57–8, 68, 82, 100; ministers' staffs and, 69; MPs and, 57–9; opposition MPs and, 57; PCO and, 62–3; PM and, 57–8, 62, 72, 75, 87; PM's court and, 82; politicians and, 227–8; program budgeting and, 150; programs linked with, 110; research institutes and, 229–30; senior public servants and, 31–2; units, 240; variety of participants in, 75

policy analysis: evidence-based, 110–11, 197; market for, 227–30

Policy and Expenditure Management System (PEMS), 69–70, 75, 232, 244

policy making: by announcement, 90; career public servants and continuity in, 209; communications and, 239–40; evidence-based, 159; Google searches and, 230; as horizontal, 110, 111; OAG and, 196; opinion and, 239–40; public servants and, 230; senior public servants and, 229–30

political parties. See parties, political

political partisanship. See partisanship

political science: and behaviour, 11, 18; changes in study of, 16; and economics, 11; and institutions, 17–18; and public administration, 11–12; public servants and, 19; and scientific language, 13 politicians: bargain with public servants, 17; career, 68; criticisms of public servants/service, 6, 16; and performance pay, 211; and policy, 227–8; on public sector management, 231; and public servants, 16–17; and scandals, 211; and self-interest, 64; and size of public service, 4

politics: administration vs., 18; and blame avoidance, 225; and bureaucracy, 111; influence as focus of study of, 11; of public spending, 8; of work of public servants, 226

The Politics of Public Money (Good), 28

The Politics of Public Spending in Canada (Savoie), 26, 62, 149, 151, 158

Pollitt, Christopher, 35, 237; *Public Management Reform*, 10, 245

power: court government and vacuum in, 91; of courts, 86; expenditure budget and vacuum in, 13–14; of House of Commons, 85; over new spending decisions, 90; of PM, 85, 86, 252; of PMO, 85; of PM's court, 91–2; of US president, 85

La Presse, on HRDC crisis, 136

Price-Waterhouse Coopers, 155

prime minister (PM): appointment of deputy ministers, 253; as boss, 76; and budget, 42; and cabinet, 67–8; as CEO, 252; chiefs of staff, 95; and clerk of PCO, 95–6, 160, 218; control vs. delegation of authority, 105; court of (*see* court of PM); and decision making, 13, 42; definition of role of, 252–3; and deputy ministers, 81; and expenditure budget, 13; and experts, 95; fallout management, 88; and focus groups, 75–6; as guardian and/or spender, 101; and House of Commons, 58; as learning on job, 87, 105; and machinery of government, 107, 108, 252; and major initiatives, 72, 73; and media, 73, 74;

and ministers, 68, 88, 204–5; and ministers' chiefs of staff, 68–9; and mission participants, 74–5; and MPs, 53, 56; number of, 105; and OAG, 160; and party discipline, 56–7; and permanent election campaigns, 88; and policy, 57–8, 62, 72, 75, 87; power of, 85, 86, 252; preparation for position, 105; and Priorities and Planning Committee, 76; as priority setter, 101; private sector executives compared with, 86–7; and program evaluation, 168–9; and public servants, 88, 247; responsibilities of, 86; and senior advisers, 96; and spending cuts, 98, 106; time spent reacting to controversies, 87–8; workload, 105

Prime Minister's Advisory Committee on the Public Service, 175

Prime Minister's Office (PMO): and Clement's G8 Legacy Fund, 78; communications officers, 213; and media events, 72; and ministers' chiefs of staff, 68–9, 81; and new spending, 96–7; power of, 85; size of, 95; and TBS role in reviewing new funding, 161

Prince Edward Island, Confederation Bridge, 97

principal-agent theory, 25–7, 37, 99–100, 192, 243–4

Priorities and Planning (P and P) Committee, 76

Prisoner's Dilemma, 26

prisons, building of new, 198

The Private Government of Public Money (Heclo; Wildavsky), 101

private sector: accounting practices, 163; and bottom line, 81–2; and CEO role in public service, 123–4; characteristics of, 227; collective bargaining in, 178; compensation in, 15; competition and, 241; consultants, 103–4; employee health/dental care, 185; executive origins/careers, 194; global economy and, 170,

219, 241–2; high-level government experience and employment in, 208; individual performance pay in, 190; machinery of government extending to, 111–12; market discipline in, 168, 180; and market share, 81–2; pensions in, 182, 184, 242; PMs compared with executives, 86–7; program/service delivery by, 111–12; return on investments in, 7; and risk, 130–1, 133–4; unions (*see* unions, private sector). *See also* private vs. public sector

private sector management: Glassco Commission and, 128; greed and, 207; and letting managers manage, 14, 128; and machinery of government, 126. *See also* private vs. public sector management

private vs. public sector: accountability in, 130; accounting in, 143–4; and bottom vs. top line, 131–2; change of public sector language to promote perspective of private, 132; collective bargaining in, 180, 242; compensation comparability in, 181–2; competition in, 130, 131; dissimilarities, 15, 82, 130–2, 138, 148, 237, 242–3, 252; employee pay/benefits in, 170, 179, 184, 190–1; employment equity in, 174; executive compensation in, 182, 191; job descriptions, 180; pensions in, 182, 184; performance measurement in, 131; public sector emulation of private, 12, 125–6, 175–9, 180, 224; public service as model for private sector, 170; risk in, 133–4; senior officials in, 133; spending cuts in, 82–3; strike method of dispute resolution in, 179; values, 242–3. *See also* private sector; public sector

private vs. public sector management: bottom line and, 129, 138, 148, 224; in coaching, 167; dissimilarities, 12, 138, 168, 219, 230, 242–3; market forces and, 129, 168; private sector

as superior to public, 12, 31, 126, 129–30; in private vs. public realms of, 132, 135; public emulation of private sector practices, 7, 8, 14, 31, 128, 240–1; public sector emulation of private practices, 7, 8, 162–3, 168, 219, 240–1; in responsibility for results, 230–1; senior public servants and, 198, 199; in US, 168. *See also* private sector management; public sector management

Privy Council Office (PCO): and accounting office concept, 122–3; on accounting officers, 251; assistant secretary to the cabinet, 108; business-inspired vocabulary of, 175; and cabinet making, 67, 68; clerks of the (*see* PCO, clerks of); communications officers, 213; and departmental programs, 162; deputy ministers' former service in, 194; and deputy ministers' self-evaluations, 134; deputy-minister-level staff, 116; and Fisheries Department scientist speaking to media, 94; *Guidance for Accounting Officers,* 123; *Guidance for Deputy Ministers,* 122–3, 155; and labelling of initiatives as from "Harper government," 73; and machinery of government, 107–8; and macroeconomic policy, 163; and MAFs, 139; and media events, 72; modelled after UK Cabinet Office, 22; and new spending, 96–7; on performance pay, 133–4; and PM's court, 89; and policy, 62–3; reclassifications in, 202; Report on Plans and Priorities, 108; size of, 95

Professional Institute of the Public Service of Canada (PIPSC), 186

program budgeting: about, 149–50; line-item vs., 128, 149–50, 168; and program evaluation, 149–50, 168; in US, 220

program evaluation: access to information legislation and, 153; and accountability, 48; and bottom line, 150, 153; Canadian Studies Program, 157; central agencies and, 150, 156; of Community Access Program, 156–7; consultants and, 151; departments and, 153, 154, 160; deputy ministers and, 154; in Environment Canada, 155–6; and expenditure budget, 152–3, 155, 158; as growth industry, 14; limitations on, 248; and line-item vs. program budgeting, 149–50, 153; MPs' and, 48; as not coming up to expectations, 33, 168; OAG on, 151–2, 196; outcome identification in, 234; PCO clerk and, 168–9; and performance, 153; PM and, 168–9; and politics, 152; problems with, 153–4, 159, 160; program budgeting and, 149–50, 168; program/strategic reviews and, 158; reports, 157–8; resources committed to, 150–1; TBS and, 150, 151, 152, 153, 156, 168, 203–4

program reviews, 102–4; about, 102; and across-the-board cuts, 100, 102; and budget surpluses, 105–6; criteria of, 158; and expenditure budget, 14; job losses, 104; majority mandate and, 241; and Manley's appeals for his department, 99; private sector executives leading, 30; and program evaluation, 158; and spending cuts, 232; sponsorship scandal compared to, 93

programs: central agencies and, 101; cuts to, 76; departmental ideas for expansion of and establishment of new, 81–2; deputy ministers and, 81–2; low-priority, 82; managers, 112–13; ministers and, 81–2; policies linked with, 110; Treasury Board and funding of, 163

PS 2000. *See* Public Service 2000 (PS 2000)

Public Accounts Committee: OAG and, 145; and performance reports, 204; UK, 122

Public Accounts of Canada: availability of, 282n65; as more detailed than estimates, 165; pensions in, 183

public administration: and accountability, 34; attack upon, 12–13; attitudes toward, 224–5; and behaviour, 18; benefits lost, 15; and bureaucracy, 9–10; changes in discipline of, 13; characteristics of, 224–5; deputy ministers in, 209; economics and, 13, 34–5, 238; ethics/values of, 209, 227; and governance, 34; identity crisis, 34–5; and influence, 11; and institutions, 17–18; need to return to roots, 12; New Public Management compared to, 125; new type of public servants and, 224; NPM vs., 30–4; political science and, 11–12; politics vs., 18; as public management, 220; and public sector operations improvement, 238; public servants and, 13, 18–19, 224–5; and public servants as career officials, 209; and reform of public service, 246–7; return to roots, 15, 251; search for comprehensive theory in, 35; and spending growth, 9; and study of institutions, 11; and theories as self-fulfilling prophecies, 244–5; theory vs. practice in, 27–8; transition to public management, 15

Public Appointments Commission, 104, 205

public choice theory, 23–5, 27, 63–4, 160, 169, 192, 237, 244

public debt, 164–5

public management: public administration and, 15, 220

Public Management Reform (Pollitt; Bouckaert), 10, 245

public opinion: on government operations, 219; on public servants' ethics, 226; on public service, 4–5, 170

The Public Purse (Ward), 39

public sector: compensation in, 15; and focus on tasks, 12; oversight in,

134–5; performance pay in, 133–4; private sector as providing solutions for, 125–6; resemblance to private sector, 11. *See also* private vs. public sector

Public Sector Employment Act, 188

public sector management, 213; access to information legislation and, 245; accountability of, 129; attempts to overhaul, 8; and blame avoidance, 204–7; characteristics of, 230–1; collective bargaining and, 15, 215, 231; courts and, 215, 216; deputy ministers and, 80, 81; empowerment of managers, 126; error-free government and, 231; as expecting the unexpected, 204; and generation of reports, 225; Glassco Commission and, 127; Glassco on, 220; horizontality and, 212; letting managers manage, 14, 127, 221; ministers and, 80–3, 81; and non-performers, 215–17, 231, 233, 235; NPM and, 14, 128, 165–6; OAG and, 195–6; officers of Parliament and, 147; permanent campaign elections and, 245; policy vs., 129; politicians on, 231; private vs. public realms of, 132; senior public servants and, 31–2; as someone else's business, 214–18; TBS and, 163; as tied to political institutions, 245; unions and, 215; up vs. down, 113, 195, 225–6. *See also* private vs. public sector management

public servants: Aboriginal, 174; anonymity of, 121–2; bargain with politicians, 17; better pay/benefits than private sector counterparts, 190–1; blame for problems, 6; as career officials, 209; Charter of Public Service and, 252; and courts, 216–17, 231; criticisms of, 237; disability claims, 191–2; dismissals, 215–17, 231; diversity of activities, 176; employee benefits, 175–6, 177; ethical standards, 207; former allies of, 16; and government agenda, 228; indi-

vidualism among, 12, 211, 225–6; and institutionalism, 18; leave, 177; loyalty to government of day, 21, 34, 52–3; ministerial responsibility and, 120–1, 122–3; morale of, 191–2, 237, 242; and MPs, 52–3, 57–8, 59–61; non-performing, 215–17, 231, 233, 235; number of, 104, 105, 171, 188, 201; and Parliament, 59; and partisanship, 53, 73, 79, 121, 239; pension plans, 175–6, 177, 181; and personal accountability, 250–1; Plato's ideas regarding, 17; PM and, 88, 247; and policy analysis, 227–8; political context of work, 135, 226, 245; and political science, 19; politicians and, 6, 16–17; and profit motive, 130, 224; promiscuous partisanship of, 198, 228; promotion of, 173, 187, 188, 194; and public administration students, 18–19; and public vs. private interests, 22; replacement new type, 224; speaking policy truth to politicians, 111; statutory responsibilities, 80; and traditional public administration, 13; training budgets for, 233; travel rewards, 167; underemployment of, 217, 218; visible minorities among, 174; in Westminster-Whitehall parliamentary model, 21–2, 120; women, 174

public service: adversarial politics and, 58; as apolitical, 18; CEO role in, 123–4; clerk of PCO and, 96; core administration, 171; costs, 186–7; criticisms of, 5–6; and democracy, 246; distinctiveness of, 246, 247, 251; divisions of, 171; elimination of positions in, 106; employment equity in, 174–5; emulation of private sector, 175–9; functions of, 172–3; growth in, 241; growth of government and, 22; as less institutionalized, 211; as model employer, 219; as model for private sector, 170, 173–5; neo-Weberian state of, 246–7; politicization of, 239; procedural controls/rules and, 246, 247; public administration and, 246–7; public opinion regarding, 4–5, 170; rebuilding credibility of, 246–54; return to roots, 12, 15, 246–7; as self-governing institution, 247; as service-delivery institution, 173; size of, 3–4, 171–2; until 1960s, 22–3; workforce restructuring, 15

Public Service 2000 (PS 2000), 96, 124, 127, 135, 161, 225, 245

Public Service Alliance of Canada (PSAC), 183, 186

Public Service Commission: as audit body, 132, 187; delegation of staffing to departments, 132; on ethical standards of public servants, 207, 226; managers and, 141; as oversight body, 132; and public service as model employer for private sector, 170; and regional breakdown of public servants, 171–2; reports on staffing, 201; and special advisers, 198–9; on termination of public servants, 217

Public Service Dental Care Plan, 177, 184, 185

Public Service Employment Act (PSEA), 80, 123

Public Service Health Care Plan (PSHCP), 185

Public Service Labour Relations Board (PSLRB), 217

Public Service Modernization Act, 215–16

Public Service Reform Act, 124

Public Service Renewal Plan, 174

Public Service Staff Relations Act, 178

Public Service Staff Relations Board, 179

Public Service Superannuation Act, 181

public service (UK), 4, 5–6

Public Works and Government Services Canada (PWGSC): excessive overtime charges in, 210; management structure, 166; real estate portfolio, 211

quantification, cult of, 155

Quarterly Financial Reports (QFRs), 143

rational choice theory, 24–5, 192, 237, 244

rational expectations theory, 13

rational self-interest, 13

rational utility maximization, 24

Rayner, Derek, 30

Reagan, Ronald: and private sector management practices, 130, 223; on public service, 6

reallocation of resources. See resource reallocation

reclassification(s), 166–7; in ACOA, 202; consultants and, 203; departments and, 187–8; deputy ministers and, 166–7, 187–8, 203; in Fisheries and Oceans Canada, 202; in Health Canada, 202; in Human Resources and Skills Development Canada, 202; number of, 177; in PCO, 202; as promotions, 188; reasons for, 202; as shift among groups, 187; TBS and, 201–2; TBS monitoring of, 189

red tape, 124–5, 137

Regan, Geoff, 48

regional offices: demands of central agencies on, 117–18; employment in Ottawa-Gatineau vs., 171–2; resource reallocation away from, 243. See also front-line workers

regions: and expenditure budget, 67; favouring of one region over another, 54; inequality among, 66; ministers and, 78–9; myths regarding, 66; new initiatives and, 78–9; political parties and, 64; process ministers and, 71; rivalry among, 65–6; senior public servants in, 201; spending and, 64

Reid, Escott, 209

Reid, Scott, 213

Reisman, Simon, 20–1

reporting: departmental overhead units and, 199; growth in demand, 197;

OAG and, 248; plethora of requirements, 14; prolific production of,
163–5, 225; time spent by managers
on, 225
Reports on Plans and Priorities (RPPs),
43, 115, 140–1, 164, 205
Representative Government (Mill),
108–9
Research in Motion, 227
resource reallocation: away from
regional offices, 243; within departments, 233–7; front-line managers
and, 235–7; from front-line offices
to NCR, 235–7; responsibility for,
231–3; senior public servants and,
234–5. *See also* spending cuts
responsible government: and
departments, 108–9; Parliament and,
37
Rights and Democracy Group, 226
Riley, Susan, 49
risk management: OAG and, 196;
public sector and, 143
risk(s): and compensation, 133–4; pay
for performance, 134, 211–12; in
private sector, 130–1; in private vs.
public sectors, 133–4
Roberts, Alasdair, 24
Robertson, Gordon, 23, 32, 203, 209
Robertson, Norman, 209
"The Role of the Deputy Minister"
(Johnson), 32
Rooney, Paul L., 194
Rose, Jonathan, 239
Royal Bank of Canada, 242
Royal Canadian Mounted Police
(RCMP): compensation, 176–7;
head office staff, 201; investigations
into wrongdoing, 211; number of
employees, 201
Royal Commission on Management,
221

salaries. *See* compensation
Samara, 50, 51; *It's My Party: Parliamentary Dysfunction Reconsidered*,
40–1; on MPs, 77; *Welcome*

*to Parliament: A Job with No
Description,* 40
Sarbanes-Oxley Act, 143, 278n64
Savoie, Donald, *The Politics of Public
Spending in Canada,* 26, 62, 149,
151, 158
scandals, 209–11; and blame avoidance, 204–7; DND use of planes,
152; and Environment Department
furniture, 137–8; HRDC Transitional
Jobs Fund, 135–7; ministers and,
226; Mulroney government and,
293n12; politicians and, 211. *See
also* sponsorship scandal
Scott, Andy, 79
self-interest: individuals as self-
interested agents, 24–5; politicians
and, 64; in public service, 208.
See also individualism; rational
self-interest
Senate: and inequality among regions,
66, 67; reform, 66, 67
senior public servants, 15; accountability of, 113, 253; administrative
discretion of, 247; association with
political leaders, 198; and at-risk
pay for performance, 134, 211–12;
and blame avoidance, 213; and
courts, 216; decision making by, 32;
enthusiasm for government agenda,
198; executive positions, 166, 171,
187, 188, 194, 201; and management
up, 113; and management vs. policy
work, 31–2; and ministers, 172;
mobility, 212; number of, 166, 171,
188, 201; and OAG, 248; past focus
on policy, 203; pensions, 207–8; and
performance monitoring, 199; policy
making, 230; and policy shaping,
229–30; and private sector management practices, 30, 31–2; and public-
private sector management resem-
blances, 198, 199; in regions vs.
Ottawa-Gatineau, 201; and resource
reallocation, 234–5; responsibilities
of, 172–3; and service delivery,
172–3; as serving collective vs. indi-

vidual purpose, 23; survey of, 245–6; training for, 226. *See also* deputy ministers

Service Canada, 215

service delivery: by private sector, 111–12; senior public servants and, 172–3; Service Canada and, 215

severance pay, 186

Shediac (NB), Supply and Services office in, 82, 98

Sheikh, Munir, 229

Siegel, David, 118, 119, 215

Simpson, Jeffrey, 104, 215

Skelton, O.D., 19, 209

spending: accountability, 15; on accountability, 248; on advertising, 72; boom-and-bust cycles of, 235, 242; caucus and, 50; constituencies and, 65; on elections, 65; federal-provincial agreements and, 65; Finance vs. line departments, 20–1; and government constituencies, 78–9; on government operations, 164–5, 245; growth in, 232; and guardians vs. spenders, 90–1; and inflation, 98; literature on, 8; Parliament and, 6, 13; PMO-PCO and new, 96–7; PM's court and, 89; politics of, 8; power over new, 90; Prisoner's Dilemma and, 26; public understanding of, 6; regions and, 64; and role of Parliament, 37–8; spenders vs. guardians and, 99–100; waste in, 6–7, 54, 65, 134, 205–6; Western crisis in, 8–9

spending budget. *See* expenditure budget

spending cuts: across-the-board, 82, 91, 100, 102, 106, 244; as ad hoc, 244; and at-risk performance pay, 134, 211–12; Bonn, 232; central agencies and, 231–2; consensus on, 232; consultants and, 197–8, 241; crises and, 246; deficits and, 105–6; departments and, 82, 98–9, 100; elections and, 65; fiscal crises and, 244; and front-line managers, 254;

Harper and, 7, 100; IMF and, 9; majority government and, 9, 241, 244; ministers and, 70, 82, 99; MPs and, 54; performance bonuses for, 134, 158–9; PM and, 98, 106; PM's court and, 91, 98–9, 101–2, 232; politicians in and out of office, 7; in private vs. public sector, 82–3; program review of 1994–97 and, 100, 104; strategic and operating review and, 82, 102–4, 158–9. *See also* resource reallocation

spending estimates: 1968 changes, 44–7; debate on, 44; MPs and, 13, 43–6, 47; opposition and, 50; Parliament and, 43–4, 49–50; Public Accounts compared to, 165; and standing committees, 43, 44–5; tabling of, 43, 47; transfers within departments and, 189; volume of, 47

spending growth: Harper and, 7; individuals and, 23–4; inflation and, 7; theories regarding, 9, 22

spin operations. *See* communications

sponsorship program, 6–7, 93–4

sponsorship scandal: and accounting officers, 81; blame in, 120, 121; *Globe and Mail* and, 73; Guité and, 137, 211; Harper and, 122; OAG and, 145, 197; old bureaucracy and, 225; and Policy on Internal Audit, 141–2; and TBS, 249; and unions, 217

"Statement of Management Responsibility including Internal Control over Financial Reporting," 143

Statistics Canada: and long-form census, 229; on morale problem, 191; on size of public service, 171

statutory appropriations, 44

Stevens, Sinclair, 293n12

Stewart, Jane, 136, 137

Stockman, David, 23–4

strategic and operating reviews, 102–4; contracting out for advice on, 159; deficits and, 106, 158; and expenditure budget, 14; and growth in public service, 241; majority mandate and, 241; and performance bonuses for spending cuts, 134; and program evaluation, 158; and public sector unions, 190; and spending cuts, 11, 82, 102–4, 232

The Structure of Canadian Government (Mallory), 17

surprises. *See* controversies; crises

Sutherland, Sharon, 196, 222

Swain, Harry, 91, 155

Tait Report, 167

Taras, David, 73

Tarte, Yvon, 179

Task Force on Public Service Values and Ethics, 113

taxes: increase in, 9; Parliament and, 38

TBS. *See* Treasury Board Secretariat (TBS)

Tellier, Paul, 114, 172–3, 175, 218, 240, 253

Temporary Foreign Worker Program, 222

Thatcher, Margaret: and bureaucracy, 6; and NPM, 30; and private sector, 12; and private sector management practices, 30, 130, 223; and public choice theory, 24; and size of civil service, 4; and spending growth theories, 22; and *Yes, Minister,* 228

Thomas, Paul, 17–18, 27, 61, 81, 88, 94, 227

Times and Transcript (Moncton), 53–4

Tobin, Brian, 57, 58–9

Tomkins, Adam, 38

Toronto Star: on modern journalism, 74; on nature of politicians, 67–8

Towers, Graham, 209

Transitional Jobs Fund, 135–7

Treasury Board: change in role of, 14–15; controls on number of employees, 189; and cuts to executive-level jobs, 166; delegation of management decision making to line departments/agencies, 132; and departmental budgets vs. programs, 221; and DPRS, 140–1; and expenditure budget, 14–15; *Expenditure Review of Federal Public Sector Compensation,* 181, 183, 184, 186–9, 191, 217; on financing of increases in salary mass, 188–9; on francophone/anglophone public service employment, 174; and Glassco Commission, 128–9; Glassco on, 220–1; "Health of the Evaluation Function," 203–4; and MAF, 138–40; on measuring productivity, 191; monitoring of reclassifications, 189; on numbers of executive-level public servants, 201; on pensions, 183, 184; president, 43, 47; and private sector emulation, 132; and private sector management measures, 162–3; program branch, 162; and program funding, 163; on public sector compensation and comparability, 176–7; and public servants' collecting travel frequent flyer/loyalty points, 167; and public service as model employer for private sector, 170; reporting demands created by, 197; on risk management, 143; and RPPS, 140–1; on severance pay, 186; and strategic and operating review, 103; tabling of spending estimates, 43

Treasury Board Secretariat (TBS): ARLUs submitted to, 41–2; budget officer role, 161–2, 219; business-inspired vocabulary of, 175; and compensation comparability, 178–9; delegation of decision making to agencies/line departments, 162; and departmental spending plans, 163, 164; and employment equity, 174–5; guardian vs. facilitator role, 162–3; Macdonell and, 221; as management board, 14, 249; on ministerial responsibility, 249; and OCG, 49, 221, 222; Office of Values and Ethics, 208, 209; and performance